O9-CFT-093

OBLIVION OR GLORY

DAVID STAFFORD

OBLIVION OR GLORY

1921 and the Making of Winston Churchill

YALE UNIVERSITY PRESS
NEW HAVEN AND LONDON

Copyright © 2019 David Stafford

All rights reserved. This book may not be reproduced in whole or in part, in any form
(beyond that copying permitted by Sections 107 and 108 of the U.S. Copyright Law and
except by reviewers for the public press) without written permission from the publishers.

For information about this and other Yale University Press publications, please contact:
U.S. Office: sales.press@yale.edu   yalebooks.com
Europe Office: sales@yaleup.co.uk   yalebooks.co.uk

Set in Minion Pro by IDSUK (DataConnection) Ltd
Printed in Great Britain by TJ International Ltd, Padstow, Cornwall

Library of Congress Control Number: 2019941061

ISBN 978-0-300-23404-6

A catalogue record for this book is available from the British Library.

10 9 8 7 6 5 4 3 2 1

For Jeanne

Midway along life's journey
I found myself in a dark wood
and the path was lost . . .

Dante, 'Inferno', *The Divine Comedy*

CONTENTS

List of Illustrations   *ix*

Acknowledgements   *xii*

Prologue: 'A Bold, Bad Man'   *xiv*

Introduction: 'A Tragic Flaw in the Metal'   1

WINTER

1   'Rule Britannia'   17

2   Family and Friends   32

3   'He Uses It as an Opiate'   47

4   A World in Torment   60

5   The Great Corniche of Life   71

6   'This Wild Cousin of Mine'   87

SPRING

7   'The Forty Thieves'   101

8   The Smiling Orchards   118

9   Tragedy Strikes   132

10 Peacemaker   141

SUMMER

11 'Where Are We Going in Europe?'   157

12 Imperial Dreams   170

CONTENTS

13	'I Will Take What Comes'	185
14	'A Seat for Life'	198

AUTUMN

15	'The Courage and Instinct of Leadership'	211
16	The Comfort of Friends	223
17	'The Dark Horse of English Politics'	238
18	Fleeting Shadows	250
	Epilogue: 'He Would Make a Great Prime Minister'	261

Endnotes	*271*
Bibliography	*286*
Index	*293*

ILLUSTRATIONS

1. Churchill strides forcefully ahead during the Anglo-Irish conference in Downing Street, October 1921. Hulton Archive / Getty Images.
2. Lady Randolph ('Jennie') Churchill, Winston's beloved mother. © National Portrait Gallery, London.
3. In the bosom of his family: the young Winston with his mother and younger brother, John ('Jack'). Time Life Pictures / Getty Images.
4. Churchill heads the family procession at his mother's funeral, July 1921. Churchill Archives Centre, Churchill College, Cambridge.
5. Clementine with daughter Marigold ('the Duckadilly'). Churchill Archives Centre, Churchill College, Cambridge.
6. Winston and his only son Randolph. Keystone-France / Getty Images.
7. A casual Winston and Clementine enjoy a rare relaxing moment in the garden. SZ Photo / Scherl / Bridgeman Images.
8. Captain Frederick ('Freddie') Guest, Churchill's favourite cousin. © National Portrait Gallery, London.
9. Clare Sheridan, Churchill's 'wild cousin'. © National Portrait Gallery, London.
10. The charismatic Boris Savinkov, former anti-Tsarist revolutionary and political assassin on whom Churchill pinned his hopes of toppling Lenin and the Bolsheviks. Hulton Archive / Getty Images.

11. Archibald Henry Macdonald Sinclair, 1st Viscount Thurso, 1890–1970, portrait by Augustus John. National Galleries of Scotland.
12. 'Winston's Bag: He hunts lions and brings home decayed cats', cartoon by David Low. From *The Star*, January 1920. LSE6215, British Cartoon Archive, University of Kent.
13. 'A New Hat', cartoon by Sidney Conrad Strube. From the *Daily Express*, January 1921.
14. Churchill takes a front row seat at the Cairo Conference, March 1921. General Photographic Agency / Getty Images.
15. Churchill, escorted by Palestine High Commissioner and former Liberal Home Secretary Sir Herbert Samuel, greets Zionist youth during his visit to Jerusalem following the Cairo Conference.
16. Churchill with Clementine, Gertrude Bell, and T. E. Lawrence ('Lawrence of Arabia') in front of the Sphinx, March 1921. Fremantle / Alamy Stock Photo.
17. Churchill with T. E. Lawrence during his Middle East trip. Library of Congress, Prints & Photographs Division, [reproduction, number LC-USZ62-65460].
18. Abdullah of Transjordan, brother to Faisal of Iraq, shakes hands with Clementine on the steps of Government House in Jerusalem, March 1921. Photo 12 / Getty Images.
19. Hazel, Lady Lavery unlocked Churchill's artistic inhibitions and played hostess to Michael Collins during the Anglo-Irish treaty talks. Library of Congress, Prints & Photographs Division, [reproduction, number LC-B2- 2990-9].
20. Michael Collins delivers a passionate speech, late 1921 or early 1922. Roger Viollet / Getty Images.
21. Churchill in Dundee with Sir George Ritchie following severe riots, September 1921. D. C. Thomson & Co Ltd.
22. The wealthy and well-connected Sir Philip Sassoon on the steps of his home at Lympne on the Channel coast in Kent. © National Portrait Gallery, London.
23. The 'Big Three' of the Coalition: Churchill seen here with F. E. Smith (Lord Birkenhead, the Lord Chancellor) and Prime Minister David Lloyd George, 1921. Fremantle / Alamy Stock Photo.

24. Churchill playing his beloved polo, 1921. Hulton Deutsch / Getty Images.
25. *Winston Churchill Painting*, portrait by Sir John Lavery. Fremantle / Alamy Stock Photo.

ACKNOWLEDGEMENTS

Over several years writing about Churchill I have benefited greatly from discussions with many friends and colleagues too numerous to list here. For this book in particular, however, I wish to thank Paul Addison and Piers Brendon, as well as the anonymous readers who made helpful and constructive comments at various stages of the project. Heather McCallum of Yale University Press UK and my agent Andrew Lownie both showed encouraging faith in the project from the start and contributed with many valuable insights and suggestions. I am also grateful to Allen Packwood, Director of the Churchill Archive Centre at Churchill College, Cambridge, who helped facilitate my stay at the College as an Archives By-Fellow in 2016, and to members of his staff, especially Natalie Adams who guided me through its digital holdings and, along with Katharine Thomson, helped with my many enquiries. Cameron Hazlehurst generously shared information about Churchill's first biographer, Alexander MacCallum Scott, as well as on The Other Club. In Scotland, staffs at the National Library of Scotland in Edinburgh and at the Dundee City Archives helped me track down useful references to Churchill and, as ever, the resources of the University of Victoria Library along with its Inter-Library Loan service proved indispensable. For permission to quote from the papers of Wing Commander Maxwell Coote, I wish to thank the Trustees of the Liddell Hart Centre for Military Archives at King's College, London, and for similar use of the papers of Gertrude Bell and of Alexander MacCallum Scott I wish to thank the Bell

ACKNOWLEDGEMENTS

Archive at the University of Newcastle and the University of Glasgow Library, Special Collections, respectively. Quotations from the Clementine Churchill Papers are reproduced with the permission of the Master and Fellows of Churchill College, Cambridge, and for those from Clare Sheridan's papers I wish to thank Jonathan Frewen.

It has been a pleasure to work with the team at Yale University Press in London. The incisive editorial comments by Marika Lysandrou along with her scrupulous guiding hand proved enormously helpful; Rachael Lonsdale, Clarissa Sutherland, and Lucy Buchan skilfully shepherded the book through its various stages of production; and Richard Mason copy-edited the text with brisk and greatly appreciated efficiency. Others I wish to thank include Matt James, Rosamund Howe, and Douglas Matthews, who compiled the index. Above all, as always, my deepest thanks go to my wife Jeanne Cannizzo for her tremendous moral and practical support, creative editorial suggestions and invaluable assistance with picture and other research.

David Stafford
March 2019

'A BOLD, BAD MAN'

Shortly before noon on Wednesday 26 January 1921 an express train bound for Shrewsbury in England was speeding towards the small rural station of Abermule, close to the Severn river in Wales. It was on a single-track line. A safety system used by the Cambrian Railway Company involving the exchange of tablets ensured that no two trains travelling in opposite directions should enter the same section. But the experienced stationmaster was on holiday and junior members of his staff made a series of catastrophic errors. As the express approached the station, its horrified crew saw a local passenger train heading straight towards them. They immediately threw on the brake. It was too late. In the shattering impact that followed, the express train mounted the oncoming engine and crashed down on the roof of the first carriage, smashing it into fragments. Many of the fragile wooden carriages of the express were brutally telescoped together, crushing and maiming their passengers. Miraculously, the express crew crawled out of the wreckage alive after jumping clear at the last moment. But both the driver and fireman of the local train were instantly killed. Fifteen passengers also perished in the collision and dozens of others were injured.

Amongst the dead was a director of the Cambrian Railway Company who'd been travelling in the express. Lord Herbert Lionel Vane-Tempest was fifty-eight years old, a Justice of the Peace, an Honorary Lieutenant-Colonel in the Durham Artillery Volunteers, and a Knight Commander, Royal Victorian Order (KCVO). More importantly, he was the youngest son of the fifth Marquess of Londonderry and owned Garron Towers, a large estate in Ireland that produced an annual income of some £4,000 (approximately £160,000 in today's values). He was also unmarried, and his heir was a first cousin once removed. Lord Herbert's name is long forgotten. But the man who unexpectedly inherited his fortune was one of the most controversial British politicians of the day: Winston Churchill, the Secretary of State for War and Air in the Coalition government of the Liberal prime minister, David Lloyd George.[1]

*

The year 1921 proved pivotal for Churchill in crucial ways. For his personal life it was, in the words of one his closest friends, both 'wonderful and terrible'. The inheritance delivered by the railway disaster helped transform his finances, as did the signing of lucrative contracts for *The World Crisis*, his multi-volume history of the First World War which established his reputation as a man of action who understood the grave issues of war and peace confronting the new century. He had also just turned forty-six, thus surpassing the lifespan of the father whose legacy and memory he idolized. 'Curse ruthless time! Curse our mortality,' he once exclaimed despairingly during his thirties. Now, he was able to imagine a longer-term future with a normal lifespan. This was also the year that he fully realized his abilities as a gifted amateur artist and enjoyed success with the first public exhibition of his works.

Yet it was also marked by tragedy and grief caused by the sudden and unexpected deaths of beloved family members as well as old friends. The end of youth and the passing of loved ones are part of the human condition. But he overcame these everyman losses with a resilience and courage that demonstrated formidable strength of character along with an acceptance of life's tragedies. 'The reflections of middle age are mellow,' he confessed to his wife Clementine. Although no less ambitious than before, he was no longer the impetuous young man in a hurry, desperate to make his mark.[2]

Politically, the year was also a milestone. When it began, his position was precarious and no one could be sure whether he was headed for oblivion or glory. Damned as impetuous and belligerent for his role in the disastrous Dardanelles Expedition of 1915, his violent denunciations of the Russian Bolsheviks and his enthusiastic support for reprisals against armed rebellion in Ireland had only strengthened this view. 'Winston has a reputation as a buccaneer,' observed one shrewd insider in British politics shortly before the year began. 'The country regards him as a bold, bad man.' Yet by the end of 1921 another critic was offering a radically different view of him, as both a statesman and a peacemaker with a shining future ahead of him: 'Were I an ambitious young backbencher I would hitch my wagon to [his] star,' he declared. 'Winston seems to be the only man in the Cabinet with a sane and comprehensive view of world politics.'[3] Churchill clearly stood at a crossroads. It was to take him two more decades to obtain the keys to 10 Downing Street and become the leader of his nation in war. But in these crucial twelve months he laid the foundations for his future glory. How he did so is the subject of this book.

'A TRAGIC FLAW IN THE METAL'

I n his early political career Churchill enjoyed dizzying success, breaking records as he hurtled his way along the political track. Elected to Parliament in 1900 at age twenty-five, by 1908 he was President of the Board of Trade and two years later he became Home Secretary, the youngest since Sir Robert Peel in the early Victorian era. When Britain went to war against Germany in August 1914 he was First Lord of the Admiralty, not yet aged forty, and responsible for the world's largest and most powerful navy. Many observers saw him as a prime minister in the making.

Then, in 1915, his career spectacularly crashed. The cause was the ill-fated naval assault on the Dardanelles Strait, the narrow stretch of water linking the Mediterranean to Constantinople (now Istanbul), the capital of the Ottoman Empire which was allied to Germany. If the British fleet could force its way through the Dardanelles, so Churchill imagined, its appearance before Constantinople could force the Turks to sue for peace, open up the sea route through the Black Sea to Britain's hard-pressed ally Russia, and prompt the Balkan states to join the Allies. It was an imaginative way to break the deadlock of bloody trench warfare on the Western Front, and a typically bold Churchillian idea. But its execution was bungled, and the results were disastrous. An expedition landed on the Gallipoli peninsula but after months of fierce Turkish resistance it was forced to withdraw with the loss of almost 50,000 Allied lives. 'Remember the Dardanelles' was to become a hostile catchphrase that was to haunt Churchill and his reputation for years to come.[1]

Responsibility for the disaster was far from his alone. But he was one of the fiercest early champions of action in the Dardanelles and became the obvious political scapegoat. He was removed from the Admiralty and shifted to the largely empty position of Chancellor of the Duchy of Lancaster. After a few depressing months he resigned his office and left for the Western Front to fight in the trenches. 'I'm finished,' he despondently told one of his closest friends, 'I'm done.' In his own graphic words, he descended into 'a sort of cataleptic trance'. Like a sea beast fished up from the depths, he wrote, '... my veins threatened to burst from the fall in pressure'. His wife Clementine later confessed that she feared he would die of grief, and he clearly came close to a severe nervous breakdown.[2] The distinguished Irish artist William Orpen completed an intense and sombre portrait of him that powerfully captures his mood in these dark post-Gallipoli days. 'All he did was to sit in a chair before the fire with his head bowed in his hands, uttering not a word,' wrote Orpen about one of their sittings: when the artist returned from a lunch break, it was to find his subject still in the same position. At four o'clock he got up, asked Orpen to call him a taxi, and left without saying a word. Yet the painting became his favourite portrait of his younger self and was to hang in his London dining room until his death.[3]

*

Gallipoli let loose the critics. Many were savage. Several had long been waiting for the chance to strike. Churchill's switch from the Conservative Party to the Liberals in 1904 in defence of free trade principles against the growing move towards protectionist tariffs by the Tories had sparked charges of being disloyal, unscrupulous, and unreliable. His overt ambition grated on the sensibilities of many. His egotism and unashamed love of the limelight hinted at superficiality and showmanship. In the new age of the photograph and the cinema his transparent delight in seeking out the camera raised dark suspicion. It didn't help, either, that he was the son of a controversial father. Lord Randolph Churchill had risen brilliantly through the Tory ranks to become Chancellor of the Exchequer in 1886, only to catastrophically self-destruct by an impulsive resignation and disappear into political oblivion before dying prematurely at the age of forty-five. Churchill idolized his father's memory. At only thirty-one he published a two-volume biography of Lord Randolph that was widely praised. Unfortunately, it also encouraged comparisons between father and son that did the younger man few favours. Many of Lord Randolph's contemporaries had regarded him as little more than an unprincipled and publicity-hungry opportunist. 'Churchill, with all his remarkable cleverness, is thoroughly untrustworthy; scarcely a gentleman, and probably more or less mad,' the fifteenth Earl of Derby had confided to his diary. Sir Henry Lucy, a veteran parliamentary sketch writer for *Punch* magazine, widely known on both sides of the Atlantic as a commentator on public affairs since the 1880s – Woodrow Wilson once credited him with propelling him into political life – lamented that for all his gifts Winston Churchill was a replica of his father and possessed 'the same arrogance of manner, the same exaggeration of speech, the same readiness to make the best of both worlds of political party'. For many contemporary critics, indeed, Churchill the younger seemed to live the life of 'a particularly wayward, rootless and anachronistic product of a decaying and increasingly discredited aristocratic order'.[4]

Neither did it help that his mother, Jennie Jerome, was an extravagant American socialite, tainting him as it did with the dreaded New World stigma of being money-grabbing, vulgar, and populist. The political alliance he forged with the radical Chancellor of the Exchequer and Welsh schoolmaster's son David Lloyd George, author of the tax-raising 'People's Budget' of 1909, only deepened misgivings. 'It is dreadful to think that we have such men in the Cabinet as Winston Churchill and Lloyd George,' complained Sir Spencer Ewart, the Director of Military Intelligence. 'The one a half-baked American politician, the other a silly sentimental Celt.' His support for Irish Home Rule further damned Churchill in the eyes of traditionalists.[5]

To Churchill's 'betrayal' of the Tories was added the unforgivable charge of being a traitor to his class. After all, he was the grandson of a duke and was born in Blenheim Palace, the ancestral seat of the Marlboroughs. His support for the reform of the House of Lords, stripping it of the power to block legislation, raised fury amongst the wealthy and the privileged. Some neither forgot nor forgave and King George V denounced him as 'irresponsible and unreliable'. Meanwhile, the Left had its own special bones to pick. As Home Secretary he took energetic measures against strikers in the coalfields, and during the national railway strike of 1911 he mobilized some 50,000 troops to stand by. Moreover, he never disguised his dislike of socialism. For the next several decades he was to remain the *bête-noire* of Labour. Hostility even extended to the myth, which still lingers today, that he ordered troops to fire on striking miners at Tonypandy in Wales in November 1910.[6]

*

Tory and Labour mistrust of Churchill came naturally. But to what degree was he even a genuine Liberal? Being true to the cause meant valuing peace. Yet there was plenty to suggest that he actually rejoiced in war. He was a graduate of Sandhurst, Britain's military academy. He fought enthusiastically in – and wrote vividly about – several of the late Victorian wars on the fringes of Empire. It was his dramatic escape from a prisoner-of-war camp during the Boer War that had first propelled him into Parliament as a 'hero of the Empire'. As First Lord of the Admiralty he demanded more and better battleships. His delight in dressing in naval uniform was undisguised. His rhetoric, whatever the subject, was invariably belligerent. Nor did he ever forget, or let it be forgotten, that he was descended from the great 1st Duke of Marlborough whose armies had won legendary victories across Europe two centuries before – and whose exploits he was to chronicle in his massive multi-volume biography written during the 1930s. 'Sunny' Marlborough, the ninth duke, was a first cousin to whom he remained close throughout his life. Churchill frequently stayed at Blenheim Palace, and when he bought a Napier car in 1911 the first thing he did was have it custom-painted in the Marlborough blue; it was at Blenheim, too, that he proposed marriage to Clementine Hozier, the young woman who became his wife. He was also fascinated by Napoleon. He avidly collected books about the French Emperor, considered him 'the greatest man of action ever known to human records', and hoped at one point to write his biography. He even kept a bust of him in his office. Whenever he moved, it travelled with him.[7]

*

One of the closest observers of Churchill at this time was the essayist and editor of the Liberal newspaper, the *Daily News*, Alfred George (A. G.) Gardiner. As early as 1908, when Churchill was at the Board of Trade, Gardiner nicely captured the disruptive impact he made on the staid Edwardian House of Commons. His dashing style, penned Gardiner, brought to mind 'the clatter of hoofs in the moonlight, the clash of swords on the turnpike road ... The breath of romance stirring the prosaic air of politics'. Five years later, with Churchill at the Admiralty, Gardiner published a collection of biographical portraits entitled *The Pillars of Society* featuring individuals as diverse as the industrial tycoon and philanthropist Andrew Carnegie, the actress Sarah Bernhardt, and the Russian anarchist Prince Peter Kropotkin. One of his subjects was Churchill. 'He is the unknown factor in politics ... [who will] write his name big in the future', pronounced Gardiner. '"Keep Your Eye on Churchill" should be the order of the day'. But Gardiner also issued a warning. They should be aware, he told his readers, that 'he is a soldier first, last, and always ... Let us take care he does not write [his name] in blood'.[8] Only a year later, during the opening shots of the First World War, Gardiner's forebodings about Churchill's natural belligerence were to seem ominously prescient.

*

In October 1914 the Belgian coastal fortress of Antwerp came under bombardment by the Germans. When the Belgian government appealed for help Churchill dashed off to the city, took personal charge of the defences, and called in reinforcements from the Royal Marine Brigade and the Royal Naval Division, both of which were under his Admiralty control. Clearly exhilarated by the crisis, he sent an impetuous telegram to the prime minister Herbert Asquith offering to resign his office and take over official command of the defences. The offer was rejected out of hand and he returned to London. Yet within hours Churchill was claiming that, having 'tasted blood' at Antwerp, he was eager for more and hoped that sooner or later – and the sooner the better – he could be relieved of his Admiralty tasks and given some kind of military command. Asquith's acerbic response was to be shared by many critics. 'He is a wonderful creature,' the prime minister concluded, 'with a curious dash of schoolboy simplicity ... And what someone said of genius – a zig-zag streak of lightning in the brain.'[9] When he read out Churchill's telegram to the Cabinet it was greeted with mocking laughter and the Conservative Party leader Andrew Bonar Law remarked that Churchill had 'an entirely unbalanced mind'. Even his close ally, David Lloyd George, believed that he was becoming a danger. 'Winston is like a torpedo,' he declared. 'The first you hear of his doings is when you hear the swish of the torpedo dashing through the water.'[10] Thirty years later, Field Marshal Sir Alan Brooke, chief of the Imperial General Staff during the Second World War, was to express similar exasperation about Churchill's impulsiveness. After one of the many furious rows over strategy he was to have with Britain's wartime leader, Brooke scribbled in his diary the following words: 'He lives for the impulse and for the present, and refuses to look at the lateral implications or future commitments. Now that I know him well episodes such as Antwerp and the Dardanelles no longer puzzle me. But meanwhile I often doubt whether I am going mad or whether he is really sane.'[11]

*

Two things saved Churchill at this time of mid-life crisis. The first was his family. Its role in his life has often been underestimated. The constant and loyal support of his wife Clementine has certainly been well recognized, and the lives of their children, especially his tempestuous only son Randolph, are relatively well known. But there also existed the extended family of his mother, brother, sister-in-law, aunts, uncles, and cousins, as well as Clementine's own many relations, all of whom formed a large private clan on which he could rely throughout his life for support and comfort. He also inspired devotion from a network of friends to whom he remained profoundly loyal. One of these was Violet Asquith, the daughter of Herbert Asquith, who remained close to him until the end of his life. Shortly after he died, she published her memories (as Violet Bonham Carter) of their relationship under the title *Winston Churchill as I Knew Him*. 'His friendship,' she wrote, 'was a stronghold against which the gates of Hell could not prevail. There was an absolute quality in his loyalty, known only to those within its walls ... This inner citadel of the heart held first and foremost his relations – in their widest sense.' It was to Violet that he confessed that he was 'done' as a result of the Dardanelles.[12]

Thanks to this wider family network Churchill was introduced to his second great source of solace after the psychic wounds of Gallipoli. The loss of the Admiralty meant that he and the family had to leave Admiralty House, and they moved in with his younger brother's family at 41 Cromwell Road, London, almost opposite the Natural History Museum. Behind the scenes, brother Jack was a constant source of advice and support to him throughout his life. Ironically, Jack was just then serving with the British forces at Gallipoli. So it was left to his wife Gwendeline (fondly known as 'Goonie') to look after their two young children and run the household. That summer, the two families jointly leased a property in the country known as Hoe Farm, near Godalming in Surrey, to which they would retreat for weekends. One day, Churchill was wandering disconsolately through the garden when he came across Goonie sketching with watercolours. After watching her for a few minutes he borrowed his nephew Johnnie's paint box and got to work. Soon he began to experiment with oils, opened an account with an artists' supply company in Covent Garden, and started making regular purchases of canvases, paints, and other artistic paraphernalia. It was the beginning of what would become a lifetime's passion for painting, with some five hundred completed canvases to his credit. This was more than the amusing hobby of a great man, deserving perhaps of a footnote. On the contrary, it was a vital thread in the tapestry of his life that reveals much about his character.[13]

It was at Hoe Farm, too, that the poet Wilfrid Scawen Blunt encountered him that same summer. Ten years before, he had been struck by

Churchill's sparkling wit, intelligence, and originality and by how much he resembled his father – only with more ability. 'There is the same *gaminerie* and contempt of the conventional,' noted Blunt, 'and the same engaging plain-spokenness … ' But at Hoe Farm, Blunt found a very different and more subdued Churchill, sitting under an old yew tree surrounded by members of the family while attempting to sketch his sister-in-law, Nellie. 'There is more blood than paint on these hands,' he abjectly told the poet. 'We thought it [the Dardanelles] would be a little job, and so it might have been if it had begun in the right way and now all these lives lost.' 'Poor Winston,' reflected Blunt, 'I imagine that but for his wife's devotion and his domestic happiness with his children and the support of a few relatives, he might have gone mad.'[14]

*

Churchill's hopes of finding a position of high command in the war were thwarted and eventually he arrived on the Western Front early in 1916 with the rank of Lieutenant-Colonel in command of the 6th Battalion of the Royal Scots Fusiliers. For a hundred days he served on the front line near the Belgian village of Ploegsteert ('Plug Street'), where he proved a successful commanding officer and won the respect of his men. Then he resigned his commission, returned to London, and began to rebuild his political career. Later in the year Lloyd George became prime minister, and in the following May an official inquiry into the Dardanelles Expedition cleared Churchill of principal blame for the disaster. The way was now open for him to return to high office and Lloyd George appointed him Minister of Munitions, and he embraced the task with his usual high energy. When the war was won Lloyd George's Coalition government of Liberals and Conservatives was returned to power with a large majority and Churchill became Secretary of State for War and Air with a seat in the Cabinet.

As the year 1921 opened, this was the position he still held. Once again he was a major national figure, his name constantly in the headlines and his future regularly a matter of feverish speculation. Brilliant he was, most critics agreed, but what to make of him? 'Restless, boundlessly ambitious, with quite wonderful gifts as a Parliamentarian,' one observer noted, 'there is no knowing what he will ever do or to what position he may ultimately reach.'[15] Few observers denied his intellect. But what about his character and temperament? The doubts sown by Antwerp and Gallipoli lingered powerfully on. Churchill's period in office had begun well. The demobilization of millions of men was a herculean task threatening chaos, but he pulled it off with aplomb. The larger world beyond British shores, however, proved more intractable. The Versailles settlement of 1919 established peace with Germany. But the war also unleashed violent and unpredictable forces of nationalism and revolution. The entire world order he had known since childhood had been uprooted, in Europe, the Middle East, and Asia. Territorial awards from defeated Germany and the Ottoman Empire had made the geographical reach of the British Empire greater than ever before; but in India, its Jewel in the Crown, the rising tide of nationalism would sweep away the Raj forever within a generation. Asia, he complained, had 'gone maggoty'.[16] The Victorian certainties were dead. In his portrait of the thirty-nine-year-old Churchill on the eve of the First World War, A. G. Gardiner had described him as 'a typical child of his time', who plunged into the world 'with the joy of a man who has found his natural element. A world of transition is made for him.' Neither man could have imagined the earthquake that was about to come. When the dust settled, Churchill emerged as a man no longer embracing change but appalled and sobered by the world he now faced. 'For the most part,' he lamented about the aftermath of the First World War, it was 'a chronicle of misfortune and tragedy . . . Events were crowded and turbulent. Men were tired and wayward. Power was on the ebb tide, prosperity was stranded; and money was an increasing worry.'[17]

These words were written later in his multi-volume history of the First World War, *The World Crisis*. At the time, however, Churchill's rhetoric was even more apocalyptic. This was especially true about the Bolshevik Revolution of 1917. 'Of all tyrannies in history,' he thundered, 'the Bolshevik tyranny is the worst, the most destructive, and the most degrading.' During his two years at the War Office, he strained every nerve and tried every trick to destroy Lenin's regime by supporting the anti-Bolshevik armies fighting in the catastrophic Russian Civil War. Lloyd George, who frustrated all his efforts, believed that at the root of Churchill's hostility to the Revolution lay his 'ducal blood' that was horrified at the wholesale slaughter of the Grand Dukes in Russia. This surely was part of it. But he was also appalled by mob rule, by the breakdown of society and social norms, and by the pitiless nature of Lenin's unforgiving regime. Across Russia, starvation was rife, and millions of the desperate and impoverished were fleeing the country. Churchill also saw Bolshevism as a dangerous form of international disorder that threatened the British Empire.[18]

These feelings he laid bare in a confrontation with Lloyd George in Paris. In Britain there was serious concern about imminent strikes and the dangers of civil violence, and Lloyd George summoned an urgent Cabinet meeting in the French capital. Churchill arrived by train in a rage about Russia. By now he bitterly accepted that the White, anti-Bolshevik, armies were finally finished. Just two days before, their leader in Siberia, Admiral Kolchak, had fallen into Bolshevik hands, his fate clearly sealed: he was shot on the banks of a nearby river and his body shoved under the ice. Over lunch, Churchill launched into a furious tirade about the world's disorder. 'Winston waxed very eloquent on the subject of the old world and the new,' noted Lloyd George's secretary and mistress Frances Stevenson in her diary, 'taking arms in defence of the former.' Above all, he was livid that the Paris peacemakers had decided to open trade talks with revolutionary Russia. Discussion became heated and according to Stevenson he became 'almost like a madman'. That night, the discussion continued over dinner at the fashionable Ciro's Restaurant. Situated on the ground floor of the Hotel Daunou in a quarter of Paris especially favoured by the growing flood of American post-war visitors to the city, it was the smartest place to be seen. Stevenson again kept a brief record. 'Winston still raving on the subject of the Bolsheviks, & ragging D [Lloyd George] about the New World. "Don't you make any mistake," he said to D. "You're not going to get your new world. The old world is a good enough place for me, and there's life in the old dog yet. It's going to sit up & wag its tail." '[19]

This was no idle threat designed simply to rile Lloyd George. As soon as he was back in London, Churchill met with close friends over dinner at Wimborne House, the principal London home of his aunt Cornelia. Amongst them was the young diplomat Alfred Duff Cooper, who during the Second World War was to serve as his representative in North Africa with the Free French leader General Charles de Gaulle. 'Winston was splendidly reactionary,' noted Cooper in his diary. Not only did he swear that his one object in politics was now to fight Labour. He also declared that he was a monarchist, that he hoped to see all the deposed European monarchs back on their thrones – including the Prussian Hohenzollerns – and claimed that the 'calamitous state' of central Europe was thanks to the new and corrupt republics. 'Thank God,' Churchill told his friends, 'that he was in no way responsible for the Peace Treaty which he would have been ashamed to put his name to.' Churchill also admitted that he was becoming more disillusioned and discontented. If he had the choice between immortality and being blown out like a candle, he confessed, he would choose the latter.[20]

*

Cartoons of the day succinctly capture the controversial public image Churchill enjoyed in the press. From his earliest appearance on the public stage he had possessed the magical quality of 'news value'. This was caught brilliantly before the First World War by a cartoon in *Punch* magazine depicting him on the Admiralty yacht the *Enchantress*, seated comfortably on a deckchair. Next to him is the prime minister Herbert Asquith. The daily newspapers have just been delivered. 'Any home news?' asks Churchill. 'How can there be,' replies Asquith, 'with you here?'[21]

Churchill fully grasped the power of such imagery. As a child he gained his first impressions of historical events from the volumes of *Punch* kept at his private school: Britannia kneeling with an unsheathed sword before the Crimean War; the British Lion leaping down on the Bengal Tiger during the Indian Mutiny; France defeated after the Franco-Prussian War, portrayed as a prostrate and beautiful woman with a broken sword in her hand.

By 1921 Churchill himself was one of the most caricatured of British politicians, resigned to the fact that cartoons invariably depicted him with a nose like a wart and wearing a variety of ill-fitting hats. The legend of his penchant for hats that were too small sprang from a single incident during the General Election of 1910, when he had unthinkingly picked up a small felt hat that he found on a hall table before going out for a walk. The scene was snapped on camera by a reporter, and since then hats had featured as one of Churchill's consistent cartoon 'props', a not so subtle hint that politically he was unpredictable and opportunistic, ready to change hats on a whim, and too big-headed for most. Only later did the cigar, the signature mark for which he now remains famous, regularly enter the cartoonists' repertoire – and it was happily pandered to by their appreciative target.

Two of the leading British cartoonists of the day were Sidney Conrad Strube of the *Daily Express* and Percy Fearon ('Poy') of the *Evening News* and *Daily Mail*. Neither had a very favourable view of Churchill, depicting him as either itching for war or hostile to the workers. But a new rival had recently entered the scene. David Low was a New Zealander of Scottish ancestry who had made his name in Australia with powerful lampoons of the country's wartime prime minister, Billy Hughes. In 1919, aged twenty-eight, he landed in England with a contract in his pocket to produce a daily cartoon for the *Star*, the evening stablemate of the Liberal newspaper, the *Daily News*. Low was a fast and ambitious learner who was quickly in demand for his caricatures of leading figures in British society. When he wrote his autobiography in the afterglow of Churchill's victorious Second World War premiership, Low would recall that when they first met, Churchill was 'one of the few men I have ever met who even in the flesh gave me the impression of genius'. In 1940, in a famous cartoon entitled 'All Behind You Winston', Low was to depict a pugnacious Churchill as prime minister, sleeves rolled up for action, with the Labour Party and the nation marching and united behind him.[22]

But in 1920–1 Low's sympathies were firmly on the Left. In contrast to Poy, he set out to ridicule, not just amuse. He had little time for Churchill's politics and regarded his demonization of the Labour Party and trade unions as more or less agents of Bolshevism to be absurd; far from Russian bears, thought Low, the British trade unions were little more than 'rabbits'. With their strong lines and high contrasts of black and white, his cartoons were radical, hard-hitting, and visually dramatic. Churchill described him with admiration as the 'Charlie Chaplin of caricature'. The fact that he was frequently a target of Low's critique bothered him not at all. To have been ignored would have been worse. Besides, he was unable to take the New Zealander's colonial radicalism too seriously. 'You cannot bridle the wild ass of the desert,' he wrote dismissively, 'still less prohibit its natural hee-haw.'[23] Low's cartoons paint him as a warmonger and a hungrily ambitious empire-builder with a record of failure behind him. One from 1920 shows him dressed in the check-suited gear of a country squire, shotgun in hand, with his 'bag' of dead animals at his feet including Antwerp, Gallipoli, and Russia. Another cartoon that same year reveals Churchill peering at portraits of Lenin and Trotsky and resembling a combination of both of them. 'Winstonsky: Horrifying effect of concentration on Russian Affairs' reads the caption. Yet another depicts him fanning the flames of war along with a foreign capitalist, a fat and well-fed 'patriot', and a 'pinhead politician', amongst others, while blocking the road for a car labelled 'League of Nations'. 'Keep the Hate Fires Burning' is its caption, playing on Ivor Novello's famous popular song from the war. The Churchill of these images was to be the stock-in-trade of critics until the Second World War and even beyond.

*

'He will never get to the top in English politics, with all his wonderful gifts,' predicted Asquith in 1915. 'To speak with the tongues of men and angels, and to spend laborious days and nights in administration, is no good, if a man does not inspire trust.'[24] Two years later when Lloyd George proposed bringing Churchill back into the government there had been howls of protest from his colleagues. 'They admitted he was a man of dazzling talents,' wrote Lloyd George. But why did he have so few followers? It was because, they argued, that while his mind was a powerful machine it contained some obscure defect, 'a tragic flaw in the metal', which must be guarded against. This was the legacy facing Churchill as the new year began.[25]

WINTER

WINTER

ONE

'RULE BRITANNIA'

C hurchill loved singing, the good life, and the company of close friends – especially if they were rich, powerful, or influential. So the New Year celebrations to herald the arrival of 1921 found him in a jovial mood. He was staying at Port Lympne, a luxurious mansion in Kent perched on a ridge overlooking Romney Marsh with views over the English Channel. His fellow house guests consisted of some of Britain's most powerful men: David Lloyd George, whose wily domination of the political scene as prime minister during the First World War and since, as well as his masterful handling of the Paris Peace Conference, had earned him the sobriquet of 'the Welsh Wizard'; Baron Riddell, the influential proprietor of one of the bestselling newspapers of the day, *The News of the World*, who had masterminded Lloyd George's relations with the press at Paris and now did so in Britain; Sir William Sutherland, nicknamed 'Bronco Bill', the political fixer and go-between who rarely left Lloyd George's side, a Glaswegian widely mistrusted as an unscrupulous manipulator, branded by Riddell as 'an amusing, cynical dog', and damned by the Cabinet Secretary Sir Maurice Hankey as 'an odious fellow, some sort of political parasite'. The Irish Secretary Sir Hamar Greenwood, a Canadian-born lawyer and Liberal Member of Parliament who had worked with Churchill at the Colonial Office before the war and now faced an Ireland in open revolt, was also amongst the company. His assigned task in the government was to exude optimism, and he was a loyal performer.

Discreetly accompanying the prime minister was his long-standing secretary and mistress, the thirty-two-year-old classics graduate Frances Stevenson, who had fallen for his charms before the war and been at his side ever since. The only other woman present was Greenwood's politically ambitious wife Margo. The daughter of a wealthy English vicar and seventeen years younger than her husband, she was rumoured to have enjoyed the prime minister's sexual favours before and possibly even after her marriage; the Greenwoods were frequent guests at weekend parties organized for Lloyd George by the ubiquitous Stevenson.[1]

*

The male guests were in their forties or fifties. The two women were in their early thirties. Close in age to both, and hovering discreetly in the background, was their host, the unmarried thirty-two-year-old aesthete and millionaire Sir Philip Sassoon. Sleek, athletic, and impeccably dressed, he was a grandson on his mother's side of Baron Gustave de Rothschild of Paris, the second cousin of the famous war poet Siegfried Sassoon, and the local Conservative Member of Parliament. Churchill knew him well, as did Clementine, who had spent several weeks in 1914 at Port Lympne recovering from the birth of Sarah, their second daughter. As private secretary to Sir Douglas Haig, the commander-in-chief of British forces on the Western Front, Sassoon had managed Haig's daily schedule and his relations with the press, drafted his letters, arranged visits for dignitaries, and garnered a host of influential contacts that were delivering him – and them – a healthy peacetime dividend by way of political influence. Churchill had made many visits to the Western Front as Minister of Munitions. 'Philip sits like a wakeful spaniel outside [Haig's] door,' he joked to Clementine. Sassoon was now Lloyd George's parliamentary private secretary and with an office next to the Cabinet Room in 10 Downing Street he now performed a similar function as he had for Haig. Frances Stevenson quipped that he was as 'amusing and clever as a cartload of monkeys'.

Port Lympne was not Sassoon's only residence. Both his grand house on Park Lane and his mansion north of London at Trent Park provided venues for an unending round of hospitality that brought together royalty, politicians, writers, stars of stage and screen, and other celebrities that was to stretch over two decades until Sassoon's premature death aged fifty in 1939. Legendary in their day, his parties resembled theatrical set pieces that according to one of their regular participants 'mingled luxury, simplicity, and informality, brilliantly contrived'.[2]

*

This visit was by no means the first that Churchill had made to Lympne. Just five months before, he and Clementine had enjoyed a summer weekend there when he had become absorbed in painting and sketching views across Romney Marsh, striving hard to capture on canvas the sparkling movement of the water. He appreciated Sassoon's hospitality, his contacts, and his discretion, as well as his interest in art. The young millionaire was soon to be appointed a Trustee of the National Gallery of Art in London and he offered Churchill encouragement and critiques of his work, lent him paintings from his own private collection to copy, and introduced him to distinguished society artists. This was not the only weekend in 1921 during which Churchill would be one of Sassoon's privileged guests.

*

Port Lympne had been built for Sassoon just before the war as a modest weekend house. But in a burst of optimism at the arrival of peace he had spent a small fortune on having it modernized and enlarged by the fashionable young architect Philip Tilden. Outwardly, the red-brick building was stylish but conservative, with terraced gardens, fountains, statues, and pavilions with classical pillars that referenced the site's historic origins as a Roman port.

Behind the bronze front door, however, Sassoon had let loose his own far from conventional creative ambitions and artistic tastes. An interior courtyard featured white marble columns, brilliant green pantiles, and orange trees, and was almost certainly inspired by a visit he had made to the Alhambra Palace in Granada, Spain. The library was lined with books bound in pinkish-red Moroccan leather and sported a green and pink carpet. In the dining room the walls were decorated with marble-effect cobalt-blue lapis lazuli, the central table was surrounded by gilded chairs with arms resembling the wings of an eagle, and the ceiling was ringed with a frieze depicting a scene from ancient Egypt of half-naked black men working with animals.

But the dramatic highlight and undoubted talking point of the house was the drawing room. Here, Sassoon had commissioned a mural by the Catalan artist, Josep Maria Sert, who had deeply impressed him with the sets he had designed for a performance of the Ballets Russes. An allegory of Germany's defeat in the recent war, it showed France as a draped and crouching female figure being attacked by German eagles and defended by the Allies in the form of children wearing headpieces from their respective national costumes, and by the Indian Empire, represented by elephants. The story ended with the German eagles being torn to pieces, feathers flying. Charlie Chaplin, who stayed with Sassoon later this same year, described Port Lympne as 'something out of the Arabian Nights'.[3]

*

It was in the drawing room, surrounded by Sert's triumphal mural, that Sassoon and his guests gathered to celebrate the New Year. Churchill was in a typically ebullient mood, vying with Lloyd George to be at the centre of attention. The two had long been friends and rivals. In the pre-war Liberal government, they had formed a 'terrible duo' that successfully steered radical social and political reforms through Parliament which made them anathema to Conservatives and the British establishment. With his clear blue eyes and mane of raffish white hair, Lloyd George was the senior by a decade. A disruptive force himself – he was the son of a poor schoolteacher and his first language was Welsh – he was more experienced, craftier, and more ruthless than Churchill. Their friendship was distinctly political, and sharply barbed. From close experience Lloyd George appreciated Churchill's talents. But he also knew their risks. As Chancellor of the Exchequer when Churchill was Home Secretary, Lloyd George had considered Churchill's plan to deal with the Welsh miners' strike 'mad' and its author wild and impulsive. 'He makes me very uneasy,' he added.[4] As prime minister, however, he felt safer with Churchill inside rather than outside the Cabinet. He had brought him back from the political wilderness to the Ministry of Munitions in 1917, and after the Conservative/Liberal Coalition victory of 1918 he appointed him Secretary of State for War and Air. Churchill was acutely aware of his dependence on Lloyd George. He knew that his protector could just as easily become his political assassin. This lent their alliance a treacherous edge. At the time of Gallipoli, Lloyd George's support had been notice-ably lukewarm. 'I assure you,' the fiercely loyal Clementine warned her husband, 'he is the direct descendant of Judas Iscariot.'[5]

But tonight, all was bonhomie. Phoenix-like, Churchill was back in the Cabinet and at the centre of British politics – and, not least, media attention. Recently turned forty-six and just under five feet seven inches tall, Churchill had clearly crossed the line from youth into middle age. He was thickening around the waist and his face was rounding out. His pale blue eyes were as alert as ever but his sandy hair was fading and he was now almost bald on top. He was still energetic, physically active, and a keen polo player, the strenuous sport he had embraced as a subaltern in the British Army stationed in Bangalore, India, some quarter of a century before. But a serious fall playing the game a few months earlier had put him out of action for several days; injuries no longer healed as rapidly as in his youth. Until two years before he had also been an enthusiastic trainee pilot. He'd given it up after almost getting killed in a crash – and in reluctant response to a passionate plea from Clementine to think of his family and the children.

*

To amuse the company Sir William Sutherland had brought along gram-ophone records of speeches by Warren Harding, the newly elected Republican President of the United States. Churchill knew more about American politics than anyone else in the company. Some he had learned from his American-born mother, but he'd acquired most from one of her oldest friends – and former lovers – the Irish-American politician Bourke Cochran, one-time Democratic congressman from New York City and close advisor to both Presidents Grover Cleveland and Theodore Roosevelt. In 1895 Churchill had arrived in New York on his way to observe the Spanish Army's campaign to crush a guerrilla uprising by Cuban rebels. It was his first visit to the United States and his mother had arranged for Cochran to take her impressionable twenty-year-old son in hand. The force of Cochran's belief in the power of rhetoric and oratory to sway politics had stayed with him ever since.[6]

As Harding's voice boomed out scratchily from the machine's gigantic loudspeaker, Churchill and Lloyd George amused the company by shouting back irreverent and caustic comments. Given the compromise nature of American politics, Churchill told his fellow guests, platitudes such as those emerging from Harding's mouth were inevitable. It was simply not safe for an American politician to venture much beyond promises that 'The sun shone yesterday upon this great and glorious country. It shines today and will shine tomorrow.'

His mimicry raised predictable laughter. But behind the mirth lay serious anxiety. The First World War had fundamentally changed the balance of world power. The US Senate had refused to ratify the Treaty of Versailles and thus blocked America's entry into the League of Nations. How would the new power of the United States, especially of its Navy, be contained? And what did its command of the seas, especially in the Pacific, mean for the British Empire, the Royal Navy, and for Anglo-American relations generally? When the gramophone emitted some grandiose claim by Harding about the American Navy, Lloyd George confessed that he would rather pawn his shirt than allow America to dominate the seas. His outburst struck a powerful patriotic chord and spontaneously the assembled company launched into a lusty rendition of 'Rule Britannia'. Churchill took the lead. As a former First Lord of the Admiralty his pride in the Royal Navy ran deep. He believed passionately in maintaining British naval superiority in the new post-war world. Only two weeks before, at a meeting of the Committee of Imperial Defence, there had been an intense discussion about Anglo-American naval relations. Lloyd George considered this the most important and the most difficult question the Committee had ever discussed. Churchill was all for close relations with Washington, and he accepted that when it came to battleships there would have to be equality – if only for reasons of economy. Overall, though, Britannia should rule supreme in ships. 'Great Britain must remain the strongest naval power,' he argued passionately. 'It would be a terrible day . . . when she ceased to be this. Great Britain, since the most remote times, had always been supreme at sea. The life of the nation, its culture, its prosperity, had rested on that basis.' Not surprisingly the evening saw him repeatedly singing out the words of 'Rule Britannia' and going out of his way to praise their beauty and patriotic fervour. The last two verses, he pronounced, would make a splendid peroration.[7]

More songs followed. Lloyd George, who had been brought up as a Baptist, was known for enjoying hymns and taking part in Wales's annual National Eisteddfod or Festival of Song and Poetry. Once, during the Paris peace talks, a junior member of the Cabinet Secretariat had gone over to Lloyd George's flat for dinner. 'As I came in,' recorded Leo Amery, '[I] heard weird doleful sounds and found L. G. [Lloyd George] singing a Welsh hymn to Miss Stevenson's accompaniment.'[8] But in the privacy of Lympne, surrounded by trusted friends, he chose something in a markedly different vein: the popular Irish song 'Cockles and Mussels'. Its opening lines – 'In Dublin's fair city, where the girls are so pretty, I first set my eyes on sweet Molly Malone' – undoubtedly evoked wry smiles, or at least private chuckles, as the assembled guests joined in with the chorus; the prime minister's relaxed attitude towards his marital vows was no secret and not for nothing was he known as 'The Goat'. In Paris he had lived openly with Frances Stevenson in a luxurious flat on the rue Nitot, quite separate from the official British delegation. After two or three more songs, and a song-and-dance routine by Hamar and Margo Greenwood, it was Churchill's turn.

As an army cadet at Sandhurst during the 1890s he had used his leave to venture into central London and enjoy one of his greatest pleasures – the music hall. This boisterous and often bawdy late Victorian blend of music, words and theatricality thrilled him all his life. As a child he loved playing with his toy theatre. He admiringly talked of his father Lord

Randolph Churchill's 'showman's knack' of drawing attention to himself. Given an audience, he once confessed to his mother, 'there is no act too daring or noble'. Lloyd George neatly captured his theatrical character after observing him once in the House of Commons. 'The applause of the House is the very breath of his nostrils,' he observed. 'He is just like an actor. He likes the limelight and the approbation of the pit.'[9]

*

The drawing room at Lympne was far removed from the orchestral pit of a London music hall. But it was certainly theatrical, and it held a captive audience. Churchill seized the moment. He had an impressive memory for words and could cite great passages of prose and poetry by heart, a gift that would provide him with a lifetime's fund of phrases and images from which he later drew to inspire the nation during the dark days of the Second World War.

But alongside the classics of literature he retained a fund of material from the old music hall. Not long before, he had dutifully accepted an invitation – although it was more like a command – to one of his mother's fashionable lunches in London. Here, for the first time, he met Ivor Novello, the brilliant young Welsh composer of the popular and enduring First World War song, 'Keep the Home Fires Burning'. They immediately took a liking to each other and throughout the meal sparked each other off by reciting the titles of music-hall songs they both knew. But Novello was puzzled when Churchill cracked an obscure joke. Only the next day did it dawn on the composer that it related to the title of a long-forgotten song from 'the old days'.[10] When they first met before the war, the Canadian press magnate Max Aitken – later Lord Beaverbrook – had quickly noted Churchill's penchant for living well, smoking expensive cigars, enjoying brandy and, in moments of relaxation, singing music-hall melodies 'in a raucous voice, and without any instinct for tune'.[11] Music-hall songs were to give him comfort for the rest of his life. During the anxious build-up to the D-Day Normandy landings in the spring of 1944, Clementine celebrated her fifty-ninth birthday with a small family gathering at Downing Street. To keep them amused while Winston worked on his papers, his private secretary 'Jock' Colville chose a selection of music-hall songs. These, he knew, were Winston's prime choice of music.[12]

One of the most popular late Victorian and Edwardian music-hall entertainers was George (G. H.) Chirgwin, the son of a circus clown, who specialized in minstrel shows. But instead of using a fully blacked-up face he painted a large white diamond shape over one eye and was thus billed as 'The White-Eyed Kaffir'. Churchill was clearly familiar with Chirgwin, and Margo Greenwood, who was keeping a diary, noted that 'Winston repeated by heart verse after verse of Chirgwin's [songs].' George Riddell, also a diarist, marvelled at how effortless it all was, even though Churchill had not heard many of the songs in years. Even the hard-bitten and cynical Sutherland was impressed. 'He's an artist in words,' he observed drily.[13]

*

So he was. Before becoming a politician, he was a writer. First as a highly paid war correspondent, then as the author of bestselling books based on his personal exploits in the imperial wars of late Victorian Britain: the North West Frontier of India, Sudan, and the war against the Boers in South Africa. Determined to vindicate the memory of the father who had so spectacularly self-destructed, he'd also written his hefty two-volume biography. Since his own political crash after Gallipoli, he was now desperately keen to vindicate himself. Over the previous few months he had been gathering documents from his time at the Admiralty to support his case, dictating the drafts of chapters of what quickly expanded from a short book about Gallipoli into a multi-volume history of the First World War to be entitled *The World Crisis*. In November he had persuaded the London literary agent Albert Curtis Brown to take on the project, and they soon secured an offer of £9,000 for British Empire rights – the equivalent today of £300,000. Then, just before Christmas, he had received more excellent news: *The Times* newspaper had agreed to pay £5,000 for serialization rights. When he arrived at Lympne, lucrative American contract talks were also well advanced. In the end, the book was to earn him some three-quarters of a million pounds in today's terms. Churchill held no religious belief in eternal life. 'Words,' he once said, 'are the only things that last for ever.' His writings about himself have effectively ensured him his own kind of immortality.[14]

The regular weekend stays at the country houses of friends and colleagues offered more than the welcome opportunity to talk, enjoy fine food, and drink champagne. He always had something creative to do as well. In good weather, this meant taking along an easel, canvasses, and an armoury of brushes and tubes of paint. At other times, he arrived equipped with pen, paper, and documents. With the generous contracts for *The World Crisis* in his pocket, this 1921 New Year's Eve he was in an especially expansive mood. So much so indeed that he boasted to Riddell that he had already written a great part of the first volume, planned to produce 300,000 words, and would then cut it down in length and polish it all up. It was exhilarating, he confessed to the wealthy press magnate, to feel that he was working for half a crown a word. He then disappeared upstairs to write more. Two hours later he returned. 'It's a horrible thought,' joked Riddell to Lloyd George, 'that while we've been frittering away our time, Winston has been piling up words at half a crown apiece.'[15]

*

Jokes about money were one thing, Music-hall nostalgia another, and mimicry of the Americans yet another. More serious was the talk about Ireland.

Here, British policy was teetering between repression and concession. Home Rule bills creating parliaments for both Northern and Southern Ireland had come into force just before Christmas. But the limited devolution they granted was not enough for Sinn Fein, which demanded a republic and full independence outside the British Empire. Its armed struggle, led by the Irish Republican Army (IRA), sparked assassinations and reprisals on both sides. Barely six weeks before the gathering at Lympne, on a Sunday morning in late November 1920, twelve British agents were hauled out of their beds at various addresses across Dublin and shot in cold blood, many in their pyjamas or in front of their wives; most were involved in anti-IRA intelligence work. In retaliation, that

same afternoon British forces raided the Croke Park Gaelic football
stadium in the city and fired into the crowd, killing twelve spectators and
injuring dozens more. 'Bloody Sunday' was followed by more reprisals
and in December the Cabinet decided to proclaim martial law in four of
Ireland's southern counties. After an IRA ambush on a British patrol a
large part of the city of Cork was burned to the ground, including the
City Hall and Carnegie Library. Ireland, said Lloyd George, was nothing
better than a 'hell's broth'. In fear of IRA assassins he had started wearing
a bullet-proof waistcoat and taking a fierce Airedale police dog with him
on walks.[16]

*

Churchill's relationship with Ireland was long, close, and complex. He
had spent part of his childhood in Dublin, had close Irish relatives, and
the small fortune he was about to inherit came from an estate in County
Antrim. Although his father had notoriously played 'the Orange card' in
supporting the Protestant unionists of the north, since before the war he
himself had supported Home Rule, although with separate provision for
Ulster. Far from being an imperialist John Bull when it came to Ireland,
his views were complex and nuanced. What he was bitterly opposed to,
however, was the IRA's campaign of violence. On this, his views were
hawkish and his rhetoric was bloodthirsty. After Lloyd George had
appointed him six months before as head of the Cabinet Committee on
Ireland, he had suggested various methods of intensifying the war
including aircraft to bomb or machine-gun Sinn Fein. To increase the
chances of a settlement, he said, it was necessary 'to raise the temperature'
of the conflict to a real trial of strength.[17] As Secretary of State for War he
was ultimately responsible for the troops in Ireland. The previous spring,
he had proposed the creation of a specially recruited auxiliary armed
force to be attached to the Royal Irish Constabulary (RIC). Known as the
'Black and Tans' because of the colour of their uniforms – a mix of police
black belts and army khaki – it was they who spearheaded the bulk of
British reprisals against the IRA, entered Croke Park with such deadly
results, and set fire to Cork. The head of the RIC was Major-General

Henry Tudor, a long-standing friend since their subaltern days together in India. Thanks to him, the force became increasingly militarized.

Churchill stoutly defended the Black and Tans' campaign of reprisals. They were 'striking down in darkness those who struck from the darkness,' he unapologetically wrote later. Nor would there be any negotiations under duress, he told his parliamentary constituents in Dundee that October. The IRA, he thundered, was nothing more than 'a miserable gang of cowardly assassins'. Not surprisingly, Scotland Yard soon received intelligence that Sinn Fein was planning to kidnap him and other British ministers. By the time he arrived at Sassoon's Port Lympne, he had been given a personal bodyguard.[18]

The Irish crisis seemed deadlocked in a never-ending cycle of violence and bloodshed. Yet behind the scenes, things were moving. Back-channel exploration with Sinn Fein had been going on for months. Just the day before travelling down to Lympne, Churchill had backed Lloyd George at a special Cabinet meeting in arguing for a temporary truce. But the generals present were strongly opposed. 'Terror could be broken,' they argued, and carried the day with martial law being extended to four more counties in the south. Lloyd George and Churchill arrived at Sassoon's nursing their defeat. Sir Hamar Greenwood was not on the original guest list. But after getting an urgent phone call from Lloyd George, he drove down in his car with Margo. As a Canadian with strong imperial instincts, he had prevaricated during the Cabinet meeting. But it was important to get him back in line and to review the situation.

General Tudor had supported the other generals in vetoing a truce. Yet Churchill was not one to nurse a grudge or take it personally. Far from it. His old friend was just standing firm as he had during the war as commander of the 9th (Scottish) Division, explained Churchill to his colleagues, and described a visit he had made to Tudor's headquarters on the eve of the massive German Spring offensive of March 1918. Together they had toured the front line and visited the trenches. The shelling on both sides was terrific. After observing the bombardments for several minutes Tudor insisted they move on. Moments later, the spot where they had been standing was blown up. Throughout, Churchill admiringly told the gathering in Sassoon's drawing room, Tudor had been quite unconcerned.

Implicitly, so had he. He was the only one present who had actively fought on the Western Front. Whatever criticisms that could be levied against him about Gallipoli, his battlefield experience gave him a moral advantage over many of his contemporaries. It also provided him with rich first-hand material for the book that he was working on upstairs in his room. His account of the episode with Tudor in *The World Crisis* is characteristically cinematic. 'Through the chinks in the carefully prepared window,' he writes graphically, 'the flame of the bombardment lit like fire-light my tiny cabin.'[19]

*

Over the breakfast table that Monday morning the talk returned to Ireland. All of those there supported peace – provided Sinn Fein was prepared to make concessions. 'Winston [punctuated] the conversation with shrewd comments,' noted Margo Greenwood. He had already confessed that he was worried about the negative effects that British repression was having on American public opinion. In one case, Kevin Barry, an eighteen-year-old medical student, had been executed in Mountjoy Prison in Dublin for a terrorist attack that killed three British soldiers. A professional hangman was specially brought in from London to carry out the sentence and Barry's death was quickly immortalized in a legendary nationalist ballad with its highly charged chorus words 'Hanged liked a dog', not shot 'like a soldier'. More notoriously, the impris-oned Sinn Fein Lord Mayor of Cork and IRA commander, Terence MacSwiney, had died in Brixton Prison after a hunger strike lasting seventy-four days. In an exquisitely choreographed show of Sinn Fein propaganda, his open coffin was carried from Brixton to Southwark's Catholic Cathedral, where 30,000 people filed past his coffin to view the corpse. MacSwiney's funeral continued to receive massive worldwide publicity as his body was conveyed by rail and ferry back to Cork. Britain was clearly losing the international war of propaganda over Ireland.[20]

Churchill, more than most of his contemporaries, was attuned to the shifting tides of transatlantic sentiment. He was also sympathetic to Irish national feelings and aware that public support inside Britain for the government's hard-line stand, already shaky, could not continue indefinitely. Yet from intelligence reports he also knew that the IRA itself was doubting it could win the war. Was it, perhaps, time for a deal?

*

Before returning to London he had one more thing to accomplish. The Lympne estate nestled in a natural amphitheatre on the edge of the sea embraced by an escarpment. Here, over a picnic lunch on New Year's Day, he asked Lloyd George for a new Cabinet position.

The fact was that he was discontented and wanted to leave the War Office. After a promising start sorting out a mess over the demobilization of millions of men in uniform and backing the creation of an independent Royal Air Force, Churchill suffered a series of failures and disappointments. Despite all his efforts, the Cabinet had refused to intervene in Russia against Lenin's Bolshevik regime and had agreed to start trade negotiations with Moscow. It had also failed to support Churchill's demand that Britain should start negotiating with Mustafa Kemal of Turkey, and frustrated some of his efforts to reduce expenditures in Mesopotamia (which in the course of 1921 became known as Iraq). Within the Cabinet, he was often isolated.

Above all, however, he feared an imminent breakdown in his relationship with Lloyd George. This was the only thing keeping him in the political game. That their relationship had survived so long was something of a miracle. Now he could see it ending. Shortly before Christmas he had bluntly set out his fears in a long and emotional letter to his long-time political friend. 'I am vy [sic] sorry to see how far we are drifting apart on foreign policy,' he began, and ended by hinting, not so subtly, at resignation. 'I have other new interests on [which] I [could] fall back,' he wrote.[21]

Lloyd George was increasingly aware of the fragility of his Coalition government and likewise feared a break. Yet Churchill outside the Cabinet would be more of a nuisance and a danger than inside. The trick was to find him a task that would absorb his energies on an alternative grand stage. Two years before, when he was pondering where to place Churchill in his Cabinet, Riddell had suggested the Colonial Office on the grounds that the colonies would pose many problems and that the position itself needed 'bucking up'. Besides, he added, Churchill could usefully make a tour of the Empire. Lloyd George had rejected the idea then. 'It would be like condemning a man to be head of a mausoleum,' he said. But Riddell's words clearly stuck in his mind. The Empire was certainly a grand stage that would appeal to Churchill's imperial instincts. Perhaps, too, it would be useful to have him out of the country for a while enjoying a grand tour of his new domain. Now, gazing out over the English Channel, the prime minister offered him the position.[22]

But Churchill did not immediately leap at the opportunity. Instead, he thought it over for three or four days. It was something of a poisoned chalice as it would include Mesopotamia (Iraq) as a British mandate. He had already struggled to reduce troop numbers there because of resistance and opposition from other ministries with overlapping interests in the country. Only if he was allowed to set up his own special Middle East Department with full powers over the issue, he told Lloyd George, would he take on the job. A few days later the two men hammered out its terms. He would formally take over the Colonial Office and relinquish the War Office in mid-February. Work on creating the new department would begin immediately and he would start thinking about making a personal visit to the Middle East to examine the issues at first hand. This perfectly fitted Lloyd George's political agenda. He knew Churchill better than did Churchill himself. 'Winston must have a stunt, he is not content to do the ordinary work that goes with his post,' he confided to Margo Greenwood.[23]

The decision also suited Churchill and was more a matter of push than pull – a way of removing himself from sources of friction and conflict with Lloyd George rather than any great enthusiasm for his new task. Indeed, his experience so far with the 'thankless deserts' of Iraq was largely negative. 'I am afraid this venture is going to break me,' he despondently told Sir Maurice Hankey, the Cabinet Secretary.[24]

TWO

FAMILY AND FRIENDS

Brimming with ideas about his new position, Churchill returned to London from the Lympne estate after his talk with Lloyd George. Home was 2 Sussex Square, an elegant early Victorian house close to Hyde Park with two mews houses at the rear, into which he and Clementine had moved less than a year before. By now they had four children: Diana aged eleven, Randolph nine, Sarah six, and two-year-old Marigold. Randolph had just been packed off to a boarding school in Surrey and was already showing signs of the ill-mannered turbulence that would make the father–son relationship one of 'storm and sunshine'. Diana and Sarah were attending nearby Notting Hill High School, while Marigold was mostly in the care of a nanny. Their parents had given them animal nicknames. Diana was 'the Gold-cream Kitten', Randolph 'the Rabbit' or sometimes 'the Chum Bolly', Sarah 'the Bumblebee' and Marigold 'the Duckadilly'; collectively they were known as 'the Kittens'. Churchill loved playing both indoor and outdoor games with his children, giving them the close parental affection lacking in his own childhood. He particularly doted on Marigold and indulged her wildly, letting her scamper round the dining table when he and Clementine had guests for lunch. She was just beginning to talk. Soon she was singing her own special tune, the hit song of the year, 'I'm Forever Blowing Bubbles'.[1]

The move to Sussex Square ended a period of chronic domestic chaos caused by Churchill's political misfortunes and his own innate restlessness. More than once the burden of finding a home for the growing family and its required retinue of servants and nannies had threatened to over-whelm him. He survived thanks only to the willing help of friends and relations. After his forced departure from Admiralty House, his aunt Cornelia was the first to come to his aid. She had long been an ardent supporter of his political ambitions and a treasured confidante. His father's sister, she had married Ivor Guest, a wealthy steel magnate who enjoyed the title of Baron Wimborne. Now a widow, she owned a town house at 21 Arlington Street lying just behind the Ritz Hotel with magnificent views over Green Park. It was there that the Churchills had briefly moved during the summer of 1915, along with Goonie and her two children, Peregrine and Johnny. But the stifling domesticity and noise of it all soon became too much for Churchill, and he fled to live with his mother in her nearby Georgian house on Mayfair's Brook Street. Later, Clementine and the chil-dren moved back to Goonie's Cromwell Road house, and here he rejoined them after returning from his soldiering on the Western Front.

But by now the dreams of owning a more peaceful, rural, retreat had taken hold in his mind and he was actively seeking a place outside London. 'I wish to find a place to end my days amid trees and upon grass of my own,' he confessed. Shortly afterwards he found the haven he sought, one that also removed his children safely away from the increasing hazards of German bombing attacks on London. Lullenden was a Tudor-built mansion house set in some 70 acres in Surrey, and over the next two years he spent as many weekends there as he could. During the week he 'camped' in various government-owned houses or flats in Whitehall near his Ministry of Munitions office. One of Lullenden's advantages was its large barn, where his boisterous young children and their cousins could be housed away from the main house, leaving him in peace and quiet for his writing. It also gave him the opportunity to try his hand at farming, although not very successfully.

By the end of the war, however, this rural idyll was proving far too expensive to run and he and Clementine began the search for a house in central London. Once again, family and friends volunteered to help. Sir John and Lady Frances Horner were long-time friends of Clementine, and their country home at Mells in Somerset frequently lent her peaceful respite from the strains of everyday family life. They also owned a town house on Lower Berkeley Street in Mayfair, and for a while they let the Churchills live there. Then Aunt Cornelia again stepped forward and they moved briefly to another house she owned in Mayfair, just off Hanover Square. Finding a permanent home in London suitable for the whole family proved tricky. After a plan to rent the house in Pimlico owned by Clementine's sister Nellie unexpectedly fell through, he was forced to move quickly and rented a small house on Dean Trench Street in Westminster, within easy walking distance of Parliament. As it was too small to house the children as well, they were left at Lullenden with the nannies while their parents visited them at weekends.

This could only be a makeshift arrangement. Unlike her husband, Clementine worried obsessively about money and knew that they were badly over-extended. Reluctantly, the hard decision was made to place Lullenden on the market, which added extra urgency to their search for a permanent home. Then in July 1919 Churchill impetuously made an offer on a large early Victorian house overlooking Hyde Park but typically failed to have an initial survey done. The bad news quickly emerged. It required extensive and costly repairs and he tried to back out of the contract. An unpleasant legal wrangle followed, from which he was rescued by his long-time friend and benefactor Sir Ernest Cassel, who purchased the lease. Meanwhile, they kept searching for the right house. Finally, they spotted 2 Sussex Square.

But this was not the end of the domestic upheaval. The house required extensive improvements and the renovations would not be finished for months. Having finally sold Lullenden to the wife of an old friend of Churchill's from South Africa days, Sir Ian Hamilton, who had also commanded the British land forces at Gallipoli, they temporarily moved in with yet another family member.

Freddie Guest was the third of Aunt Cornelia's five sons and Churchill's favourite cousin. Close in age – they were only six months apart – they had been polo-playing friends and political allies for years, and were to remain so until Freddie's premature death from cancer aged only sixty-one. Like Churchill, he had quit the Conservatives over the issue of free trade and was a Liberal Member of Parliament; for a short while before the war he had even served as his cousin's private secretary. Thanks to a distinguished military career in both the Boer and First World Wars, he was usually referred to as 'Captain Guest', although to Churchill he was always just 'Freddie'. Genial and sociable, he was sometimes wrongly dismissed as no more than a lightweight, a snob, and a playboy. His real importance lay behind the scenes. During the war he had headed the National War Aims Committee whose goal was 'to resist insidious influences of an unpatriotic character', for which it received money from the Secret Service to disseminate anti-socialist and anti-pacifist propaganda.[2]

More significant now was Freddie Guest's role as the Coalition Liberals' Chief Whip, a fierce promoter of Lloyd George, and a cunning and ruthless backroom fixer. This made him a fund of useful knowledge for Churchill about internal Coalition politics, and a useful go-between when Winston and the prime minister were at odds. Guest was also in charge of raising money for Lloyd George's political fund. This relied mostly on the selling of honours, a murky business that was to erupt the next year into a major scandal that would see him fiercely denounced as Lloyd George's 'evil genius'. Already, during this first week of 1921, the Conservatives were bitterly complaining that he was unscrupulously poaching on their own financial terrain. Freddie was also a keen aviator and like his cousin fought fiercely for the institutional independence of the Royal Air Force. When Churchill moved to the Colonial Office, Lloyd George rewarded Guest for his loyalty by appointing him Secretary of State for Air. This made him more useful to Churchill than ever.[3]

Freddie's marriage was as fragile as Churchill's was secure. His wife was Amy Grant, a fellow aviation enthusiast and the daughter of Henry Phipps Jr, a wealthy Pittsburgh iron master and business partner of Andrew Carnegie, the great American steel magnate and philanthropist. Templeton, their house in Roehampton, to which the Churchills moved while waiting to occupy Sussex Square, lay some six miles from central London and had its own tennis court. For Clementine, an avid player, this was a delight. It was not the first time the two couples had 'bunked' together. After their marriage in 1908 the Churchills had stayed with Freddie and Amy while their first London house was being renovated, and at Templeton they now had several children between them. It was with relief, however, that Clementine was finally able to move out. She disliked what she termed 'the Guest tribe', and sometimes found Amy infuriating – 'Suffragetty, Christian Sciency, and Yankee Doodle', she complained to her husband. Once, while the Churchills had been staying as guests before the war, Amy became so furious that Freddie was staying up late playing cards with Winston that she locked him out of their bedroom and ignored the resounding blows on the door delivered on Freddie's behalf by his cousin – who, in 'family solidarity', was demanding to be let in. By 1921 the Guests' marriage was fraying visibly at the edges. Before the year was out, Freddie was openly talking about marrying another woman.[4]

Once installed in his new home Churchill immediately began dreaming up even more improvements. These included the conversion of the two mews houses into a library and a painting studio for himself. Typically, this cost more than anticipated. But armoured with his aristocratic sense of entitlement, he rarely let expense be a barrier to his lifestyle. Visits to his bank manager were frequent, and he relied heavily on loans secured against his shareholdings or guaranteed by dependable friends such as Freddie. When the war ended he had debts of £16,000 (more than £600,000 in today's terms). His post as Secretary of State for War gave him an annual salary of £5,000. Yet this fell short by at least £300 per month of what he was spending, and he was running a substantial overdraft. The sale of Lullenden had somewhat eased his position. But the building works at Sussex Square quickly overran the budget. Simultaneously, his portfolio of shares was losing its value thanks to a general weakening in the stock market. The only thing keeping his bank manager happy was the promised contracts on *The World Crisis*. When he returned to London from his New Year's stay at Lympne, the debts were relentlessly piling up.[5]

*

Back at the War Office, he launched on a frenzied bout of action readying himself to take over the Colonial Office the following month. As its

Under-Secretary for two years before the war, he had been mostly concerned with Britain's colonies in Africa. But the institutional responsibilities added since that time had vastly expanded to take in territories across the Middle East formerly ruled by the Ottoman Empire but handed over to Britain as mandates by the League of Nations. At their core lay Palestine and Mesopotamia – the latter consisting of the old Ottoman provinces of Basra, Baghdad, and Mosul, the former an ill-defined area both to the east and west of the River Jordan. Victory over the Turks had ended with a million British and Indian Army troops in occupation of territory that stretched from the eastern Mediterranean shore to the Persian Gulf. To a government pledged to cutting the budget back to peacetime levels, the cost of maintaining them was unacceptable. During his two years at the War Office, Churchill had already forced through massive reductions in expenditure. But with drastic cutbacks in personnel, how was the peace to be maintained amongst simmering ethnic and religious conflicts and political rivalries? How were these territories to be governed?

His first priority was to set up the new Middle East Department he had agreed on with Lloyd George. He consulted with civil service mandarins in Whitehall, fired off telegrams to Baghdad, and kept the Foreign Secretary, Lord Curzon, informed since Mesopotamia had been a Foreign Office responsibility. Above all, Churchill made sure that Lloyd George remained on board. The immediate administrative details apart, the outline of a longer-term political solution was already forming in his head. To help him, he sought out the views of someone with his own unique and first-hand experience of the Arab world.

*

On the morning of Saturday 8 January 1921 a slight, fair-headed thirty-three-year-old man with piercing blue eyes and untidily dressed was ushered into Churchill's office by Edward Marsh, the civil servant who had served as his private secretary through his various ministerial posts since 1905. With his lispy voice, upturned eyebrows, and quizzical regard, many people found Marsh a cold and distant figure, a marked contrast to the hot-blooded Churchill. But the two of them fitted comfortably

together, and the fastidious Marsh – always known affectionately as
'Eddie' – had even survived the gruelling challenges of accompanying
Churchill in his pre-war tour of East Africa. With a double first-class
degree in Classics from Cambridge, he possessed strong literary interests
and was a ruthless proofreader for many distinguished writers. As an intimate friend of the poet Rupert Brooke, who had died of sepsis en route to
Gallipoli in 1915 aged twenty-seven, he was also his literary executor.
Later this year, Marsh would present to the British Museum the manu-
script of Brooke's most celebrated sonnet, 'The Soldier', with its moving
opening lines:

> If I should die, think only this of me
> That there's some corner of a foreign field
> That is for ever England.

Brooke had died in the Aegean and was buried on the Greek island of
Skyros.[6]

'Tactful and patient,' one historian remarks, 'Marsh translated the
furious energy of his demanding superior with his own quiet and metic-
ulous administrative skills.' The two men enjoyed a good, joking relationship. Once, when Marsh drafted a skilful letter smoothing over a
ruffled personal friendship for his signature, Churchill appended a few
appreciative words. 'You are a good little boy & I am vy [*sic*] fond of you.
W.' Clementine felt the same way. 'I am so glad you will let me be your
friend too,' she told Marsh after first meeting him.[7]

The man he now showed into Churchill's office was Colonel T. E.
Lawrence, who was already being widely celebrated as 'Lawrence of Arabia'.
After the failure at Gallipoli, British attention had turned towards
subverting Turkey by promoting an Arab uprising. Lawrence, an Oxford-
educated archaeologist-turned-wartime intelligence officer based in
Cairo, had been sent to Jeddah to support a revolt already hatched by
Hussain, the Sharif of Mecca and leader of the Hashemite family. In
Hussain's third son Faisal and his army of Bedouin warriors, the romanti-
cally inclined Lawrence found the ideal personification of the legendary

'noble Arab'. During the last two years of the war he and Faisal spear-headed increasingly successful guerrilla raids. Their targets included the all-important Hejaz railway and supply line linking Medina to Damascus, and key centres on the fringes of the main British advance. In October 1918 General Allenby had marched triumphantly into the Syrian capital. During the Paris Peace Conference, frequently dressed in his flowing Arab robes, Lawrence passionately promoted Faisal's claim to the Syrian throne. But he was thwarted by the French, who considered Syria their own special domain. Just months before Lawrence appeared in Churchill's office, they had driven Faisal out of the country into exile. Ever since, Lawrence had been promoting the alternative idea of making him King of Iraq.[8]

The heroic image that clung to Lawrence was a complex mix of truth, rumour, and invention. Some of this was due to Lawrence himself. Most of it, however, was thanks to an enterprising American journalist and war correspondent named Lowell Thomas, who had met Lawrence in Jerusalem after its capture by the British. Dressed in full sheik's costume including robe, headdress, and dagger, the barefoot Lawrence had instantly bewitched the youthful American. The mud and mechanized slaughter of the Western Front trenches offered nothing heroic. Keen to find a positive story about the war for Americans, Thomas forged instead a powerful and emotional story about the adventures in the desert of the man he described glowingly as Britain's modern 'Coeur de Lion' – Richard I, or Richard the Lionheart – the king who had led the Third Crusade in Palestine to victory over the great warrior Saladin. Ironically, Lawrence had once himself compared Faisal to the same medieval English monarch.[9]

Using coloured slides and dramatic live film footage shot from the air, Thomas skilfully crafted a two-hour-long multi-media extravaganza accompanied by a symphony orchestra playing Arab-inflected music. Entitled *With Allenby in Palestine*, and presenting Lawrence as the liber-ator of the Arabs, the show opened in New York early in 1919 and in August transferred to London and the Royal Opera House, where the words *and Lawrence in Arabia* were quickly added to the title. On most evenings Thomas himself would stride onto the stage to introduce the spectacle. 'This blue-eyed poet,' he would tell the enraptured audience, referring to Lawrence, 'succeeded in accomplishing what no caliph and no sultan had been able to do in over a thousand years. He wiped out centuries-old blood feuds and built up an army and drove the Turks from Holy Arabia.' The show was a huge hit. Its originally scheduled two-week run was extended to six months and from the opera house it moved on to the Royal Albert Hall and after that to the Queen's Hall. Some million or so people flocked to see it including Queen Mary, celebrity writers such as Rudyard Kipling and George Bernard Shaw, and dozens of school groups. Allenby himself even turned up one night, to considerable fanfare. The show arrived in the British capital with the blessing of the English-Speaking Union, an organization dedicated to promoting a sense of a common Anglo-American destiny. At a luncheon it hosted in his honour Thomas said that from the moment he first met Lawrence he had known that he was a man destined to go down in history as 'one of the most remarkable characters of modern times'. Both fascinated and appalled at the extravaganza, on several occasions Lawrence himself anonymously slipped in to view the show. Lloyd George also went to see it and echoed Thomas in declaring that Lawrence was one of the most remarkable and romantic figures of modern times. In one of the British press's most over-the-top reviews of Thomas's show, the *Daily Telegraph* lauded it as a celebration of 'British grit' and 'British resourcefulness'.

Churchill was predictably swept away by the spectacle. Seizing on its power as propaganda, he urged Thomas to prolong its life in London and even extend it to other British cities. 'It would be of great public advantage,' he told him, 'that this impressive tribute from an impartial quarter to some of the most striking achievements of the British Army should be as widely known as possible.'[10]

By his own confession, he knew little about the Middle East. But, as always, he was determined to be on top of his brief. Seduced by the Lawrence legend, he turned to its hero as his principal advisor on Arab affairs. Reluctant at first, Lawrence was soon enthusiastically playing the part. Each man saw in the other something to admire. Both were brave, energetic, visionary, and enjoyed reputations as being brilliant but wayward. After Lawrence was killed many years later in 1935 while riding his motorbike, Churchill declared that he had possessed the 'full measure of the versatility of genius'. Thanks to Lowell Thomas, he was also an American hero, and the *New York Herald Tribune* hailed him as 'the most romantic figure that the world has brought forth in modern times'.[11]

*

Three days before Lawrence was ushered into his office, Churchill found a file in his in-tray. Classified 'Most Secret', it consisted of intercepts of Bolshevik telegrams, reports from British agents keeping an eye on the Reds' activities around the world, the diplomatic communications of various countries including the United States, and some of the Secret Intelligence Service's (SIS) own evaluations of the Russian scene.

It was almost exactly twelve months since Admiral Kolchak, leader of the anti-Bolshevik forces, had been captured and murdered by the Communists. Since then, despite continued fighting in the Crimea, Lenin had consolidated his grip on Russia. Just months before, Lloyd George had welcomed the arrival in London of a Soviet delegation to negotiate a bilateral trade agreement with Britain – the first time a representative of the new Bolshevik state had been received officially by the leader of any of the Great Powers. Lloyd George had no liking for Communism. But he was convinced that the best antidote to revolution was trade and European economic recovery, and for that the Russians had to be involved. Outwardly, the head of the Russian delegation, Leonid Krassin, was a reassuring figure. A veteran Bolshevik and former financier and supplier of weapons to the party, he resembled a solid member of the bourgeoisie. After meeting him at the Savoy Hotel in Berlin, one British special correspondent described him as 'the best-dressed Communist in the world', with his morning coat and trousers obviously hailing from Bond Street. 'His linen is immaculate,' he rhapsodized, 'and a silk tie sets off a valuable tie pin. A gold ring and wrist watch hardly suggest Moscow.' Such powerful visual impressions helped nourish the idea that Krassin was a moderate – and that there were others like him in Lenin's entourage who could be wooed by the West. The location of the Bolshevik office in the British capital encouraged such a hope – New Bond Street, in the very heart of Mayfair.

But Lloyd George's conciliatory approach to the Bolsheviks bitterly divided British opinion. Many Conservatives were strongly opposed to any dealings at all with a regime that openly espoused revolution, while the Left prayed for the survival of the new socialist state and vocally opposed any efforts to undermine it. The protests climaxed in the summer of 1920, when Soviet and Polish forces clashed outside the gates of Warsaw amidst fears of Western intervention to help the Poles. 'Hands Off Russia' became the watch cry on the Left.

Churchill led the vanguard of those determined to destroy Lenin's regime. He saw nothing good in Krassin's presence in London. To him, a Bolshevik was always a Bolshevik and he had a more clear-eyed view than many of his contemporaries of the tyranny that Lenin and Trotsky were imposing on the Russian people. It was also obvious that Krassin's London office was far more than a trade office – it was a significant base for Bolshevik espionage, as he knew from the dozens of secret intercepts being produced by the British codebreakers.

Despite what they revealed, Lloyd George refused to expel Krassin, and the Cabinet voted to continue the trade talks. Churchill's fury remained unabated, especially as he believed that the Russians would be paying for Western goods with gold and diamonds plundered from their owners – in effect, he protested, 'the proceeds of piracy'. Across the Cabinet table, Lloyd George openly disagreed with him. 'The Russians are prepared to pay in gold and you won't buy,' he scoffed, and went on to quip that after all Britain traded with cannibals in the Solomon Islands. Humiliated and close to resigning, Churchill sat out the meeting, white-faced and silent. That night he travelled to Oxford and told students at the Union that there would be no recovery in Europe while 'these wicked men, this vile group of cosmopolitan fanatics, hold the Russian nation by the hair of its head and tyrannize over its great population'. The policy that he would always advocate, he said, would be the overthrow and destruction of that 'criminal regime'.

It is easy to scoff at his overblown rhetoric on the topic, and many biographers have done so. But Churchill's critique of the Bolsheviks' reign of terror and its suppression of freedom and basic liberties has been amply vindicated by history. Moreover, his bloodthirsty language was no worse than that emanating from the Bolsheviks themselves. Indeed, even in Britain, the rhetoric attacking him from the Left was often toxic. At a huge 'Hands Off Russia' rally at the Royal Albert Hall that same month to commemorate the third anniversary of the Russian Revolution, Cecil Malone, a Communist Member of Parliament and decorated former army officer, proclaimed to wild cheers that the hanging of 'a few Churchills and Curzons from the lampposts was a price worth paying for revolution.'[12]

*

As 1921 opened, any hope that Lenin could be brought down by the organized forces of the 'White' (anti-Bolshevik) armies was clearly in vain. Stubbornly, Churchill continued to believe that the Bolsheviks could be crushed by other means using secret service sources. Since the creation of both MI5 (the domestic security service) and MI6 (the foreign intelligence service, otherwise known as the Secret Intelligence Service, or SIS) under the pre-war Liberal government of Herbert Asquith, Churchill had been amongst their strongest supporters. As Home Secretary he had given MI5 the power to use general warrants to intercept the mail, and at the Admiralty he had thrown his weight behind the creation of Room 40, its top-secret unit for the breaking of German codes and ciphers, avidly reading the raw material it produced. Only a few months before, he had strongly resisted peacetime cutbacks to the budgets of the individual intelligence services. Better, he argued, would be to create a unified service to produce more effective results. 'With the world in its present condition of extreme unrest and changing friendships and with our greatly reduced and weakened military forces,' he told his Cabinet colleagues, 'it is more than ever vital to us to have good and timely information.' He also strongly supported the creation of the Government Code and Cypher School (GC&CS), the successor to Room 40 in breaking foreign codes and ciphers.[13]

Now, secret service reports from a wide variety of sources were regularly landing on his desk. Delivering them was his personal military secretary, the man who that morning had placed the file of intercepts in his in-tray. This was 'Archie' Sinclair, his battalion second-in-command from 'Plug Street' days. With his fine features, black hair, and dark complexion, Sinclair resembled 'a Spanish grandee rather than the Highland Chieftain he really was'.[14] Educated at Eton and Sandhurst, he had joined the 2nd Life Guards in 1910 and two years later succeeded to his grandfather's baronetcy as Viscount Thurso, along with some 100,000 acres of land in northern Scotland. 'There were few more glamorous young men in society than Archie,' writes one historian. 'His good looks, charm, and romantic highland aura were spiced with a touch of daredevilry that led him to experiment with a primitive aircraft which he flew before breakfast.'[15]

Although Archie was sixteen years Churchill's junior, they had much in common. Archie's mother, like his, was the daughter of a wealthy New York businessman. Her death a few days after Archie's birth, followed by that of his father when he was only five, meant that he too, although for different reasons, felt deprived of proper parental attention. Both Sinclair and Churchill were cavalry officers and relished the thrills of polo and flying. During the war Churchill shared some of his most intimate thoughts and feelings with the young officer whom he treated with close to paternal affection. In several letters addressing him variously as 'Archie dear' or 'My Dear', and signing off with 'Best Love', 'Yours always', and 'Yours affectionately', Churchill opened his heart to him about his despair at the fall-out from the Dardanelles disaster. In one, handwritten only two weeks after his removal from the Admiralty and marked 'Very Private', he confessed that the hour was 'bitter', that he was 'profoundly unsettled', and that he had no idea of what to do or which way to turn.[16]

In 1921 Sinclair was Churchill's principal channel into British intelligence, one of a network of friends working with, or for, the SIS. This was thanks largely to Archie's personal friendship with a fellow officer and Scot in his regiment who had worked on the intelligence staff at GHQ France, Stewart Menzies – the man eventually destined to become 'C', or head of SIS, and who was to serve as Churchill's 'spymaster' during the Second World War. It was Sinclair who first introduced the two men.

Cryptically, Menzies remarked that he found Churchill 'an entertainment'. Archie acted as 'cut-out' with the intelligence services, served as gatekeeper against importuning White Russian supplicants, and provided a discreet and reliable conduit to the major players. All this, in Churchill's own scribbled words on a secret file he kept in his papers, he described as 'Archie's work'.[17]

Two other vital links with British intelligence emerged at this time. The first was Major Desmond Morton, another Eton-educated young officer who was connected – like Sassoon and Sinclair – with GHQ in France. In fact, as ADC to Haig, Morton lived at its epicentre. Frequently tasked with escorting visitors to the front, he established lasting connections with a number of ministers and dignitaries. More importantly, he made significant contacts in the world of intelligence. Morton at age twenty-five was a year younger than Sinclair, and already a badly wounded holder of the Military Cross when he first met Churchill painting a canvas at Ploegsteert in 1916. Later he frequently escorted him round the front lines and they had lengthy talks about technical issues that concerned them both. 'Together,' Churchill recorded later, 'we visited many parts of the line. During these sometimes dangerous excursions, and at [Haig's] house, I formed a great regard and friendship for this gallant officer.'[18] When the war ended Morton moved into SIS – and Churchill claimed to have arranged the transfer. True or not – firm evidence is lacking – by 1921 Morton was SIS's expert on Soviet activities directed against Britain.[19]

Equalling Morton in importance as an intelligence source for now and in the future was Brigadier Edward Louis Spears, who had performed brilliantly during the war as British Liaison Officer with the French Deuxième Bureau (Secret Service) and War Office. He was now head of the British Military Mission in Paris, with the Military Cross and Croix de Guerre to his name. A fluent French speaker born in Paris, the twenty-nine-year-old Spears had conducted Churchill around the French front lines in 1915. In the younger man Churchill instantly spotted a similar spirit to his own: a man of courage, high intelligence, nonconformist views, and something of an outsider. Soon they were in regular correspondence. The next year, after

Spears was seriously wounded for the fourth time, he sent him a passionate letter. 'You are indeed a Paladin worthy to rank with the truest knights of the great days of romance,' he wrote. 'Thank God you are alive. Some good angel has guarded you amid such innumerable perils, & brought you safely thus far along this terrible and never-ending road.'[20] It was no wonder that Spears was Churchill's first (but rejected) choice as his battalion second-in-command on the Western Front, and that more than two years after the war Spears was still supplying him with intelligence about French affairs. So much so, indeed, that their personal link created a crisis with the British ambassador to France, Lord Derby. 'Spiers [the original spelling of his surname] is a sort of political spy for [Churchill],' he complained bitterly to Curzon.[21] This forced Spears to leave Paris, but he remained a key link for Churchill with his anti-Bolshevik contacts.

The documents Sinclair placed in his tray this January morning confirmed all Churchill's darkest fears about the Bolsheviks. Even as he was preparing to join Lloyd George for the New Year's celebrations, he now learned, Krassin had sent a message to Moscow advising Lenin that signing the trade agreement would cut the feet from under hostile elements such as Churchill and thus free Moscow from 'the English political and economic cabal'. Once an agreement was signed, argued Krassin, threats to break it by Moscow would provide the Bolsheviks with a powerful weapon. 'We must boldly conclude an agreement and naturally be prepared for further struggle,' he told Lenin, 'since no treaties will save us from a struggle until communism is victorious in the West.' On reading the file, Churchill's response was short and blunt. 'All these telegrams,' he responded, 'illustrate the perfidy and malice of these ruffians.'[22]

THREE

'HE USES IT AS AN OPIATE'

With Parliament recessed until mid-February, on the morning of Monday 10 January Churchill left with Clementine by train for the French Riviera for a long-needed break. It was the first real holiday for the couple since the war. As a younger man he had considered holidays mostly a waste of time. Once, he had even confessed that he would not mind at all being condemned to live the rest of his life within the square mile that embraced Westminster. Even worse, during their pre-war honeymoon in Venice, he had disappeared into a newspaper shop and emerged with a bundle of copies of *The Times* under his arm, sat down on a stone, and buried himself in the headlines, oblivious to the beauties surrounding him, including his new bride.[1]

But now, having discovered the delights of painting, he had plenty to occupy him. Clementine also needed a rest. She was physically and emotionally exhausted after the stresses of coping with their new baby and managing a household with young children, nannies, and governesses. The recent domestic moves and disruptions had not helped either. Then, just five days before their departure, her maternal grandmother Blanche, the Countess of Airlie, died aged ninety at her home in London. Although they were not especially close, the death brought back family memories tinged with grief about Clementine's older sister Katharine ('Kitty'), who had tragically died aged sixteen of typhoid fever, leaving her a lonely and isolated figure in her family.

Their departure from London also promised to put behind them another grief – the collective sorrow of a nation mourning the deaths of hundreds of thousands of young men killed on battlefields around the world. Both had friends who now lay buried in foreign fields. Black armbands of mourning were still being worn, and until recently *The Times* had included 'Death by Wounds' in its announcements column. Only a few weeks before, Churchill had stood solemnly alongside Lloyd George and other Cabinet colleagues in Whitehall as King George V unveiled the newly built Cenotaph, Sir Edwin Lutyens's severe granite memorial to 'The Glorious Dead' of the British Empire. Only yards in front of them, resting on a gun carriage, lay the coffin of an anonymous British soldier disinterred from the battlefields of France – 'the Unknown Soldier'. Draping it was the faded and bloodstained Union Flag that a British padre on the Western Front had used both as an altar cloth and to cover shattered bodies. Carefully placed on top of it was a dented helmet and a soldier's webbing belt. Such basic military equipment was intimately familiar to Churchill from his Ploegsteert days. Of those standing beside him, he was the only one to have served in the trenches, where he had witnessed the real face of war. 'Filth and rubbish everywhere, graves built into the defences and scattered about promiscuously, feet and clothing breaking through the soil, water and muck on all sides,' he told Clementine.[2]

The very simplicity of the burial of the Unknown Soldier was overwhelming in its emotive power. To millions, the coffin and the man within it represented a son, a father, a brother, a friend they had lost. Or, as *The Times* observed, 'All could mourn for him the better because he was unknown.' As Big Ben began to chime eleven o'clock, the King pressed a button and released the flags that had been veiling the Cenotaph. After ten more strokes – at the eleventh hour of the eleventh day of the eleventh month, two years from the moment when the Armistice finally muzzled the guns of war – silence fell – the 'Great Silence' of two minutes' duration that had been inaugurated the year before. People bowed their heads, lost in thoughts and memories of the dead. For some, the silence was too much and they broke out sobbing. Others appeared simply numb. No one moved for what seemed like an eternity. Then bugles broke the silence with the clear notes of the 'Last Post'. When they finished, the frozen tableau began to move again. Slowly it made its way towards Parliament Square and Westminster Abbey and here, after a short funeral service, the coffin was lowered into its carefully prepared resting home in the floor of the central nave.

The whole ceremony was a brilliantly conceived idea and a nationally cathartic moment. If any single event marked the psychological transition from war to peace, it was this. Now it was time to move on, to look forward not back, to start living again and enjoy what life had to offer.[3] This is what the Churchills were now trying to do.

*

They broke their journey in Paris, where Winston was the guest of honour at a dinner party given by Louis Loucheur, his opposite number as Minister of Munitions during the war. He also spent an hour with the French President Alexandre Millerand discussing the future of Germany, Eastern Europe, and the Middle East. Aligning their interests was testing Anglo-French relations to the limit, especially over the issues of German reparations and the future of Syria and Mesopotamia.

Churchill's main contact in the city was an old contemporary from Harrow and Sandhurst days, Major Gerald Geiger, who was head of the British Military Mission in the French capital. During his twenty-four hours there he took time out with Geiger to visit one of the city's most prestigious commercial art galleries. Accompanying them was a Swiss art critic whom he had first met in Paris during the war. Charles Montag had once been a painter himself, specializing in impressionistic landscapes, and he was friendly with several of the leading Impressionists and Post-Impressionists including Monet, Degas, Pissarro, and Renoir. He was also a professional arts organizer and not long before had held a one-man show of his own paintings at the gallery they were now visiting. The Galerie Druet was situated in the heart of the city on the rue Royale linking the Place de la Concorde to the Place de la Madeleine, and had been founded by Eugène Druet, who made his name photographing the sculptures of Auguste Rodin. Just four years before, it had exhibited several dozen drawings and paintings illustrating the campaign in the Dardanelles, a break with its normal peacetime practice of showing the works of contemporary French artists.

But the reason for visiting the Galerie Druet was not to view any of the rich crop of local artists flourishing in post-war Paris. Instead, it was to inspect a small collection of works by an unknown painter identified as 'Charles Morin'. The three of them spent some forty minutes discussing and criticizing the canvases and Geiger reported back to Archie Sinclair in London that Churchill was 'very interested'. This was hardly surprising. The exhibition had actually been organized by Montag, and Charles Morin was none other than Churchill himself. It was not the first time he had used a pseudonym when visiting France. During the war as Minister of Munitions he had sometimes travelled as 'Mr Spencer', the name which had been his first suggestion for the exhibition.[4]

By now he was a serious amateur artist. Since first picking up his nephew's paint brush at Hoe Farm he had made rapid progress. This was thanks both to his typical enthusiasm and energy for anything that fired his imagination, and to the help given to him by leading professional artists of the day. Two close neighbours when the Churchills were living on London's Cromwell Road were John and Hazel Lavery, who became lifelong friends. The Belfast-born Sir John Lavery was one of Britain's most accomplished portrait artists and Hazel, a striking American beauty some twenty years younger than her husband, was a fashion model who had posed for some of the leading photographers of the day. She had her own artistic talents and a ready gift for organizing *soirées* that brought together noted artists, politicians, and writers.

It was Hazel who took the first crucial step of unlocking Churchill's artistic inhibitions. Finding him one day at Hoe Farm paralyzed by the blank space in front of him, she had simply seized a brush, filled it with paint, and splashed several large and fierce slashes of colour on the canvas. 'Anyone could see that it could not hit back,' he recalled later with his typical ironic humour. 'No evil fate avenged the jaunty violence. The canvas grinned in helplessness before me. The spell was broken.

The sickly inhibitions rolled away ... I have never felt awe of a canvas since.'

From then on he never lost an opportunity to paint, whether in Lavery's London studio, on the battlefront at Ploegsteert, staying the weekend with friends in the English countryside, with his family amidst the delights of Lullenden, or at Freddie and Amy Guest's house at Roehampton. His mother once found him painting at Blenheim. 'His last paintings are very good,' she enthused to her sister Leonie. 'Lavery says that if Winston could take up painting as a profession he could, but of course he uses it as an opiate.'[5] During the previous spring he had spent several days at the Duke of Westminster's vast estate at Mimizan south of Bordeaux, struggling to capture on canvas the dark and serried ranks of pine trees that dominate this stretch of the Atlantic coastline. 'How I wish Lavery were here to give me a few hints,' he lamented to Clementine; 'it would bring me on like one o'clock ...' The Irish artist held a high regard for his efforts, recording that he knew of few amateur painters with a 'keener sense of light and colour, or a surer grasp of essentials', and that had he chosen painting instead of statesmanship he would have been 'a great master with the brush'.[6]

Clementine, too, gave him great support. His new interest in art was as sudden as it was unexpected. Until he was forty, he had never visited an art gallery. So the two of them went off to the National Gallery in Trafalgar Square. The first picture they came to Clementine thought was 'very ordinary'. Nonetheless, Winston spent half an hour studying it minutely. The next day they were back again, although this time Clementine insisted they use a different entrance to ensure he did not return to the same picture.[7]

So it was with a significant body of work behind him that he visited the Galerie Druet. It was his first commercial exhibition and six of the paintings were sold. Unfortunately, history does not record which, nor for how much. But as his youngest daughter Mary was to write many years later, it must have given her father much pleasure to know from his first public showing that his paintings had a market.[8]

Mostly landscapes, Churchill's paintings are traditional, safe, and reassuring, giving no hint of the incendiary and provocative trends that were then shaking the foundations of European art and culture. The post-First World War Paris that welcomed his first exhibition was also a city echoing with the revolutionary and discordant tones of American jazz and the provocative nihilism of its artistic twin, Dadaism, as represented by poets and artists such as Tristan Tzara, André Breton, and Francis Picabia. All were a repudiation of the post-war cries for a 'return to order'. Yet the restoration of order was precisely what Churchill craved, as he had so fervently told Lloyd George almost exactly a year before in the same city, where the peacemakers were still wrangling over the future. Conservatism in art was his mantra, and remained so. Three decades later, at the prompting of President Eisenhower, he agreed to a travelling exhibition of his paintings in America. When it opened in Kansas City it was visited by former President Harry Truman, who pronounced 'Damned Good. At least you can tell what they are and that is more than you can say for a lot of the modern painters.' Churchill beamed.[9]

This did not mean that he was averse to learning new tricks. After their visit to the Galerie Druet, Montag took him to some other galleries in Paris and for the first time he got to see in person paintings by some of the leading French Impressionists. But it was only when he reached the remarkable sunlight of the Riviera that he was fully able to absorb and admire their techniques.[10]

*

If he hoped that the name of Charles Morin would throw people off the scent about the real name of the artist on display at the Galerie Druet, he was mistaken. By now the fact that painting had become his consuming passion was a widespread topic of newspaper gossip in Britain, and 1921 was to see the easel and other artistic paraphernalia added to the miscellany of eccentric and undersized hats as one of the standard Churchill props delighted in by cartoonists. It was also the year that saw him write an article that would firmly anchor his reputation as a gifted amateur artist. This was 'Painting as a Pastime', which was to appear in the *Strand* magazine as a two-part article over the winter. Illustrated with nineteen of his paintings, mostly in colour, the journal also featured distinguished writers such as P. G. Wodehouse and Arthur Conan Doyle. Churchill would later publish these reflections on painting as a small book after the Second World War. It proved to be one of his most popular and successful; expanded and revised it has been more or less constantly in print ever since. Even as he left for Paris, he was mapping it out in his head.

His artistic endeavours offered hostile observers ready weapons for ridicule. The *Daily Herald* was one of his most savage critics. The newspaper of the Labour Party was bitterly hostile to his attacks on the party and his belligerence towards Russia. Over the previous year it had been engaged in a bitter vendetta with him over funding it had received from Moscow and for disciplinary action taken by the War Office against those soldiers opposing intervention on behalf of the White forces in the Russian Civil War. Churchill in turn denounced the paper for encouraging 'mutinies, strikes, and riots'. In retaliation, the *Herald* published a bitterly satirical poem by the author Osbert Sitwell that savaged Churchill's support for Admiral Kolchak, denounced him for wasting 'a million lives' at Gallipoli, and painted him as a bloodthirsty warmonger for whom wars were 'nothing more than a form of sport like football or kiss-in-the mouth'.[11]

News about the French exhibition of his paintings had leaked to the *Herald* and three days before he left London its Paris correspondent went to town with the news. In an article headlined 'Winston, the Painter' he referred to four pictures entitled 'Southern Scenes' being exhibited in a 'well-known picture gallery on the Rue Royale'. 'Broad, audacious, and highly coloured,' he wrote, they had been favourably reviewed by local art critics who were apparently unaware of the true identity of Charles Morin. They all agreed, he claimed tongue-in-cheek, that the artist should continue painting and leave whatever other work he was engaged on to devote himself entirely to art. Not surprisingly, the *Herald* threw its weight behind the critics' advice – probably concocted by itself – to keep off other, meaning political, activities.[12] Whether or not Churchill was aware of this leak is unclear. In any event, after two days in Paris he and Clementine boarded the night sleeper train bound for the south of France.

The Riviera had long been a magnet for Britain's upper classes migrating swallow-like from the cold grey damp of their north Atlantic winters. Dozens of once small and impoverished fishing villages and ports had been transformed into sunny winter resorts, and after the arrival of the railway in the 1860s grand and luxurious hotels catering for the rich had sprouted up in places such as Cannes, Nice, and Menton. The casino in Monte Carlo opened in 1866, followed by its grand opera house thirteen years later. European royalty increasingly wintered on the Riviera, and in the last two decades of her life Queen Victoria stayed there on nine separate occasions. She made her last visit in 1899 by which time she had settled on Nice as her favourite destination – or, to be more precise, Cimiez, an ancient Roman settlement 400 feet above the coastal city and linked to it by electric tram. With its boulevards lined with plane trees and magnificent vistas of the valleys below and the mountains above, it was an exclusive and idyllic spot featuring two luxurious hotels, the Grand and the Excelsior Regina. The latter, a 'shining colossus of marble and stucco', was Victoria's favourite.

This was now also the Churchills' destination. At the railway station in Nice they were welcomed officially by the British consul and the local French prefect and then driven to their hotel. Here the host for their stay was one of the richest men in Britain, Sir Ernest Cassel.

*

Churchill's connection with Cassel went back many years. The son of a Jewish banker in Cologne, Cassel had accumulated his vast fortune through shrewd investments around the globe in railways, mining, and government loans. But he was best known in Britain as the personal banker and closest male friend to King Edward VII. He also physically resembled the monarch with his portly figure, heavy beard, and penchant for double-breasted suits – so much so, indeed, that the two were sometimes mocked as 'the Windsor-Cassels'. He had lived in Britain for fifty years, was a naturalized citizen, a Privy Counsellor, a noted philanthropist, and a convert to Catholicism – although this provided little protection against the insidious anti-Semitism that infected much of the British upper-class society with which Churchill mingled.

The link with Churchill was a family one. Cassel was a close friend of Lord Randolph and was generous to both his sons. He found a job in banking for Jack, and holidays for Winston had become something of a tradition. An early one included a trip down the Nile on Cassel's yacht in 1902 to witness the opening of the Aswan Dam, for which he had arranged the finances. At least two summer holidays were spent at his sumptuous villa in the Swiss Alps, where Churchill enjoyed long walks while working on his father's biography. Brook House on Park Lane in Mayfair, Cassel's principal residence, sported six marble-lined kitchens and an oak-panelled dining room that could seat a hundred guests. Churchill also benefited handsomely from Cassel's investments of the money he made from his early literary efforts and speaking tours. When Winston married Clementine in 1908 Cassel gave him £500, which was then a really generous wedding gift.

But Cassel's gilded life was also marked by tragedy. His English wife died only three years after their marriage and his only child, a daughter, succumbed in her early thirties to tuberculosis. Since then he had lavished his affections on his two grandchildren, especially the elder, Edwina. Named in honour of her godfather, King Edward VII, she was now a vibrant and glamorous twenty-year-old living in Brook House and acting as Cassel's social hostess. It was no surprise, therefore, that she was present in Nice to help host the Churchills and his other guests. The following year, in one of the most glamorous weddings of the season, she married Lord Louis Mountbatten, then a young naval lieutenant. Two decades later, under Churchill's wartime leadership, Mountbatten would be appointed the Supreme Commander of Allied Forces in South-East Asia before becoming the last Viceroy of India, tasked with the granting of independence to India. Thirty years after that, he was to be assassinated in Ireland by IRA terrorists.[13]

*

The Riviera played such an integral part in the social calendar of British society during this era that *The Times* included a separate section of its 'Court and Society' column devoted entirely to its affairs. This was the year that saw visitors at last returning on the scale of the years before the war. The exodus to the sun saw London hotels deserted while berths in sleeping cars to the Riviera were fully booked up for a month ahead. Monte Carlo – 'the Mecca of the Mediterranean' – was once again a magnet for visitors. Now, thanks to a new and efficient bus service linking its glittering white casino to the other great resorts along the coast, visitors at last had an alternative to the slow, dirty, and uncomfortable journey by rail. No longer would first-class passengers have to wait around in draughty stations for trains that rarely arrived on time.

Now, of course, for more comfortable personal transport there was also the motor car and the chauffeur, an increasingly common sight along the Corniche as the rich and famous returned to bask in the warmth under endless blue skies. The only downside was their magnetic draw for pickpockets and thieves. Cimiez itself was the scene of one of the largest robberies of the 1921 season when £20,000 worth of jewellery and cash was stolen from a bedroom at one of its largest hotels while the occupants, a Paris-based diplomat and his wife, were asleep. The mystery of why they did not wake up during the burglary was subsequently solved by the discovery of a strange device described as an 'asphyxiating gas revolver' that emitted fumes ensuring the victims remained asleep.[14]

Germans, as well as Russian aristocrats, had been part of the Riviera scene before the war. Now, in their absence, it was more than ever a British enclave. Indeed, it could well have been renamed Mayfair-sur-Mer. It was not just that the Churchills were staying with their Mayfair neighbour Cassel. They were also rubbing shoulders with friends such as the Duke and Duchess of Westminster, the Duke of Marlborough, and the press magnates Lords Beaverbrook and Northcliffe. There were fine restaurants for dining such as Ciro's, and plenty to do. Most Riviera resorts sported golf courses, polo grounds, and tennis courts, and new ones were appearing all the time.

For the athletically inclined Clementine, tennis was a passion. So it was a treat when she and Cassel motored over to Monte Carlo at the end of January to join the cream of British society wintering in the south for the official opening of new lawn tennis courts in Monte Carlo. Not only did she love playing the game herself. This year she could also watch the first female tennis celebrity in person. The flamboyant twenty-one-year-old French player Suzanne Lenglen had won Wimbledon for the previous two years, was ranked amongst the top ten players in the world, and dominated this year's Riviera tournament. One of Clementine's most exciting moments came when she herself won a few games in a doubles match against opponents who included a pre-war Wimbledon champion while being cheered on by a sympathetic crowd that included Lenglen. 'Dizzy with glory' was how she felt.[15]

Churchill had his own new special passion to pursue and preferred to give tennis and golf a miss. He happily dined at Ciro's with Beaverbrook, took lunch with the local French prefect, and hobnobbed with Northcliffe. The mornings he devoted to business. Telegrams followed him from London that demanded action, and throughout his Riviera stay he remained on top of War Office business. But every afternoon he got into a car and motored a little way out of Nice, chose a picturesque spot, and got to work on a canvas. It was a routine he was to follow over the many decades to come on his visits to the south of France.

The press followed his new pastime with interest. When he left towards the end of the month *The Times* reported that 'He has put in some good work with his paint brush during his short sojourn, and is thus taking back to England several souvenirs of the many beauty spots which abound close to hand.' But it was more than additional canvases that Churchill took home. He returned from the Riviera having learned a different way of seeing.[16]

*

In 1885 Hugh Macmillan, a minister in the Presbyterian Free Church of Scotland and a devout believer in the moral and spiritual truths to be revealed by nature, published a richly illustrated book based on his personal travels entitled *The Riviera*. His introduction was a rhapsody to the region's scenic beauty and grandeur that highlighted the 'peculiar quality of the light that shines on sea and shore'. It was a land, he went on, 'where the brilliant sunshine and translucent atmosphere gives the feeling of vast aerial space [and where] the light has a sparkling crystalline lustre, as if each particle of air through which it passes was the facet of a gem. It transfigures every object, makes a dead leaf to shine like a ruby, and converts the meanest and most squalid scene into a picture.'[17]

By the time Churchill arrived at Cimiez many French painters had long since discovered the same magical and transformative quality of light in the south of France. Vincent van Gogh and Paul Cézanne were trailblazers, soon to be followed by other Impressionists and Post-Impressionists such as Paul Signac, Auguste Renoir, Camille Pissarro, André Derain, Raoul Dufy, Pierre Bonnard, and Claude Monet. In the spring of 1921 those still living were joined by Henri Matisse, who moved permanently to a two-roomed apartment in the old city of Nice, a mere stone's throw away from the sea.[18]

The presence of these masters attracted a host of other lesser artists seduced by the unique light of the Mediterranean. During a brief visit to the small Provençal fishing village of Cassis the previous autumn, Churchill had closely studied their technique. It was a revelation. He realized that they viewed nature less as a matter of form and surface than as 'a mass of shimmering light ... which gleams with beautiful harmonies and contrasts of colours'. Until then, he had painted the sea with long, smooth, horizontal strokes of mixed pigment. Now he saw that it could be done in an entirely different way, through innumerable small points of colour, sometimes even vertical rather than horizontal daubs, each of which emitted a vibration peculiar to itself and so created canvases that were brilliant and alive, quite unlike those of previous centuries. He was smitten. 'Have not Manet and Monet, Cezanne and Matisse rendered to painting something of the same service which Keats and Shelley gave to poetry after the ceremonious literary perfections of the eighteenth century?' he asked. 'The beauty of their work is instinct with gaiety, and floats in sparkling air.'[19]

From now on his own paintings reflected their quest for light and gaiety. For the most part they are bold, bright, and well-composed. He used military metaphors to describe his method. Painting was 'like fighting a battle' and required reconnaissance, a plan, a knowledge of 'the great Captains of the past' and 'strong reserves' – which he defined as Proportion or Relation. Yet these belligerent images give a misleading guide to his character and state of mind. The end result of his artistic struggle with the canvas is not disharmony, dissonance, or turmoil and there is nothing violent or disturbing in his paintings. On the contrary. His landscapes reveal a profound search for tranquillity, peace, and harmony. Professor Thomas Bodkin, one-time Director of the National Gallery of Ireland and the Barber Institute at the University of Birmingham, once summed up the essence of his paintings: 'Light and peace, those qualities which all wise men most value in life, are indubitably those which chiefly distinguish the scenes that he prefers to paint.'[20]

FOUR

A WORLD IN TORMENT

After two weeks on the Riviera, Churchill returned to London, and broke his journey with a couple of nights at the Ritz hotel in Paris to meet Lloyd George, who was discussing German reparations with the French prime minister Aristide Briand. Back at Sussex Square he took up the slack of managing the household in Clementine's absence. Randolph was away at his boarding school, and because of a series of coughs and colds Diana and Sarah had been taken temporarily out of their Notting Hill school to the healthier climate of the coast in Kent. This left only Marigold at home. She was now a bubbly and vivacious two-year-old full of curiosity, who brought a welcome sparkle of laughter to his life. He adored her. Every morning a nursemaid brought her to his bedroom to say hello, and when a letter arrived from Clementine enclosing a photograph of herself he delighted in explaining that it was 'Mumma' and watched as she affectionately kissed it. He hated it when she fell sick with one of her frequent colds and had to be confined to the nursery. The other children pleased him, too. Thirteen-year-old Diana was shaping into 'a beautiful being', and Sarah was full of life. Twice he drove out to visit Randolph at his school, once with the two girls who were eager to see their brother. He found his son well and sprightly, although the headmaster preferred the word 'combative' and said he mixed himself up in fights and quarrels on any excuse.

Childish fisticuffs were one thing. Quite another were terrorist threats to life and limb. The previous November, Scotland Yard had got wind of a

Sinn Fein plot to kidnap leading British politicians including Lloyd George, Hamar Greenwood, and Churchill himself. Since then Churchill had been protected by a Detective-Sergeant Hunter. But in February he was suspended from duty after becoming involved in a divorce case and was replaced by Detective-Sergeant Walter Henry Thompson, a Special Branch veteran who had previously been bodyguard to Lloyd George. From now on Thompson, armed with a fully loaded Colt 45 automatic, would sleep in the house and accompany Churchill on all his official and private journeys.[1]

*

At the War Office he energetically continued his campaign of retrenchment by peppering his officials with probing questions about its bloated budget. Why should there be three times as many army doctors and chaplains now as there were before the war? Or more veterinary officers, even though tanks and mechanical transport were replacing horses? Why had the number of officers doubled since 1914? It was a scandal and at least three thousand of them should be discharged before the end of March. Such were some of his typical missives throughout January as he wrapped up his War Office business in preparation for taking over the Colonial Office. His cost-cutting measures contrasted sharply with contemporary cartoons depicting him as a man of war.

Yet he remained fiercely bullish in his opinions. At Cabinet meetings and in a stream of memoranda he bombarded his colleagues with his views on a wide range of international issues. In the post-Versailles world, he saw challenges for Britain on every front. Peace had not broken out when it was officially declared. Instead it had resulted in conflict across the globe: struggles for national liberation, strife over borders, rebellions and revolutions and civil wars, behind many of which he saw the hand of Moscow. It was a world in torment with shifts in the balance of power that were potentially ominous for Britain and the Empire. Prime amongst them was the extraordinary new power of the Japanese and American navies, which challenged Britain's traditional supremacy of the seas and hence the global reach of its foreign and imperial policies.

He insisted that Britain should maintain its global naval supremacy by building four battleships a year for the next four or five years. Just a decade before, he had headed Britain's naval race with Germany. 'I do not see,' he now argued, 'how the foreign or Colonial policy of our Empire can be carried out on the basis that we have ceased to be the leading naval power [and] I [would] not personally agree in any circumstances to take part in anything that [could] lead up to this.'[2]

Nor was he happy about Egypt, which had effectively been governed by Britain since the 1880s and was officially a British Protectorate. When nationwide riots and strikes in favour of independence prompted a committee of inquiry headed by Lord Milner, the Colonial Secretary, to recommend the end of the Protectorate and the granting of self-government, he was incensed. So far as he was concerned, the nationalists were little more than tools of a Moscow seeking, yet again, to deprive Britain of its rightful place in the world. His interventions on this and other issues exasperated the Foreign Secretary Lord Curzon, who protested bitterly to Lloyd George that Churchill was trying to be 'a sort of Asiatic Foreign Secretary'.[3]

But it was affairs in Europe that particularly troubled him. For all his grandiose rhetoric about the Empire, he knew that Britain's security depended crucially on events across the English Channel. He was unhappy about the Paris peace settlement and sceptical about the League of Nations. Relations between France and Germany were poisoned by the running sore of reparations, 'absurd ideas' about what Germany should pay, and the cession of wealthy Upper Silesia with its large German population to the newly created Poland. British troops still occupied parts of the defeated enemy that was torn by revolution, threats to civil order, and paramilitary violence. Growing nationalist grievances had already spawned Adolf Hitler's radical and anti-Semitic Nazi Party. Only when a stable Germany and a secure France were reconciled, he believed, could Europe truly declare peace. Meanwhile the danger grew of an alienated Germany and a hostile Russia overcoming their ideological divide and joining forces against the Western powers – which indeed was to happen the following year when Berlin and Moscow unexpectedly signed a treaty at Rapallo. But now Churchill was eyeing an even more sinister possibility. What was there, he wondered, 'to prevent Russia developing under German guidance enormous plans for the armament of Russia and the re-armament of Germany?' This was remarkably prescient. Indeed, such secret feelers were already under way. A few months later, German Army officers travelled to Russia to explore the ground and soon afterwards Junkers started building military aircraft there. Such collaboration helped prepare the ground for Hitler's massive rearmament programme of the 1930s.[4] Churchill's main source of information about Russia remained Archie Sinclair's network of intelligence contacts and diplomatic intercepts. But during his final week at the War Office he received a letter personally addressed to him from one of Russia's leading anti-Bolsheviks.

Boris Savinkov was a former anti-Tsarist revolutionary, political assassin, and one-time Deputy Minister of War in the post-Tsarist government of Alexander Kerensky. Churchill had first met him in Paris lobbying for Allied intervention to help the White Army. With a bushy crop of reddish-brown hair atop a heavily lined face with parchment-like skin, the forty-year-old Russian possessed charisma and a flair for the dramatic. He indulged in stylish clothes, expensive restaurants, exotic brothels, and enjoyed a string of mistresses. He mixed with poets and artists such as Apollinaire, Modigliani, and Diego Rivera. He wrote a novel, *The Pale Horse*, which was a thinly disguised fiction of the assassination of Grand Duke Sergei, the Governor of Moscow and uncle of the Tsar, that Savinkov himself had planned. He was also the author of a youthful play about the escape from Elba of his great hero, Napoleon, in which he himself played a major role. Churchill was instantly mesmerized. 'I had never seen a Russian Nihilist except on the stage', he wrote later, 'he was singularly well cast for the part . . . remarkable grey-green eyes in a face of almost deathly pallor . . . an unusual personality, of veiled power in strong restraint . . .' Since their first meeting in Paris, he had consistently embraced him as the saviour of Russia.

Savinkov now headed the Union for the Defence of the Motherland and Liberty and was living in Paris. Despite the defeat of the White armies he still believed that Lenin's regime could be overthrown.

Continuing unrest, internal dissent, and peasant uprisings against the Bolsheviks all kept his hopes alive and he pleaded for financial help to support a small army of some five thousand men. This, he told Churchill, 'would form the nucleus of the revolutionary force and would be able to restore order after a successful revolution'. Previously, he might have received a positive response. But by this time Churchill's endless optimism about ridding the world of Lenin's regime was starting to wear thin. Besides, he now had other things on his mind such as Iraq. So his instructions to Sinclair were firm and blunt: for the time being at least, Savinkov should be given no sympathy or encouragement for his plans.[5]

*

As Secretary of State for Air as well as War, Churchill keenly supported the creation of the Royal Air Force as an independent arm of warfare and had appointed as its chief of staff – effectively its head – Air Marshal Sir Hugh Trenchard, who had headed its predecessor the Royal Flying Corps in France during the war. A major post-war challenge was to balance drastic national budgetary cuts against the urgent need to place the fledgling service on a secure foundation. 'No more complicated service has ever been brought into existence in this world,' Churchill told the House of Commons this winter. Thirty highly skilled trades, for example, were involved in the production and repair of an aeroplane. The establishment of training schools alone posed an enormous challenge, and not just for teaching flying but for all of the air force's unique technical needs: wireless control, air gunnery, observation, aerial bombing, and so on. 'The training establishments are the plum-trees,' he explained in an oddly chosen metaphor, 'as the fighting squadrons are the plums themselves.' Most urgent of all, however, was the need to protect the fledgling service against predatory attacks by the army and navy, above all by finding a convincing and persuasive strategic role for it. An effective air force was also a matter of Great Power politics. 'It was vital that Great Britain should occupy the leading place as a scientific air power,' he told the Cabinet early in the New Year.[6]

An effective air force did not, however, include airships. The Germans had deployed Zeppelins for bombing raids on British cities, and the air force and Admiralty had experimented with their use. But when the war ended they could see no further military use for them, and as part of the post-war cost-cutting programme it was decided to halt their construction. 'It was a melancholy decision,' he informed the House of Commons, although this reflected the feelings of others rather than his own, which were adamantly opposed to their value as weapons of war. It had also meant the abandonment of airship construction for civil purposes, and efforts began to find private companies willing to take over the task. As for civilian aviation in the British Isles using aeroplanes, he remained cautious. In his personal view, the country's notoriously poor weather characterized by fog, wind, and rain, combined with an excellent and competitive rail and road network, made it a dubious commercial prospect. There was one spectacular exception, however. It was a route that he knew well and frequently used – that between London and Paris, which eliminated the lengthy and tedious sea crossing of the English Channel. 'There is no more striking experience than to travel by air from London to Paris,' he enthused to the Commons in visually graphic terms. 'One really has a sense of enchantment when, in less than two hours ... there is the beautiful city of Paris, with the Eiffel Tower and the Golden Dome of the Invalides, revealed in the sunlight far below.'[7]

*

Shining light on the murky transactions of the world's troubled affairs was another matter, however. As a senior minister he had always relied heavily on secret intelligence and was on the list of those who regularly received top secret diplomatic intercepts of foreign powers. Anxious to continue receiving these after leaving the War Office, he persuaded the Foreign Secretary Lord Curzon, head of the Cabinet's Secret Service Committee, to add the Colonial Office to the list of recipients. Walter Long, the First Lord of the Admiralty, agreed to do likewise for naval intercepts.[8] In the dangerous and uncertain post-war world that Britain faced, Churchill continued to see the intelligence services, whose birth he had fostered before the war, as a vital weapon, both sword and shield of the state. As a member of the Cabinet's Secret Service Committee, he had strongly resisted post-war Treasury cuts to the budgets of both MI5 and MI6 (SIS). While it took five to ten years to build up an effective secret service, he argued, it could all too easily be destroyed by the stroke of a pen. Instead of cuts, he proposed the creation of a more cost-effective and unified intelligence service. 'With the world in its present condition of extreme unrest and changing friendships and antagonisms,' he told the Cabinet, 'and with our greatly reduced and weak military forces, it is more than ever vital to us to have good and timely information.' He had lost the argument for unification. But other weapons were added to the national security armour with the passing of a new and more drastic Official Secrets Act and the establishment of the Government Code and Cypher School (GC&CS), the forerunner of the famed Second World War Bletchley Park; over the next few years, it enjoyed striking success in breaking the diplomatic communications of many countries. For the remainder of his life at the top, he was to be one of the most eager consumers of these intercepts.[9]

*

If the world beyond Britain's shores remained dark and troubled, at home the roaring twenties of the bright young things were well under way. No one symbolized the new era better than the heir to the throne. The unusually youthful-looking twenty-seven-year-old Prince of Wales possessed a charm and refreshingly easy manner that contrasted sharply with the House of Windsor's stiff formality. His undisguised enthusiasm for nightclubs and nightlife was fully in tune with the spirit of the new age. 'A dear thing, with beautiful eyes, but such a boy,' remarked Frances Stevenson.[10]

In Churchill's rarefied social circle it was an open secret that the prince had a mistress. Mrs Freda Dudley Ward was just a few weeks younger than the heir to the throne and the wife of a much older and complaisant Liberal Member of Parliament. Lord Riddell, who observed her during one sociable weekend at Lympne, thought she was 'a clever, perceptive sort of woman, always on the move, singing, dancing, smoking, talking or playing tennis'.[11] She certainly bewitched the prince. Since meeting him three years before, she had become his constant companion at private events. A man who craved being mothered, the prince doted on her. Churchill had met him in Paris during the Peace Conference and advised the palpably nervous young man on how to deliver a public speech. It was better to memorize it, he advised; but if he chose to read it he should deliver it openly and speak slowly. Thanks to this, the prince had pulled off a creditable performance. No doubt he now had a better opinion of Churchill than immediately after Gallipoli, when he had denounced him as 'an intriguing swine'.[12]

Times had changed, and it was in a completely different milieu that Churchill now met the youthful prince again. The first occasion came in early February, when Sir John and Lady Lavery threw a private party for the heir to the throne in the painter's studio in Kensington. Freda was there, as were Lloyd George and Philip Sassoon. Churchill found the whole evening an 'amusing affair', marred only by his misfortune in standing on the future monarch's foot while dancing and causing him to yelp out loud. All was forgiven, however, and a week later Churchill was invited to a party at Freda's private residence. Again the doting prince was at her side. Dancing went on well until the early hours and this time Churchill quickly picked up on a distinct *frisson* in the air. Amongst familiar faces such as Philip Sassoon he also spotted Michael Herbert, the wealthy younger brother of the Earl of Pembroke whose country seat Wilton House near Salisbury consisted of some 14,000 acres of prime agricultural land. The prince was fiercely jealous of any rival, and in 1921 Herbert headed the pack. As he observed the rivals circling each other, Churchill ruminated on life's puzzles. Even the monks must have their worries, he supposed, except in their case more disagreeable. Serve them right, he mused, and shared his thoughts in a letter to Clementine.[13] He was a great respecter of the British monarchy, but not necessarily of individual monarchs. He held no high opinion of the current occupant of the throne, King George V, and as First Lord of the Admiralty had once dismissed his opinions on the Royal Navy as 'cheap and silly drivel'. But he viewed the King's son and his mistress with a detached and ironic eye. 'The little prince was there idolising as usual,' he told Clementine, capturing the essence of the royal affair and adding that he thought the prince was wearing himself out. It was also obvious that people were getting a bit tired of the affair with Freda and thought it should soon be resolved one way or the other.[14]

His readiness to look past the future King's human frailties was evident at the Laverys' party. In studying him at close quarters, Churchill was reminded of the portrait in Hampton Court of Henry VIII by Hans Holbein, the Reformation King's official artist. It was of a decidedly rotund monarch. Nonetheless, in the studio of one of Britain's leading portrait artists of the day, his painterly eye spotted a marked resemblance to the slim young Prince of Wales. 'What a strange thing heritage is,' he mused, 'we are really only variants of what has gone on before.' He himself never forgot his own heritage as a direct descendant of the great Duke of Marlborough, the victor of Blenheim.[15]

*

During Clementine's absence on the Riviera he threw himself into an energetic social life. He enjoyed dinners at Philip Sassoon's Park Lane mansion with fellow politicians and friends, spent a couple of weekends basking in the luxuries of Lympne, visited his cousin Freddie Guest at Templeton, and regularly attended social occasions within the privileged square mile of Mayfair including dinners thrown by his mother, who remained an inveterate socialite. He relied heavily, too, on the company of his brother Jack and his wife. In most biographies the quiet and unassuming John ('Jack') Strange Churchill is a largely absent figure. Six years younger, and a practised if only modestly successful stockbroker, he eschewed publicity and remained in his brother's shadow for the whole of his life. Yet they were always close and Jack was to spend the Second World War living in private quarters at 10 Downing Street. As 1921 opened, he was poised to become a partner in the distinguished City of London firm Vickers da Costa. It was not the career he had hoped for. But lack of family money had denied him entry to Sandhurst and instead, thanks to the family connection with Sir Ernest Cassel, he had entered the world of finance. He had fought with distinction in South Africa and held staff positions at GHQ France and at Sir Ian Hamilton's headquarters at Gallipoli, from where he provided his brother with a useful unofficial channel of communication. Jack had emerged with the Croix de Guerre, the Légion d'Honneur, and the Distinguished Service Order. Goonie his wife – otherwise known as Lady Gwendeline Bertie – was the daughter of the Earl and Countess of Abingdon and a society beauty whose glamour was splendidly captured at age thirty by Sir John Lavery as she wore a fur coat and hat and dark leather gloves. Jack and Goonie had two boys and a girl. The Churchill parents and cousins frequently lived, socialized, and holidayed together. Jack was especially useful for financial advice, and particularly in sorting out the tangled mess of their mother's money affairs.[16]

Despite such close-at-hand family support, Churchill missed Clementine badly and eagerly looked forward every morning to receiving a letter. On the page his love was unbounded. Often twice a week, and sometimes on successive days, he brought her up to date with his life in London. It was not just a marriage and a family they shared. Both were social animals and Clementine cared deeply about her husband's political career and ambitions. In return, she painted detailed pictures of her life on the Riviera and offered her reactions on significant issues of the day. At other times, their letters were of an intimate, personal nature. Clementine worried about the prying eyes of the household servants at Sussex Square, so Churchill assured her that he kept her letters securely locked up in a special box in his desk. It seems certain from indirect clues in their correspondence this winter that Clementine was also dealing with a gynaecological problem that demanded medical attention. It might have involved birth control, or perhaps fertility treatment, or something else. Whatever it was, he was deeply anxious about her health and even discussed it personally with her doctor in London, urging her to follow his advice and take it easy.

Meanwhile, between family and work he found little time for painting or writing. Returning from the Riviera burning with his new-found enthusiasm for light and colour, he immediately found fault with the new studio. The problem was the windows. Their frames were so wide that they cut out a third of the light, and light, he insisted, 'is life'. He immediately started chasing the builder to have them altered. But a week later he was frustrated that nothing had been done. In any case, he had now decided that the best solution was simply to install a single large sheet of plate glass and store away the offending frames for some future use. In addition, he also wanted to add a skylight to let in direct sunlight. Without it, he found the studio depressing, and he was impatient to get into it. The skylight would have the added benefit of giving the whole space the feeling of a proper art gallery, where pictures were illuminated from above.

If he couldn't get behind an easel, at least he could write about his new-found passion. The *Strand* magazine had already offered him some £1,000 for two illustrated articles on the subject and he was eager to accept it. But Clementine was alert to the need to re-establish his political credibility as a man of *gravitas*. She worried that the project would give both professional art critics and his political rivals gratuitous ammunition with which to attack him. 'I do not think it would be wise to do anything which will cause you to be discussed trivially as it were,' she urged him from Cap Ferrat. But he bluntly disagreed. It would be no worse than a Cabinet colleague writing about their hobby of golf or chess, for example. As for the art critics, he would make his articles light and amusing. In any case, he argued, he wanted to encourage other people to experiment with the brush and see if they got as much pleasure as he did out of painting. So he went ahead.

The fee, of course, was also welcome. So was the contract he received in January from Charles Scribners' Sons for the American rights to *The World Crisis*, with its handsome terms of 20 per cent royalties, tax free, and an advance of $16,000. With his customary generosity he lent some of this money to help Clementine's sister, who needed a loan to open a hat shop. He had also guaranteed a loan to Montagu Porch, his mother's third husband, and helped Clementine's mother, Lady Blanche, with her own financial affairs. He took such family obligations seriously, even while he continued with his own ambitious and spendthrift ways.[17]

FIVE

THE GREAT CORNICHE
OF LIFE

Churchill's relationship with money was a high-wire act that always teetered on the brink of disaster. As the grandson of a duke, he expected and relished the trappings of aristocratic life – grand houses, personal valets and servants, fine food and drink, expensive clothes, first-class travel. The problem was that he lacked the assured income to fund it. He received only a modest allowance when his father died and was forced to make his own financial way in life. This he did brilliantly by earning a small fortune through his early books and journalism. But what he earned was quickly spent. Never afraid to take on debt or run financial risks, by 1921 he was spending more than he was earning as a Cabinet minister. Meetings with his bank manager about juggling loans had become distinctly fraught. He could count on covering some of the gap between income and expenditure thanks to the lucrative contract he had just signed for *The World Crisis*. Still, the situation was precarious. Bills for the renovations and additions to the new house continued to mount. 'We must try to live within our income,' he sternly admonished Clementine.[1]

But that same day, twenty-four hours after the railway accident in Wales, his solicitors were officially informed of his inheritance of the Garron Towers estate lying on the coast of County Antrim in Ireland. Following the recent sale of most of the estate's houses it consisted mostly of farmlands, quarries, a lime works, and a harbour. The proceeds of the sale were safely invested in government bonds and stocks that yielded an annual income of some £4,000 (£240,000 in today's terms). Combined with his Cabinet salary it meant that he was suddenly a wealthy man, one of the many reasons that made this year an important turning point in his life. For the first time, he now had a secure income independent of any parliamentary or ministerial salary, or of what he could earn from writing. Adding to the rosy financial picture was the news this same month that his wildly spendthrift mother had sold her Mayfair house for a clear profit of £15,000, and was thus rescued from the depressing prospect of having to move across the Channel in search of a lower cost of living, as Clementine's mother had done. 'No more need to [live] abroad!' he sighed with relief on her behalf.[2]

Observers were quick to speculate on what his inheritance would mean for Churchill. One of them was Thomas Power O'Connor, an Irish Nationalist Party Member of Parliament and a living link with the politics of the 1880s and the glory days of Churchill's father. With almost fifty years of continuous service in the Commons, he now enjoyed the title of 'Father of the House'. By profession he was a journalist and a long-time correspondent for the *New York Herald*, and he wrote regular columns for *The Times*. After noting that one of the assets of the Garron Towers estate was a large and gloomy house that for years had been let as a hotel, O'Connor went on to make the point that while there was not quite so much money as originally rumoured, nonetheless it opened new doors to Churchill's ambitions and prospects:

> But still there will be enough left to make Mr. Churchill's position pecuniarily [*sic*] much more satisfactory than it has been. He also is like Mr. Lloyd George in finding politics the master passion of his life. Restless, boundlessly ambitious, with quite wonderful gifts as a Parliamentarian – which have steadily improved in the last few years – there is no knowing what he will ever do or to what position he may ultimately reach.[3]

*

Churchill was never reluctant to celebrate good fortune in extravagant style. The day after receiving news of his inheritance, in an escapade missed even by the official biographer, he headed back to the Riviera to rejoin Clementine at Cimiez. Passing through Paris, he met briefly with Gerald Geiger, who reported eagerly to Archie Sinclair that 'the blessed railway accident' had seen their mutual friend leaving for the south of France in 'an atmosphere of geniality possibly more exuberant than normal owing to the rosy visions which the prospect of an additional £6,000 pa [*sic*] doubtless engenders'. Travelling with Churchill in the train south were the Curzons, and on arrival at Nice he found Clementine waiting happily at the station along with various local dignitaries. He was in time to take in some of the colourful winter carnival and stayed for three or four days before returning home.[4]

*

To Clementine the inheritance came as a massive relief. She had never shared her husband's tolerance of debt and financial risk. Since he had left Nice two weeks before she had continued the good life on the Riviera. She was there for the Festival of Flowers, played tennis, socialized with friends, and spent money she knew they could ill afford; in fact, she had just sent her husband a bill for some new clothes. So her first natural reaction to the news was to hope they could pay off their debts. However, after a few days' reflection, she began to relish the prospect of an easier and grander life. Dreams of again owning a large house in the country swam into view.

By now she had moved on from Nice to stay with Adele, the widowed Countess of Essex, another old friend, who owned a villa named Lou Mas at St Jean Cap Ferrat. An American heiress and former society beauty, she was a close neighbour in Mayfair of Churchill's mother and divided her time between London and the Riviera. One day she and Clementine met for lunch in Monte Carlo with Jean, Lady Hamilton, the co-owner with Sir Ian of the Churchills' lost lamented Lullenden. The encounter sparked nostalgic musings that revealed that both Clementine and Winston were now already nursing hopes of repeating the country house experience – though Clementine ruefully accepted that even with the Garron Towers inheritance a place like Lullenden itself would be too costly to run.[5] Shortly afterwards, she moved to the gleaming white *belle époque* Hotel Bristol in nearby Beaulieu-sur-Mer, where she stayed until the end of February. She felt lonely in this vast hotel surrounded by middle-class English people, but she kept up her tennis, continued her casino visits, and was especially delighted when John and Hazel Lavery arrived for a lengthy stay at nearby Cap d'Ail. The artist's previous Mediterranean visits had been to North Africa. Now he hoped to capture the visually exciting landscape of the Riviera.[6]

*

Clementine was no passive or subservient observer of her husband's political career, and actively promoted his cause with other sun-seekers on the Riviera. One day, at her special request, Adele invited J. L. ('Jim') Garvin, the voluble editor of the influential Sunday newspaper, the *Observer*, for lunch at Lou Mas. He was one of the few Conservatives to have defended Churchill over the Dardanelles. 'He is young. He has lion-hearted courage. No number of enemies can fight down his ability and force', he had written. 'His hour of triumph will come.' So gratified was Churchill by this that he had nominated Garvin to write his biography, although this never in the end transpired. The lunch was a relaxed event full of London gossip, and Clementine learned that Lord Northcliffe was bursting with curiosity about Churchill's art and wanted to know how much his 'Charles Morin' paintings in Paris had sold for. Yet memories of war still cast their shadows over the Riviera's febrile glitter. Garvin's only son had been killed on the Somme in 1916, and his wife had died of influenza during the post-war pandemic. The Hotel Bristol itself had only recently re-opened after serving as a military hospital. More consequential, however, was a lengthy conversation Clementine had at the Bristol with another powerful media figure. But this one was known as an outspoken foe of her husband.[7]

*

'Thank God, we are once more on British soil!' declared the fresh-faced twenty-six-year-old Churchill as he stepped off a train from Boston at the Windsor railway station in Montreal. It was just before Christmas 1900. He was heavily bundled up against the cold and on his way to Ottawa and Government House to enjoy the season's festivities with the Governor-General of Canada and his wife, Lord and Lady Minto. Afterwards, he would continue with a speaking tour he was making of North America. It was his second visit across the Atlantic, and the first to Canada. Since his dramatic escape from the Boers, he had spun it into a highly lucrative lecture tour and tale of personal adventure that earned him enough to fund his lifestyle for several years to come. He had also just been elected as a Conservative Member of Parliament. In New York he had been introduced to his audience by the legendary author Mark Twain, and in Boston by his namesake (but no relative), the American novelist Winston Churchill. He had met President McKinley in Washington, and dined in Albany with the Governor of New York, Theodore Roosevelt. After Christmas with the Mintos, he returned to Montreal to give his lecture before going on to Toronto and Ottawa and finishing his tour in Winnipeg.

In Montreal he delivered his talk to a packed audience at Windsor Hall. It followed the format he had perfected, a skilled confection of vividly told highlights of the British campaign against the Boers woven together by the scintillating thread of his personal adventures and illustrated by carefully selected photographs. For his rapt audiences north of the border he added some suitably laudatory words about the performance of the Canadian troops. By all press accounts it was a great success. The English-language *Montreal Gazette* noted approvingly that 'Lord Randolph's son . . . caught the sympathy and interest of his audience and retained it throughout.'[8]

Yet one listener took away a distinctly negative impression of the ambitious young politician from Britain. Colonel John Bayne Maclean was the son of Scottish immigrants to Ontario. A former journalist who owned a number of trade magazines, he had put an enormous effort into publicizing the talk as well as arranging a lunch and a dinner afterwards for the speaker. But he was disappointed to find that Churchill had little to reveal about the Boer War that the twelve hundred or so paying listeners did not already know. What was worse, he came across as 'boastfully arrogant' by claiming that one day he would be the British prime minister. The son of Lord Randolph, thought Maclean, had been 'shamefully disgusting and offensive to all', and his negative opinion had only hardened over the years.

This winter Maclean had joined the swelling wave of North Americans flooding to the post-war Riviera to mingle with the rich and famous of European society. By this time, he was a grandee of Canadian publishing and had accrued a media empire that included *Maclean's*, an influential news magazine reporting on politics and current events that was read across the country. To have it as an enemy could be disastrous. Clementine was well aware of Maclean's influence in Canada. So she deployed all her considerable charms against the tycoon whom she found 'naif, vain, touchy, kind-hearted, horribly energetic, and vital'. The blunt-speaking Maclean was sufficiently diplomatic not to mention his reaction to her husband's 1900 visit to Montreal. Instead, urged on by Clementine, he enthused at length about Canada and himself. By the end of their conversation he was a convert to the Churchill cause.[9]

The dividend came several weeks later when *Maclean's* published a special feature on Churchill carefully timed for the Imperial Conference in June. Spread over several columns, the hefty article described him as 'the most striking figure in British politics'. The author of the laudatory article was well chosen for the purpose. Sir Ian Hamilton had first met the young Churchill as 'an eager chubby-faced shipmate' while they were sailing home together from India in 1897. Ever since, they had formed something of a mutual admiration society. Churchill's fifth book was a glowing account of Hamilton's triumphant march on Pretoria during the Boer War. As commander of the Allied forces at Gallipoli, Hamilton in turn had deplored Churchill's dismissal from the Admiralty. 'What a tragedy that his nerve and military vision have been side-tracked,' he lamented; 'his eclipse projects a black shadow over the Dardanelles.'

To anyone reading Hamilton's profile of Churchill it was clear that in the new Colonial Secretary the Empire had found a man of courage, vision, and genius. 'Is he perfect?' asked Hamilton rhetorically. 'Heavens, no! A genius he is, but wayward and self-absorbed. In company he falls often into a sort of trance ... [but] ... really he is dreaming with an intense concentration and is clearing the decks for action ...' Above all, he emphasized, Churchill was the man for action. 'He is in every sense courageous, and he never gets frightened unless danger is still a long way off; then he does get the wind up but that is because he sees very far ahead and is miserable, wretched, when his colleagues wish to wait-and-see. He sees. He doesn't want to wait; he wants to make ready for the storm. Yet once let it break and the last thing that will break under it is Winston's nerve.' It was almost as though Hamilton was writing the advance script for Churchill as he urged rearmament on a reluctant Britain in the 1930s.[10]

For Clementine, Maclean's conversion was a considerable coup and demonstrated not for the first time that she was her husband's strongest and most faithful ally. It was also a sign that his reputation across the British Empire was recovering from its low point of five years before. To have the leading Canadian magazine of opinion come out so powerfully in his favour was excellent news. From now on, Canada to Churchill would always be 'The Great Dominion', a land of huge opportunity and potential vital to the security and future of the British Empire. His faith was powerfully enforced when at the end of the decade he crossed the country by train with his son Randolph, brother Jack, and Jack's son, Johnny. 'The immense size and progress of this country impresses itself upon one more every day,' he enthused. 'The sentimental feeling towards England is wonderful. The United States are stretching their tentacles out in all directions, but the Canadian National Spirit and personality is becoming so powerful and self-contained that I do not think we need fear for the future.'[11]

*

Still basking in the glow of his inheritance, and with a now carefree Clementine at Cap Ferrat dreaming of a new Lullenden, Churchill motored out to the Chiltern Hills some forty miles north-west of Downing Street and another grand house within easy reach of London. Nestling close to the ancient village of Ellesborough in a quintessentially English landscape thickly wooded with beech trees lay the ancient Tudor mansion known as Chequers, or Chequers Court. After entering its fine wrought-iron gates set between two lodges, he passed down 'The Victory Way', the long drive built during the war with the help of German prisoners of war, and soon caught his first glimpse of the house that during the Second World War was to become almost a second home to him and Clementine.

The surrounding Buckinghamshire countryside was rich in historical associations. John Hampden, a principal leader of the parliamentary opposition to King Charles I during the English Civil War, had lived close by, as had Benjamin Disraeli, the great leader of the Victorian Conservative Party and twice prime minister. Chequers' own history went back to the Domesday Book of 1086, and its name derived from an earlier house once owned by a twelfth-century Exchequer official. Just four weeks before his visit, Lloyd George had formally taken possession of the keys from Sir Arthur and Lady Lee, who presented it in perpetuity to the nation as a place of rest and relaxation for British prime ministers. Churchill was one of his earliest guests. Along with him he brought Marigold.

Like Churchill himself, Chequers was the product of an Anglo-American union. Arthur Hamilton Lee had been a commissioned artillery officer in the British Army, where one of his earliest postings was to the Royal Military College in Kingston, Ontario. It was there that he met Ruth Moore, the daughter of a wealthy Wall Street banker, whom he soon married. Later he served as the British military attaché with the United States Army in Cuba and made friends with the leader of the legendary 'Rough Riders', Colonel Theodore Roosevelt, who was to stay at Chequers several times over the coming years. In 1900 Lee left the army and was elected as a Tory Member of Parliament in the same 'Khaki election' that saw Churchill also enter the House of Commons. During the First World War, Lee fell under the spell of Lloyd George, worked for him at the Ministry of Munitions and the War Office, and was knighted for his efforts. Two years later he was raised to the peerage as Baron Lee of Fareham.

It was Ruth Lee's Wall Street inheritance that created the Chequers the couple gave to the British nation. They spared no expense in lavishly modernizing and furnishing it throughout with seventeenth-century oak panelling, hanging the walls with almost two hundred historic portraits and other paintings, and stocking it with antique furniture and countless artefacts of historic interest. Amongst them was Napoleon's scarlet and gold dispatch case, the octagonal table the deposed French Emperor used while an exile on St Helena, and a large collection of Cromwelliana, including a mask of the Lord Protector himself. One of the first sights to greet Churchill was a large collection of enemy trophies on display in the Great Hall.

In giving the house to the nation, the Lees' hope was twofold. First, that during an epoch of radical change in the nation's history it would act as a moderating influence on its rulers. 'To the revolutionary statesman the antiquity and calm tenacity of Chequers and its annals might suggest some saving virtues in the continuity of English history and exercise a check upon too hasty upheavals,' wrote Lee in the deed of settlement, 'whilst even the most reactionary could scarcely be insensible to the spirit of human freedom which permeates the countryside of Hampden ...' These were words that Churchill himself could have written, anxious as he was about the rising tide of socialism in Britain and revolution abroad, yet powerfully committed to a romantic view of English history that saw it as the steady march towards freedom embodied in a stable parliamentary monarchy. He had little religious belief. It was history, or this special version of it, that lay at the heart of his faith.[12]

The Lees also hoped that the rural tranquillity of Chequers would benefit the personal health of prime ministers. 'The better the health of our rulers,' declared Lee, 'the more sanely they will rule.' Ironically, during Churchill's first official use of the house starting in 1940, it was to be far from a tranquil retreat from the cares of office. On the contrary, it became a buzzing hive of frantic activity and a powerhouse of strategy. Relatively safe from air attack, it was to serve as his command centre second only to the underground war rooms in Whitehall. Characteristically, one of the first changes he made was to install a direct telephone line to Downing Street. Another was to have the book-lined Long Gallery converted into a temporary cinema for the use of its wartime staff and himself after a long day's work – a far cry from the quiet walking and contemplation of nature so lovingly envisaged by the Lees.

Churchill was deeply impressed. On the Sunday he sent a letter to Clementine from the house. 'It is just the kind of house you admire,' he wrote, 'a panelled museum full of history, full of treasures,' and added that Marigold had marched into his bedroom that morning in 'blooming health' but with no 'special communication' to make. Perhaps, he noted, Clementine would one day get to see it herself.

She was now at Cap Ferrat, a haven with its own seductive charm. Backed by precipitous white cliffs topped by the medieval village of Eze, the peninsula dangled like an earring into the Mediterranean and was an especially favoured spot for the wealthy. The drive from Nice had taken her along the French Corniche, the twisting road running high above sea level through cactus and pines that offered magnificent views of the Mediterranean. So when she sat down in Adele's villa to write a letter expressing her optimism and joy at her husband's new situation she readily fell back on images of the luxury that surrounded her. What with his new and exciting task at the Colonial Office, the visit to Chequers, his book, and his painting, it must feel, she wrote, that he was 'soaring like an aeroplane above the great Corniche of life'. As for herself, she enthused in a later letter, she was now free of haunting care and felt like 'a cork bobbing on a sunny sea'.[13]

*

Churchill took possession of his room at the Colonial Office on Tuesday 15 February, the first day of the new parliamentary session. It was twice as big as his old one in the War Office and reminded him of the days he had spent writing in the saloon at Blenheim Palace. 'Fine and sedate ... but well-warmed,' he glowed. With him came Eddie Marsh, to whom it was familiar territory. It was here, as Under-Secretary of State for the Colonies, that Churchill had first taken him on, and Marsh had actually started his civil service career there some ten years before that. It seemed fitting, remarked one of his fellow civil servants, that the immaculately dressed Marsh 'should spend his days in heavily-carpeted rooms, locking and unlocking Cabinet boxes with one of the four keys that dangled from a slim silver chain'.[14]

Churchill's fresh surroundings matched the global scope of his new responsibilities. Britain had emerged from the Paris Peace Conference with an imperial reach wider than ever before in its history. Not only had it acquired the mandated former Ottoman territories in the Middle East, but also several former German colonies. Along with the Indian Empire and the Dominions of Canada, Australia, New Zealand and South Africa, they made the British Empire the largest in the world.

Yet for him politically, at any moment the aeroplane soaring above the great Corniche of Life could stall and come crashing to earth. The reason was simple. Politically, he was almost completely dependent on Lloyd George. It was the Welsh Wizard who had brought him back to high office after the Dardanelles disaster, and he could still now make or unmake him. This would leave him isolated. He had a coterie of loyal personal friends, but he lacked any strong and independent political base. 'He was not interested [in other people and their opinions],' observed Violet Asquith. 'Nor did he seek to conceal his indifference by any softening subterfuge. To save his life he could not have pretended an interest he did not feel ... He enjoyed the ovation of the crowd but he still ignored the necessity of having a personal following.' Alexander MacCallum Scott, his first biographer, noted the same weakness. 'He was not a man who encouraged intimacies,' he wrote. 'His brusqueness often verged on rudeness, and alienated many a well-wisher.' This stood in sharp contrast to Lloyd George, who possessed the gift of demonstrating genuine interest in others' opinions. During their lifetime the two men promoted the image of a close and enduring friendship. Yet Clementine's private gibe about Lloyd George and Judas Iscariot was easily matched by Lloyd George's own, that Churchill 'would make a drum out of the skin of his own mother in order to sound his own praises.'[15]

But if Churchill was dangerously reliant on Lloyd George, the prime minister himself was precariously placed. He had stormed to power in the 1918 General ('Victory') Election by leading his Coalition of National Liberals and Conservatives to win over 500 seats in the House of

Commons. Combined with his personal standing as the prime minister who had won the war, this gave him two years' mastery of the political scene. But as 1921 opened, his grip on the Coalition and the country was patently weakening. It was a grim winter. The post-war boom was over. Unemployment was rising steeply, and the Labour Party was gaining more and more popular support. Amongst diehards on the Conservative backbenches, pressure was growing for reductions in state spending. The Treasury, which was under Conservative control, took the same line. To keep them happy, Lloyd George was forced to cut back on some of the progressive measures the government had introduced to make the country 'fit for heroes', his great electoral promise. In January the victory of an 'anti-waste' candidate at a by-election in Dover increased the pressure, which was spurred on by a virulent anti-Lloyd George press campaign. Spearheaded by the Northcliffe press, owner of *The Times* and *Daily Mail*, it began to cast doubt on the very survival of the Coalition. On the very day that Churchill was luxuriating in his bed at Chequers hinting to Clementine that one day, too, she might be able to enjoy its splendours, *The Sunday Times* declared roundly that 'Everyone knows that the present Coalition cannot last indefinitely.'[16]

As rumours of a possible general election spread, Lloyd George moved firmly to strengthen his political base. The Liberals had split when he displaced Asquith as prime minister in 1916. His followers took the designation of 'National' (or 'Coalition') Liberals', while those remaining loyal to Asquith became known as 'Independent Liberals'. It was a bitter schism. The Independents kept control of the Liberal Party machine and funds, as well as the National Liberal Club in central London. Here, relations between the rival Liberal factions became so acrimonious that both Lloyd George and Churchill saw their portraits rudely relegated to the basement. In response, the Lloyd George Liberals set up an alternative club known as the 1920 Club. Formed shortly before Christmas 1920 and cheekily situated almost next door, it held its first general meeting in mid-February at the Central Hall in Westminster, just off Parliament Square. Moving the vote of thanks for its creation was the Chief Liberal Whip – none other than Captain Frederick (Freddie) Guest, Churchill's cousin and shrewd political crony.[17]

As the first British prime minister to fully appreciate the power of the press, Lloyd George went out of his way to court press magnates and avidly read the newspapers to gauge public opinion. Thanks to Freddie, he even possessed one of his own after Churchill's cousin master-minded the purchase of the *Daily Chronicle* as his personal mouthpiece. Baron Lee, who was now First Lord of the Admiralty, also pitched in by purchasing the weekly journal *Outlook* as a pro-government organ. In October 1920 the *Lloyd George Liberal Magazine* had also been launched, specifically to bolster the Coalition. Guest was one of the principal electoral architects of the Coalition government and a figure key to its continuing survival. As a leader with no party machinery or treasury behind him, Lloyd George needed a war chest to finance his political activities. Here, Freddie proved indispensable by building up a fund eventually reaching £3 million through the sale of honours such as knighthoods and other forms of political patronage. Although there was little new about the trading of honours for political purposes, the scheme was becoming a growing target for Lloyd George's political enemies. Freddie's dubious dealings were one of the reasons why Clementine disapproved of him. Now, as the political ground beneath his feet began to shake, Lloyd George turned to Churchill's cousin once again for help.[18]

The day after Churchill returned from his weekend at Chequers, the prime minister sent Guest to the West Country, Yorkshire, and Lancashire to bolster support for the National Liberals against attacks by their Independent Liberal rivals that threatened to weaken his political base. Here, Guest strongly banged the anti-socialist drum by telling an audience at the Manchester Reform Club that only the Coalition could prevent a Labour government from coming to power – a theme that Lloyd George was to embellish himself at the inaugural dinner of the 1920 Club held the following month at the Savoy Hotel in London.[19] In a similar talk at Leeds, Guest concluded by referring to the Liberal Club's removal of its Lloyd George portrait to the basement. They should remember, he joked, that Guy Fawkes had once stored gunpowder in a cellar.[20]

But gunpowder is volatile and unpredictable. Outwardly the relations between Churchill and Lloyd George were civil and friendly. But they were far from seeing eye to eye on many issues, and at Cabinet meetings Churchill was often 'a brooding source of discontent'.[21] Contrary to popular myth, he was no reactionary. In the pre-war Liberal government, he had argued vigorously for active social reform, and its radical scheme of unemployment insurance was his personal brainchild. During the war he had argued for massive state intervention in the economy and in 1918 favoured the nationalization of the railways. He also strongly and consistently pressed for the taxation of war wealth – the amount by which personal wealth had increased during the war. When the Cabinet had rejected the idea the previous June, he made sure that his dissent was recorded in the official minutes. He also remained committed to the government's housing programme, which was now coming under increasing attack. His own experience and lifestyle were privileged and aristocratic. But since 1908 he had been a Member of Parliament for Dundee, an impoverished and heavily working-class town dominated by the jute trade and hit badly by the current slump. After one of his earliest visits to Scotland, he had been struck by the unfriendly and disaffected attitude of the working classes. 'They evidently [mean] trouble,' he remarked. Now, unemployment was increasing steeply and poor relief was hard to get, as he was reminded almost daily by angry and anguished letters from his constituency. The swingeing cuts to social programmes being contemplated by the Cabinet seriously troubled him. When he visited his constituency later in the year he was shocked to see men in bare feet and children who were clearly starving and under-nourished. 'Should our policy remain the austere bankers' policy?' he caustically asked Lloyd George.[22]

*

It was on foreign policy issues, however, that he was most seriously at loggerheads with the prime minister. Over the Bolsheviks they had frequently come to metaphorical blows, and there was now an uneasy truce. It was Turkey that now divided them. Two years before, eager to profit from the collapse of the Ottoman Empire, Greece had invaded the Anatolian mainland of Turkey and seized the city of Smyrna with its Greek population exceeding that of Athens itself. A former Ottoman army officer called Mustafa Kemal, known as 'Ataturk', was now leading a national war to drive out the Greeks. Lloyd George was passionately pro-Greek and an unqualified supporter of Prime Minister Eleftherios Venizelos, whom he hailed as 'the greatest statesman Greece had thrown up since the days of Pericles'. By contrast, Churchill wished to see Turkey kept as intact as possible as a bulwark against Bolshevik Russia and because he feared that a humiliation of the Turks would alienate Muslims across the Middle East and within the British Empire. The two men had frequently quarrelled over this. Shortly before Christmas, Churchill had accused Lloyd George of waging 'a vendetta' against the Turks.[23]

Things were to get worse. While he was holidaying on the Riviera with Clementine, he received an urgent plea from his friend Edwin Montagu, the Secretary of State for India, who was married to Clementine's cousin and lifelong friend, Venetia Stanley; their home at Breccles in Norfolk frequently played host to the Churchills. Lloyd George was about to go to Paris and would be pressing his views about the Greek–Turkish war on the French. 'His mood is violently anti-Turkish and he is dreaming in *Greek*,' wrote Montagu. 'Come back or go to Paris but *act now* and *save the world*.' Five days later Churchill arrived in the French capital. He found Lloyd George in 'a cursed bad humour' and determined to keep on backing the Greeks. The next morning, the two men continued their row after Lloyd George accused him of having driven Turkey into the First World War in the first place when he was at the Admiralty. Back in London, Churchill wrote him a furious letter correcting certain facts, hinting strongly that he might resign, and pointing out that Lloyd George's anti-Turkish stance would badly harm his own chances of finding a Middle East settlement.

His anger climaxed later in the month. Amongst a bundle of secret intercepts that landed on his desk he spotted the text of a telegram sent from the Greek Foreign Office in Athens to its legation in London, which revealed that in a recent conversation with Venizelos, Lloyd George had expressed his total support for the Greeks even against the advice of the Foreign Office. The next day, Churchill furiously confronted him with the evidence. If he did not stop his anti-Turk crusade, he warned, the Turks would be thrown into the arms of the Bolsheviks, Mesopotamia would descend into disorder, and Muslims everywhere would be alienated from Britain. 'I am deeply grieved at the prospect and find myself so utterly without power to influence your mind even in regard to matters with which my duties are specially concerned,' he wrote bitterly. He was all the more distressed, he added, because they agreed on many other issues and because, he concluded, 'of our long friendship & my admiration for yr [*sic*] genius and work'. With his relations with Lloyd George in such a febrile state, it was just as well that after a few hours' reflection he decided not to send the letter. Instead, a few days later, he left the country bound for Cairo.[24]

SIX

'THIS WILD COUSIN OF MINE'

f the political family was under strain, Churchill's wider family had troubles of its own. Even as he was waving goodbye to Clementine on the Riviera, his mother was bidding farewell to her beloved only niece, the daughter of her elder sister Clara. Tall, lithe, and graceful, at age thirty-five Clare Sheridan was bound for Liverpool, the Cunard liner *Aquitania*, and New York. Behind her she fled a scandal that left London society sniggering and Winston fuming. Most families have at least one black sheep within the fold, and Clare was the Churchills'. For that reason, she has been excluded from most mainstream Churchill biographies. Yet her exploits bring into sharp focus Churchill's continuing obsession with the Bolsheviks, as well as the too often understated importance of family in his life.

Clare was his only female cousin, a satin-gowned bridesmaid at his wedding. The Jerome sisters kept their families close. Jennie played the role of family matriarch and took a special interest in Clare, who had suffered an unstable childhood marked by chronic parental neglect. Her parents flitted between various homes in London, Sussex, and Innishannon in County Cork, Ireland, where her father Moreton Frewen owned a landed estate on the banks of the River Bandon; his speculative financial ventures frequently crashed, bankruptcy always threatened, and not for nothing was he mockingly dubbed 'Mortal Ruin'.

Unlike her two brothers who were privileged with an Eton education, Clare suffered the usual home schooling reserved for girls of her class and ended up at a convent in Paris and a finishing school in Germany. At age seventeen she was taken to London to 'enter society'. The three Jerome sisters were living together in a cluster of houses on Great Cumberland Place, and every morning Clare would cross the street to visit Jennie and read out loud to her *The Times*' editorial while she took breakfast. Lady Randolph also coached her on becoming a debutante. 'My Aunt Jennie became my second mother,' Clare remembered, 'I was a wild animal being tamed . . .'[1]

She saw her cousin Winston regularly at family events. But he was a full decade older and often seemed distant and intimidating. The cousin she felt closest to was John Leslie, the son of her aunt Leonie and Sir John Leslie of Glaslough in County Monaghan, Ireland, who owned an estate of almost 50,000 acres. Born in the same month and year as each other, the cousins shared an artistic and rebellious streak. In his twenties, John declared for Irish Home Rule, changed his name to its Irish variant 'Shane', and formally embraced Catholicism. It took Clare longer to find herself. Her literary ambitions received scant encouragement, and unfulfilled as a social butterfly, at age twenty-five she married William (but always known as 'Wilfred') Sheridan, a London stockbroker and descendant of the playwright Richard Brinsley Sheridan – of whom, revealingly, she had never heard. In 1912 she gave birth to a daughter. Another quickly followed but was sickly from birth and soon died of meningitis. A year later her husband was killed at the Battle of Loos only days after the birth of their third child, a son. Clare was now a war widow with two small children to support.

At this point she turned to her cousin Winston. Once before, from the dismal convent in Paris, she had written to him about her misery and received a sympathetic if patronizing response. 'My dear Clare,' he wrote, 'Do not be low-spirited. It is something after all to be fed and clothed and sheltered: more than most people in the world without constant and unwearing [*sic*] toil. Cultivate a philosophical disposition; grow pretty and wise and good . . .'[2] Now she asked her cousin to find out the details of her husband's death. Winston had liked Wilfred, whose body was missing in German-held territory, and did his best to find out more but without success. Dressed in her black widow's weeds and with her baby boy and small daughter accompanied by a governess, shortly before Christmas 1915 Clare travelled to London. Churchill was with his regiment on the Western Front and for a few nights she stayed with a sympathetic Clementine at Jack and Goonie's Cromwell Road house. 'My darling,' reported Clementine to her husband, 'I don't know how one bears such things. I feel like I could not weather such a blow – she has a beautiful little son 8 weeks old but her poor "black puss" [Wilfred] sleeps in Flanders.'[3]

Clare was also broke. On his return to London, Winston did what he could to help. Her problem was that widows of men who had volunteered for service did not qualify for pensions, Wilfred's parents lived on a fixed income, and her own father, as usual, was in a financially fragile state. Eventually the War Office gave her a pension of £250 pounds a year. Together with support from her aunts Jennie and Leonie, this was just about enough to live on.[4]

But she needed a life, and found it in art. Churchill was also just discovering its magic, and it brought them closer. Sculpture rather than painting was her salvation. Grieving over the loss of her infant daughter she had found unexpected comfort and pleasure in working with clay to make the child a memorial. Art schools and classes followed, and thanks to family connections and friends in high places she received tuition and advice from some of the leading sculptors of the day. Sitting for Jacob Epstein, she intently observed him at work and adopted some of his revolutionary techniques. Celebrities such as H. G. Wells, Hazel Lavery, and Lady Diana Manners – the wife of Duff Cooper – sat for her, as did the Canadian air ace Billy Bishop V.C.; it was a coup when his bust was purchased by the Canadian War Museum. An exhibition of her sculptures under the auspices of the National Portrait Society brought her more commissions and she splashed out by buying a Buick and hiring a chauffeur. She took a small studio in St John's Wood in London, and here the up-and-coming society portrait artist Oswald Birley captured her wearing bright red lipstick and an artist's smock. In her mid-thirties, she now blossomed into a vibrant and self-confident woman enthusiastically breaking Edwardian taboos and calling herself a pacifist and anarchist.

Her biographer Anita Leslie, Shane's daughter, who came to know her well, described her as 'instinctive, emotional, devoid of logic, uncontrollable, blazing with love and indignation in turn'. Candle-lit dinner parties in her studio became a magnet for an upper-class Bohemian set thrilling to the jazz beat of post-war London.[5]

Events had brought her directly into Churchill's orbit after Freddie Guest decided to collect the sculptured heads of celebrities who happened to be his friends. As Winston and Clementine were temporarily living with him at Templeton, Clare eagerly seized on her cousin as an obvious subject for a portrait. Freddie had generously converted a north-facing room of the house into a studio where Churchill happily spent his Sundays painting. Lord Beaverbrook turned her down, but another of his close friends was more than willing to sit for her.

Lord Birkenhead had been a spectacularly successful lawyer in Liverpool before emerging as an equally brilliant backbench Tory MP famed for his robust attacks against Home Rule for Ireland and reform of the House of Lords. Born in 1872 as Frederick Edwin Smith – and hence forever known as 'F. E.' – he was tall, darkly handsome, and athletically naturally gifted. Outwardly he had little in common with Churchill except for intense ambition, a gift for high-speed verbal repartee, and a lust for adventure and pleasure. Each quickly recognized in the other a kindred soul, and across the political divide they formed an unlikely bond that was to endure until Smith's death in 1930. Together the two rising young stars 'played soldiers' in the pre-war Oxford Yeomanry, staying up late during the summer field exercises drinking and playing cards until the early hours. Smith was the first to hear of Winston's engagement to Clementine when they were staying at Blenheim Palace together, and later the Churchills moved to live close to Smith and his family in Eccleston Square in London, where each man became godfather to the other's son. 'Our friendship was perfect,' Churchill once said, and Smith reciprocated by saying that there was 'no man in public life in England with a heart so warm, with a simplicity so complete, with a loyalty so unswerving and so dependable'.[6] In 1919 Lloyd George had appointed Smith as Lord Chancellor with the title Lord Birkenhead (the place of his birth). Shortly afterwards, Birkenhead helped save Churchill from committing political suicide. In a fury over Lloyd George's policy toward the Bolsheviks, Churchill had teetered perilously on the brink of resignation. Only Birkenhead's strongly worded advice held him back from carrying out the threat.[7]

As well as being a heavy drinker and gambler, F. E. was a notorious womanizer and had long set his eyes on Clare. Over several weekends his car collected her from her studio and drove her to Templeton, where she spent hours sculpting the three male friends. Churchill was the hardest to do because he found it impossible to sit still and was impatient to get on with his painting. Sunday, he said, was the only free time he had. 'I waited, I watched, I snatched moments, I did and undid and re-did, at times in despair,' she complained. Sometimes Freddie would plead with him to give her a chance, and he would be contrite and promise to sit still. He managed to do so for three minutes and then began to fidget. As the day faded, she recalled, he would invariably turn excitedly to the window to paint the sunset. 'His canvas had been prepared, the cedar tree in the foreground was already painted, he went straight for the colour. On one of these occasions he said to me, without looking round: "Sometimes I could *almost* give up everything for it." '[8] One day Clare returned to Templeton about midnight to find the three friends still up and talking. Guest was wrapped in a bath towel, Birkenhead was wearing vivid strawberry-coloured pyjamas, and Churchill was clothed in a Jaeger dressing gown 'borrowed' by Freddie from a German prisoner of war. After they plied her with champagne, Winston announced fiercely: 'In my next incarnation I mean to be a woman, I mean to be an artist, I shall be free, and I shall have children.'[9]

Meanwhile, Birkenhead continued his pursuit at Clare's St John's Wood studio. Much taken with his sardonic humour, she tolerated his amorous pleadings and agreed to join him and Churchill on his yacht during the summer. Society was soon buzzing with gossip. Her Aunt Jennie, much concerned, urged her to be careful and pointed out that in her own affairs she had never taken on a married man. She riposted that it wasn't an affair; she was simply enjoying a man's company. Whatever the truth – and Birkenhead's official biographer makes no mention of her despite acknowledging at least one other of the Lord Chancellor's sexual affairs – Churchill demonstrated his usual tolerance and refused to be scandalized. So far as he was concerned, they were both special and whatever they did was fine by him. Clare particularly, after her wartime suffering, could do no wrong – or so he thought.[10]

*

One day Clare invited Winston to lunch at her studio with her brother Oswald, the portrait artist Ambrose McEvoy, and the gallery owner Colin Agnew, who had promised her an exhibition in the West End. The lunch came at the climax of Churchill's crusade against the Bolsheviks. The Red Army had reached the gates of Warsaw but had then been dramatically turned back by the Polish Army in what history remembers as the 'Miracle of the Vistula'. Boris Savinkov seized the moment to urge Churchill to release British war materiel for use in a 'push' across the Soviet frontier, collecting 'a huge snowball of anti-Bolshies' to crush the regime in Moscow. The Cabinet also knew from secret service intercepts that Leonid Krassin and Lev Kamenev, his fellow Bolshevik at the Soviet Trade Office on New Bond Street and Trotsky's brother-in-law, had been carrying out propaganda contrary to all their promises.

This was exactly what Churchill had predicted. A keen reader of the intercepts, he had seen with his own eyes messages revealing Soviet duplicity and deception and on one of them, a telegram from Kamenev to Moscow, he furiously scribbled, 'This is unmistakable avowal of *mala fides* [bad faith].' But his demand for the immediate expulsion of Kamenev and Krassin was rejected by Lloyd George. As the Cabinet had already ruled out any military action against Russia, he was also compelled to reject Savinkov's plea for military assistance.[11] Over lunch with Clare he let loose his frustrations at having his hands so firmly tied. '[Winston] said nobody hated Bolshevism more than he, but Bolsheviks were like crocodiles,' noted Oswald in his diary. 'He would like to shoot every one he saw, but there were two ways of dealing with them – you could hunt them, or let them alone, and it was sometimes too expensive to go on hunting them for ever.'[12]

Luckily for his enjoyment of their lunch Churchill had no idea what Clare was up to. While he raged about the Bolsheviks, she kept quiet about the sitter who had come to her studio earlier that morning – none other than the 'crocodile' Kamenev himself. Captivated by the notion of adding Bolshevik heads to her forthcoming show, and not a little thrilled by the forbidden lure of Bolshevism itself, only three days previously she had paid a visit to the Soviet offices on New Bond Street. Here, she was warmly received by a smiling Kamenev who assured her that, far from obliterating art as was widely rumoured, the Soviet government was anxious to surround itself with culture and that artists were its most privileged class. Promising to sit for her, he had turned up promptly at her studio three hours before her lunch with Winston. While she sculpted, Kamenev talked almost non-stop about the wonders of the new society in Russia. Not surprisingly given her family situation, he heavily empha- sized its support for children whose parents were too poor to clothe, feed, and educate them. In turn, she enthused about her lifelong love of Russian literature, art, music, and dancing. 'You should come to Russia,' he responded. 'You can come with me and I will get you sittings from Lenin and Trotsky.' Thinking he was joking, she hesitated, but only for a moment. 'Let me know when you are going,' she said, 'and I will be ready in half an hour.' The next morning Churchill's other Bolshevik 'crocodile', Leonid Krassin, also came for a sitting. 'He has a beautiful head and sat almost sphinx-like, serene and expressionless most of the time,' she noted. 'He has no smile like Kamenev and his piercing eyes just looked at me impas- sively while I worked. It's rather uncanny.'[13]

By contrast, she was bewitched by Kamenev's charm offensive. He sent her a bouquet of roses, and throwing caution to the winds the two of them lunched openly at Claridges and strolled round the Tate Gallery. In Trafalgar Square they ran into a 'Hands Off Russia' demonstration. The speaker was George Lansbury, the editor of the socialist newspaper the *Daily Herald*, who was a staunch supporter of the Bolsheviks and bitter opponent of Churchill whom he regularly denounced as an imperialist and a warmonger. Lansbury quickly noticed Clare and Kamenev in the Trafalgar Square crowd. 'Gangway please for Comrade Kamenev' went up the cry and they were wildly cheered. But aware of the threat of expulsion hanging over him, Clare's new-found Bolshevik friend prudently declined to speak. Then the couple visited Hampton Court and rowed on the Thames with Kamenev humming Volga boat songs. 'Twelve hours with Kamenev,' she noted ecstatically in her diary when she came home at midnight.

Meanwhile Churchill continued his high-level fulminations against 'the crocodiles'. His campaign was given extra fuel by Sir Henry Wilson, the robustly opinionated Chief of the Imperial General Staff, who was convinced that the British Empire was facing an existential crisis and that Lloyd George's tolerance of Krassin and Kamenev must have an explanation sinister enough to merit a coup d'état. Several times Churchill discussed with Wilson the stream of intercepts from the code-breakers proving Kamenev's involvement with the revolutionary excitement sweeping the British labour movement, and encouraged him to put his fully documented case on paper. On the day after his lunch with Clare, he was sufficiently wound up on the topic to tell Lloyd George that 'a veritable plot was being hatched against England and France', and he sent him a damning intercept in which Kamenev talked of buying arms for the working class. But if Wilson was fantasizing about treason, Churchill trod a far more careful path and concentrated again on demanding the expulsion of the Russians. This time he suggested full publication of the intercepts to prove the extent of Bolshevik meddling. 'Are we really going to sit still,' he asked, 'until we see the combination of money from Moscow, the Kameneff-Krassin [sic] propaganda, the Council of Action, and something very like a general strike, all acting and reacting on one another, while at the same time our military forces are at their very weakest?' To add force to his argument, he also pointed out the political dangers of permitting the Russians to stay: it gave encouragement to Labour, which was a growing political threat, while at the same time alienating the Conservatives who were part of the Coalition. Less than ten days had passed since Kamenev's visit to Clare's studio. But Churchill's appeal fell on deaf ears. Lloyd George was far less alarmist about the Bolsheviks and their impact on the British labour movement, and the

Cabinet refused to publish the intercepts. He did, however, throw Churchill a bone. Krassin could stay, but Kamenev would be given his marching orders. After a stormy interview with the prime minister at 10 Downing Street, Clare's favourite Bolshevik was told to pack his bags and leave Britain. This did little to appease Churchill's fury. 'As long as any portion of this nest of vipers is left intact,' he fumed, 'it will continue to breed and swarm.'[14]

Clare was sculpting in her studio when she received the news. Infatuated with her romance and seduced by the prospect of being able to sculpt the heads of both Lenin and Trotsky, she blithely abandoned the promised cruise with Birkenhead and Churchill, cashed a £100 cheque, purchased her ticket at Thomas Cook's, bought a new hat, had her hair washed and cut, scribbled a few letters, hastily packed a couple of suitcases, and left the next morning with Kamenev for Moscow. Almost the entire Soviet trade delegation saw them off. Krassin, ever the gentleman, even presented her with a large box of chocolates tied up with a red ribbon.[15] The only people she told in advance were Shane and her brother Oswald. 'I'd rather she didn't go,' the latter confided to his diary, 'but she has got "Bolshevism" badly ... and I think it may cure her to go and see it. She is also her own mistress and if I thwarted her by telling Winston she'd never confide in me again.' Shane also kept the secret and took the full brunt of Churchill's anger during a massive family row over the escapade. 'Clare's in Russia with those filthy communists,' he raged. 'She's mad, I tell you. Mad! It's absolutely typical of Clare, but this time she's really gone too far. I'll not forgive her.'[16]

*

Clare's stay in Moscow was an artistic triumph. In the freezing cold of a makeshift studio in the Kremlin she sculpted all the top Bolsheviks including Trotsky, Zinoviev, Dzerzhinsky, and even Lenin himself. The Soviet leader was taciturn but ventured the opinion that Russia's greatest enemy was the sculptor's cousin, Churchill himself. 'All the forces of your Court and your Army are behind him,' he pronounced, thus revealing a cartoonish view of British politics that was to bedevil other Soviet leaders as well. By contrast, Trotsky was flirtatious and kissed her hand. 'Even when your teeth are clenched,' he whispered seductively, '*vous êtes encore femme*.' 'I will tell them in England how nice you are,' she replied. 'Tell them,' he murmured back, 'that when Trotsky kisses he does not bite.'[17]

But socially the venture was a disaster. News of her departure quickly leaked out and, although aunts Jennie and Leonie loyally defended their niece, London society was scandalized. Clare's return in late November was a press sensation. *The Times*, under the banner headline 'WITH LENIN AND TROTSKY', published daily extracts from the diary she had kept in the Soviet capital. 'There is a certain piquancy in the mere event,' it noted in an editorial, 'which is not lessened by the fact that Mr. Churchill's cousin is a lady, and that her sympathies appear to be rather with her Russian hosts than her kinsmen.' This was true. 'I love the bedrock of things here, and the vital energy,' she wrote on the eve of her departure from the Soviet capital. 'I am appalled by the realization of my upbringing and the futile viewpoint instilled by an obsolete class tradition.'[18]

For Churchill, the timing could hardly have been worse. It was barely two weeks since the Albert Hall had echoed with cheers at the image of him being hanged from a lamp post, so it was no surprise that she quickly received word that he would refuse to meet her. A similar message came from Birkenhead and others who rapidly ostracized her. Instead, new friends of a very different ilk came forward. Many were members of the 'Hands Off Russia' campaign, such as William Coates, its secretary, Cecil Malone, the Communist MP who had conjured up the lamp post image, her cousin's nemesis George Lansbury, and William Ewer, the *Daily Herald*'s foreign editor. 'I like my new friends,' she noted happily, 'I talk heart to heart and soul with them.'[19] Early in the New Year, while Churchill was painting happily on the Riviera, Ewer and Lansbury took her out for lunch, and before the meal was over she agreed to sculpt Lansbury's head. Yet the company and sympathy of her new-found friends was not enough to guarantee her financial future. She needed wealthy patrons. The London *Times* extracts of her diary had also appeared in the *New York Times* – Churchill family news was always good copy in the home of the Jeromes – and when she received the offer of a lucrative and all-expenses-paid speaking tour of the United States, she leapt at the chance.

*

It was this domestic wrangle and social scandal that, at 8 a.m. on the icy morning of 22 January 1921, brought Lady Randolph Churchill to the platform at Paddington Station, bidding farewell to her tempestuous niece as she boarded the train for Liverpool. As if deliberately flaunting her notorious Moscow escapade, Clare was wearing a Cossack hat and a Siberian ponyskin coat. As the family matriarch, Churchill's mother was in protective mode. 'If you are not happy,' she said, putting her arm affectionately through her niece's as they walked down the platform, 'come straight back. You have a powerful family who love you and we are all here to open our arms to you.' But she also offered a blunt admonition. 'Remember,' she wrote in a farewell letter, 'that you are the nearest thing to a sister that Winston ever had, and apart from the embarrassment you can cause him when your unusual doings are associated with his name – he can be deeply wounded. So don't do that again.'[20]

Clare was thankful for their loyalty. But she, too, was wounded and felt badly let down by her cousin's refusal to see her. Although they were at loggerheads over Bolshevism, she genuinely admired his qualities of boldness and bravery. In Moscow, she had even discussed them with Trotsky and noted afterwards in her diary: 'Winston is the only man I know in England who is made of the stuff that Bolsheviks are made of. He has fight, force, and fanaticism.'[21] Why, she wondered, could he not admire her sense of adventure that matched his own in younger days, venturing off to distant and exotic places to bring back news, and even risk his life?

Once on board the *Aquitania* and bound for New York, she took pen and paper to write him a bitter and emotional letter about her feelings of betrayal and disappointment. Whereas she had always told people that he had heart and was loveable, she could say that no longer, she lamented. 'You never waited to hear what I thought,' she raged. 'You did not *want* to know what I had seen. What I could tell no-one else, but *would* have told you, did not interest you ... you just turned your back on me.' She would never forget his unkindness, she continued, and he should know that if she now had Bolshevik tendencies these were the result of her treatment in England, not in Moscow. 'I will only think of you as in the past,' she concluded, 'with affection, Your Cousin Clare.'[22]

But to Churchill family was important, and even though Clare had maddened and embarrassed him he had an essentially forgiving nature. Despite her angry outburst, he sent her a gracious reply explaining that having nothing to say to her that was pleasant on her return from Moscow, he had thought it better simply to remain silent until a better time arrived. But he still regarded her with affection, admired her gifts, would always do his best to help her, wished her well in America, and hoped she would come back 'with a healthy gap between you and an episode which may have faded and to which we need neither of us ever refer'. Privately, he also felt deeply protective towards his younger wayward cousin. Without telling her, he found her a guardian angel in New York in the form of Bernard Baruch, who had been his opposite number in the United States dealing with munitions production. The American had made his fortune before the age of thirty on Wall Street, chaired the United States' War Industries Board, and served as a staff member to Woodrow Wilson during the Paris peace talks. He and Churchill had first met at the Hotel Majestic when their talk quickly turned to the atmosphere of revenge clouding the negotiations. 'I remember how he turned from the mirror, before which he was adjusting a black satin tie,' recalled Baruch, 'and said to me earnestly: "I was all for war when it was on. Now it is over, and I am all for peace." ' Now, writing to his wartime friend, Churchill asked him to keep an eye on 'this wild cousin of mine – she's brave,' he added, 'but has no judgement and might get into trouble.'[23]

SPRING

SEVEN

'THE FORTY THIEVES'

Churchill left London on the evening of Tuesday 1 March and travelled by train to Marseilles, where he met up with Clementine. Here they embarked on the *Sphinx*, a steamship of the French company *Messageries Maritimes* that regularly serviced the route between Marseilles and Beirut and had recently served as a hospital ship. It was large and comfortable and Churchill escaped sea-sickness. Six days later they arrived in Alexandria and booked into the Savoy Palace Hotel. The idea of accompanying him to Cairo had been Clementine's. After several weeks alone on the Riviera she was missing him badly and longed for more time basking in the Mediterranean warmth. She also knew that they could now comfortably cover her own expenses as well as those of her personal maid.

Churchill immediately seized the opportunity to visit Aboukir (Abu Kir) Bay, just east of the city. Here, just before sundown on 1 August 1798, Admiral Horatio Nelson's ships had surprised Napoleon's French fleet at anchor, sunk his flagship *L'Orient* and eight other ships, and destroyed the future Emperor's grandiose hopes of vast Eastern conquests. For Churchill, battles marked the tectonic collisions that shaped the destinies of nations, and he treasured exploring them in person. 'The British Fleet was once again supreme in the Mediterranean,' he wrote years later. 'This was a turning point.'[1]

The Cairo Conference was also a milestone in history, building a new order in the Middle East out of the ruins of the Ottoman Empire.

Churchill and his party left Alexandria for the Egyptian capital the next day, including the ever loyal Archie Sinclair. Joining them was another young man of Archie's age who had greeted them at the docks. Twenty-eight-year-old Captain Maxwell Henry Coote was an Eton-educated member of the Anglo-Irish gentry. Badly wounded as an artillery officer at Gallipoli, he had later flown as a fighter pilot in France and marked up several 'kills' of enemy aircraft. Now, posted with the Royal Air Force in the Middle East, his main duty as temporary aide-de-camp to Churchill was to escort Clementine around the sites. He found her charming and looked forward to the task.[2]

Few of Churchill's overseas travels were without risk. The train to Cairo was the Sultan of Egypt's own with a special coach containing a saloon and dining car. Clementine took out a book to read, Churchill opened one of his official boxes, and Inspector Thompson positioned himself close by. The new Colonial Secretary's opposition to Egyptian independence was well known. An unfriendly crowd had greeted him at the docks and three of the demonstrators had been shot and killed. The British-led Egyptian police were on full alert. Sweating profusely in the heat, Thompson grew increasingly uneasy as the train crawled at a snail's pace through the crowded suburbs of Alexandria. Suddenly, as it slowed down even more on approaching a crossing, there was the sound of breaking glass. A crowd outside was throwing stones and the carpet outside the compartment was quickly covered in debris. Thompson drew his revolver and braced himself for an attack. Churchill stopped reading, looked up briefly, and smiled. Clementine put down her novel. Both remained cool. Then the train picked up speed, quickly left the crowd behind, and they calmly went back to their reading.[3]

But the danger was not over. As they approached Cairo an orderly appeared with a message saying they should get out of the train at the small suburban station of Shubra because a large and angry crowd had gathered at the main terminus. The ploy worked perfectly. When the train finally arrived in Cairo half an hour late, all it disgorged of the party were five hatboxes and other baggage. Churchill and the others had duly been met by cars at Shubra and driven, unnoticed, to the Semiramis

Hotel. Many of the frustrated demonstrators, shouting 'Down with Churchill', picked the wrong hotel and gathered instead outside the much patronized but less glamorous Shepheard's.[4]

After checking in, Churchill and Archie Sinclair paid a courtesy visit to the British High Commissioner, Viscount Allenby. Egypt's status was ambiguous. Before the war it was technically part of the Ottoman Empire under its own *khedive* (or ruler), one of whom built himself a grand residence in Cairo known as the Abdin (or Abdeen) Palace. In reality, however, Egypt was a quasi-British colony. British troops had occupied the country in 1882 and then formally declared it a protectorate and imposed martial law when the Turks entered the war on the side of Germany. Throughout the conflict Cairo had resembled a huge military base and recruiting ground for Egyptian labour to help the British war effort. After a nationalist uprising was crushed in 1919, General Allenby, who had captured Jerusalem from the Turks, was sent out as High Commissioner to take charge, and a commission of inquiry under Lord Milner recommended an Anglo-Egyptian treaty giving the country independence. Churchill, amongst others, bitterly opposed this. But when he arrived in Cairo the future of Egypt still remained open – a *khedive* and prime minister were in place but Allenby and London were still calling the shots.

The official British Residency was a grand Victorian mansion with splendid gardens stretching down to the banks of the Nile. Allenby had a notoriously bad temper for which he was nicknamed 'the Bull'. He was also an avid birdwatcher and kept a pet marabou stork. It, too, had its moods. While it devotedly followed Allenby around as he strolled in the gardens, and even gently unlaced his shoes, it viewed strangers with considerable animosity. Its long beak could be painful through a light summer dress and sometimes, as they were enjoying tea in the gardens, visitors would find their hats suddenly tweaked from their heads. Fortunately, Churchill and Sinclair were spared such ignominy.[5]

*

It was one of Churchill's many gifts to realize the importance of theatre in politics. The conference was carefully staged with himself as the leading man supported by a cast of lesser yet still notable characters, and it had been mostly scripted in advance thanks to the assiduous efforts of numerous advisors. Some of them travelled with him to Cairo, to be joined there by governors and army commanders of various British-held territories across the Middle East. All in all, they numbered about forty. The proceedings were kept strictly secret. But the fact of the conference was highly public. Cairo, like Nice and Cannes, had its winter season for Europeans, and this was the year that also marked its recovery from the war. *The Times* noted the 'Revival of Gaiety' in Cairo, and the city was full of visitors enjoying tennis, croquet, and other pastimes. Many were staying at the Semiramis Hotel, which became almost too crowded for comfort. An exhibition of paintings by Bridget Keir, an accomplished British watercolourist, opened in the hotel but soon moved to Ciro's, where Winston and Clementine paid it a visit.[6]

If the British Residency was spectacularly sited, so was the Semiramis. A vast Edwardian palace that overlooked the Nile, it was the grandest and most exclusive hotel of its day in the Egyptian capital and was named after the legendary queen of Assyria and conqueror of Mesopotamia who was reputed to have built the city of Babylon. From the rooftop garden visitors could enjoy spectacular views towards the pyramids of Giza and the desert beyond. Its vestibule was lined with marble and grand mirrors. To the austere Lawrence of Arabia, it was all too much. 'Very expensive and luxurious,' he complained, 'horrible place: makes me Bolshevik.' It had been recommended as the conference site by Allenby, who himself was no stranger to the carefully choreographed moment. When he had entered Jerusalem just before Christmas in 1917 as the first Christian to capture the Holy City since the Crusades, he did so on foot as a show of humility to reassure its people that he came as a liberator rather than conqueror – and made sure that the scene was amply captured on film and camera. Besides its spectacular location and large number of rooms, the hotel also had security advantages, protected on one side by the Nile and on two others by Residency guards and a nearby British barracks.[7]

Adding to the sense of an exotic and grand Oriental spectacle were two baby lions. Brought by one of the participants, Sir Geoffrey Archer, the

Governor and Commander-in-Chief of forces in Somaliland which had recently crushed a revolt led by the religious leader Mohammed Abdullah Hassan ('the Mad Mullah'), they were destined for onward shipping to the London Zoo. Churchill quickly sensed a photo-opportunity. In one of the many conference photographs, he made sure that the lions featured prominently, posed near his feet. They also came close to causing an avian tragedy when Archer took the cubs along to a party at the Residency. To everyone's horror, they quickly spotted Allenby's pet marabou stork and went bounding after it. They were stopped only at the last moment by Archer and their keeper, a sergeant in the King's African Rifles.[8]

Churchill knew that success in Cairo was a vital step in his political comeback. Visible press coverage had a crucial role to play. Above all, it should be positive. Predictably, the hostile *Daily Herald* was already denouncing him as an 'amateur Alexander'. But even the more sober *Sunday Times* was mocking him for strutting 'his Eastern stage'. He had to ensure that solid results emerged from the spectacle.[9]

*

On the first evening, T. E. Lawrence joined the party at the Semiramis Hotel. Three days after taking over the Colonial Office, Churchill had drafted an outline of his proposed agenda for Cairo, and on the eve of his departure he approved the collective view of his officials in the Middle East Department about the decisions to be ratified. It would now be a matter of sorting out the details and making sure that the major actors were on board. Lawrence would later joke that the Cairo decisions had really been decided in the Ship Inn, a well-known watering hole frequented by Whitehall civil servants. The quip contained considerable truth. King Faisal had already secretly travelled to London and agreed in principle to become ruler of Mesopotamia, a solution Churchill instantly saw as offering a rapid solution to the problem – provided that Sir Percy Cox, the Baghdad-based High Commissioner, could stage-manage affairs so that Faisal appeared as the genuine choice of the local population. The influence of Lawrence on Churchill was palpable. His view of the scholar-soldier came close to hero worship.[10]

The next morning Churchill and Sinclair drove out to the Royal Air Force base at Heliopolis, in the Cairo suburbs. Clementine accompanied them and inspected the married quarters, reviewed them with a critical eye, and listened to guarded complaints by some of the occupants. Greeted by a Guard of Honour, and with a strong wind whipping sand into his eyes, Churchill carefully inspected heavy bombers of No. 70 Squadron. At his side was Sir Hugh Trenchard, who had travelled out with him from London. Churchill's cost-cutting plan for Mesopotamia depended crucially on the air force taking over desert policing from the army, and he was relying on the Chief of the Air Staff to get the job done against strong opposition, especially from Cox. He was also eager to see an air route opened between Cairo and Baghdad; later that day Trenchard was able to confirm that all the machinery was now in place to complete the route for both automobiles and aircraft. That night, Churchill dined in the mess at Heliopolis with Archie and a few months later the squadron duly moved to Iraq in accord with his grand plan.[11]

*

The Cairo Conference officially opened at the Semiramis Hotel on Saturday 12 March. As it was Churchill's show it was choreographed to his habits. This meant a late morning start after a leisurely breakfast, with every afternoon devoted to visiting a range of historic sites armed with his easel and paints. He had arrived fully equipped for his battles with the canvas and brought all the colours he needed to capture the yellow desert, purple rocks, and crimson sunsets. The official biography gives the impression that most of the time in Cairo was passed in conference. But Churchill's passion for painting meant that he built a lengthy afternoon excursion with his paints into every day of the proceedings. Meanwhile, escorted by Captain Coote, Clementine busied herself exploring the bazaars and other sites in and around the capital.

Churchill organized the conference with the same brisk efficiency he brought to his painting. Two committees were created, one to deal with political matters, the other with military issues. He personally chaired the former and General Congreve, the GOC Egypt and Palestine, the latter; occasionally they met jointly. From the start, he dominated the proceedings and came straight to the point by emphasizing the urgent need to co-ordinate all aspects of British policy in the region, and above all to control expenditure, the nub of the matter. As if to emphasize the point, the Director of Finance at the War Office had also journeyed from London to sit alongside the generals and diplomats around the table. This obsession with expense quickly made itself felt. General Haldane, the commander of British forces in Mesopotamia, promised that all outlying army detachments would be withdrawn to concentrate defence on the Mosul–Baghdad–Basra axis of the country and described the procedures that had been ordered for units leaving the country and the fate of the equipment they were leaving behind. Immediately, Churchill demanded to know what was being done about their animals – horses and mules – and how many of them there were. The number ran into thousands. He then asked if fodder would have to be brought in for them after the start of the approaching financial year, which began on 1 April. The answer to this was that, yes, a lot would have to be brought in. His response was abrupt and shocking. 'Have them all shot before the commencement of the financial year,' he ordered.

There followed a moment of deathly silence. Eventually one of the generals rose to his feet. 'Sir,' he said, 'in the name of all humanity I must protest against such ruthless cruelty to poor defenceless animals, which have served us well.' Another long silence followed. This time it was broken by General Sir Edmund Ironside, the commander of British forces in North Persia. Standing at six feet four inches, the solidly built forty-year-old – inevitably nicknamed 'Tiny' – was an impressive figure never afraid of speaking his mind. Patiently, he explained that there were strict War Office rules on how to dispose of surplus animals and that these were being scrupulously followed. There were thousands of animals to be dealt with, but only a handful of army vets available. Standing orders were not to sell off any animals, fit or unfit, in the Middle East, where they would be cruelly treated. Every single animal had to be inspected by a vet and only those with no more than another two years' service were to be destroyed at once. The remainder were to be shipped off to other places in the British Empire.

Churchill knew full well about war horses and their fate. As Secretary of State for War, just two years before he had stepped in to save thousands of horses which had served Allied forces on the Western Front. Shipping problems and official bungling had caused lengthy delays in rescuing them from France and Belgium, where they were at serious risk of disease or slaughter at the hands of local butchers. Only his very forceful intervention had speeded up their repatriation. But his brusque intervention now was typical of his operational style: the impetuous response that flew to the heart of the issue – in this case expenditure – countered by the informed view of an expert that forced a re-think. Ironside had Churchill's respect. They had known each other since the Boer War. Only two years before, Ironside had been commander of the British forces at Archangel that Churchill was hoping to help topple the Bolsheviks. He was not a man to be challenged on such an issue. So Churchill let the matter drop. Nor did he hold a grudge. A couple of days later, over a friendly cup of tea in the hotel, he offered Ironside command over the remaining troops in Mesopotamia after Haldane stepped down later in the year.[12] As for the horses, they were disposed of according to War Office rules, as he later explained himself to the House of Commons. Between April and August there was wholesale destruction of some 30,000 animals that could neither be fed nor transported elsewhere and that would not be guaranteed humane treatment if left to the local population.[13]

On the political front Sir Percy Cox dutifully followed the conference script by declaring that Faisal would undoubtedly be chosen as King by the Mesopotamians themselves. Predictably, Lawrence also backed Faisal. He explained that this was not just because he was his friend but because the country was 'backward and half-civilized', with a number of rival candidates for the throne that meant it needed an active and inspiring candidate to pull it all together. Faisal's brother Abdullah, reputed to be something of a sybarite with a taste for European opera, was unsuited for the task.

Churchill endorsed Lawrence's view. But he had a broader perspective. The British government was already heavily subsidizing Faisal's father Hussein in Mecca. Abdullah was also emerging as a possible candidate for Transjordan and would require financial support. By backing all three for the vacant thrones, he pointed out, each would know that the position of his brothers depended on his own good behaviour. Thus Britain's dominance in the region would be assured. This revealed a truly Churchillian streak of *Realpolitik*. It also reflected much of Lawrence's thinking. Historians now refer to it as 'the Sharifian solution' – a mosaic of client states ruled by the Hashemite family and watched over by Britain.

The morning's business done, after lunch Churchill departed by car with Clementine and Archie to view the pyramids, and that evening threw a large dinner party at the Semiramis for the major players. Maxwell Coote was a wide-eyed observer of the spectacle. Some wag, he noted, had tagged the participants 'The Forty Thieves', which tickled Churchill enormously. But the young officer's eye was mostly drawn to the solitary woman amongst them. Her name was Gertrude Bell.

*

Sometime during the conference a photographer snapped a black-and-white picture of the fifty-two-year-old Bell sitting behind a be-suited Lawrence in the desert squinting at the camera under the bright Egyptian sun. She is dressed in an unfashionably long skirt and broad-brimmed hat. Neither is smiling, and the photographer has titled his work 'The True Monarchs of Mesopotamia'. In the flesh, Bell had greenish eyes and light auburn hair, and was rarely seen without a cigarette in her hand. Brilliant and opinionated, she has been dubbed by contemporary observers as 'Queen of the Desert' (or 'Desert Queen'), as well as 'Maker of Nations', for her contribution to the conference.[14]

Like Lawrence, she was a trained archaeologist and expert on the Middle East with a degree from Oxford – and in her case also the record of being the first woman to receive a First Class degree in Modern History. She had climbed Mont Blanc and the Matterhorn, and before the war had led two expeditions to Mesopotamia. On her chosen stage of the Orient she was the only female star. She had worked for the wartime Arab Bureau and arrived in Baghdad in 1917 as an intelligence officer. Since then she had settled in the city and become a close and trusted advisor to the tall and taciturn Sir Percy Cox. Few Europeans knew more about the country than her, and locals called her 'Al-Khatun' (the Lady). She spoke Arabic, it was said, like a nightingale. She and Lawrence knew each other well as professional colleagues and both had taken part in the Paris Peace Conference, where she was impressed by the 'charm, simplicity, and sincerity' of the emerging hero of the Arabian desert.[15]

'Gerty' – as she was privately called by Lawrence – arrived in Cairo by train on the eve of the conference, and he escorted her to the Semiramis Hotel. Here, closeted in her room, they spent an hour discussing business before she left to introduce herself to Clementine. Meanwhile Cox, who had journeyed with her from Baghdad, disappeared to have a long discussion with Churchill. She arrived in Cairo with a highly negative view of the Colonial Secretary. Some of it stemmed from her family background. Her baronet grandfather was a wealthy Newcastle iron-master and Liberal Member of Parliament while her father, who ran the family steelworks in Middlesbrough, had been High Sheriff of Durham and Lord Lieutenant of the North Riding of Yorkshire. For such traditional Liberals, the maverick Tory Radical Randolph Churchill's renegade son, who had turned against Asquith to join forces with the firebrand Lloyd George, was undoubtedly an anathema. It may have counted, too, that the great but unconsummated love of Bell's life, a British Army officer, had been killed at Gallipoli.

A personal encounter with one of the Churchill tribe can only have fuelled her disdain. In January, Clare Sheridan's brother Hugh Frewen, who had survived six months' fighting at Gallipoli, arrived in Baghdad, sent by the army to compile a gazetteer of Mesopotamia. He was also in the midst of divorcing his first wife, the daughter of an Italian duke. Bell was infuriated by what she considered his incompetence and laziness as he presented her with a series of written questions that she dismissed as 'either pure tosh or . . . things that you can't know'. Finally, she lost patience and suggested sharply that before he bothered her again he might consult a few articles in the *Encyclopedia Britannica*. Then, in her own words, she 'bowed him out rather abruptly'.

To Bell, Frewen's very presence in Baghdad exemplified the British military's extravagance and wastefulness, which to her was ultimately the fault of the War Office of which Churchill was then the minister. That same month, when she heard that he would be taking charge of the Middle East and had already crossed swords with Cox over the future of the country and the pace and level of troop withdrawals, she erupted in fury. 'With a man like Winston in command there is no further talk of honour,' she complained bitterly, 'if we retain the mandate we must spend the money on which it depends.' Cox, she went on, would make this clear. But would 'rogues like Winston and Lloyd George' be honest about this to the British public? To her, there was no doubt. They would go on with their 'hanky-panky' until it led to terrible disaster in Mesopotamia. It was with considerable forebodings, therefore, that she arrived in Cairo.[16]

Yet she need not have worried. The second day's proceedings saw the choice of Faisal as King in Mesopotamia ratified and plans for troop reductions agreed. Before leaving London, Churchill had promised Lloyd George that he would save him millions of pounds, and he successfully pressed the military chiefs at the conference table for even larger and faster cuts than they proposed. Satisfied by his victory, after lunch he drove out to the pyramids to paint and only returned after dark. Meanwhile, Bell went shopping with Clementine and returned to the hotel laden with red and green slippers they had purchased in a local bazaar. Amongst her many other attributes, Bell was noted for a preoccupation with clothes and had her hats and dresses sent from London and Paris.[17]

But that night it was neither Gertie nor Clementine who filled Churchill's thoughts. It was Archie Sinclair. During the day the temperature of his wartime second-in-command had shot up to an alarming 105 degrees and a nurse from the Anglo-American Hospital was urgently summoned. It was a case of typhoid fever, probably from drinking contaminated water. When Maxwell Coote broke the news, Churchill was seriously upset and feared the worst. 'Winston … is evidently a bit of a pessimist where illness is concerned and was apt to be very anxious,' noted his aide-de-camp. That night, he and a brooding Churchill dined alone together, and in spite of the champagne ordered by the latter it was a largely silent affair until they discovered that each was familiar with the same stretch of the wartime frontline in France. After that, there was no lack of topics for conversation and the meal ended with a now relaxed and amiable Churchill asking Coote to take over as much of Archie's work as he could until his old friend recovered. Soon, Coote was taking down dictation for telegrams that Churchill was regularly dispatching to keep Lloyd George informed of progress. Without the Welsh Wizard's full backing, he would be a politician adrift.[18]

The third day followed the same pattern. Churchill relentlessly insisted that more should be done to reduce expenditures and then, after lunch, disappeared again to paint. Coote was impressed by the results. 'Another really most clever picture of Cairo and the hills looking back from the Pyramids,' he noted. Clementine returned from yet another shopping expedition with her own trophies of perfume and cigarettes, although, with her usual prudence, she refrained from buying a carpet that caught her eye because she felt it was too expensive. Old habits died hard, and she hadn't yet fully absorbed their new-found wealth.[19]

*

Gertrude Bell was feeling better about things each day. It had been a relief to find on arrival that the briefing papers provided for her coincided with her own ideas. She also proved a strong ally in the grand plan by Churchill and Trenchard to gradually hand over the main responsibility for security across the Middle East to the Royal Air Force – a task that could be covered at a fraction of the cost of maintaining large numbers of troops on the ground. Trenchard was something of an odd man out amongst the army generals and civilian pro-consuls at Cairo. As an oddity herself amongst a gathering of men, Bell took a liking to him. She noticed how he emphasized his words with a stab of his pencil each time he answered one of the many hostile critics opposed to the Royal

Air Force – a new and untested force whose longer-term future still hung in the balance. One day, leaving the conference room, she innocently asked him: 'How many pencils do you get through in a conference, Air Marshal?' This broke the ice between them and she became convinced that provided the air weapon was used with restraint it would work as an effective force.[20]

Bell's satisfaction with the results also extended to even the contentious and potentially divisive issue of Kurdistan. Churchill arrived in Cairo open to the idea of giving the Kurds their own separate state. This would provide a buffer between Turkey and Mesopotamia and mean *not* placing them under an Arab ruler, who might oppress them. But in the course of the fourth day's discussions he conceded to the strongly held opinion of both Bell and Cox, who favoured a united Mesopotamia with Kurdistan inside its borders.[21] Having also squeezed yet more expenditure cuts out of the military, that evening he sent a telegram to Lloyd George telling him that everyone was on board. Relieved also to learn that Archie Sinclair's temperature was finally back to normal, he took off riding in the afternoon and returned again only after dark. This time he brought back a painting of the pyramids themselves. The admiring Coote thought it was the best he had yet done.[22]

The young air officer was being kept busy. The next day Winston and Clementine explored the great Mohamed Ali Mosque atop the Cairo Citadel, visited the local hospital, and walked around the legendary 'City of the Dead', the sprawling Muslim necropolis inhabited by thousands of Cairo's poor and dispossessed. It was located on the edge of the Mokatta Hills, and that afternoon Churchill set up his easel there and painted. Again, he had good reason to feel pleased with the morning's progress. Trenchard's scheme for the air control of Mesopotamia was approved and Churchill had sketched out his own views on the importance of air power for the future of the Empire. An air route from Cairo to Karachi, for example, would shorten the journey from England to Australia by eight or ten days. His imperial gaze also encompassed Arabia. Here the tribal chieftain Ibn Saud was a rival to Hussein in Mecca. Already, Britain was subsidizing him to the tune of £60,000 a year. Sir Percy Cox wanted to double the amount and Bell agreed on the grounds that it would keep the Saudi ruler happy as compensation for seeing Faisal and Abdullah receive kingdoms from Britain. In the end it was agreed that Hussein and Ibn Saud should each be given an annual subsidy of £100,000 to keep them in line with British objectives. That evening Churchill and Clementine were the guests at a ball given by General Allenby. One of those present was Bekir Sami Bey, the Turkish Minister of Foreign Affairs, and Churchill seized the chance to extract a promise that Turkey would not interfere with Britain's interests in Mosul in northern Mesopotamia.[23]

The following day, undeterred in his search for economies, Churchill insisted that before too long Mesopotamia should start making a financial contribution to the cost of maintaining British troops in the country. Afterwards, he motored out to an old Dervish monastery carved out of sandstone hills. Coote watched intently as he worked his magic on the canvas and marvelled at how Churchill would slap on paint and then, if he wasn't happy, simply scrape it off. 'He is very clever,' he observed, 'and has a great eye for colour.'[24]

The urgent need for budget cuts continued to dominate Churchill's mind, not least because it affected the future of the Coalition at home – and hence his own political career. With his eyes set on following his father to the Exchequer, he had to demonstrate that he was a responsible guardian of the nation's finances. Britain's presence in the Middle East was to be decidedly 'Empire-Lite'. So was his own, and he made much of the fact that rather than bringing out cipher clerks from London at great expense he was relying on Allenby's staff in the Residency. He kept them exceptionally busy. To Lloyd George alone during the conference he sent at least a dozen telegrams. Most of them were lengthy accounts of the proceedings. But sometimes he asked for help in clearing administrative roadblocks in London, such as mobilizing shipping to get more troops back to Britain sooner. He also kept in constant touch with other colleagues. No one could claim that Churchill did not keep them informed or that the Cairo decisions were anything other than collective. The most sensitive question for Lloyd George was how they would affect

Anglo-French relations, which he was eager to improve. The French considered Faisal 'treacherous', had thrown him out of Syria, and were strongly opposed to placing him on the throne in Mesopotamia from where they feared he would undermine their control of Syria. So how could this be managed without causing a break with Paris? The answer would be to present him as the free and spontaneous choice of the local population, which would make it difficult for the French to resist. Accordingly, Churchill assured Lloyd George that between them he, Cox, Bell and Faisal himself could ensure the creation of a 'spontaneous' movement that would produce the desired result. In the meantime, it was agreed that nothing should be announced to the French and that Faisal should return secretly to Mecca and gain his father's and brothers' consent to the deal.[25]

*

Suddenly, in the midst of all this, Churchill's future was dramatically thrown into high relief by unexpected news: Andrew Bonar Law, the Conservative Party leader and lynchpin of the Coalition – effectively deputy prime minister to Lloyd George – had abruptly resigned for reasons of ill health and his most likely successor was Austen Chamberlain, the Chancellor of the Exchequer. If this happened, who would take over charge of the nation's finances? Churchill immediately telegraphed Eddie Marsh to find out what was happening. His ambition to follow in his father's footsteps to the Chancellorship was no secret, and he even kept his father's robes of office clean and ready to wear.

For the next ten days Lloyd George pondered the decision. Churchill, stranded in the Middle East, could only wait and wonder about his fate. The British press was quick to pounce. 'To have given immortality to the Pyramids on his canvas,' noted one drily, 'must seem a poor consolation for such an inopportune occasion.' But that great things could emerge for him out of the Coalition crisis was clear to at least one perceptive observer, who firmly saw him as his father's son with a Tory allegiance. 'Mr. Churchill must not be forgotten in these times because he is away painting the Pyramids,' observed 'Scrutator' of *The Sunday Times*:

One can imagine circumstances in which he would have made a bold bid for the leadership of the Tory party, but not now. His time will come later, when the reshaping of parties begins, and in these times he will be found working with Lord Birkenhead: for the dominant motive of Churchill's life is his attachment to his father's memory. Sooner or later, he will appear in the role of second founder of the Tory Democratic party.[26]

*

Sunday 20 March marked the grand finale of the conference. At 9.45 a.m., seated in the last of a convoy of cars alongside Clementine and Captain Coote, Churchill was driven to the Mena House Hotel. Surrounded by luxurious gardens and almost literally standing in the shadows of the Great Pyramids of Giza, the hotel was a favourite destination of European royalty and celebrities. Here he was greeted by the Sheik of Mena dressed in purple and gold and mounted on a horse bearing the same coloured trappings. Recently the hotel had served as a makeshift hospital for Australian troops wounded at Gallipoli – yet another reminder of the shadow that still clouded Churchill's reputation.

But it was camels that now required his urgent attention. Several were waiting for his party, although some of the guests cried off at the last minute, perhaps afraid of losing their dignity. Camels are notoriously difficult to mount, and even the youthful Coote struggled with the task. But Churchill managed gallantly, as did Clementine, and there was time for him to pose for the camera with Bell and Lawrence in front of the Sphinx before they set off for Sakkara and the ruins of the ancient city of Memphis with its famous stepped pyramid a few miles to the south. Along the way the saddle on his camel slipped, and he fell off. Unharmed, he took it as a great joke. Clementine, meanwhile, seemed entirely comfortable on her mount. After lunch at Sakkara, the chief archaeologist showed them around the tombs. But Churchill declined the offer and wandered off with his easel and paints. Later, after the others had returned to the Mena House Hotel, he and Lawrence made their own way back, riding their camels through the desert at full trot all the way as if warriors together flush with victory.

The next morning began with a formal photograph of all the participants and concluded with a grand dinner that, at his own insistence,
included the wives of all the participants. The following day saw him pay
a visit with Allenby to the Sultan at the Abdin Palace and have lunch with
the Egyptian prime minister, after which he sent Coote off to buy gifts for
the detectives who had been protecting him, including cigarette cases,
a silver wrist watch, and a travelling clock. Finally, before leaving the
Egyptian capital, he and Clementine were driven out to the Nile Barrage
(or Great Dam) where he set up his easel once again and began painting.
On the way back their car collided with another and the front ends of
both cars were damaged. But no one was injured and Churchill's main
concern was the state of his canvas which, fortunately, was also undam-
aged. With a series of successful paintings behind him, and a conference
that had gone happily to plan, he left Egypt a contented man knowing
that the Cabinet back in London was satisfied with what he had achieved.
He had, he informed a reporter, enjoyed every minute of his stay.[27]

Both Bell and Lawrence felt the same way. 'We're a very happy family
[and] agreed upon everything important,' wrote the latter to his brother
from the Semiramis Hotel. As Bell journeyed back to Baghdad, she took
time to report to an old friend. 'It has been wonderful,' she wrote.

> We covered more work in a fortnight than has ever been got through
> in a year. Mr. Churchill was admirable, most ready to meet everyone
> half way and masterly alike in guiding big meetings and in conducting
> the small committees into which we broke up ... The general line
> adopted is, I am sure, the only right one, the only line which gives us
> a real hope of success.[28]

EIGHT

THE SMILING ORCHARDS

Churchill and his party left Cairo by train shortly before midnight on Wednesday 23 March, headed for Jerusalem. At the last minute Archie Sinclair decided he was still too ill to travel, so Maxwell Coote continued to stand in for him and shared a sleeper compartment with T. E. Lawrence. Gertrude Bell was making her own way back to Baghdad. Her elderly father, who had accompanied her to Cairo, joined the Churchill group to travel back home. Coote thought him a cheery old man with a keen sense of humour.

The young air force officer by now was feeling relaxed around his ward. At first he had been apprehensive. But after two weeks together he had got used to Churchill's demanding habits and developed skills to manage him. They were badly needed at dawn the next day when the train had to cross the Suez Canal. There was no fixed bridge. So the carriages were uncoupled two at a time from the train and shunted onto a ferry that took them to the other side, where they were attached to an onward waiting train. Coote was all too aware that Churchill was a notoriously late riser and constitutionally incapable of arriving anywhere on time. Because of this, the train was late in leaving and there was now a serious risk they would miss the connection to Palestine. So before departing Cairo, Coote arranged that breakfast would not be served until they were safely across the Canal and installed in the carriage that would take them on to the Holy City. The stratagem worked brilliantly. Churchill sat himself down with three minutes to spare and was soon tucking contentedly into his food.

The train's only restaurant car was used by other, carefully vetted, travellers. One was the society hostess Mrs 'Ronnie' Greville, widow of the Honourable Ronald Greville, a horse-racing chum of 'Bertie' (King Edward VII), and a Tory MP for whom Churchill had once campaigned. The illegitimate daughter of the Scottish millionaire brewer William McEwan and a ferocious gossip, she was also a notorious social climber and friend of Queen Mary. As a couple the Grevilles had been privately mocked as 'the Grovels', and it was once said of Mrs Greville that she had to be 'fed royalty like sea lions fish'. Maxwell Coote, observing her at work in the restaurant car, decided that she was definitely a 'tuft hunter' – meaning a snob – who liked to sprinkle her conversation with remarks such as 'the nicest king I have ever met'. Also sharing the carriage was the Baroness de la Grange, a Frenchwoman who had made her château a centre of hospitality for the British Army during the war. Both Allenby and Jack Churchill had been visitors there and the press had dubbed her the 'Mother of the British Army'. Lawrence, however, was convinced that she was working as a French spy. He disliked the French for having expelled Faisal from Syria and was determined, as were Churchill and Lloyd George, to keep their current negotiations and plotting with Faisal about the throne of Mesopotamia secret from their allies in Paris for as long as possible.

One of the more distinguished of the passengers, however, was not to be seen mingling with this pseudo-house party on the train as it chugged eastwards through the Sinai. He and his small party remained in their own special carriage. It was only after lunch, when the train crossed the border and stopped at Gaza, that he linked up with Churchill.[1]

*

Sir Herbert Samuel was the British High Commissioner for Palestine. Four years older than Churchill, he had also been a radical member of the reforming pre-war Liberal governments of Campbell-Bannerman and Asquith, and had served as a wartime Home Secretary. He was the first British minister to promote the idea of a Jewish state and enjoyed the reputation of being a resourceful and resilient administrator. He had arrived in Cairo shortly before midnight on the night of Allenby's grand ball and Churchill had immediately quit the dance floor to confer with him. Samuel's appearance marked a new and more contentious phase of the discussions.[2]

Palestine was a League of Nations mandate under British control. By the terms of the Balfour Declaration of November 1917, Britain had also pledged it as the site of 'a Jewish National Home' – provided that this did not impinge on the civil and religious rights of the existing non-Jewish communities there. Fleeing pogroms and discrimination in Europe, Jews had begun arriving in large numbers since the 1880s and violence between them and Arabs had been increasing. Churchill was sympathetic to Zionist aspirations, but not uncritically so. Samuel was one of the few Jews in the top reaches of British politics. Churchill hoped that he would be able to play tough with the most vociferous Zionists.

One of the other issues to be discussed was that of Transjordan – the territory east of the River Jordan that was technically part of Palestine but mostly desert and almost exclusively Arab. In preparation for Cairo, Churchill's advisors had concluded that Transjordan should be separated from the rest of Palestine and set up as an Arab state. The Balfour Declaration promise was to be confined to the lands west of the Jordan. Lawrence strongly supported this view, and Churchill accepted it. Transjordan, they both agreed, should be an Arab state with Abdullah as its most likely monarch.

When Churchill officially announced this on the sixth day of the conference, Samuel had been dismayed. But he was outmanoeuvred and outnumbered. Abdullah had already set himself up in Transjordan, Britain's 'Sharifian' policy was in play, and he could not be removed without bringing down the entire edifice of indirect British rule in the Middle East so carefully constructed over the previous five days. As a sop to Samuel, however, both Churchill and Lawrence promised that everything would be done to ensure that Abdullah stamped down on any anti-Zionist agitation. The next day at the conference Samuel also lost out over the maintenance of law and order in Palestine, an increasingly troublesome issue. He wanted a Jewish military force rather than a simple *gendarmerie* to defend Jewish settlements. This time Churchill was on his side. But both were thwarted by the local military authorities, who opposed any separate Jewish army.

*

The main purpose of the visit to Jerusalem was to meet with Abdullah and get him firmly committed to the British grand plan. When the train stopped in Gaza, Churchill and Samuel were met by a police guard of honour and driven into the town. It had been badly shelled during the war and many of its buildings lay in ruins. The population consisted of some 15,000 Arabs and fewer than a hundred Jews. As they toured the streets, the two were greeted by enthusiastic crowds shouting in Arabic, 'Cheers for the Minister', and also cheers for Great Britain. But as neither understood the language they remained happily unaware that mingled with these greetings were cries of 'Down with the Jews' and 'Cut their throats'. Lawrence, who understood perfectly, remained silent. If the British nurtured any illusions that settling differences between the Arabs and the Jews was going to be easy, this made it abundantly clear that Arab hostility ran deep.

Churchill arrived in Jerusalem after dark. There was a full moon, and on the drive up the Mount of Olives to Government House he caught glimpses of the distant Dead Sea shining in the moonlight. The next day was Good Friday and Maxwell Coote escorted Clementine to St George's Anglican Cathedral for the midday service. Dedicated barely twenty years before as the focal point of worship for Anglican Christians in the Holy Land, the Victorian Gothic edifice had been shut down during the war and its adjacent Bishop's Residence used as the home and headquarters of the notoriously brutal commander of the Fourth Ottoman Army. Jemal Pasha had terrorized the city by ruthlessly deporting or hanging opponents he suspected of treachery or nationalist leanings. It was here, too, that the surrender of the city had been signed in December 1917. The Anglican Bishop, the Harrow-educated Rt Reverend Rennie MacInnes, was well known as a supporter of the Palestinian Arabs – especially Christians – against the Zionists, whose demands he denounced in a pastoral letter that year as 'unjust and intolerable'.[3] Afterwards

Clementine visited the Church of the Holy Sepulchre, built in the fourth century to enclose both the site of Christ's crucifixion and the tomb where his body was laid. From this most holy of Christian sites she proceeded to the Temple Mount to see the massive Western (or 'Wailing') Wall, a remnant of Herod the Great's Second Jewish Temple and the holiest place where Jews are permitted to pray. She followed this by visiting the gleaming white marble of the Islamic shrine of the Dome of the Rock, one of the world's most potent symbols of Islamic power.

Churchill decided against joining this whistle-stop tour of the holy highlights of Jerusalem. Instead, he opted to pursue his own very personal source of spiritual solace. Setting up his easel in the gardens of Government House, he spent the afternoon happily painting a view over the Jordan Valley. Maxwell Coote liked the result, but thought that the oils failed to capture the soft and subtle colouring of the Palestinian landscape. The political landscape, however, was far from serene. That same day in Haifa demonstrators massed to protest against continuing Jewish immigration and police shot and killed two Arabs, a woman and a thirteen-year-old boy. In the anti-Jewish riots which followed, ten Jews and five policemen were wounded. Over the next few days Churchill would have plenty to ponder on as he tried to capture the troubled topography of the Holy Land.[4]

That night, true to form, he kept the Samuels waiting for dinner. Their official residence on the Mount of Olives was based in a vast church-hospital complex originally named after Augusta Viktoria, the wife of Kaiser Wilhelm II who had visited Jerusalem some twenty years before, nursing dreams of establishing a German empire in the East. Built to resemble a Hohenzollern Castle, it was notoriously cold and uncomfortable – an 'icebox' thought Coote. This perhaps suited Samuel, an austere and buttoned-up figure once described 'as free from passion as an oyster'. But after the heat of Cairo and the luxurious comforts of the Semiramis Hotel, the Churchills suffered. Feeling distinctly chilled when she went to bed, Clementine lit the oil stove. Within minutes it was belching out thick black smoke and soot rapidly covered the bedcovers. Churchill managed to clear enough of it off for them to clamber between the sheets. But it was a wretched night and when Clementine's maid arrived in the morning she described the Colonial Secretary and his wife as looking like a couple of 'coal heavers'.[5]

Yet the couple were nothing if not hardy and game. After breakfast Clementine went off to play tennis and Churchill attended a memorial service at the British Military Cemetery nearby on the Mount of Olives. In an emotional debate in the House of Commons barely twelve months before, he had supported the recommendation of the War Graves Commission which favoured the burial of fallen soldiers close to the foreign fields where they had died rather than the repatriation of their bodies home. Now, as he stood alongside Bishop MacInnes, he gazed over the graves of some 2,500 soldiers of the British Empire killed during the Palestine Campaign. As always on such occasions, he was deeply moved and fluent in his words that set the scene in historic perspective and gave meaning to the lives of the dead. 'These veteran soldiers lie here where rests the dust of the Khalifs and Crusaders and the Maccabees,' he said. 'Peace to their ashes, honour to their memory and may we not fail to complete the work which they have begun.'[6]

The next day was Easter Sunday, the holiest in the Christian calendar. After attending morning service at the Cathedral – which Coote applauded as nice and 'thoroughly English' – Churchill was taken in hand by Sir Ronald Storrs, the civilian governor of the city. Something of an artistic connoisseur who favoured white suits and flamboyant buttonholes, he was a Cambridge-educated classicist and long-time friend of Lawrence with whom he had worked in the Arab Bureau in Cairo. The forty-year-old Storrs was intimately familiar with British policy towards the Arabs and especially Abdullah, and since arriving three years before in the wake of the British Army had thoroughly explored Palestine. Now, he was bent on putting a British stamp on Jerusalem. Determined to preserve and enhance its historic buildings and antiquities, and to prevent it from becoming 'an inferior Manchester or Baltimore', he had recently founded the Pro-Jerusalem Society. Funded by Arabs, Jews, and Christians alike along with many international banks and millionaires such as Mrs Andrew Carnegie and J. P. Morgan Junior, its subscription list also included Sir Basil Zaharoff, the most notorious arms dealer of the day – and an important British intelligence asset. Storrs had visited him in his villa outside Paris during the Peace Conference to find him lying in the garden with one foot swathed for classic gout and an electric bell-push in a cedar tree for communicating with his secretary. After Storrs showed him his plans for Jerusalem, Zaharoff pushed the bell and immediately wrote out a generous cheque – 'the millionaire of my dreams,' recalled Storrs.[7] Amongst the Society's first acts were the restoration of the Dome of the Rock, the founding of a Chess Club and a School of Music for both sexes, and a Dramatic Society, whose first performance was Shakespeare's *A Midsummer Night's Dream*.[8]

Storrs had briefly met Churchill in Paris two years previously and now showed him the sites of old Jerusalem that he had missed the day before, such as the Church of the Holy Sepulchre and the Temple Mount. Afterwards, he drove both the Churchills six miles south to Bethlehem. The Emperor Constantine had built the Church of the Nativity over the cave where Jesus Christ was believed to have been born and the town was a major site of pilgrimage for Christians around the world. Storrs knew it well. He had visited the town on his first Christmas Eve in Palestine to attend midnight mass and afterwards descended the steep stone steps into the Crypt of the Manger. Its walls and ceilings were hung with heavy satin brocade and Storrs had watched entranced as a baby doll on a little gold bed was lowered reverently into the recessed niche of the Manger. Despite the dozens of holy fakes being hawked on the streets, he found the town and its church to be of 'surpassing merit'. So he was able to give his guests a thorough and genuinely enthusiastic guided tour through the church.[9]

Churchill, however, seems to have been more moved by the fact that although he had taken along his easel and equipment, the weather was too cloudy and dull for him to make use of his brushes. Storrs singled out this obsession in his memoirs. After applauding how briskly and efficiently Churchill dealt with business, he noted that after appreciating the beauty of the Temple Mount by moonlight, the Colonial Secretary had seemed 'thereafter to grudge every moment spent away from his easel'.[10]

*

Painting notwithstanding, the main order of the day was Churchill's first face-to-face meeting with Abdullah. The day before, Lawrence had driven across the Jordan to the ancient trading city of Al-Salt high in the hills between Jerusalem and Amman to brief Abdullah on what he could expect Churchill to say. At dinner that night they both dined with Yusuf al-Sukhar, a wealthy Christian merchant, and in the morning were driven in a British military car to Jerusalem via Jericho. Arriving at Government House in the afternoon, Abdullah was ceremoniously greeted with flags, a Guard of Honour, and a band, and afterwards took tea with the Samuels.

That night there was a large dinner in the grand hall. Here Churchill finally met Abdullah. Short and thickly-built with dark brown eyes and a heavy beard, the thirty-nine-year-old emir exuded intelligence, energy, and charm. A devout Muslim who had spent most of his youth in Istanbul, he possessed a good sense of humour and, an avid chess player, he was astute and ambitious. In moving from Mecca to Transjordan his eyes had been set on Damascus rather than Amman, and Churchill knew it. For the sake of Britain's wider relations with France, he had to make it clear to Abdullah that Transjordan should not become a base for attacks on the French. Over dinner he promptly raised the issue by mentioning a recent attack by desert tribesmen on a French border patrol and said that the British government was blaming it on Abdullah's influence. 'But luckily,' he laughed, 'I have two broad shoulders to carry the Government's protest for you.' This made it easier for Abdullah, too, to distance himself from the dispute by pleading ignorance but, he added, he couldn't prevent people from defending their own country. He then made a gesture of friendship. The dinner over, he took some snuff from a golden box enamelled green with the rays of the setting sun in red and offered it to Churchill. Seeing that the snuff was French, he took some, and then sneezed violently. They both took this as a great joke, laughed, and amiably set nine thirty the next morning for their first meeting. Churchill described Abdullah as 'a very agreeable, intelligent, and civilized Arab prince'.[11]

*

Over the next three days he had three separate meetings with him, interspersed with several events designed to signal to all communities in Palestine that their future was assured under the new British mandate. From the start Churchill made it clear that the Balfour Declaration would stand and that there could be no question of having an Arab ruler for both Palestine and Transjordan – an idea that Abdullah initially tried floating but that he instantly squashed. Instead, Abdullah would continue to govern in Transjordan with the support of a British political agent and a handful of military officers to assist his local levies. In addition, he would receive a subsidy of £5,000 a month. Aware of Abdullah's wider ambitions and to make it all more palatable, Churchill hinted that perhaps, in the not too distant future, he might eventually end up being installed by the French in Damascus. But, he quickly added, this was not something that the British could guarantee.[12]

What he could promise, however, was a neighbouring military and air force presence to bolster Abdullah's position and impress his opponents. To make the point, he took Abdullah to witness a grand military review at the barracks at Jaffa where they viewed a march past featuring units of the Indian mule corps and cavalry, infantry from the South Lancashire regiment, and light cars and armoured cars. As they stood together on the podium while the National Anthem played, Bristol fighters from No. 14 squadron swooped overhead. This was military theatre to warm his heart and he was delighted. For Abdullah, a realist, it showed where power lay. Transjordan was at least a stepping stone to something larger, or so he hoped. So he accepted the deal and promised he would stamp down on Syrian exiles in his country who were stirring up cross-border trouble with the French. For this, he was to pay a heavy price. It made him enemies amongst Arab nationalists who had pinned their wider hopes of Arab liberation on his shoulders, and it alienated his Palestinian allies by accepting that Britain was bound by the Balfour Declaration, even though Churchill promised that it would not apply to Transjordan itself. In the longer run too, there was to be yet a further price. Abdullah remained confined for a lifetime in Amman, a town of fewer than 5,000 inhabitants, ruling over a territory of no more than 300,000 people – a 'falcon trapped in a canary cage', as one observer cruelly noted. Churchill was well aware of the risks Abdullah was taking. 'I hope he won't get his throat cut by his own followers,' he told Curzon. Thirty years later the fears were to come true. On 20 July 1951, three years after the creation of Israel, Abdullah was assassinated by a young Palestinian on the steps of the Al-Aqsa mosque as he entered for Friday evening prayers.[13]

Britain also paid a penalty in Churchill's attempts to find a middle way between competing visions of the future. Throughout his talks in Jerusalem he received petitions from both Jews and Arabs about the future of Palestine. Following his second meeting with Abdullah at Government House, on Easter Monday, the Haifa Congress of Palestinian Arabs presented him with a lengthy protest against Zionist activity and bluntly demanded he rescind the Balfour Declaration, put an end to Jewish immigration, and create a government elected by those in Palestine who had been there before the war. The protest was also rife with anti-Semitic stereotypes that could have been lifted verbatim from the infamous forgery, *The Protocols of the Elders of Zion*. Churchill dealt with the protesters briskly, refused their demands, and urged the Arabs instead to work creatively with the Jews to create a prosperous Palestine.[14]

Then it was the turn of the Jewish National Council to present him with its own lengthy statement, which stressed its acceptance of Arab rights, the hope of reaching an understanding with them, and the immense progress already made by the immigrants in trade, industry, and agriculture. In response, he expressed his strong support for the Zionist dream but asked that the pioneers should be 'picked men, worthy in every way of the greatness of the idea and of the cause for which they are striving' – a thinly disguised warning against socialists and revolutionaries. That same night he was a guest at a reception given in his honour by the leading Zionists in the city, and the next day he visited the still uncompleted Hebrew University on Mount Scopus. Here he was greeted by a guard of honour of the Palestine Police and presented with a scroll of the Law by the Chief Rabbi. 'Personally, my heart is full of sympathy for Zionism,' he declared. But he repeated yet again that Britain's promise included assurances to the non-Jewish inhabitants that they would not suffer as a result. If the Zionists worked for *all* Palestinians, he declared, the country would 'turn into a Paradise and will become . . . a land flowing with milk and honey'. Then he was handed a tree to plant. But it broke off from its root as he tried to place it in the hole. No one had thought to provide a spare. He looked annoyed and Samuel was embarrassed. Finally, a small palm tree was substituted. But, as one disgruntled observer remarked, it would not even grow there. It was an ill omen for the smooth implantation of a new society.

That same afternoon Samuel threw a huge reception in Government House for representatives of all religions in Palestine, taking care to personally greet them all. Lawrence was also present and introduced the wide-eyed young Maxwell Coote to two Christian sheiks from Al-Salt dressed in the full finery of their traditional robes. Alongside patriarchs of the Abyssinian Christian Church and other grandees it was all, in the young officer's words, 'far more interesting than any European or Egyptian show could be'.[15] More useful, however, was a frank discussion Churchill was able to have with a French diplomat named Robert de Caix, a veteran advocate of France's hereditary rights to Syria and Palestine as the original land of the Crusades and now Chief Secretary to General Henri Gouraud, the commander of French forces in Syria. Bluntly, Churchill charged him with being 'extremely hostile' to Britain, and complained that the French were causing great difficulties for Britain in the Middle East. De Caix's denial, along with his strongly expressed fears that Transjordan could become a staging ground for anti-French action, was equally robust. But after Churchill explained that a 'keystone' of the deal with Abdullah was the prevention of such acts, and de Caix on his side outlined what the French were doing to soothe nationalist sentiment, both men calmed down and Churchill felt satisfied. 'He seemed an honest man,' he reported to the Foreign Secretary Lord Curzon, 'and on the whole I got on with him.'[16]

*

Meantime, events in London were never far from his mind. There was still no news about whom Lloyd George would appoint as Chancellor of the Exchequer. This may explain why Coote became involved in some urgent reshuffling of Churchill's travel plans, although it may simply have reflected his ward's habitual impetuosity. Already by the time Churchill arrived in Jerusalem he had changed his initial plans to sail home from Alexandria on the Italian liner the *Esperia* and instead booked berths for a later sailing on the French ship the *Lotus*. But on the day of Abdullah's arrival in Jerusalem he reverted to his original plan. Barely had Coote fired off telegrams to take care of this than Churchill announced yet another change of schedule, this time asking his young aide-de-camp to book a special train back to Alexandria that would leave in the evening rather than on the morning of his last day in Palestine, thus giving him an extra few hours to pack in more visits. This seemed settled. But the next day, from Cairo, Archie Sinclair sent a telegram saying that a 50 per cent penalty charge would have to be paid for cancellation of the *Lotus* reservations. At this Churchill flew into a fury and dictated an enraged reply. He then wondered whether they should after all cancel the arrangements for the special train, which by now had been painstakingly arranged. The issue was left hanging until just before dinner, when Coote was summoned yet again. This time he found Churchill wallowing in the bath. The conversation was somewhat intermittent while he submerged himself fully under the water on at least four occasions. But in the end it was agreed that he would stick with the 'special' night train after all and board the *Esperia* the next day.

Coote took all this with amazing good humour. He was neither the first nor the last of those who worked for Churchill to find him both infuriating and endearing. 'Winston is a wonderful man truly, to work with,' he noted, 'he always changes his plans literally every day and would drive one demented, I think, in time if one had the job of always fixing up his arrangements, but I like him for it and he can never receive "No" as an answer to anything he would like.' Churchill in turn had taken a shine to Coote, jokingly calling him 'Coûte que Coûte' ('Cost what may') and always asking him if he was happy and having a good time. 'I have grown quite fond of him on this trip,' noted Coote on their final day together, 'although I never expected I should during my first few days with him.'[17]

*

Churchill's last day in Jerusalem was Wednesday 30 March. It was a packed schedule that began with an unprecedented early morning rise at 5.30 to drive to Jericho for breakfast with the local Arab Governor. Back in Jerusalem by ten o'clock, he visited a Muslim school with Samuel before witnessing a fly past at the Royal Air Force base at Ramleh – both a boost to the local squadron and a re-affirmation of his faith in British air power as an economical peacekeeper in the Middle East.

Afterwards, he visited three of the most impressive new Jewish settlements in Palestine. The first was Tel-Aviv, where he was met by its mayor Meir Dizengoff who, like thousands of others, was an immigrant from the Russian Empire. As Churchill proudly explained, Tel-Aviv was only twelve years old and had been 'conquered by us on sand dunes'. The next stop was the small pioneer settlement of Bir Yaakov, which was wholly settled by Russian Jews. 'Were they Bolsheviks?' enquired Churchill. 'Certainly not' came the reply, they believed in hard work and self-help. Duly impressed, he went on to his last stop: the small community of Rishon-le-Zion (First in Zion). Founded forty years before, again mostly by Jews from Russia, and sponsored by Baron Edmund de Rothschild, it had a population of some 2,000 inhabitants housed in modern red-roofed houses set amidst verdant vineyards and flourishing orange groves created by assiduous cultivation and irrigation. Churchill was especially impressed by the youth and vigour of its workers, both men and women, and lauded how the Jews had not just made their own land flourish but raised the standards around it. 'I am talking of what I saw with my own eyes,' he told the House of Commons later. 'All around the Jewish colony, the Arab houses were tiled instead of being built with mud, so that the culture from this centre has spread out into the surrounding district.' For Zionists, this was a sure sign that in Churchill they had a friend. For Palestinian Arabs, however, while his emphatic support for the Balfour Declaration persuaded some to abandon their opposition to it, to others it merely hardened their determination to resist it.[18]

*

Churchill's train left Ludd station that evening bound for Alexandria. He was exhausted but cheerful, enjoyed his dinner, and stayed up talking for quite a while. He was up early next morning and watched intently in his bedroom slippers as the coach was ferried across the Suez Canal. Then, thanks to plentiful hot water from the engine, he enjoyed a hot bath, as did a grateful Clementine. In Alexandria he was reunited with Archie Sinclair, who was now recovered from his typhoid fever, and at three o'clock in the afternoon, with Royal Air Force planes circling overhead, he embarked on the *Esperia* bound for Genoa. The next morning it was announced in London that Lloyd George had appointed Sir Robert Horne as his new Chancellor of the Exchequer.[19]

NINE

TRAGEDY STRIKES

O n hearing about Sir Robert Horne's promotion, Churchill delayed his return to London and after disembarking at Genoa rented a car and headed for the French Riviera, where he and Clementine checked into the luxurious Grand Hotel Eden at Cap d'Ail. Sandwiched between Monte Carlo and Beaulieu-sur-Mer, it was described by *Bradshaw's* – the essential railway and hotel guide of the time for British visitors to the Continent – as 'one of the most salubrious and picturesque spots of the Riviera'. Here they were joined by his mother, who took an adjoining room. No record of what they talked about survives, and indeed their reunion has escaped the attention of most biographers, some of whom have claimed that he rushed back to London to confront Lloyd George. Yet seeking out his mother's company to soothe his bitter feelings about being denied the high position once enjoyed by his father was completely natural, and it is safe to assume that Lady Randolph sought to reassure him that this was not the end of his career, merely another bump along the road to his ultimate success. This was certainly her strong belief. Visiting an old friend in Italy soon afterwards she spoke fervently of her 'unswerving faith' in her elder son's abilities, and pronounced that his shoulders were broad enough to bear any burden. Alice Keppel, the former mistress of King Edward VII, who also met her in Italy at this time, recalled that she spoke with pride and love about her son.[1]

He also found solace with his easel and canvas. Sir John and Hazel Lavery had recently arrived on the Riviera and were also staying at the

Eden. Over the next four days he joined them on painting expeditions along the Corniche. Like many of his artist contemporaries, Lavery craved the Mediterranean light. Before the war he had worked in North Africa but now preferred the South of France. Having just been elected to the Royal Academy, he was planning an exhibition later in the year. One of the outstanding works that he produced for it was simply entitled *The Bay, Monte Carlo* and showed Hazel sitting on a terrace overlooking Cap Ferrat. Churchill painted the identical view, but without Hazel. It was on one of these expeditions that Lavery also painted him standing before his easel on a cliff above the Mediterranean, brush in hand, attempting to reproduce its brilliant light. Entitled *The Blue Bay: Mr Churchill on the Riviera*, before the year was out it had been reproduced in such American newspapers as the *Brooklyn Daily Eagle*.[2]

His passion for painting was now a lively topic of public conversation. Not long after this Riviera sortie, the critic and avant-garde artist Wyndham Lewis offered the typically provocative opinion that it was no use trying to educate the masses but that instead Britain's political leaders should be educated in art. 'They tell me,' he wrote, 'Mr. Churchill turns out ever so many pictures a week.' Sadly though, true artists were both rare and frequently judged insane. 'There was the Mad King of Bavaria. They considered him mad because he liked music,' he added. 'If Mr. Churchill liked painting more than he does, he also would be considered mad.'[3]

*

Mad, Churchill was not. But he was certainly still angry when he returned to London, convinced that in his absence he had been cheated of the chance to become Chancellor of the Exchequer. 'Winston has come back . . . as cross as a bear with a sore head,' noted Austen Chamberlain. Lloyd George's decision continued to rankle throughout the spring. Churchill avoided him at Cabinet or other official meetings, and in his letters no longer addressed him as 'Dear LlG' or even 'My dear David', but instead deployed the cooler and more formal 'Dear Prime Minister'. In turn the prime minister confessed that he was sick of Churchill and wouldn't care if he resigned.[4]

Amidst this stormy political weather, Churchill also had to cope with several personal issues. These included sorting out financial details of the Garron Towers inheritance. Although Jack took care of some of them, one in particular required his own intervention. His legacy had included some emeralds and other jewels, but a few items of these had gone missing, been stolen, or sold by the Londonderrys. Whether or not to confront them legally about this caused both him and Clementine some heart-searching. But in the end, after discussing the matter with F. E. he sorted it out amicably with Lord Londonderry for the sake of family harmony.

All this soon paled into insignificance in the face of a real tragedy. Lieutenant-Commander William ('Bill') Ogilvy Hozier was Clementine's younger and only brother, a retired naval officer who had commanded two destroyers and a cruiser at the Dardanelles. Early in April he flew to Paris and checked into the Hotel Jena. On the morning of Thursday 14 April he paid his bill and sent out a servant to buy the newspaper. When the man returned shortly after 9 a.m. it was to find the door to Hozier's room locked. Persistent knocking received no answer and it was not until late in the afternoon that the door was finally forced open to reveal the thirty-three-year-old dead in his pyjamas with a bullet wound in his right temple.

Clementine was devastated by her brother's suicide and his twin sister Nellie even more so. Although his gambling had long been a worry to the family, he appeared to have no current debts, had paid his bill, and showed no signs of depression. Nor did he leave a note. Clementine and Nellie rushed over to Dieppe to be with their mother, Lady Blanche Ogilvy, who had been living in France for several years, and they decided that Bill should be buried there. As a suicide he could not be interred in consecrated ground. But eventually an English clergyman was found who would take the funeral service. 'It is cold and snowing,' Lady Blanche wrote to her son-in-law in a hurriedly scrawled note the night before the burial, expressing her concern about Nellie's mental state and praising Clementine for her tender support. 'I would like it said in *The Times* and other papers,' she added, 'that we three were here – dear Winston I am so thankful that Clemmie has such a husband as you are.' Churchill found time to go by train and ferry over to Dieppe for the funeral, and returned the same night to attend a Conference of Ministers the next day that had been postponed for his benefit.[5]

*

Two weeks later he received another hurriedly scrawled note, this time from his mother. Enclosed was a long letter from his wayward cousin. The letter he had sent to Clare in January had never reached her and she was keen to mend fences and bring him up to date with what she had been doing in New York, as well as her future plans. Bernard Baruch had found her difficult to handle. 'She ran around New York like a fire engine out of control,' he said years later, '... sometimes I had to wonder if Winston was deliberately playing a joke when he gave me this exotic creature to "look after". She was impossible.'

Fire engine or not, Clare had met with some of her Jerome cousins and family, and dined with Winston's old friend Maxine Elliot, the American-born star of stage and film. She gave talks about Bolshevism, saw a great deal of the painter Ambrose McEvoy who was also visiting the city, made several sculptures, and was now contemplating a visit to Mexico City to sculpt a bust of the revolutionary General, and now President, Álvaro Obregón. If she did, she would make a detour to California to see Charlie Chaplin to whom she had a letter of introduction. 'Bless you Winston dear,' she concluded. 'I hope your feeling about me is what mine is about you – always devoted, Clare.' Then she added a PS: 'Don't you think you might send me to Moscow as British representative or Ambassador? ... My tact, diplomacy & pacifist character should fit me for the job ... In these days when women do things it ought to be appropriate.' After all, she reminded him, he had said more than once that he would vote for her if she stood for Parliament.[6]

It is hard to imagine that she considered this extraordinary suggestion anything other than an ironic joke. But with Clare it was hard to be certain; she was just as capable of being naively sincere. Certainly, society gossip about her exploits in Moscow had not ceased with her departure to New York, as Lady Jean Hamilton discovered during a stay at Taplow Court on the River Thames in Buckinghamshire, the home of Ethel ('Ettie') and William ('Willie') Grenfell, Lord and Lady Desborough. With its spreading cedars, walled fruit garden, and 200 acres of land, the house was a favourite weekend gathering point for members of London society including politicians, writers, and poets. Churchill had been a steady Taplow *habitué* since returning from the Boer War, and at a couple of high-spirited parties had been flung into the Thames where he coolly continued to swim in his top hat and spats. Taplow was always a hub of society gossip. This time it was his cousin who provided its principal fodder. 'Everyone,' noted Jean Hamilton, was discussing Clare. How could she, they protested, live in looted houses and ride in motorcars belonging to her class so brutally murdered by her new hosts? It was all so 'unspeakably dreadful and *cheap*'. Especially so when she occupied the Tsar's box at the opera dressed all in red but without, the gossips noted, the courage to wear her white gloves![7]

Clare still featured in the British newspapers as well. Reviews of her sculpted heads of the Communist leadership appeared, as did advertisements for her new book. In any case, Churchill left little doubt as to how he felt. 'It is rather pathetic how she hankers after your goodwill,' the forgiving Jennie told him, '[but] don't be hard on her.' He wasn't. But his dictated, typewritten reply was brief and cool in tone, wishing her well in America and promising to welcome her back as a friend provided that she was not still associated with 'these Bolshevik butchers'. He simply ignored her suggestion about going to Moscow as an ambassador. If it was serious, it was fatuous. If it was a joke, it wasn't funny.

*

In Churchill's dealings with Clare his mother was always a significant presence. This was equally true for other aspects of his social life, and it was rare for much time to pass when they did not meet for lunch or dinner; scarcely had he returned to London than she invited him and his brother over for dinner with John and Hazel Lavery. Jennie was now a white-haired sixty-seven-year-old, and enjoying her third marriage.

Montagu Porch, a former officer in the Colonial Service and three years younger than Winston, was visiting Nigeria. Like her elder son, Lady Randolph had always relied heavily on credit to sustain her lifestyle. Unusually, however, she had recently received an infusion of cash after selling her Mayfair house at a healthy profit and moved into a new home in Bayswater, close to Winston and Clementine.

After leaving them at Cap d'Ail she had travelled to stay with an old friend in Florence and Rome, where as usual she indulged in expensive shopping expeditions and returned to London with a new pair of high-heeled evening slippers made by Rome's finest shoemaker. Resuming her normal hectic social round, she found time to look in on a private view of Lavery's Riviera paintings at his home accompanied by her smoke-grey chow dog before heading off to the country to stay with Sir John and Lady Horner, whose daughter Katharine was a lifelong friend of Clementine's and whose home at Mells Manor in Somerset had frequently provided a welcome rural retreat for the Churchills; Katharine's husband Raymond Asquith, son of Herbert Asquith, had been killed on the Western Front. One evening, hastening downstairs, Jennie slipped in her new shoes, took a heavy fall, and broke her left leg just above the ankle. The bones were set and two days later she was taken by ambulance back to her London home to recuperate. All seemed well.

But ten days later gangrene set in. Soon she developed a high fever. An anxious Churchill promptly phoned a surgeon and within hours her leg was amputated above the knee. Family members hastened to her side. If ever it was clear that Churchill belonged to a tightly knit family, this was the proof. His aunts Leonie and Clara – Clare's mother – were beside themselves with anxiety. Churchill's brother was distraught. 'I knew there was death in the house,' he told Oswald, Clare's brother, as they walked back to Jack's house one night. 'I had a presentiment of it. I only did not know who it would be.'

Yet Jennie quickly recovered and was soon joking cheerfully about her missing leg with her sisters and friends. Churchill was vastly relieved, and when Sir Ian and Lady Hamilton came for lunch he was able to assure them that she was out of danger – a message he repeated in a telegram he sent to Montagu Porch the following day. But on the morning of Wednesday 29 June, after eating a hearty breakfast, his mother suddenly suffered a massive haemorrhage of the main artery in her thigh and fell unconscious. Urgently summoned by phone, Churchill rushed over from home still dressed in his pyjamas but could do nothing to help. Jack had been nursing her diligently night and day for the previous five weeks and had just started again to sleep at his own house after the doctor declared that the danger was past. He, too, now rushed to the scene. Quite by chance Bourke Cochran and his wife were in London and they also turned up, bringing Leonie with them.

Before noon, Churchill's mother was dead, having never recovered consciousness. Hurriedly, he scrawled a note to Bernard Baruch, who was also in town, cancelling a lunch they had planned that day at Sussex Square. 'I deeply grieve to tell you that my mother died this morning,' he wrote, adding that he still remained anxious to talk with him as soon as he could.[8] At three o'clock that afternoon Lady Randolph was laid in her coffin. Churchill and his brother, cousins and aunts went to pay their last respects. 'I wish you could have seen her as she lay at rest – after all the sunshine and storm of life was over,' he wrote to a friend. 'Very beautiful & splendid she looked. Since the morning with its pangs, thirty years have fallen from her brow. She recalled to me the countenance I had admired as a child when she was in her heyday and the old brilliant world of the eighties and nineties seemed to come back ...'[9] Her death was a stark reminder that the days of his youth were now over. It was a major emotional loss. 'She shone for me like the Evening Star,' he was to write of her in *My Early Life*. 'I loved her dearly – but at a distance.' But this oft-quoted avowal refers to his childhood days and reflects the detached irony of his memoir. Mapping out his ambitions in his youth, he had depended heavily on her strong emotional and practical support, and after marrying Clementine he had sometimes turned to his mother at moments of stress, as he had done when overwhelmed by the crowded domestic scene during the war.

On Saturday 2 July the family travelled by train to Oxford in a reserved coach, the blinds half down. A car drove them the last eight miles to

Bladon and the small and peaceful church nestled close to Blenheim Palace. Here Jennie's body was already laid out amidst a wealth of flowers framed by two altar lights that had burned all night, a scene captured by Lavery in a painting. 'Jack and Winston were like widowers,' Shane Leslie wrote to Clare in New York. 'Her sons and sisters were affected almost beyond the grief that is claimed by ties of flesh and blood ... Winston was bowed under the greatest grief of his life.' After the service, when her coffin was finally lowered into the freshly dug grave next to his father, a tearful Churchill threw in a spray of crimson roses. At the same hour, in St Margaret's Church in Westminster, a memorial service took place attended by dozens of Jennie's friends, relatives, and members of London society including the American ambassador, Sir Ernest Cassel, the Curzons, and the Wimbornes. The Churchills' two daughters Diana and Sarah were also present. Freddie Guest, Archie Sinclair, and Eddie Marsh served as ushers. The King and Queen sent official representatives, and Sir William Sutherland represented Lloyd George. At Bladon, the lesson was read by the sub-dean of the Chapels Royal.

Lady Randolph's death received headline coverage across the Atlantic as well as in the British press. After all, as the *Boston Evening Globe* put it, she was not only Lord Randolph's widow and the mother of Winston Spencer Churchill, but 'Miss Jennie Jerome of New York'. Her conquest of British society was a common theme of American obituaries, and the *Boston Post* described her as the United States' 'Best Ambassador' in Britain. Inevitably, her death also focused eyes on her son Winston, whose name by now was familiar to many Americans. 'She died,' noted the *Post*, 'before she realized the ambition of her life – to see her son Winston Churchill as Prime Minister.' Back in New York, Bernard Baruch, who was still grieving his own father's recent death, picked up the same theme. 'I am watching with intense interest your broadening career.'[10]

More letters of sympathy poured in. Many recalled the glory days of his mother's prime – and of theirs – but some gave voice to more reflective thoughts. 'Life's work will soon absorb you again, as indeed it is right it should,' wrote his ever loyal aunt Cornelia. 'But don't lose sight of that rift in the heavens which reminds us of the life beyond and which can only inspire you to right thinking and doing.' Other close friends chimed in. Only the weekend before, Winston and Clementine had spent another of their regular stays at Taplow. 'Your spirit is brave & will stand fast,' wrote 'Ettie' Desborough, 'but I cannot bear to think of *you* in the dark country of grief.' But it was his cousin Ivor Guest, Freddie's brother, who undoubtedly captured its true significance for Churchill himself. 'For her doubtless it was a release from crippled age,' he wrote, 'but to lose one's mother is to be severed from one's own youth, and begets a new sense of isolation in confronting destiny henceforth.'

That Churchill had to accept that the final curtain had fallen on a major scene in his life he made clear to Millicent ('Millie'), the Dowager Duchess of Sutherland, a near contemporary who had directed field hospitals in France during the war. 'I find it difficult writing this afternoon that she is gone,' he penned from the Colonial Office as the finality of his mother's death began to sink in, 'that there is no chance of Eddie opening my office door to say she has come to see me – as she often did – that I shall never have one of our jolly talks again.' And to Lord Curzon, one of his mother's oldest friends, he made it clear that he saw her death as a major milestone in his life. 'I am deeply touched by the kindness of all you write,' he told the Foreign Secretary. 'You have ever been a true friend. We all keep moving along the road.'[11]

His mother's death also completed the transformation of his finances, as he now received his half share of both his parents' trusts. This was complicated, as it involved extracting money due from his Jerome grandfather's settlement in New York, but eventually it produced another tranche of income. Three days after Jennie's funeral, he met with Sir Reginald Cox, the senior partner at his personal bankers, to discuss his future financial arrangements. By the end of 1921 his family's entire net worth stood at £100,000, or £4,500,000 in today's values – a level it would not reach again until close to the end of the Second World War. All too predictably, however, his annual spending continued to outrun his income. This gave him even more incentive to get on with writing *The World Crisis*, as well as producing articles for newspapers and magazines that would pay him well.

TEN

PEACEMAKER

Churchill came home from the Middle East to find Britain in crisis. The post-war slump was deepening, wages were falling, and unemployment had rocketed from some 600,000 at the start of the year to almost 2 million, prompting mass demonstrations by the unemployed. While he was contentedly painting with Lavery at Cap d'Ail, the coalminers had gone on strike against a hefty cut in wages. The transport workers and railway men promised to follow suit. In response the Cabinet declared a state of emergency and mobilized the armed forces. Reservists were called up, vehicles were requisitioned for emergency food distribution, and a special volunteer Defence Force was created. Although the threatened work stoppage was abandoned, the miners remained defiantly out and the reservists were not released until June. To alarmists, there was a distinct whiff of civil war in the spring air. 'The strike news is bad. Everyone discusses revolution,' noted Duff Cooper the day that Churchill finally arrived back in London.[1]

*

Yet across the Irish Sea things were far worse. Since the partial imposition of martial law, violence on both sides had intensified and feelings polarized even further. Attacks by the IRA on the British Army and Royal Irish Constabulary were countered by ruthless official reprisals – the burning or blowing up of the houses of suspects along with their furniture and other possessions. These had a chilling effect on the civilian population and soon the IRA began to encounter silent but stubborn hostility to its campaign of attacks on British forces, even in areas of the south and south-west where nationalist sympathies ran deep. Those found guilty of murder in the courts continued to be executed. As victory for Sinn Fein proved elusive, paranoia amongst IRA units about spies and informers within the civilian population mounted. 'Civilian spies were considered by us as the most dangerous of all,' recalled one IRA intelligence officer from County Cork, the epicentre of its guerrilla campaign. Suspects received threatening letters, suffered economic boycotts, or were forced into exile. Women seen consorting with British soldiers had their hair forcibly cut. In the most serious cases, those deemed guilty were simply shot. By May, some seventy-three bodies had been discovered with placards attached announcing 'Traitor. Shot by the IRA.' County Cork saw the most killings – amounting to almost half of all those carried out in the whole of Ireland during the war of independence. One of them indirectly impinged on the Churchill family.[2]

*

At 9.30 on the night of Thursday 31 March a man named Frederick Stenning heard a knock on the front door of his house in the village of Innishannon in County Cork, where he lived with his wife and three adult children. Two armed men stood on the doorstep. He tried to slam the door shut. When he couldn't, he fled back down the hallway followed by the men. Drawing a revolver, he turned and opened fire on his pursuers, who shot him dead. The assassins belonged to the West Cork Brigade Flying Column of the IRA, which had identified him as an important informer for the Royal Irish Constabulary. The Protestant Stenning was a well-known loyalist and the father of a British soldier killed in the First World War. He had been spotted watching the local IRA unit preparing an ambush before cycling off to the RIC barracks in the town. The fifty-seven-year-old was also the sub-agent for Clare Sheridan's father, Moreton Frewen, the owner of the nearby Innishannon House and proprietor of most of the houses and shops in the village, as well as the local fishing and shooting rights. Originally hired to create a fish hatchery by the entrepreneurial but unreliable Frewen, Stenning collected the rents and served as his gamekeeper and wood ranger. Frewen had once been the nationalist MP for Cork North-East but now lived in his English family home in Sussex.[3]

Things were to get much worse. Just a few weeks later the IRA launched a full-scale campaign of punitive counter-reprisals against the British by targeting 'Big Houses' belonging to the largely Protestant gentry. Again the heaviest hit area was County Cork, where a 'devil's competition' of burnings erupted between the two sides. Here, in June, some eighteen grand mansions went up in flames along with their often priceless collections of furniture, paintings, and antiques.

After Stenning's murder his widow and her children left Innishannon for England. But in the last week of June the IRA returned to the town, attacked the post office, and sabotaged its telephonic and telegraphic equipment – a classic guerrilla technique designed to paralyze army and police communications. In addition, they burned down the Stennings' empty home along with four local 'Big Houses' along the River Bandon including the historic Coy Castle. Innishannon House, which was now occupied by a retired British officer, was burned that same day. 'On Friday the miscreants put the torch to my pretty home,' wrote Frewen to his Irish-American friend Bourke Cochran, Churchill's one-time American mentor. Clare quickly learned of its fate from her father in a letter he sent her in New York. She had loved playing in its grounds as a child and remembered it well – 'a mere square shooting lodge, comfortable but plain'.[4]

Churchill had stayed at Innishannon before the war. But there were other strong Irish links as well. His aunt Leonie spent much of her time across the Irish Sea, having married into the Anglo-Irish Leslie family of County Monaghan. As pre-war Home Secretary, Churchill had happily introduced her son Shane to John Redmond, the leader of the nationalist Irish parliamentary party for which he stood twice – unsuccessfully – as a Member of Parliament. During the war Shane sailed to the United States and linked up with Cochran, married the Irish-American's sister-in-law, and worked with the British ambassador in Washington DC in a campaign to soften Irish-American hostility to Britain. Back in London, he provided Churchill with a useful conduit to Irish nationalist feeling, and it was after a discussion with him that Churchill warned Clare against simplistically equating the Irish with the Bolsheviks. 'Don't confuse [them],' he told her, 'The Irish all believe in God, uphold the family, and love their country.' Clare admired and respected Shane and the two spent many happy hours together at Innishannon.[5]

Then there were the Laverys, who in 1921 were playing a major part in the Churchills' social life. Both had strong feelings about Ireland, and although the socially ambitious and successful Sir John was careful what he said in public, his paintings often carried a powerful message. His massive 1916 canvas recording Sir Roger Casement's unsuccessful appeal against his death sentence for high treason in seeking German help for the Irish rebels, showed the full machinery of the state directed towards the hapless Casement's extinction. More recently, he had painted Terence MacSwiney's coffin leaving Southwark Cathedral, a shaft of sunlight dramatically highlighting the green, white and orange Irish tricolour draped over the Republican martyr's coffin. One day, when Churchill visited Lavery in his studio, the artist placed the painting on his easel without comment. 'Well,' said Churchill after gazing at it for a few moments, 'what could we do?' Lavery stayed silent and Churchill continued to study it. 'He was a brave man! They are fine people,' he said finally. 'We cannot afford to lose them. We shall be shaking hands together in months.'[6] These strong personal links with Ireland and the Irish made Churchill more receptive to Irish national feelings than many of his colleagues.[7]

*

'If you were their leader you would not be cowed by severity and certainly not by reprisals which fall like the rain from Heaven upon the Just and upon the Unjust.' So wrote Clementine from the French Riviera about the rebels to her husband, urging him to adopt a more moderate line over Ireland.[8] This was a typically blunt piece of advice from his liberally inclined and politically savvy wife. But it only reinforced the view he had already reached himself. Since December he had been urging a truce, and the escalating violence over the winter and spring only strengthened his

1. A top-hatted Churchill strides forcefully ahead during the Anglo-Irish conference in Downing Street, October 1921. He had strong family connections with Ireland, was amongst the first to call for a truce during the war for independence, and played a principal role during the negotiations. The man at the very back on the right is his Special Branch bodyguard, Detective-Sergeant Walter Thompson, appointed because of assassination threats, and a constant presence at his side.

2. 'She shone for me like the Evening Star.' Lady Randolph ('Jennie') Churchill, Winston's beloved mother, was born in Brooklyn, the daughter of a wealthy Wall Street speculator. Her first husband and father to Winston, Lord Randolph Churchill, died at age forty-five, and she remarried twice. She had numerous lovers, was reckless with money, and died suddenly in June 1921 after tripping down stairs while staying with friends in Somerset. Her vast network of society contacts was invaluable in boosting Churchill's early career.

3. In the bosom of his family: the young Winston (right) with his mother and younger brother, John ('Jack'). By profession a stockbroker, Jack is largely absent from most Churchill biographies, but the two were close and he campaigned for Winston, advised him on finances, and sorted out their parents' complicated estates. He and his wife 'Goonie' (Lady Gwendeline Bertie, daughter of the Earl and Countess of Abingdon) regularly lived and holidayed with Winston and Clementine along with their children.

4. Churchill (extreme left) heads the family procession at his mother's funeral in July 1921 at St Martin's church, Bladon, close to Blenheim Place, where she was buried alongside Lord Randolph. He is followed by his brother Jack and nephew Johnnie. Behind, other close members of the family include Clare Sheridan's mother and brother, as well as Clementine and Goonie. Churchill himself was buried at Bladon in 1965, close to his parents and Jack who pre-deceased him.

5. Clementine with daughter Marigold ('the Duckadilly'), whose favourite song was 'I'm Forever Blowing Bubbles'. Churchill took her to Chequers during his weekend stay there in February 1921. Her sudden death in August while on holiday in Kent caused her parents inconsolable grief. She was buried in Kensal Green cemetery in London, where they could easily visit her grave. All their other children are buried at Bladon, as is Clementine.

6. Winston and his only son Randolph, whose headmaster complained that he was 'combative', seen here together at about this time. The father–son relationship was to be one of 'storm and sunshine', and Randolph's personal and professional lives as husband, politician, and journalist proved turbulent. He became his father's official biographer and wrote the first two volumes of the eight-volume set that was eventually completed by Sir Martin Gilbert.

7. A casual Winston and Clementine enjoy a rare relaxing moment in the garden. Note the cigar, already a regular prop. With her cloche hat and drop-waist belt, Clementine has clearly embraced the brave new world of post-war fashion. Privately a sometimes severe critic of her husband, she was also the emotional anchor that moored him firmly to the home and family that provided the vital bedrock of his life and career.

8. Married to a wealthy American heiress, the genial and sociable Member of Parliament and decorated army officer Captain Frederick ('Freddie') Guest was Churchill's favourite cousin, and remained close to him politically and personally throughout his life. A son of Lord Randolph's sister Cornelia (Lady Wimborne), he was also the Coalition Liberals' Chief Whip, a cunning backroom fixer, and successful raiser of finances for Lloyd George's political fund. In April 1921 he was appointed by Lloyd George as Secretary of State for Air in succession to his cousin.

9. Another of Churchill's close relatives, his 'wild cousin' Clare Sheridan, with whom he shared fond childhood memories of Ireland, was widowed during the First World War and left with two small children. Naïve and idealistic, she was also a serious sculptor who enraged him by heading for Moscow to sculpt Lenin, Trotsky, and other top Bolsheviks. On her return to London in 1921 she was briefly 'exiled' by the family to the United States, but she and Winston were eventually reconciled and she sculpted him as prime minister during the Second World War.

10. The charismatic Boris Savinkov, former anti-Tsarist revolutionary and political assassin on whom Churchill pinned his hopes of toppling Lenin and the Bolsheviks. A bon-viveur who mixed with poets and artists and had a string of mistresses, he once authored a play about Napoleon's escape from Elba in which he himself played a major role. A mesmerised Churchill described him as 'an unusual personality of veiled power in strong restraint'. In December 1921 he personally took Savinkov to meet with Lloyd George at Chequers.

11. The dashing and daredevil 'Archie' Sinclair, Churchill's wartime comrade-in-arms, link with the secret intelligence service, and trusted handler of his confidential files on anti-Bolshevik affairs. Younger by some sixteen years, he too had an American mother, was a trained cavalry officer, and enjoyed flying and polo. Their intimate relationship resembled that of father and son, and during the aftermath of the Dardanelles disaster Churchill privately confessed to him that he was 'profoundly unsettled'. During the Second World War Sinclair served as his Secretary of State for Air.

12. A typically acerbic David Low cartoon entitled 'Winston's Bag' with the caption 'He hunts lions and brings home decayed cats'. Wearing plus-fours, Churchill is shown big game hunting but with only small dead cats lying at his feet, labelled with episodes held against him such as 'Russia' and 'Antwerp'. Like the accompanying Strube cartoon, it illustrates the negative reputation enjoyed by Churchill at the start of the decade.

13. A cartoon by Sidney Conrad Strube reflects the widespread contemporary view of Churchill as restless and ambitious. Captioned 'A New Hat', it mocks Churchill and his many career and political hats as journalist, painter, and Cabinet Minister, the latest being Colonial Secretary. His beaming ally and prime minister, David Lloyd George, rubs his hands in approval.

14. Churchill takes a front row seat at the Cairo Conference in March 1921. On the second row, left, stands 'The Queen of the Desert', the archaeologist and wartime intelligence officer Gertrude Bell. She spoke Arabic, it was said, 'like a nightingale'. Note the two lion cubs also in attendance. The ever-faithful Sinclair stands at the very back, wearing a bow tie. The conference established important contours of the post-war Middle East settlement, especially the creation of Iraq. 'It has been wonderful,' declared Bell at its close, 'Mr. Churchill was admirable.'

15. Churchill, escorted by Palestine High Commissioner and former Liberal Home Secretary Sir Herbert Samuel, greets Zionist youth during his visit to Jerusalem following the Cairo Conference. He was enthused by what he witnessed of the pioneering Jewish settlements and sympathized with the Zionist dream. But he found balancing Jewish and Arab interests increasingly frustrating.

16. Churchill on a camel in front of the Sphinx in March 1921. On his right Clementine; on his left Gertrude Bell and T. E. Lawrence ('Lawrence of Arabia'). With painting now his premier private passion, Churchill spent most afternoons during the Cairo Conference disappearing into the desert with his canvas and paints, while Clementine explored the principal tourist sites and went shopping with Bell in the bazaars of Cairo.

17. Churchill with T.E. Lawrence during his Middle East trip. Seduced by the romantic 'Lawrence of Arabia' myth created by the enterprising American journalist Lowell Thomas, Churchill appointed him as his principal advisor on Arab affairs. Along with Gertrude Bell, Lawrence strongly supported the cause of the Hashemite Sheikh Faisal as King of the newly created Iraq. On Lawrence's death in 1935, Churchill declared that he had possessed the 'full measure of the versatility of genius'.

18. Abdullah of Transjordan, brother to Faisal of Iraq, shakes hands with Clementine on the steps of Government House in Jerusalem in March 1921. Churchill considered him 'a very agreeable, intelligent, and civilized Arab prince', and he was to rule over Transjordan until his assassination in 1951 by a Palestinian nationalist. While Clementine chose to visit some of the holy sites in the city, Churchill opted instead to go off once more with his canvas and paints.

19. Hazel, Lady Lavery unlocked Churchill's artistic inhibitions and played hostess to Michael Collins, the thirty-three-year-old director of intelligence for the IRA, during the Anglo-Irish treaty talks. This strikingly beautiful American-born model, fashion innovator, and socialite was unreliably rumoured to have had an affair with Collins, and her portrait later featured on banknotes of the Irish Free State.

20. Michael Collins delivers a passionate speech in late 1921 or early 1922. During the Irish Treaty negotiations, he and Churchill accorded each other an important measure of respect. Sinn Fein was bitterly divided about the agreement, and Collins told a friend that in putting his signature to it he had signed his death warrant. Nine months later, during the civil war between pro- and anti-Treaty forces that followed, he was shot and killed by a Republican assassin.

21. Churchill in Dundee with Sir George Ritchie, his political guide and friend in the city, in September 1921 following severe riots. Famed for its jute industry, Dundee had been Churchill's constituency since 1908 and was suffering from high unemployment and dismal poverty. Bodyguard Detective-Sergeant Walter Thompson can be spotted on the right staring at the camera.

22. The wealthy and well-connected aesthete and Member of Parliament Sir Philip Sassoon, a frequent and generous host to Churchill during 1921, seen here on the steps of his home at Lympne on the Channel coast in Kent. Previously private secretary to Sir Douglas Haig, the commander-in-chief of British forces on the Western front, he was now Lloyd George's parliamentary private secretary. The prime minister's mistress, Frances Stevenson, quipped that he was as 'amusing and clever as a cartload of monkeys'.

23. The 'Big Three' of the Coalition: Churchill seen here in 1921 with F. E. Smith (Lord Birkenhead, the Lord Chancellor) and Prime Minister David Lloyd George. They were also the principal founders of The Other Club, a cross-party and exclusively male dining club founded before the First World War that in addition to politicians included artists, writers, entertainers, and members of the press. Its day-to-day running was largely left in the hands of Freddie Guest.

24. Churchill playing his beloved polo in 1921. He described it as 'the prince [and sometimes emperor] of games' and he rarely missed an opportunity to indulge in it. He also enjoyed the danger and thrill of flying, but reluctantly gave that up after a crash and many entreaties by Clementine to think of the future of his family. Churchill's love of risk was also evident in his gambling and finances.

25. One of Britain's most accomplished and celebrated portrait artists, the Belfast-born Sir John Lavery actively nurtured Churchill's artistic ambitions and, along with the considerably younger Hazel, quietly supported the Irish nationalist cause. During 1921 he and Churchill painted together on the French Riviera, and in the catalogue for a show of Lavery's landscapes in October Churchill highlighted the artist's use of 'brilliant and beautiful colour'. Here, Lavery captures Churchill at work with his canvas.

conviction. Four weeks after the murder at Innishannon, and with the IRA's scorched-earth campaign against Ireland's Big Houses fully ablaze, he also argued that the planned elections for the two new Irish parliaments should go ahead, even if this almost certainly meant a landslide victory for Sinn Fein in the south. 'How are you worse off if all returned are Sinn Fein?' he asked his Cabinet colleagues in April. 'The election would be a new situation which might lead to negotiations.' With the elections finally fixed for a month ahead, he again argued strongly in Cabinet for a truce, on the plausible grounds that British forces were finally getting the upper hand and that continuing the war could only worsen Britain's reputation around the world. 'We are getting an odious reputation,' he declared, '[and] poisoning our relations with the United States.'

Yet it wasn't just across the Atlantic and in the Dominions that British 'frightfulness' was generating hostility. It was in Britain itself. No one was a more avid daily reader of newspapers than Churchill, and he knew full well that the major Liberal and Labour papers had opposed the war from the start. But the country's distinguished newspaper of record, *The Times*, had also now come out strongly against reprisals and the 'reign of terror' being inflicted on the Irish. 'If only the people of England knew ... Why do these things happen?' it asked. 'Why are the servants of the Crown charged with pillage and arson and what amounts to lynch law, and even with drunkenness and murder? How can the reign of terror be stopped?' Even as Clementine was penning her own plea to her husband, in the House of Commons the Liberal leader Herbert Henry Asquith called for a truce to end 'the ghastly state of affairs' in Ireland. The Archbishop of Canterbury joined him in the Lords by denouncing the government's policy as 'morally unjust'. Sir John Simon, a former Liberal Home Secretary, also described the reprisals as 'politically disastrous and morally wrong ... exposing us to the scorn of the world'. Even some Conservatives began to voice doubts. If nothing else, the relentless violence in Ireland was now threatening the coherence of Lloyd George's Coalition.

Churchill's case for a truce was helped by the actions of Sir James Craig, the leader of the Irish Unionists, who now decided to meet secretly with Eamon de Valera to see what direct discussions between the two men could achieve. The answer was virtually nothing – except that the encounter raised the pertinent question: if Craig could meet with the Sinn Fein leader, why not Lloyd George?[9] But when the issue of a truce again came to a vote in Cabinet, Churchill found himself once more in a minority against the prime minister. The violence and the burnings continued and spread to the British mainland. In mid-May several night-time attacks were launched against the homes of Royal Irish Constabulary men in London, Liverpool, and Scotland. The methods in each case were remarkably similar. Gangs of between three and sixteen men, all masked and carrying revolvers, broke into houses, soaked carpets, curtains, and furnishings with petrol or paraffin, and set them ablaze. No one was killed, but some of the occupants were shot and wounded. At one house, the 'hands up' order was met by a determined one-legged Royal Navy veteran who simply hurled a sewing machine at the raiders.[10]

As Churchill predicted, the elections later that month produced a landslide victory for Sinn Fein in the south and a healthy majority for the Unionists in the north. The next day an IRA company of 120 men seized control of the Customs House in Dublin, set it on fire, and destroyed most of the Irish Local Government Board records that underpinned the British civil administration of the country. It was a propaganda coup for Sinn Fein. Yet in the subsequent battle with the police six of the attackers were killed, and over the following weeks a significant surge of British troops along with major intelligence swoops inflicted heavy damage on the rebels. More worryingly for the IRA, internal discipline was beginning to fray. This lent force to Churchill's argument for a truce. At a Cabinet meeting in the first week of June he confidently claimed that his old friend and head of the Royal Irish Constabulary, General Tudor, was clearly 'getting to the root of the matter'. He was not wrong. The intensification of IRA actions represented a degree of desperation. While it was clear they could continue guerrilla warfare for quite a while, it was also obvious that they could never prevail.[11]

The conditions were ripe for a deal. Behind-the-scenes peace-feelers had never ceased. King George V had long expressed his dislike for the Black and Tans' methods, and when he travelled to Belfast to open the new Northern Ireland Parliament he openly appealed for all Irishmen 'to pause, to stretch out the hand of forbearance and conciliation, to forgive and to forget, and to join in making for the land which they love a new era of peace, contentment, and goodwill'. Two days later, Churchill strongly supported Lloyd George when he floated the idea of seizing the moment to send a letter to both de Valera and Craig inviting them to enter into negotiations. 'I believe in striking while the iron is hot,' he said. The next day, his uncle Moreton's Irish home was torched – a clear sign that the campaign of official reprisals had simply encouraged the IRA to raise the stakes and intensified the deadly spiral of destruction.[12]

With the ruins of Innishannon still smouldering, an American delegation from the state of Virginia arrived in England to present statues of George Washington to St Paul's Cathedral and to Sulgrave Manor, the ancestral home of the United States' first President that had recently been purchased by public subscription to mark a century of peace between Britain and the United States. Churchill was the guest speaker at a London lunch hosted by the English-Speaking Union. He used the occasion to celebrate the growing closeness and common sense of purpose between Britain and America as witnessed so recently on the Western Front, but coupled it with a warning that a 'grave impediment' to its future was the troubled Ireland. Happily, he pointed out, an opportunity had now arisen to place Anglo-Irish relations on an honourable, free, and enduring foundation. 'It would be foolish to anticipate what the course of events may be,' he said. 'No one can tell. Once more, unreason may dash away the cup.' It was important, therefore, for the British people to appreciate that their relations with Ireland and the Irish involved far more than the United Kingdom, but had a global impact. Ireland, he hoped, would soon no longer provide 'a source of peril and of reproach to the British Empire'.[13]

The momentum for peace was gathering force. Over the next few days, several Sinn Fein leaders were released from prison. When General Jan Smuts, the prime minister of South Africa, arrived in Britain for the Imperial Conference, he offered his services as an intermediary. Travelling to Dublin, he drew on his experience of fighting against the British in the Boer War to urge the Sinn Fein leaders to accept the olive branch being offered. Their response was grudging, but encouraging enough that when Smuts reported it to the Cabinet Churchill warmly welcomed the news. 'I would go a long way to humour them,' he declared.

*

The week before the King's speech in Belfast, Churchill addressed the House of Commons about his settlement for the Middle East. He had been preparing it for weeks, knowing full well that his performance could make or break his political future. One of his great skills as a speaker was to make complex issues comprehensible. But he only succeeded after laborious and lengthy preparation and practice. His speeches always went through several drafts, and he would frequently read them out loud to himself to gauge their rhythms and effect. Early in his parliamentary career he had once tried to speak to the Commons without notes, only to forget in mid-sentence what he was about to say and be forced to resume his seat to a shocked silence in the House. Traumatized, he rarely again tried to speak without carefully constructed notes.[14]

Complex events in the Middle East required a simplifying narrative for Members of Parliament. For one thing, there had been continuous unrest in Palestine between Jews and Arabs. Only about 10 per cent of its population of just over 600,000 was Jewish, and of these only a small minority were recently arrived Zionists. So the mark they left on the physical and demographic landscape of Palestine was minor. But even this was too much for local Arab nationalists. They complained about an increasing proportion of Jews taking jobs in Palestine's civil administration and feared a future in which Jews might predominate. With Zionist immigration picking up again after the end of the war, they also took aim at even historic Jewish communities long established in the Holy Land. The first week of May saw an outbreak of violence in Jaffa between Arabs and Jews with shops looted, several people killed, and troops brought in to restore calm. The violence spread to recent Jewish settlements, and the Royal Air Force dropped bombs to scare away the attackers. In a radical effort to calm Arab fears, Sir Herbert Samuel ordered a temporary halt to all Jewish immigration, and even refused to allow two boatloads of

Russian Jews to land at Jaffa. As a result, other groups of Jews already embarked for Palestine were held up in Europe.

Samuel's decision took Churchill by surprise. The Jews en route could hardly be left stranded in Vienna. But when the High Commissioner told him that Arab unrest had been prompted by the presence of some two hundred recently arrived Jewish Bolsheviks from Russia, Churchill threw his weight behind the decision and urged him 'to purge the Jewish Colonies and newcomers of Communist elements and without delay have all those who are guilty of subversive agitation expelled from the country'. Samuel's reference to 'Jewish Bolsheviks' was guaranteed – and possibly deliberately designed – to spark Churchill off. In his many fiery rhetorical tirades against the Bolsheviks since Lenin's seizure of power, Churchill had more than once equated Jews with Bolsheviks and dubbed the latter as 'Semitic conspirators' or as 'Jew Commissars'. Bolsheviks apart, however, he saw Jews in a highly positive light. This made him a marked anomaly in being free of the the ingrained hostility to Jewry typical of the English upper class, and indeed of a number of his friends and social contacts. Duff Cooper, for example, had recently been forced to send a grovelling letter of apology to Philip Sassoon after denouncing him with an offensive anti-Semitic slur for not lending him and Diana his car after a party – despite the fact that thanks to his generosity the two had spent their honeymoon night at Lympne. 'Bendor', the Duke of Westminster, frequently a welcoming host to Churchill, was a deep-grained and unapologetic anti-Semite. 'Sunny' Marlborough, his cousin, was little better.[15]

As for Zionism, Churchill had long advocated a Jewish homeland on the grounds that it rectified an historical injury and was a positive and civilizing force. It also, he argued, provided an antidote to Bolshevism. What he had seen with his own eyes at Rishon-le-Zion left a profound and permanent mark on his ideas about Palestine. 'You have changed desolate places to smiling orchards,' he told its pioneer inhabitants, 'and initiated progress instead of stagnation.' When he briefed the Cabinet before his Commons speech he went out of his way to emphasize that the Zionist colonies had created 'a standard of living far superior to that of the indigenous Arabs'. His pro-Zionism was a sincere and lifelong commitment, although it was always tempered by his pragmatic views about British interests and his own political priorities.[16]

This became dismayingly clear to his military advisor in the Middle East Department, Colonel Richard Meinertzhagen. A tall and imposing figure some four years younger than Churchill, and with a decorated career as a soldier and spy in Africa and the Middle East to his credit, he was an even greater myth-maker than Lawrence of Arabia. His real-life story was interesting enough. Yet he felt compelled to embellish it with dozens of tall tales, faked many of his diary entries, and indulged in some shameless fraud and theft. An enthusiastic ornithologist, he gifted his collection to London's famed Natural History Museum, but years later it was discovered that he had stolen dozens of specimens from other museums, incorporated them into his own collection, and then claimed to have discovered them in new locations. He even took specimens from the Museum, re-labelled them, and presented them back to it.

Such practised deception seems also to have applied to many of the stories he told about himself. One of the most celebrated was the so-called 'Haversack Ruse', a deception plan during Allenby's campaign in Palestine in which a haversack containing false battle plans to fool the Turks was planted and led to British victory at the Battle of Beersheba. In reality, Meinertzhagen probably neither planned nor executed the operation. But his claim to have done so guaranteed him a formidable reputation at the Paris Peace Conference, where he served as a military advisor to the British delegation. 'He struck me as being one of the ablest and most successful brains I had met in any army,' enthused Lloyd George. Lawrence of Arabia, who got to know Meinertzhagen well in Paris and recognized something of a kindred soul, described him in his *Seven Pillars of Wisdom* as 'a silent laughing masterful man ... who took as blithe a pleasure in deceiving his enemy (or his friend) by some unscrupulous jest, as in spattering the brains of a cornered mob of Germans one by one with his African knob-kerri. His instincts were abetted by an immensely powerful body and a savage brain, which chose the best way to its purpose unhampered by doubt or habit.'[17]

Churchill was often drawn uncritically to charismatic men of action. So he was attracted to this wealthy and well-connected banker's son who had once been dangled on the knees of the elderly Charles Darwin, and whose aunt was the formidable Fabian socialist, Beatrice Webb. During the same week in January that Churchill recruited Lawrence as his advisor on Arab affairs, he and Freddie Guest met with Meinertzhagen at a London club and over lunch offered him the post of Military Advisor. By this time, the legendary Colonel's pro-Zionist views and friendship with Chaim Weizmann had already produced clashes with his army superiors; he provided a much-needed balance to their strongly pro-Arab views. It took three months for the appointment to come through. When it did, Meinertzhagen was dismayed to discover what he viewed as Britain's betrayal of its commitment in the Balfour Declaration.[18] He also took strong exception to the decision by Sir Herbert Samuel to appoint the mild-mannered twenty-six-year-old Al Hajj Amin al-Hussayni, the scion of a distinguished Palestinian family, as the new Mufti (later Grand Mufti) of Jerusalem, a position of significant influence in the Muslim community. Only the year before, Hajj Amin had been convicted *in absentia* to ten years' imprisonment for his part in stirring up anti-Jewish riots, and his family was well known for its hostility to Jews. But Samuel believed that Arab grievances had to be met and that Hajj Amin could be coaxed into enforcing a more peaceful line with the local Palestinian population.

To Meinertzhagen, the decision was 'pure madness'. He predicted that nothing but trouble would come of it – and indeed the Grand Mufti was eventually to be expelled from Palestine and ended up broadcasting anti-Semitic tirades from Hitler's wartime Berlin. But Churchill's response was simply to shrug and say he could do nothing about it. His reply to another complaint was equally infuriating to his pro-Zionist advisor. Meinertzhagen had not attended the Cairo Conference and believed that the decision to separate Transjordan from Palestine was a betrayal of Britain's pledge to the Jews. His fury led to a stormy meeting in Churchill's office. 'I went foaming at the mouth with anger and indignation,' noted Meinertzhagen in his (far from reliable) diary. 'I told him it was grossly unfair to the Jews, that it was yet another promise broken, [and] that the Balfour Declaration was being torn up by degrees . . .' Churchill eventually calmed him down with some soothing comments.

But his policy on the issue remained unaffected. He was not a minister to be easily swayed by any of his advisors, however passionate or like-minded. It was already becoming dismally clear that in Palestine he and his successors would be tested to – and beyond – the limit in finding a path acceptable to both Arabs and Jews. Meinertzhagen neither forgot nor forgave. In 1964, at age eighty-five, he wrote scathingly that 'Churchill, encouraged by Lawrence, gave the whole of Transjordan to that miserable Abdullah ... [In 1921] I remonstrated. He put on that ridiculous bull dog expression but nothing could be done to remedy Churchill's stupidity.' He then added bitterly, 'I do not share the general admiration for Churchill. No living man has done so much harm to this country as Churchill, yet he is venerated as a God.'[19]

*

After the Jaffa riots and Samuel's restrictions on immigration, a temporary calm descended on Palestine. After spending a weekend with Clementine at Philip Sassoon's Trent Park home in company with the Curzons, Ettie Desborough, and others, on Tuesday 14 June Churchill returned to Westminster to paint a relatively bright picture of the Middle East to the House of Commons. Skilfully, he began by stressing that Mesopotamia and Palestine were obligations inherited from the defeat of the Ottoman Turks. Whatever the challenges, they could not be abandoned. 'We cannot,' he said, 'leave the Jews in Palestine to be maltreated by the Arabs ... nor can we leave the great and historic city of Baghdad and other cities and towns in Mesopotamia to be pillaged by the wild Bedouin of the desert.' It was Britain's duty to succeed, and the key to that was to reduce expenditures to within reasonable and practicable limits. This solemn overture was followed by a lengthy account of the impressive troop and budgetary reductions he had been able to force through, thanks largely to decisions at Cairo. Even as he spoke, he told the House, Faisal was on his way from Mecca to Baghdad, and although popular opinion would have to be taken into account, he was clearly the most suitable candidate for the throne.

Then Churchill turned to Palestine. Here, he admitted, the problem was 'more acute', and he made no effort to disguise the contentious issue of Jewish immigration and the Arab response. But he strongly defended the principles of the Balfour Declaration, again painted a glowing picture of what he had witnessed at Rishon-le-Zion, and reiterated his strong belief that Jewish immigration would benefit *all* the inhabitants of Palestine. In Transjordan, he said, the arrangements he had made personally with Abdullah in Jerusalem had all been successful. Finally, like the masterful orator he was, he concluded by returning to where he had begun – the collapse of Ottoman rule and the chaotic legacy this had left. 'All [our] efforts will be frustrated and brought to naught,' he pronounced, 'unless we can combine them with a peaceful and lasting settlement with Turkey.'[20]

It was a tour de force. It presented him as the man who had brought order out of chaos, saved millions of pounds of taxpayers' money, and established the foundations of a solid peace in the Middle East. Simultaneously, however, he distanced himself sufficiently far from events to ensure that any failures could plausibly be blamed on a situation that he had inherited, not created. More importantly, it offered him a get-out clause. Only a few days before, he and other Cabinet ministers had met at Chequers for a brainstorming session on the Middle East where Lloyd George had suggested offering both Palestine and Mesopotamia to the United States. Over lunch, Churchill had discussed this idea privately with Curzon. Afterwards, he told Lloyd George that he was 'much taken' with the idea and would like to announce it in his forthcoming speech. But Lloyd George dropped the idea almost as quickly as he had floated it, and that was the end of it. Clearly, Churchill did not consider either Palestine or Iraq as vital to Britain's security, nor was he personally committed to the settlement he had overseen. Two weeks beforehand, he had unbur-dened himself over the issue during lunch with Thomas Marlowe, the editor of the *Daily Mail*. 'So far as he is concerned they are inheritances,' Marlowe noted. 'He did not initiate any of the liabilities there ... Mesopotamia and Palestine are twin babies in his care but he is not the father.' Churchill also told Lloyd George privately that in Mesopotamia 'We live on a precarious basis in this wild land filled with a proud and impecunious chief [*sic*] & extremely peppery well armed politicians.'[21]

More significant in the long term was the problem he turned to in his concluding words – Turkey. Here, the nationalist government of Kemal

Ataturk was engaged in a bitter war with the Greeks and had yet to sign a peace treaty with the Allies. It was also the issue on which he was at constant loggerheads with the prime minister, a fervent supporter of the Greeks. The entire Middle East settlement, Churchill told the House, depended in the last resort on a peaceful and lasting settlement with Turkey, which, if it chose, could stir up Arab unrest throughout the region.

The speech proved a personal triumph. The Conservative leader Austen Chamberlain believed that it had changed the whole atmosphere of the House of Commons on the Middle East question. Curzon commented on its 'brilliancy [sic] and success'. Even Lloyd George, the target of Churchill's concluding comments, felt bound to congratulate him. 'Your Mesopotamian performance was one of your very best. Hearty congratulations on its conspicuous success,' he wrote. Predictably, Churchill's old nemesis, the *Daily Herald*, poured scorn on what it scathingly denounced as his 'oriental visions of squandermania'. But *The Times* applauded his speech as the most interesting of the parliamentary session. 'He has lost none of his old skill,' it commented. The veteran journalist Herbert Sidebotham, a long-time observer and commentator on his parliamentary performances, wrote that he had never known the House more interested in any speech, 'or a speaker more easy and confident in his power'.

Yet the most fulsome praise came from a Conservative backbencher who had entered the House just three years previously. Neville Chamberlain shared the ambivalent view of Churchill held by many of his fellow MPs. 'I never quite know whether most to admire his great gifts,' he confessed privately, 'or to be alarmed at his impulsiveness and hasty judgement.' But after listening to his panoramic survey of the Middle East, the later architect of appeasement dethroned by Churchill as prime minister in 1940, lauded him with unstinting praise. 'Winston's speech on Mesopotamia was a brilliant performance,' he told his sister. 'He kept the House amused and interested for 90 minutes interspersing arguments and policy with anecdote and description and exercising great art in delivery.' And, he added, 'his speeches are worth ten of [Lloyd George's] as he takes so much more trouble on them'.[22]

SUMMER

ELEVEN

'WHERE ARE WE GOING IN EUROPE?'

I reland was burning, the miners were striking, and the dole queues
lengthening. But the annual rituals of Ascot, Wimbledon, and Test
Match cricket against Australia were played out as usual. With the
burial of the Unknown Soldier in Westminster Abbey, the 'great silence'
of collective grief was finally ending. Churchill had already experienced
the Riviera's return to its usual pleasure-seeking routine. Now it was
London's turn to embrace renewal. Nothing better symbolized this celebration than the first Anglo-American Polo Test Match to take place
since before the war. Held at Hurlingham Park, the 'spiritual home' of
polo in Fulham in south-west London, it was another symbol of the
intensifying sense of transatlantic friendship so firmly embraced by
Churchill in his address to the English-Speaking Union. The captain of
the American team was an Oxford Blue.

On a Saturday afternoon shortly after his Commons speech on the
Middle East, he and Clementine joined hundreds of enthusiastic spectators including a generous sprinkling of dukes, duchesses and other ranks
of the nobility to enjoy the first of the two matches. It was also a grand
royal occasion. The first of the Windsors to arrive was the Prince of
Wales, followed shortly afterwards by Queen Alexandra, his grandmother and widow of King Edward VII, as well as several of the royal
princesses. Then at three o'clock, in blazing sunshine and greeted by the
massed bands of the Brigade of Guards, the King and Queen arrived in
their luxurious open carriage drawn by two bay horses. The King wore a

silk hat and dark frock coat, while the Queen was dressed in a gown of hyacinth blue satin covered by a heavily beaded black and silver cloak and sporting a double necklace of pearls. Joining them in the Royal Box were the Duke of York – the future King George VI – and the Duke of Connaught, the elderly third son of Queen Victoria and Prince Albert, who as a young army officer based in Montreal had helped repel a Fenian raid from across the border with Vermont. Making it clear that such hostile episodes were firmly interred in the past, that Anglo-American friendship was now the name of the game, and that the Canadian-American border was friendly and open, the American ambassador and his wife sat comfortably next to royalty in the Royal Box.[1]

Accompanying the Churchills were Philip Sassoon as well as the ubiquitous Freddie Guest, who regularly helped organize the annual Commons versus Lords polo match. Since his Sandhurst days, horses had engaged some of Churchill's deepest passions. He had emptied his pockets hiring horses from nearby livery stables for point-to-point races and steeplechases. Gazetted at age twenty to the Fourth Hussars, a cavalry regiment, he had spent hours in the riding school and stables. He loved the glittering jingle of the cavalry squadron manoeuvring at the trot. Famously, he had taken part in the 400-horse cavalry charge of British troops at the Battle of Omdurman in Sudan in 1898 and seen more than twenty of his comrades killed.

'Never, never, give up' was one of life's lessons he had learned on the barracks square. 'Many a time,' he writes in *My Early Life*, 'did I pick myself up shaken and sore from the riding school tan [track] . . . and with what appearance of dignity I could command, while twenty recruits grinned furtively but delightedly to see their Officer suffering the same misfortunes which it was their lot so frequently to undergo.'[2] It is hard here not see a metaphor for his entire political career – and perhaps it consciously was, as he wrote these words well after his misfortune and recovery from the Dardanelles.

Risk and danger were his aphrodisiacs. Only the year before, when he was not busy painting, he had spent hours breathlessly chasing wild boar on horseback through the vast estate in south-west France belonging to his friend Bendor. But it was polo that really captivated him. Since leaving the army he had been a regular player, including at Hurlingham. In India, so he recalled with self-mocking irony, this was the only serious purpose of being a subaltern. On arrival at Bangalore, he and his fellow junior officers had purchased ponies to form a regimental team; a mere six weeks later it broke records by winning one of India's most prestigious tournaments. In his memoir he describes a typical day under the blistering sun at the garrison. On parade at six in the morning, an hour and a half practising manoeuvres, then breakfast, cleaning out the stables, and long before eleven the officers retire to their bungalows to sleep until emerging at five o'clock as the shadows began to lengthen. 'Now,' he writes, 'the station begins to live again. It is the hour of Polo. It is the hour for which we have been living all day long.' But his own playing days were almost over; he was to enjoy his last match six years later at age fifty-two. Yet his youthful passion remained alive and well. To share it, for the second match against the Americans he brought along his friends General Smuts, Hazel Lavery, and Lady Diana Cooper. England lost both matches. But the game was the thing. 'Polo,' he later pronounced, 'is the prince of games.'

After the first match at Hurlingham there was tea on the lawn. But the Churchills couldn't linger over the cucumber sandwiches. That evening, they drove into Kent to spend the weekend with Winston's wartime friend, Edward Spears.[3]

*

By now, the acerbic Spears had made a sufficient number of enemies in high places to have been forced to resign his position in Paris and settle in England. But Churchill still considered him a first-rate source of intelligence about Russian and Bolshevik affairs and remained convinced that Lenin could still be toppled. Just as he had arrived in Cairo, the Bolsheviks had gathered for their Tenth Party Congress in Moscow. It should have been a cause of celebration. Instead, the economy was stricken by famine, strikes, and peasant revolts. 25 million people were close to starvation. Well over a million – possibly two – had fled abroad. In the region of

Tambov 300 miles south-east of Moscow, a 70,000-strong peasant army was in open rebellion. In Petrograd, workers went on strike and demanded free elections and the end of Bolshevik dictatorship. Eddie Marsh, who was taking care of 'Archie's work' during his absence in Cairo, cabled Churchill with even more dramatic news. Sailors at the huge Russian naval base on the fortress island of Kronstadt that guarded the entrance to Petrograd had once formed the shock troops of the Revolution. But now they had joined the strikers, burned their Party membership cards, and denounced the 'Communist usurpers' and the Cheka. Lenin ordered Trotsky to crush the revolt. After twenty-four hours of bloody fighting, Red Army troops captured the fortress at the cost of nearly 10,000 men. Many of the rebels escaped across the ice to Finland. But some 15,000 were captured, to face either immediate execution or a lifetime in the prison camps now multiplying across the Soviet utopia.[4]

To Churchill, this justified all his fierce loathing for Lenin's regime and confirmed his long-aired predictions about the tyrannical path the Bolsheviks would inevitably take. But it also gave him some hope that dissent might still be ignited against the Reds. So he was making sure to keep in touch with the plotting of anti-Soviet forces. Here, the role of Spears was crucial. From Paris, Boris Savinkov was pushing grandiose plans to open up Poland, the Ukraine, and Rumania to Western capital. Spears was ambitious, keen to enter the world of business, and eager to make a fortune. So he had strenuously cultivated his links with Savinkov and was collaborating in a number of his schemes. Churchill was also in touch with another shadowy player in the anti-Soviet game: Sidney Reilly, the legendary and unpredictable 'Ace of Spies', who had only just escaped with his life after spying for the SIS in Moscow. Since then he had been travelling constantly between Moscow and Paris reporting on the plans of Savinkov and other White Russian activists, as well as campaigning for more positive action against the Bolshevik regime, which he denounced as 'the worst form of autocratic tyranny in history'. After meeting him in Paris, Churchill recognized a kindred soul and they had kept in regular touch by letter or phone, using Archie Sinclair as a go-between. Both Spears and Reilly were valuable as links to Savinkov's plans for an anti-Bolshevik uprising, and each was in touch with Sir Mansfield Cumming, the SIS boss.[5]

The Spears were renting Ightham Mote, a half-timbered fourteenth-century moated manor house hidden deep in the Kentish countryside. Spears' wife was the American novelist Mary ('May') Borden, the daughter of a Chicago millionaire and a former lover of the avant-garde artist and poet, Percy Wyndham Lewis. Quick-witted and intelligent, and with large and expressive grey-green eyes, she was a divorcee and former suffragette who had spent time in a police cell after smashing windows during a demonstration in Parliament Square. Clementine disliked many of her husband's male friends, and at first Spears found her difficult. But the ice was broken by a hearty game of tennis and the hosts' customary charm and hospitality. For Churchill, who was godfather to the Spears' young son, there was the typical pleasure of painting. The canvas he produced shows the ancient lattice-windowed house with its shimmering reflections in the surrounding water.

Spears also knew Churchill well enough to have invited a guest for Sunday lunch as lively conversational foil. The local clergyman proved well up to the challenge as Churchill peppered him good-naturedly with questions such as 'Should the clergy be patriotic?' and by provocative declarations like 'Jesus Christ would not have taken sides in this war.' When he tired of the verbal sparring, Mary Borden, who was herself a lively and accomplished conversationalist, fascinated him with stories about her mobile field hospital in wartime France. All in all, the weekend was a success in cementing further the personal bond linking Churchill to the leading conspirators against Lenin's regime.[6]

*

The weekend with Spears may well have stimulated a more domestic project. Churchill was still yearning for his own home in the country, and he and Clementine had been searching for properties ever since his Garron Towers inheritance came through. Shortly after visiting Ightham Mote, he went to view 'Peelings', a seventeenth-century house with an adjoining estate on the East Sussex coast owned by the Duke of

Devonshire. But Clementine worried about her husband's grandiose visions of running a farm as well as a large family home. Why risk their new-found fortune on a venture where they had no experience? she asked in exasperation. What with his political career, painting for leisure, and polo for excitement and danger, what need did he have for more? She, too, longed for a country house. But she wanted it to be a rest and a joy, not a fresh preoccupation. 'I want to lie in the sun & blink & wake up now & then to eat a mouse caught by someone else & drink a little cream & doze off again,' wrote 'the Cat'.[7]

In fact, she was already doing plenty of dozing and eating, enjoying the lazy days of early summer. With the older children still at school, she and Goonie were guests of the Horners at 'Menabilly', a large old house on the Cornish coast that her friends had rented for the summer. Neglected but endowed with lush sub-tropical gardens and a huge kitchen garden with buttressed walls, its lethargic atmosphere entranced her as a place that time seemed to have forgotten. A decade later it was to be fictionalized by the novelist Daphne du Maurier as 'Manderley', the home of the villainous Maxim de Winter and his sinister housekeeper, Mrs Danvers, in her best-selling novel, *Rebecca*.

Clementine's appeal to her husband may have had some effect. Within days 'Peelings' was forgotten and he was enthusing about another property he had just seen. This one was in Kent; perhaps he had been drawn to the attractions of the county by his stay with Spears. It was called Chartwell Manor and lay about twenty-five miles south-east of London. It enjoyed commanding views over the Weald of Kent and on its southern side featured a small lake fed by a natural spring – the Chart Well. By this time Clementine had left Cornwall to join a tennis party at nearby 'Fairlawne', another country house owned by an old friend and future Member of Parliament, Victor Cazalet. At Winston's urging, she went over to view Chartwell herself. She was enthusiastic. 'I can think of nothing but that heavenly tree-crowned Hill – It is like a view from an aeroplane being up there,' she told him. 'I do hope we shall get it – If we do I feel we shall live there a great deal & be very, very, happy.' This would be especially so if they could immediately build a new wing for Jack,

Goonie, and their children. However, on second thoughts and after a further viewing she turned against it as requiring extensive modernizations and additions beyond their financial means. But her husband had set his heart on it. A year later, without consulting her, he bought it.[8]

*

Busy though the domestic scene was, politically the summer was even more demanding. The Imperial Conference opened in London on Monday 20 June and lasted six weeks until early August. The word 'conference' is misleading. In reality it consisted of a series of closed meetings at 10 Downing Street between Lloyd George and British ministers and officials on the one hand, and the Dominion prime ministers on the other: William ('Billy') Hughes of Australia; Arthur Meighen of Canada; William Massey of New Zealand; Jan Christian Smuts of South Africa; and, representing India in a somewhat anomalous position, V. S. Srinivasa Sastri, a member of the Council of State of India. Interspersed were several meetings of the Imperial Defence Committee for a discussion of major strategic issues.

As Colonial Secretary, Churchill might have been expected to act as *major domo*. But Lloyd George was determined to set the course for Britain's place in the post-war world himself and chaired all the sessions. Churchill added this to his growing list of grievances against his old rival. Lloyd George, he complained to the *Daily Mail*'s editor Thomas Marlowe over lunch one day, was stealing the limelight. He was, so Marlowe told his newspaper's owner Lord Northcliffe afterwards, 'very sore' about it.[9] Once again, it was painfully evident which of the 'terrible twins' was the senior partner. To the man who had donated Chequers to the nation and was now First Lord of the Admiralty, Lord Lee of Fareham had plenty of time to observe the two rivals duelling verbally at Cabinet meetings. 'L.G.'s domination of the Cabinet is complete and wonderful,' he told his wife. 'Winston, who talks a great deal, and usually in a stimulating and interesting way, is the only Minister who even tries to measure swords with him.' But, he added, 'if it comes to a serious contest L. G. never has any difficulty downing him in argument'.[10]

Churchill's feelings were understandable. The Colonial Office with its global reach sounded very grand. By drawing Mesopotamia and Palestine into its orbit he had put it firmly in the headlines. But the Dominions essentially now ran themselves, and looking after British colonies in Africa, the West Indies, South-East Asia and the Far East was mostly run-of-the-mill business and tediously mundane: currency problems in East Africa, postage rates in the Crown colonies, citrus fruit production in Jamaica, and so on. He happily delegated most of these issues to his subordinates.

One episode, however, brought him credit from an unexpected source, and has been curiously neglected by previous biographers. One of the first parliamentary questions he faced as Colonial Secretary was about child slavery in Hong Kong. *Mui-tsai* – the Cantonese for 'little sister' – were young Chinese girls sold by the poor, who could not afford to keep them, as bonded domestic servants to wealthier families. It was a long-established cultural practice also to be found in Malaya and Singapore. But it had been roundly denounced as child slavery by Western missionaries and organizations such as the Anti-Slavery Society, and frequently came accompanied by lurid allegations of sexual abuse and prostitution. As a result, the *Mui-tsai* system had come under hostile press and parliamentary scrutiny as 'a disgrace and scandal under the British flag'.

Churchill's predecessor Lord Milner had done little about it, thanks largely to resistance from the Governor of Hong Kong and Colonial Office officials who argued that it was an essentially philanthropic cultural tradition that helped the poor provide for their children. At first, Churchill was inclined not to cause trouble in the colony by pressing the issue. But when public criticism intensified and publicly defending child slavery became an embarrassment, he abruptly changed tack and told his officials that he was not prepared to go on defending it. When the Governor protested that abolishing the system would cause ructions in the island colony, he instantly snapped back. 'I do not care a rap what the local consequences are,' he wrote. 'You had better make it clear that [freedom for the *Mui-tsai*] must be real.' Later he followed this up with a telegram curtly instructing the Governor to issue a proclamation declaring that the system would no longer be recognized in the colony. His decision made him friends in unfamiliar places. The *Manchester Guardian*, a frequent critic, applauded his decisive action as 'handsome and sensible', and congratulated him for having 'cut through all sophisticated official defences by which this piece of humanity has been resisted so long by the bureaucrats'. The issue had by now also become something of a feminist cause, and Lady Gladstone of the Anti-Slavery Society, the *doyenne* of humanitarian lobbyists with numerous friends in high places, declared that Churchill's name 'would go down to history for this in glory'.[11]

*

Nonetheless, he regarded such incursions into distant Imperial affairs as inferior to most Foreign Office business and continued to speak his mind on its activities whenever the mood took him. This was much to the annoyance of Curzon. Already this year, the Foreign Secretary had complained that Churchill seemed to be behaving like some sort of 'Asiatic Secretary'. The sinner was happy to compound the offence. A week before the Imperial Conference opened, he travelled to Manchester, the heartland of Britain's cotton manufacturing industry, where he had held his first seat as a Liberal in the Commons. Here, at a luncheon for the city's Chamber of Commerce, he painted a vivid panorama of the post-war world coloured by the extremes of violence and peace, prosperity and poverty, despair and hope. Ireland was teetering on the brink. International trade held the key to prosperity but was stalled by mountains of debt and unrealistic demands on Germany for reparations that it couldn't pay. As for Russia, under Lenin it was a case study in folly. 'Probably seven or eight million have lost their lives, and many more have had their lives ruined in order to teach Monsieur Lenin the rudiments of political economy,' he mocked. Things would only get worse for Russians. But at least other nations would be saved by her example. The lesson, he assured his audience, was written in glaring letters – 'the utter failure of this Socialistic and Communistic theory, and the ruins which it brings to those subjected to its cruel yoke'.[12]

But it was potential failure closer to home a mere twenty miles across the English Channel that truly worried him most. 'Where are we going in

Europe?' he demanded. 'Has the Great War brought us the assurance of a lasting peace? Can we be quite sure that our children will not be exposed to a repetition of the horrors through which we have, with difficulty, lived?' Talk of peace was all very well, he went on, but it was no good trusting in 'a paper League of Nations'. Peace had to have the backing of the Great Powers. The only real way to prevent another terrible war was to establish a solid settlement between Britain, France, and Germany. His audience hardly needed to be reminded that since the Peace Conference there had been endless disputes about German reparation payments, and that in March Allied troops had marched into the Ruhr cities of Dusseldorf and Duisburg over defaults on payments.

Recent headlines had also shone an alarming spotlight on violence in Upper Silesia, a significant region of Germany awarded to Poland by the Paris peacemakers. Its loss was dire for the Germans as it produced a quarter of the country's coal and was rich in iron and steel mills; at least a third of its population was German-speaking. After powerful protests, the Allied victors decided to hold a plebiscite allowing inhabitants to decide of which nation they wished to be citizens. In the months leading up to it violent Polish resistance broke out, especially after former German residents were granted the vote and began flooding back to the region in their tens of thousands. In March, four battalions of British troops had been rushed in to restore order amidst widespread intimida-tion, assaults, and raids from across the Polish border. In the ballot, the Germans obtained a large majority, but much of the coal-producing area opted for Poland. How precisely to divide the region in light of the results provoked yet more violence. By the time Churchill was speaking to his Manchester audience, the Upper Silesia question had flared into a broader argument pitting Germany on one side and Poland and France on the other. As well, fighting between German and Polish paramilitary forces had seriously escalated. The dispute seemed to be threatening peace in Europe itself. 'If the Treaty [of Versailles] can be reduced to waste in one quarter,' thundered *The Times*, 'it will soon become pulp in others.' Anglo-French relations in particular seemed threatened. Just days before Churchill spoke, British troops had once again been in action.

A sergeant from the Black Watch who was shot 'by unknown outlaws' was buried with full military honours. 'Allies Floundering in Silesia' warned *The Times*.[13]

Combined with Anglo-French disputes over Syria and the Middle East, traditional anti-French feeling was mounting in Britain. But this was dangerous, argued Churchill. People had to be fair to France, and understand the anxieties its people felt about the ex-enemy nation of some 70 million just across its border compared to their own more modest 40 million. 'We must,' he declared, 'understand their point of view.' In pursuing post-war reconstruction, it was for Britain to help navigate the rancour between these two European nations. 'Let that be the part of Britain,' he exhorted, 'to mitigate the dangerous poisons still rife in Europe, and to consolidate the world upon the basis of the victory which our lads have won.'[14]

He may well have concluded on his customary upbeat and patriotic note – this, after all, was a speech delivered to natural-born Liberal businessmen in a county that had sent tens of thousands of 'lads' off to war. But his reference to 'dangerous poisons still rife in Europe' offered a necessary and timely caution about radical nationalist trends across the English Channel. His words proved remarkably prescient. 'You may be sure,' he warned his listeners, 'that deep in the heart of Germany, certainly in their universities and in those powerful forces dethroned by the war, there must be lurking ideas dangerous to the peace of Europe.' Criticisms that Churchill lacked judgement were then, as they remain today, commonplace. Yet he also possessed a much rarer and more valuable quality: that of insight. As history was to show, German universities did indeed nurture strongly nationalist sentiments, and some of them capitulated easily to the Nazis and their ideology. Meanwhile, 'dethroned' by the war, elements within the German armed forces and elsewhere were busily doing their best to destroy the Weimar Republic. Only weeks after Churchill's Manchester speech, an embittered ex-corporal from Austria named Adolf Hitler, who had also fought on the Western Front, was elected as sole leader – 'Fuhrer' – of the radically nationalist and anti-Semitic party in Munich known as the National Socialist German Workers Party, or NSDAP – the Nazis.[15]

*

Lloyd George formally opened the Imperial Conference in 10 Downing Street at noon on Monday 20 June. Evoking the unity that the Empire had displayed during the Peace Conference, he stressed the need to uphold the treaties they had all signed and pronounced friendship with the United States 'a cardinal principle' for the future – especially if agreement could be reached on naval armaments. 'We cannot forget,' he said, evoking his most bullish patriotic sentiments, 'that the very life of the United Kingdom, as also of Australia and New Zealand, indeed the whole Empire, has been built up on sea power – and that sea power is necessarily the basis for the whole Empire's existence.' His final remarks acknowledged changes in the nature of the Empire created by the war. Four blood-soaked years had fuelled growing demands for independence from what was still frequently described in the white Dominions as 'the Mother Country'. If Australian and New Zealand boys could die in their thousands at Gallipoli, and Canadians at Vimy Ridge, then it was clear that any future commitments to fight should be the result of decisions made in Canberra, Wellington, or Ottawa, not in London. At Paris, each Dominion had been granted its own delegation. Lloyd George acknowledged the new reality. 'There was a time when Downing Street controlled the Empire,' he declared. 'Today the Empire is in charge of Downing Street.' This was inflated rhetoric. Forging a new constitutional relationship between the Dominions and London that would balance their growing sense of autonomy while maintaining the integrity of the British Empire proved too complex and controversial to deal with, and the issue was shelved until a later conference.

But for now, the warm glow of victory and wartime comradeship smoothed the path of co-operation, helped by the common British heritage shared by those sitting around the Downing Street table. Billy Hughes, the Australian prime minister, a dozen years older than Churchill, had been born in Pimlico, less than a mile away from Downing Street; New Zealand's William Massey came from Londonderry; and while Arthur Meighen of Canada had been born in Ontario, his paternal grandfather had come from the same Ulster city as Massey; while his mother, who had travelled with him from Canada, was visiting her family relatives in Scotland and Ireland. Meighen was the youngest of the Dominion prime ministers at the conference, a 'debutante among a tribe of dowagers'.[16]

Churchill was one of the only four British Cabinet members sitting round the Downing Street table to hear Lloyd George's opening remarks. The next day he formally delivered his own *tour d'horizon* by reporting on the Crown Colonies and other territories administered by the Colonial Office. It was a subject he had already covered the week before in a speech that pre-empted much of what Lloyd George had just said. At a dinner in the House of Commons given by the Empire Development Parliamentary Committee to welcome the delegates, he promised they could look forward to the British Empire's future as 'a super-unit', one that would deal with 'our cousins and brothers in the United States on terms of amity and equal friendship'. That was the dream, he suggested, one that would secure the peace and safety of 'all who spoke the English tongue'. The route was through increasing inter-Imperial trade and improving and extending communications by air and sea. Not least, he told them, 'we must spread our valiant manhood over the British Empire, we must spread our soldiers and citizens as numerously as possible in the great Dominions of the Crown and in that way facilitate the steady growth of inter-Imperial sentiment and common interest'. His comments on India came almost as an after-thought. 'Not yet a Dominion,' he acknowledged, it was heading in that direction thanks to the reforms being introduced by the Secretary of State for India, Edwin Montagu; eventually, Churchill promised, it would join the others as a powerful partner.[17]

TWELVE

IMPERIAL DREAMS

Aweek after presenting his survey of Colonial Office affairs to the Dominion prime ministers, Churchill hosted a dinner at his home. In addition to some family and close friends – Clementine, brother Jack, Eddie Marsh, John and Hazel Lavery – it embodied the Imperial Conference in miniature: Lloyd George with his wife Margaret; Sir Thomas Smartt, the South African Minister of Agriculture, and his daughter; Sir James Allen, wartime acting prime minister of New Zealand who had once tangled with Churchill over developing a national naval force separate from the Royal Navy; sitting beside his wife, he was now his country's High Commissioner in London. Also at the table with his wife was Lord Byng of Vimy, the British general who had overseen the withdrawal of Allied troops from Gallipoli and as Commander of the Canadian Corps led Canadian forces to their famous victory at Vimy Ridge in April 1917; he was now awaiting his final confirmation as the new Governor-General of Canada. Two single women also graced the table. Lady Sybil Grey was the second daughter of Earl Grey and had turned her home at Howick Hall in Northumberland into a wartime hospital before establishing an Anglo-Russian hospital in St Petersburg's Dmitri Palace; she still carried the scar of a shrapnel wound from standing too close to a grenade practice at Minsk. Representing Australia was Lady Coghlan, daughter of the New South Wales agent-general in London, who had thrown her wartime energies into providing humanitarian relief to Serbia.[1]

The principal guests of honour, however, were the Canadian prime minister Arthur Meighen and his wife, Isabel. The product of small-town rural Ontario, Meighen disliked social events, and his wife was there to help with the exhausting round of pomp and ceremony surrounding the conference: a state dinner and ball at Buckingham Palace; luncheons with the Prince of Wales and the Duke of Connaught; and his own swearing in as an Imperial Privy Counsellor at Buckingham Palace. He was awarded the Freedom of the City of London, and he and Isabel journeyed north to Scotland where he was granted the Freedom of Edinburgh, both of them elaborate civic affairs involving numerous speeches and formal meals. One evening he also attended a party at Cliveden House, the mansion on the Thames occupied by Lady Astor, the first female Member of Parliament to take her seat in the House of Commons. The Virginian-born Astor had assembled a glittering array of guests to meet him. One of them was the sculptress Lady Kennet, widow of the polar explorer Robert Falcon Scott – 'Scott of the Antarctic' – who boasted how she had enjoyed his company. 'Ridiculously young and so alive,' she enthused. 'I danced with him with a crowd looking on and I didn't care a blow ... He is an adorable one.'[2]

Meighen was just five months older than Churchill and had celebrated his forty-seventh birthday the week before. His transatlantic exchanges with the Colonial Secretary over who should become the new governor-general had produced some testy moments as he tried to pin him down on candidates during his lengthy absence in the Middle East. Byng had only emerged as a contender at the very last moment. In addition, Meighen shared the general suspicion of Churchill allegedly widespread in the Dominions – or so *The Times* had recently claimed – as 'autocratic, restless, [and] immensely ambitious'. Some of this wariness sprang from the Gallipoli legacy. It was difficult for Churchill to shake this off. John, the son of Sir James and Lady Allen, had died fighting there, and privately the New Zealand High Commissioner considered the expedition still being vigorously defended by his dinner host as 'ill-conceived and mad'.[3]

Churchill did his best to soothe any fears Meighen harboured about the depth of his commitment to the Dominions. Three days before the dinner, he told an audience including the Prince of Wales that he would bend all his energies to improving Canadian trade with the West Indies. 'Canada,' he said, 'was not complete commercially or geographically unless she was associated with the tropical islands of the West Indies.' But this was not the real reason he was so keen to court Canada's prime minister.[4]

*

The major issue confronting the conference was the future of the Anglo-Japanese Alliance. Signed in 1902, it saw each of the two powers agree to remain neutral in any war fought by the other, and it was now up for renewal. But Washington was deeply suspicious of Japan's Pacific ambitions and hostile to the treaty's extension. Meighen was opposed to anything that could damage good relations with Canada's giant southern neighbour. 'Every possible effort,' he told Lloyd George long before showing up in London, 'should be made to find some alternative policy to renewal.' Churchill's view was similar, and in Meighen he found a powerful ally. The best way forward would be through a multilateral conference of all those involved, including Japan. This way, he believed, naval armaments could be limited and a dangerous crisis over the Pacific averted.

His desire to keep in good standing with Washington was inspired by more than his benevolent feelings for the 'English-Speaking World'. As graphically illustrated in the New Year sing-along with Lloyd George at Lympne, he was profoundly worried about the challenge posed by the United States Navy to Britannia's traditional ruling of the waves. But nor did he wish to alienate the Japanese, who themselves possessed a powerful navy. In May, the twenty-year-old Crown Prince Hirohito had paid a lengthy visit to Britain as part of a charm offensive aimed at renewing the alliance. Shortly before hosting Meighen, Churchill received Baron Gonsuke Hayashi, Japan's ambassador in London, who sounded him out about the future of the alliance. Churchill courteously told Hayashi that he hoped some 'great international instrument' could be drawn up that would ensure peace for all parties in the Pacific for the next twenty or thirty years, but explained that Britain's most important object was to avoid a naval rivalry with the United States. Subject to that, he assured the ambassador, he was 'a well-wisher of Japan'. He had studiously made no reference to renewing the alliance. The dinner at his home was a signal that he and Meighen were of one mind on the issue.[5]

On Friday 1 July, Dominion Day, Curzon formally introduced the topic of the Anglo-Japanese Alliance to the assembled prime ministers in Downing Street and argued for its renewal following suitable consultations with China and the United States. Lloyd George, Australia's William Hughes, and New Zealand's William Massey all agreed. But Meighen bluntly rejected the idea because of its negative effects on relations between the United States and the Empire. If war ever broke out between them, he said, 'Canada would be the Belgium of the conflict'. Instead, the best way forward would be through a conference with the United States and Japan to discuss the whole issue of naval rearmament in the Pacific. Churchill clearly had a reliable ally in Canada.

*

By the time the Canadian prime minister spoke, however, Churchill was overwhelmed by the business of planning his mother's funeral. While Lloyd George and the Dominions debated whether or not to bury the Anglo-Japanese Alliance, he was laying his mother to rest in the church-yard at Bladon. Yet within hours of returning to London he was back at his desk furiously catching up with his files. He had already missed one crucial meeting of the conference. Determined to have his opinions heard, he dictated a lengthy memorandum for his Cabinet colleagues. It was Monday 4 July – American Independence Day – when they gathered round the table at 10 Downing Street to encounter his powerful verbal barrage aimed against renewal of the alliance. Its only value to Tokyo, he argued, could be as a support, open or veiled, against the United States. Pressure for a 'Big Navy' would grow irresistibly in America, sparking a naval race that would broaden into a larger antagonism. 'We went through all this with Germany in the years before the war,' he warned. 'What a ghastly disaster it would be if such a process began between Great Britain and the United States.'

His obsession with US naval power was neither new nor unfounded. American admirals made no secret of their traditional jealousies of the Royal Navy. Since the end of the war the United States had built more warships than the rest of the world put together. 'Don't let the British pull the wool over your eyes,' the American Chief of Naval Operations had instructed Admiral Sims when sending him to London to co-ordinate wartime plans with the British Admiralty. 'It's none of our business pulling their chestnuts out of the fire. We would as soon fight the British as the Germans.' In Washington such hostile attitudes still simmered below the surface. Churchill, with his close interest in American affairs, was more aware of them than many of his other colleagues, and it made him even more determined to strengthen the London–Washington axis. Significantly, the Cabinet colleague closest to him on this subject was Lord Lee of Fareham. 'The political relations of Britain and America,' the donor of Chequers told the Cabinet, '[are] of transcendent importance [and outweigh] in every way those with other powers or any combination of powers.'[6]

Churchill's heavy guns provoked angry counter-fire. Curzon was outraged. Relations between the two men were always rocky. Curzon had been a strong ally over Gallipoli and had recently welcomed Churchill and Clementine along with Ettie Desborough and Adele Essex to his grand Palladian home, Hackwood House in Hampshire, for the Whitsun holiday weekend. To Churchill the visit evoked vivid memories of happier pre-war times between the two of them, and he suggested that perhaps they could revert to their former habit of addressing each other in official correspondence as 'Dear Winston' and 'Dear George'. When Churchill's mother died, Curzon wrote him a deeply felt and genuine letter of sympathy. Yet their private cordiality was accompanied by deepening political animosity. Over Egypt, where Churchill was adamantly opposed to the slightest concession to nationalist feeling, they had repeatedly clashed in Cabinet and Curzon bitterly described him as 'difficult and insolent'.[7]

This time he furiously scribbled a note and pushed it in front of Lloyd George. 'It seems to me entirely wrong that the Colonial Secretary should on an occasion like this air his Independent views on an F.O. question. I would not presume on a Colonial Office question, either to intervene at all or to take a line independent of the C.O. [Colonial Office].' 'I quite agree,' wrote Lloyd George back, 'I have done my best to stop his fizzing ... It is intolerable.' Austen Chamberlain pitched in with his own contribution to this bizarre game of pass-the-note. 'I think you are right to show Winston that you profoundly resent his constant and persistent interference,' he scrawled to Curzon. 'It goes far beyond anything that I at least have ever known in Cabinet even from the most important member of a Government.' Encouraged by this show of solidarity, Curzon pushed a missive of his own directly towards Churchill.' 'My dear Winston,' he addressed him in the manner so recently agreed upon, 'I wonder what you would say if on a Colonial Office [question] I felt myself at liberty to make a speech at this Conference – quite independent of the Colonial Office and critical of the attitude adopted by its chief.' Unrepentant, Churchill fired back. 'You may say anything you like about the Colonial Office that is sincerely meant,' he replied. 'But there is no comparison between these vital foreign matters [which] affect the whole future of the world and the mere departmental topics with [which] the Colonial Office is concerned. In these matters we must be allowed to have opinions!' That nicely summed up his real opinion about his job as Colonial Secretary – distinctly inferior to Curzon's and responsible for 'merely departmental' topics. It was typical, too, of Churchill's habitual refusal to stay within the boundaries of his own ministerial tasks and of his determination to speak out on any issue that interested him, even if it ruffled his colleagues.

He tried Curzon's patience again three days later when the conference turned its gaze on Europe. Newspapers were once more headlining France's support for Poland in the crisis over Upper Silesia. Curzon opened the debate by dismissing any idea of giving a security guarantee to France, whose diplomacy he privately considered double-faced and untrust-worthy. Dominion leaders followed suit. Prime Minister Smuts of South Africa in particular disliked and mistrusted France. Its policy, he declared, had for centuries been the curse of Europe and with Germany 'down and out' the French were using the reparations issue as the instrument of their dominion in Europe. 'The British Commonwealth,' he said, 'must stand up to France.'[8]

Churchill took a radically different view. 'May I say a word, Prime Minister?' he began, this time giving at least a nod to Curzon's sensitivities by stating that he agreed with the Foreign Secretary's sentiments, but only wanted to 'say a word from a slightly different angle'. Predictably, the word lengthened into a short but forceful speech. It essentially re-hashed what he had already told his audience of businessmen in Manchester the month before. 'No one should doubt,' he told the Dominion prime ministers, 'the deep-rooted nature of the fear which this poor, mutilated, impoverished France has of this mighty Germany which is growing up on the other side of the Rhine.' His own hope was to achieve an 'appeasement of the fearful hatreds and antagonisms which exist in Europe'. This certainly involved reconciliation with Germany. But to allay French fears some sort of treaty had to be found that would bind the whole Empire to protect France against unprovoked aggression. If this were not done, the Franco-German struggle would be renewed. 'It is from this point of view,' he concluded, 'that I have been an advocate of our giving such a guarantee to France, even if America would not come in, though I agree,' he added, 'this is not the moment to do it.'[9]

*

But it was the Pacific that remained the greatest of concerns to the Dominions. 'Sea Power,' declared Lloyd George in his opening comments to the conference, 'is necessarily the basis of the whole Empire's existence.' One of its decisions was to have momentous consequences for the Empire – and, twenty years later, for Churchill personally.

While he had been busily presiding over the conference in Cairo, the commanders-in-chief of the China, East Indies, and Australian naval stations of the Royal Navy had gathered on board the British heavy cruiser HMS *Hawkins* anchored off the island of Penang on the west coast of the Malayan peninsula and approved the construction of a permanent new naval base on Singapore. The small island off the southern tip of Malaya, acquired from the Sultan of Johore a hundred years before by Sir Stamford

Raffles of the East India Company, had grown into one of the world's greatest transport hubs with a population of half a million. Now it was destined as well to become the Royal Navy's main base in the Pacific. The idea had first been floated by Admiral Lord Jellicoe, hero of the Battle of Jutland, who urged the need to project British power in the Far East both to counter a possible Japanese threat and to deter Australia and New Zealand from turning their backs on the Empire and looking instead for protection to the United States. A Britain impoverished by war could not afford to keep a battle fleet permanently in the Far East. But if war with Japan broke out, the Royal Navy would have time to send its fleet to Singapore, where it could dock and refuel its largest warships. At Penang, the assembled British admirals agreed that Singapore was the 'key' to British power in the Far East. As well as major docking and refuelling facilities, it would also have an advanced command headquarters and a Naval Communications and Intelligence Centre. Their proposal travelled up the chain of command to the Admiralty in London and then to the Cabinet, which approved it just as the Dominion prime ministers were assembling for the conference. It was vital to show them that Britain actually had a naval policy for the Pacific. 'It would be disastrous to the prestige of Great Britain,' pronounced Arthur Balfour, the former Conservative prime minister and Acting Chairman of the Committee of Imperial Defence, 'if she were to abandon the Pacific by omitting to take the steps necessary to permit the British fleet operating there.' The decision in principle was more important than the reality. Treasury objections meant that no construction could actually begin for at least two more years.[10]

The Singapore base finally came before the conference on the same day as the game of notes played across the Cabinet table. Briefing it was Admiral David Beatty, the First Sea Lord and former Naval Secretary when Churchill was at the Admiralty. If war with Japan broke out, he told them, the object of the British battle fleet once it was readied at Singapore would be to destroy the Japanese Navy. So just holding Singapore would deter Japan in the first place from attacking either Australia or New Zealand. 'So long as Singapore remains in British hands,' he promised, 'there is nothing to fear.' Pointed questions followed and Prime Minister

Hughes, for one, was not convinced. If it took six weeks for the British battle fleet based in home waters to reach Singapore, in the meantime what would happen? Could Australia rely on the United States for its defence? No, replied Beatty; the United States Navy would take far longer to get there – if at all. This brutally frank reply silenced Hughes and put a stop to further discussion. Construction of the base was duly approved. It would, Beatty promised, be 'impregnable'.

The decision was momentous in its implications. Actual use of the base would only be contemplated in the event of a war with Japan. Yet the Anglo-Japanese Alliance was still in force and would remain so until the Washington Conference. This frightened Lloyd George. If news about Singapore leaked out, he remarked, it 'would blow up the whole East'. Churchill agreed, and with no one dissenting he moved that to guard the secret only one copy of the minutes should be kept.[11]

He was profoundly impressed by Beatty's defence of the Singapore base. Three months later, as pressure mounted on government finances and threatened yet more political trouble for the Coalition, Lloyd George appointed a Committee of National Expenditure to recommend cutbacks on a whole range of government spending and Churchill was appointed to chair the Cabinet Committee examining the proposals for the armed forces. One of them was to abandon the Singapore base. To this, he firmly put his foot down. It was vital, he argued, 'to continue the discreet building up of the fuelling stations and of the base in Singapore which alone can enable our fleet to offer some protection to all our interests in the Pacific, including Australia and New Zealand'. In the end construction went ahead, although to appease the Treasury only with much reduced urgency spread out over time. Twenty years later Singapore was to surrender to the Japanese in what Churchill, then prime minister, was to deplore as the largest capitulation in British military history.

*

Churchill is frequently described as an imperialist, and he was – at least in his head, where dreams of the Empire's glory imprinted in his Victorian childhood inspired his writing and rhetoric until the day he died; on becoming Colonial Secretary, he had even suggested that his title might be changed to Secretary of State for Imperial Affairs. Yet his imperialism was largely rhetorical. In the real world of action, he rejected ideas of imperial federation, trade preference, and tariffs; most of these were politically 'dead ducks' anyway. Thanks to the peace settlement, the world's map was coloured in large daubs of red. But what did he actually know of it? He left India – 'the Jewel of the Empire' – in 1898, never to return, and the same went for South Africa after 1900, the last full year of Queen Victoria's reign. At age thirty-three he had made his trip to East Africa, but he never visited West Africa, or Australia, or New Zealand, or indeed any of Britain's Far East possessions about which he so frequently waxed eloquent. He visited Canada on several occasions, but invariably as an adjunct to longer and weightier visits to the United States. As for the newly acquired territories such as Mesopotamia and Palestine, events in 1921 demonstrated that far from rejoicing in their 'possession' by Britain, Churchill frequently lamented their acquisition and did his best to ensure that they cost as little as possible.[12]

Insofar as he cared deeply about the Empire, it was largely in relation to the security of Britain itself – and this crucially hinged on events just twenty miles away across the English Channel. Keeping the balance of power in Europe was historically a central plank of Britain's foreign policy, and Churchill's urgency about post-war Franco-German relations was heartfelt. Yet even here, things were changing. Heated disagreements about the Anglo-Japanese Alliance between the Dominion prime ministers rapidly cooled down after back-channel talks prompted an invitation from President Warren G. Harding to Washington later in the year to discuss arms and security in the Pacific. Meeting at Chequers on Sunday 10 July, the Dominion prime ministers immediately and unanimously accepted the offer with relief. It was good news for Lloyd George, too, coming as it did just twenty-four hours before the Irish truce came into effect.[13]

Churchill embraced the idea of the Washington Conference with enthusiasm. 'Properly and wisely handled,' he told his Cabinet colleagues in late July, '[it] might well lead to a lasting peace in the Pacific.' Brusquely, he torpedoed the idea floated by some of his colleagues of holding a preliminary conference in London as a waste of time, on the grounds that all decisions would in the end have to be referred to Washington anyway. Rather, he preferred talks in the American capital to start as soon as possible. In the event, they opened in November and lasted until early the next year. As a bargaining tool with the Americans, he also vigorously supported the construction of four new heavy cruisers and four new battleships.[14]

The Imperial Conference marked a turning point for Britain. No longer could it maintain the balance of power in Europe without the help of American muscle. The 'special relationship' between Britain and the United States is frequently credited to (or blamed on) Churchill's Second World War relationship with Franklin D. Roosevelt. In reality, however, its seeds were planted here, in 1921. Churchill's recognition of the reality that Washington now held the keys to Britain's security was an insight uncomfortable to many of his contemporaries. But it was to give him credibility and authority as a statesman when the burden of leadership was thrust on his shoulders some twenty years later.[15]

*

Naval affairs dominated the conference. But air matters were also much on the minds of its delegates and in the midst of business the prime ministers were invited to the London suburb of Croydon, site of the recently opened London air terminal. Commercial flight was still in its infancy, but already there were daily passenger flights to Paris and Brussels. Whatever their differences over tariffs, trade, or the Anglo-Japanese alliance, the prime ministers were unanimous about the need for better inter-Imperial communications and intrigued by the enticing prospects of travel by air. All had been present at the annual dinner of the Royal Colonial Institute on the eve of Dominion Day to hear the Prince of Wales declare, to cheers, that a united Empire depended almost more than anything else on personal connections and that 'the future of rapid Imperial communications lies in the air'. As a former trainee pilot himself at Croydon, the youthful heir to the throne was a committed flying enthusiast. He went on to say – again to cheers – that he hoped delegates to the next Imperial Conference would be able to reach London thanks to Imperial air routes. Turning to New Zealand's Massey and Australia's Hughes, he noted that each had travelled over 12,000 miles to take part in the Conference. 'I am sure,' he smiled, 'that Mr. Hughes will be happier the day he leaves the Old Country when he knows that it will take him 10 days instead of six weeks to arrive at his destination.'[16]

Hughes certainly would. The Australian prime minister was feisty and opinionated and strongly opposed – as was Arthur Meighen – to a plan put forward by Smuts for a federal Imperial Constitution, 'constitutional tinkering' as he caustically dismissed it. Nonetheless, he strongly favoured improved communications to bind the Empire together and believed that Australia's best and indeed only future lay within it. 'What should we be outside the Empire?' he asked rhetorically. At Croydon, he caught a glimpse of how that future might look.

Officially receiving the Dominion leaders at the Croydon airfield was Freddie Guest, now the Secretary of State for Air in succession to his cousin. They watched aeroplanes taking off and landing, and listened in to their pilots communicating with ground control on their radios. But the highlight of the visit for Hughes came when he clambered up an inside stairway to the top of a tall wooden mast where a giant airship, numbered R33, was firmly moored. The Prince of Wales' vision of a ten-day journey between Australia and Britain had been of travel by airship, not aeroplane. These giants of the air had been developed as weapons of war, the dreaded Zeppelins of the First World War. Now they were serious candidates for inter-continental commercial flight. Just two years before, the giant British airship R34 had made the first ever transatlantic round trip by air, completing the westbound journey to New York in just over four days. Some of the Dominion prime ministers had already been taken on a short flight on a sister airship, the R36, and three days into the conference banner headlines broke the news that the successful maiden flight of the world's largest airship had taken place over southern England. This was the six-engined R38. Fully loaded with 30 tons of petrol, the almost 700-feet long dirigible was capable of flying at a cruising speed of 60 miles per hour at an altitude of 25,000 feet for 6,500 miles, roughly the distance from England to Tokyo.

It was little surprise that Hughes was captivated by the potential of airship travel, nor that he was quick to put an enthusiastic case for an Imperial airship service officially before the conference. But here he ran head on into an opponent who could be as bull-headed and opinionated as himself. Churchill, who had reluctantly given up the thrilling speed of piloting an aeroplane only after the passionate pleadings of his wife, knew his mind about airships. He was against them, whether for civilian or military use. Unlike their winged rivals they were slow, vulnerable, and unmanoeuvrable. 'Had I had my own way,' he declared in *The World Crisis*, 'no airships would have been built by Great Britain during the war.' But after he left the Admiralty, he deplored, 'forty millions of money were squandered ... in building British zeppelins, not one of which on any occasion ever rendered any effective fighting service.'[17]

Eventually his successors at Admiralty House had reached the same decision and abandoned airships, and as Secretary of State for War and Air he had closed down the Royal Air Force's airship division, cancelled airship construction and trials, and sold off existing machines. Indeed, by the time of the R38's headline-catching maiden flight, it had also been handed over to the American government for use by the United States Navy, which remained keen to exploit its potential for military or commercial purposes. It now had an Anglo-American crew readying to fly it across the Atlantic to Lakehurst in New Jersey for a journey expected to take some 90 hours. Freddie Guest was as ruthless about airships as his cousin, and before the conference opened had announced that the government would wash its hands of all airships at the beginning of August. Hughes fought a powerful rear-guard action to reverse the decision, and the conference set up a special committee to explore commercial schemes that might still keep airships in the air. But the odds were stacked against the Australian prime minister. Guest was the chairman of the committee, and Churchill spoke powerfully against the whole idea of Imperial airship travel as being impossibly expensive. An airship cost

£320,000 to build, against £10,000 for an aeroplane, and three or four would be needed for an effective service. In addition, the five or six mooring masts needed to dock the airships would each cost £300,000. In all, he explained, they would be looking at a cost of some 3 million pounds. Even if Britain could afford to pay half the bill, the Dominions would have to find the other half; and it was doubtful whether they would, or could. No decision was made by the time the conference ended, which effectively put an end to Hughes's scheme. Churchill also successfully opposed another ambitious plan by the Australian to build a network of powerful radio transmitters in each Dominion to improve communications. Instead, he offered a cheaper version of his own. In both cases, he vetoed the plans on the grounds of cost.[18]

*

But what really finished off the hope of airships as the future of Imperial travel was the catastrophic fate of R38. On the morning of Tuesday 23 August the gigantic airship left its mooring mast at Howden aerodrome in Yorkshire with a mixed British and American crew for its final trials over the North Sea before leaving for New Jersey. After a flight lasting thirty-five hours, much of it in thick fog, it was returning to its base when two violent explosions ripped it in half over the city of Hull. It crashed in flames into the River Humber, killing all but five of the forty-nine people on board. The disaster was a massive setback to hopes of future airship travel. The New Zealand prime minister put a brave face on the news by repeating his faith in the prospects. Nonetheless, he had to admit that 'we have to face things as they are and it means a long setback'.[19]

The tragedy also prompted an outpouring of national mourning on both sides of the Atlantic. In early September a memorial service for the victims was held in Westminster Abbey, where the national anthems of the United States and Great Britain were played by the Band of the Royal Air Force and the congregation sang the Battle Hymn of the Republic. Simultaneously, the Stars and Stripes-draped coffins of the American victims were solemnly transported to Devonport, escorted by a Royal Air Force guard of honour, to be placed on board the British light cruiser

HMS *Dauntless* and taken home to the United States. Eddie Marsh repre-sented an absent Churchill for the service in the Abbey while in New York Freddie Guest, who was on a private visit to America, attended the funeral service for the American victims. The elaborately choreographed ceremonies were testimony to a new-found sense of Anglo-American kinship that appeared to underpin the grandeur of the nation's post-war global reach.[20]

THIRTEEN

'I WILL TAKE WHAT COMES'

The fallout from the Cairo Conference kept Churchill busy over the summer and he rapidly descended into gloom about the prospect of reconciling Jews and Arabs. 'I do not think things are going to get better, but rather worse,' he told the Cabinet.[1] He had a head-on collision with Chaim Weizmann, who insisted that the Balfour Declaration presumed an ultimate Jewish majority in Palestine, and later in the summer at a meeting with a Palestinian delegation of Muslim and Christian Arabs in London he encountered a different brick wall – their demand that the Balfour Declaration be repealed and a point-blank refusal to talk directly with the Zionists. Even before the delegation arrived, he confessed to the Cabinet that the situation in Palestine was causing him 'perplexity and anxiety. The whole country is in ferment,' he lamented, 'both Arabs and Jews are arming, ready to spring at each other's throats.'[2]

He could barely conceal his exasperation with the Palestinian demands. Shortly after the end of the Imperial Conference he met privately with Shibley al-Jamal, the delegation's head, but made no headway. A week later, he spent the morning receiving the entire delegation. As he had already explained to Shibley al-Jamal, he had no power to change the Balfour Declaration, nor could he agree to an elected assembly for Palestine, which would inevitably place the Jews in a permanent minority and certainly impose a ban on any future immigration. He used blunt talk about the Palestinians' refusal to compromise. 'Do you really want to go back to Palestine empty-handed?' he asked, and appealed to them – 'without any great hope', he admitted – to be more flexible. That was all he could do. The Palestinians remained obdurate. The Cabinet, not surprisingly, had no solution either for Palestine. All that his equally exasperated ally Birkenhead could offer was the idea that the mandate should be offered to the United States.[3]

Things were looking brighter in Iraq, however, where Churchill's driving concern remained cost-cutting. To Sir Percy Cox, his consistent message was the need for economies. It was essential that Faisal and a stable Iraqi government be installed in Baghdad as soon as possible – and that the Royal Air Force officially become the primary keeper of order in the desert. As the Imperial Conference was winding up in early August, Churchill laid out his plans to the Cabinet. Thanks to Cox's heroic (not to say Machiavellian) efforts in buying support for the British choice for the throne across the country, Faisal was gaining acceptance as the country's first monarch. This meant that Britain could look forward to an independent native state casting 'hardly any burden' on the Empire. The country would be run by 'the same cheap, makeshift machinery which the Colonial Office have successfully employed ... in East and West Africa', he promised. There would be no Imperial troops stationed at great expense outside Baghdad, and instead the RAF would keep order. Iraq, he told them, was a 'vexatious country', and spending any more on it would be a misapplication of resources. As he insisted personally to Lloyd George, the Colonial Office should be given full control over War Office expenditures in the country. This was agreed, and two weeks later he happily announced that Faisal had finally been chosen by the people as their ruler after a referendum that produced a literally incredible 96 per cent approval for the Hashemite King.[4]

*

'The first duty of the Royal Air Force is to garrison the British Empire', Churchill had impressed upon the House of Commons in 1919, and at Cairo he made clear that this new arm of war would play the major role in policing Iraq. By then even the army had come to admit their rival's value in quelling disorder across the new country's sprawling terrain. While he was enthusiastic about what air power could do, he also remained cautious. The sudden appearance of airplanes dropping bombs from the sky could have an enormous deterrent effect. But with British troops becoming thinner and thinner on the ground, such actions might increasingly be seen as a bluff, and hence perhaps dangerously discounted. Air power should be used with circumspection, he cautioned Sir Percy Cox after one such episode in July on the Lower Euphrates. With that proviso, he assured the High Commissioner, he was a great believer in its legitimate use.

What did he consider legitimate? Quelling disturbances and enforcing order met the test, but supporting measures such as the collection of taxes did not. That same month, he was shocked to learn that Royal Air Force planes had fired on women and children taking refuge in a lake. 'By doing such things we put ourselves on the lower level,' he berated Sir Hugh Trenchard. 'Combatants are fair game and sometimes non-combatants get injured through their proximity to fighting troops, but this seems to be quite a different matter.' He was surprised, he told the Chief of the Air Staff, that the officers responsible had not been court-martialled. Yet his reprimand appears to have had no effect on the ground. A year later, the same RAF officer whose report had so shocked him wrote with gusto about a hundred bombs having been dropped on a village that formed 'a hotbed of malcontents', after which it had been burnt to the ground by troops.[5]

Razing a village full of 'malcontents' was a brutal but not unusual aspect of colonial policing. Far more controversial is Churchill's alleged use of poison gas against Iraqi rebels. The charge has been widely accepted by many of his critics. Yet it is far from accurate, largely because of Churchill's own confused use of the term 'poison gas' when he was actually referring to non-lethal tear gas and not the far more deadly chlorine or phosgene gas. 'It is sheer affectation to lacerate a man with the poisonous fragment of a bursting shell,' he had declared as Secretary of State for War and Air, 'and to boggle at making his eyes water by means of lachrymatory gas.' This was not the view of the Cabinet, however, which held that Britain should only use gas in warfare in retaliation against its first use by others. Besides, the League of Nations was actively discussing the idea of banning chemical weapons altogether. For Britain to use any sort of gas with talks under way would cause serious political and diplomatic complications.

However, the next year during a rebellion across Iraq, Sir Aylmer Haldane appealed for the use of gas to be considered – both from the air and by ground troops. Trenchard's view was that gas dropped in bombs from the air was probably far less effective than regular high-explosive bombs. But Churchill authorized Haldane to use whatever gas shells he had; and when it was discovered that there were none available in Iraq, he gave him permission to acquire 5,000 rounds of sixty-pound SK chemical (tear gas) shells from stocks in Egypt. Now, just days before Faisal was officially enthroned as Iraq's new monarch, Haldane told Churchill that he was 'arranging to do some bombing by moonlight'. Then he added: 'I wish that we could have authority to use gas bombs, but the air ministry are [sic] awaiting for the Cabinet's decision in the matter. I am allowed to use them from my guns – but where the guns can go they cannot use gas shells with advantage – but in the hilly country of the Kurds gas would be far more effective than in the hot plains where the gas is very volatile.' From this it is clear that gas bombing from the air was *not* being carried out, because it was unauthorized. Nor was shelling using tear gas being deployed, even though permitted, because of the terrain. This appears to have remained the case for at least the rest of 1921.[6] Despite her support for Trenchard at Cairo, Gertrude Bell realized the limits of what bombing could achieve. Shortly before Christmas she told her father that 'between ourselves, aeroplanes are no good in mountainous country. You can't so much as see a Kurdish mountain village from the air; its' [sic] flat mud roofs look like a part of the hillside. And even if you do locate it you can't do much harm. The people take refuge under any convenient rock and your bombs are comparatively innocuous. Oh for peace.'[7]

As for tear-gas bombs dropped by air, Cox discussed their use with King Faisal in November that year and gained the Iraqi monarch's consent – 'provided they were not lethal or permanently injurious to health'. Buoyed up by this, shortly after Christmas Churchill agreed to the supply of such bombs to the air force in Iraq. No sooner had he done this, however, than he revoked the order. Ironically, this was thanks to a decision by the disarmament conference in Washington whose meeting he had so warmly supported. Article 5 of its Disarmament Treaty prohibited the use of 'asphyxiating, poisonous, or other gases'. Faced with a major political embarrassment if his decision became public, he lost no time in beating a retreat and the order was quickly countermanded. Similar instructions were sent to the army.

In short, Churchill would gladly have approved using tear gas in Iraq if circumstances had permitted. But thanks to a combination of practical, legal, and political obstacles, he never did. Otherwise, his enthusiasm for policing by air remained undimmed for so long as he remained Colonial Secretary. Subsequently the Royal Air Force suppressed several Kurdish insurrections, ensured that Faisal's writ ran effectively across his kingdom, and also kept Abdullah on the throne of neighbouring Transjordan.[8]

*

No one this summer could accuse Churchill of not doing his best to follow the Cabinet's determination to pare military expenditure to the bone. Ironically, his relentless search for cuts contrasted sharply with his never-ending personal desire to spend more. Using his Garron Towers estate inheritance, he increased Clementine's household allowance by a third. He also visited his bank manager to discuss arranging a new consolidated loan of £30,000. Then, the day after the 'game of notes' with Curzon round the Cabinet table, he met with Sir Reginald Cox, the senior partner of Cox and Co., to discuss his financial affairs. As soon as Parliament rose for the summer recess, he promised, he would produce a detailed blueprint of his plans. He was true to his word. Early in August, after providing a list of his outstanding loans and an overdraft totalling £35,000, he asked whether they could be consolidated into a single loan to be paid off slowly over eleven years. At this, however, the bank baulked. Instead, it agreed to a small overdraft and a loan of £30,000, to be reduced 'substantially' in the following year. Meanwhile, Churchill pressed on with his search for a grand country home. Clementine's confession of her desire to lie in the sun and 'eat a mouse caught by someone else' came the day after he attended the meeting at Chequers where the Cabinet accepted President Harding's proposal for the Washington Conference.[9]

*

Other items on the personal front also kept him happily busy. His painting was going well and drawing compliments from friends. During the British-American polo match at Hurlingham, Lady Jean Hamilton had visited his studio to look over the paintings he had brought back from his Middle East journey as well as others he had painted that year, and to his delight she purchased one. 'I am steadily improving,' he enthused to Charles Montag in Paris, and invited the Swiss painter over to London so that together they could explore the Tate Gallery where there were many 'fine pictures' to be examined. Montag was unable to come, but instead arranged for a Paris bookseller to have a package of books sent to him via the British Embassy in Paris. One was a volume on the doctrines of Confucius. The others were lengthy studies on the art of Corot, Renoir, and Cézanne, and he valiantly began to struggle through them in French.[10] 'Painting is the joy of my life,' he told Lord Riddell over lunch one day as the Imperial Conference was nearing its end. Meanwhile, the *Strand* magazine visited his studio and chose the eighteen paintings it planned to use as illustrations for his article on 'Painting as a Pastime'. Most were landscapes painted at the homes of friends with whom he spent weekends, such as Lympne and Breccles. But the selection also included a handful from that year's visits to the Riviera as well as one of the pyramids outside Cairo. Two more were also carefully packed to go with him to Dundee, where he was due to visit his constituency in the autumn.

*

Nor was he neglecting his other great passion. Vindicating his record at the Admiralty was central to his political comeback and long-term political ambition. The week before lunching with Riddell, he sent off yet another draft chapter of *The World Crisis* for comments to Admiral Thomas Jackson, a pre-war head of naval intelligence who had served as his Director of Operations at the Admiralty including planning for the

Dardanelles. The chapter covered his account of the Battles of Coronel and the Falkland Islands fought early in the war against the German Navy in the south Atlantic. In addition to having Jackson check, correct, and amplify his account, Churchill asked for any suggestions or criticism he might have from the naval point of view. 'I am most anxious ... to do justice to the Navy and to the Sea Lords on the Boards of Admiralty with whom I was associated,' he stressed. Yet he made no attempt to disguise the fact that he intended to place himself at the centre of the story. 'I feel fully justified in showing the part which I played personally,' he told him.[11]

*

On the domestic front, plans for the summer holidays were well advanced. During the first half of August all four of the children would be sent off to the seaside resort of Broadstairs in Kent in the care of Rose, their young French nursery governess. Once Parliament recessed in mid-month, their parents would travel up to Scotland to stay with the Duke and Duchess of Westminster at Lochmore Lodge on their vast estate in county Sutherland. The children would join them there. In the mean-time, with Winston still taking care of Middle Eastern and Imperial matters, Clementine would go on her own to stay with the Westminsters at their English home at Eaton Hall near Chester, for a tennis tourna-ment. When she left, she would join the children on the train taking them north where the family would be reunited for a holiday amidst the moors and glens of Scotland.

He had a few special summer treats planned for himself as well. The same day that he informed the Cabinet of Faisal's forthcoming corona-tion, he celebrated the receipt of his first advance for *The World Crisis* by purchasing one of the most expensive cars of its day, a Rolls-Royce 'Silver Ghost' Cabriolet (Convertible), so-called because of the ghost-like quiet of its engine. It cost him £2,595. In homage to his ducal heritage, he ordered it to be painted in Marlborough blue. It was to remain at the coachbuilders until he returned from his visit to Scotland at the end of September. Meanwhile, he grandly hired another 'Silver Ghost' to use over the weekend.[12]

There was just one small cloud on the horizon. 'Winston v anxious about his sick child,' noted H. A. L. Fisher, the President of the Board of Education, after the Cabinet meeting. Childhood diseases were still a cause for concern in these pre-antibiotic days, and especially so in the immediate shadow of the great influenza pandemic. Only the previous month, while Clementine was staying with Goonie at Menabilly, Sarah had fallen ill and Churchill was profoundly anxious until the family doctor telephoned with the good news that it was 'only' measles. He was vastly relieved to hear it, and she soon recovered. The only inconvenience was that he had to cancel a dinner he had planned for the Prince of Wales – the heir to the throne had never had the highly contagious disease and didn't want to risk his approaching holiday.[13]

This time it was Marigold who was sick. Along with her brother and two sisters, she had been in Kent since the beginning of the month. From the start she had suffered from a slight cold and a cough. The local doctor did what he could. But by mid-August her throat had become seriously sore. Alerted by the landlady at Broadstairs, Clementine rushed down from Eaton Hall and the other three children travelled to Scotland as planned accompanied by Bessie, her maid. Marigold was now gravely ill, with septicaemia. A specialist was called in, but could do nothing. Two days after voicing his anxieties to Fisher, Churchill told Curzon that Marigold was a little improved but that he and Clementine were still dreadfully anxious about her. That evening, Monday 22 August, Clementine was sitting by Marigold's bedside. 'Sing me Bubbles,' she said suddenly and her mother bravely began singing her favourite song. But she had not gone far when Marigold whispered, 'Not tonight . . . finish it tomorrow.' On the following evening she died, with both of her parents at her side. She was just two years and nine months old.

The day should have been one of celebration for Churchill. Early that same morning on the banks of the river Tigris Gertrude Bell, wearing her CBE star and three war ribbons, had watched proudly as Sir Percy Cox announced that Faisal had been elected King of Iraq and there followed a twenty-one-gun salute and a playing of 'God Save the King'.[14] Instead, it was one of intense private sorrow. Clementine, so Winston later recalled, 'gave a succession of wild shrieks, like an animal in mortal pain'. Three days later, Marigold was buried at Kensal Green cemetery in London, close enough to their London home for her parents to make regular visits to the grave; subsequently, it was marked by a headstone carved by the renowned artist Eric Gill. Press photographers were present at the burial but at Churchill's request none of the pictures were used. That evening, 'stupefied by grief', he and Clementine took the sleeper train north to join the other children at Lochmore Lodge. 'My mother never got over Marigold's death,' recalled her youngest daughter, Mary, 'and her very existence was a forbidden subject in the family.'[15] For Churchill, Marigold's death appears to have been so closely associated with his purchase of the Rolls-Royce that he couldn't bear to use it. Shortly after returning from Scotland, he sold it to his ever supportive Aunt Cornelia.

Marigold's death generated widespread sympathy. From New York, Bernard Baruch wrote a heartfelt letter of sympathy and Gertrude Bell sent her own special condolences to Clementine from Baghdad; only five months before, they had been happily exploring the bazaars of Cairo together. 'What a cruel year this has been for you,' wrote Venetia Stanley, 'and this last blow seems the most cruel and wanton of all. That divine perfect little creature!' John and Hazel Lavery were in Edinburgh when they received the news. 'Dearest Winston and Clementine,' read their telegram, 'we are so deeply grieved for you our tenderest love and sympathy.' From Taplow, Ettie Desborough addressed a letter to Winston. 'The baby of the family always seems in a way the focus point,' she wrote, '& Marigold was such a wonderful, darling & beautiful little child – everything that was bright seemed to lie open before her, the little Duckadilly ... My deepest heart is with you,' she added, 'no one, no one, knows what the pain of losing a darling child is but those who have borne it.' Ettie knew of what she wrote. Two of her three sons had been killed on the Western Front.[16]

His political colleagues added their voices, and Lloyd George took the opportunity to mend relations between them; he himself had lost his favourite young daughter some fourteen years previously, a death that finally killed off his own religious faith. Following his mother's death, this was the second family loss that Churchill suffered that summer. 'You were saying the other day how closely death had pressed home to you this year,' wrote Lord Grey of Fallodon, 'and now it has come again in a particularly poignant form.' Sir Abe Bailey expressed a similar sentiment. 'My dear Winston,' he wrote, 'You seem to be getting quite your share of trouble and family losses & might well say "How much more."'

The answer came soon enough. Thomas Walden had been butler to Lord Randolph and stayed with the family, served loyally and bravely as Churchill's valet in South Africa, and shared his Boer War dangers. Shane Leslie knew him well. 'Strong and faithful,' he recalled, 'he valeted Randolph and Winston whose dress was often almost ragged until he reached the period of uniform.' Walden died in early August and both Winston and Jack attended his funeral, and paid its expenses. A quarter of a century before, he had also stood by the freshly dug grave of his childhood nanny, Mrs Everest, 'my dearest and most intimate friend during the whole of the twenty years I had lived,' he later wrote in *My Early Life*. Now another important link with his childhood was severed. 'What a wonderful and terrible year this has been for you. Full of political triumph and material good fortune but crossed with too much sadness,' wrote Archie Sinclair from his family seat at Thurso Castle in Caithness.[17]

For two weeks the Churchill family stayed together as guests of the Westminsters at Lochmore Lodge. No record exists of what they did, what they said, or how they coped. Afterwards, Clementine left for London with the children to prepare them for school while Churchill went to stay with the Duke of Sutherland at Dunrobin Castle, as he had arranged the month before over a dinner at Philip Sassoon's. A vast baronial mansion north of Inverness designed by Sir Charles Barry, architect of the Houses of Parliament, the castle had served as a naval hospital during the war and after a disastrous fire in 1915 had recently undergone considerable refurbishment at the hands of another renowned architect, Sir Robert Lorimer. It also enjoyed its own private railway station and ran its own carriages as well as a special locomotive equipped with an upholstered seat high up at the back of the driver's cab for special guests such as crowned heads of state and members of Royalty. This year they included the Prince of Wales and his brother, the Duke of York – the future King George VI. They were met by the duke at Inverness station and escorted in his private train to the castle. There were some thirty or so guests during Churchill's stay. Mrs Dudley Ward, as well as her husband, was amongst them.

By this time – as *The Times* put it – 'everybody who is anybody will now be found north of the Tweed'.[18] King George V and Queen Mary were firmly ensconced at Balmoral. Grouse shooting had begun as always on 12 August ('the Glorious Twelfth') and Highland lodges and grand houses were packed with shooting parties. Other members of the Royal Family also headed north, many of them solemnly attending the unveiling of war memorials now being completed in towns and villages across Scotland. Soon, the Highland Games were also under way at Ballater.

But Churchill was in no mood for heavy socializing. Besides, he found the company at Dunrobin, many of them there for tennis, to be 'extremely young' – a sure sign that he himself was now feeling distinctly middle-aged. Instead, he preferred to wander off by himself with his brushes and easel and paint. On one cool but brilliant afternoon, under a cloudless sky, he went out and painted what he described to Clementine as 'a beautiful river in the afternoon light with crimson and golden hills in the background'. He was so refreshed by the outing that he declined an invitation the next day from the duke to join a grouse-shooting party and instead went off again with his canvas. When rain kept him indoors he spent time reading *Amelia*, a domestic novel by Henry Fielding describing the hardships of a newly married young couple in London. 'It's saltly [*sic*] written', he told Clementine.

There were other distractions, too. One morning a Royal Navy destroyer dropped anchor in a nearby bay and gave him the chance to go over it with an expert eye. He knew his ships and noted immediately that it was far larger than any destroyer from his own time at the Admiralty, almost as large as a cruiser. 'I expect they have gone too far in the direction of size for a vessel which has no armour and now becomes such a very easy target,' he mused critically. He also spent time corresponding with his brother about his personal finances. They were due money from their grandfather Leonard Jerome's settlement on their mother. But getting their hands on it proved difficult and they had to hire an American lawyer. 'I should be glad to get it ferried safely across the Atlantic and invested here,' he told Clementine. 'There are so many splendid things going cheaply now.' In the end it provided him with some more useful income.[19]

Most of his time, however, he spent on mapping out the speech he planned for his approaching visit to Dundee. It would give a *tour d'horizon* of the major issues facing the government: unemployment, Ireland, and the forthcoming Washington Conference. 'I intend to make a very careful and thoughtful speech,' he wrote.

*

Introspection was not one of Churchill's most obvious qualities. But spending these long summer days in the Highlands after Marigold's death gave him ample time to ponder life's tragedies and its unpredictable brevity. Close by, there were other reminders, too. The duke's brother, Alastair, who had been awarded the Military Cross while fighting with a machine-gun regiment, had died of malaria just four months previously aged thirty-one, and lay buried next to his father in a grave by the sea. This raised more ghosts from the past. He penned a note to Clementine:

> It's another splendid day: & I am off to the river to catch pictures – much better fun than salmon. Many tender thoughts my darling one of you & yr [sic] sweet kittens. Alas I keep on feeling the hurt of the Duckadilly. I expect you will all have made a pilgrimage yesterday. 'Tis twenty years since I first used to come here [when] Geordie [the Duke of Sutherland] & Alastair were little boys ... Another twenty years will bring me to the end of my allotted span even if I have so long ... I will take what comes.[20]

He had to. Two days later Sir Ernest Cassel died suddenly of a heart attack at his Park Lane home in London. Not only had he often helped

Churchill financially, he was also a treasured link to the past and to his father. Only a few months before, Winston and Clementine had been his personal guests on the Riviera. The loss struck Churchill deeply. 'He was very fond of me and believed in me at all times – especially bad times,' he told Edwina Ashley, Cassel's granddaughter, the future Lady Mountbatten. 'The last talk we had – about six weeks ago – he told me that he hoped he wd [sic] live to see me at the head of affairs . . . I have lost a good friend whose like I shall never seen again. This year has been vy [sic] grievous to me.'[21] Clementine shared his grief. 'I have been through so much lately that I thought I had little feeling left, but I wept for our dear old friend, he was a feature in our lives and he cared deeply for you.' Four days later, they both attended the Requiem Mass for Cassel held at the Church of the Immaculate Conception in Mayfair, which concluded with the playing of Chopin's Funeral March. Afterwards, Cassel was interred, like Marigold, at Kensal Green cemetery.[22]

At age forty-six, Churchill had suffered several heavy personal losses. They had not unnerved him, or made him any less ambitious, but they had made him more reflective and aware of his mortality. No longer was he simply 'the bold, bad man' of the year before. He was now a more vulnerable figure, an everyman who had suffered personal tragedies, and with whom ordinary people could identify.

FOURTEEN

'A SEAT FOR LIFE'

M eanwhile, Irish affairs had not stood still. With both the commander of British troops in Ireland and General Tudor in favour, a truce finally came into force on Monday 11 July. 'The die was now cast,' wrote Churchill in the final volume of *The World Crisis*, '. . . The gunmen emerged from their hiding-places and strode the streets of Dublin as the leaders of a nation as old and as proud as our own . . . the attempt to govern Southern Ireland upon the authority of the Imperial Parliament had come to an end.'[1] Three days later, the Sinn Fein leader Eamon de Valera met Lloyd George in the Cabinet Room at 10 Downing Street. Hanging on the wall was a large map of the world with parts of the British Empire vividly marked in red. The Imperial Conference was still in daily session. Lloyd George pointed out the chairs being occupied by the various prime ministers, Smuts here, Meighen there, and so on. His message was clear: the Empire was a sisterhood of nations and Ireland could join them round the table as one of the Dominions.[2]

Shortly afterwards de Valera was officially presented with the British government's proposals. While the north made its own separate arrangements with London, southern Ireland could enjoy Dominion Home Rule including control over its finance, taxation, police, and army affairs. There would be tariff-free trade across the Irish Sea, but Imperial defence would remain in British hands: 'The Royal Navy alone must control the seas around Ireland.' In Dublin, the Sinn Fein leadership debated and prevaricated for a month before rejecting the terms and demanding full independence. De Valera scorned the British offer as little better than 'second-rate political margarine'.[3]

The reply heralded the opening salvo in a barrage of letters between the two leaders that went on for weeks. Meanwhile, no arms were surrendered and violence continued. Ireland once more seemed poised for war. Lloyd George decided another Cabinet meeting was vital. But by late August, Parliament was in summer recess and many ministers had dispersed abroad or to the Highlands, including the prime minister himself. On doctor's orders he was resting with his wife at Flowerdale House, outside the small village of Gairloch on the remote coast of Ross-shire.

Besides tranquillity and a golf course, for the Welsh-speaking prime minister who relished playing the role of Celtic outsider it had at least one other draw. Soon after arriving, he attended a two-hour service conducted in Gaelic at the Free Church of Scotland. Although a keen singer of hymns, he struggled to find the psalms and Bible readings. Only the promptings of Sir Hamar Greenwood – assisted by the whisperings of a 'Highland lass' in a nearby pew – helped him through the service. The sermon, given in Gaelic, seemed interminable. Yet throughout, Lloyd George gallantly maintained an attitude of close attention.[4]

For significant business, however, Flowerdale House proved impossible, even with help from the indefatigable Frances Stevenson. One small room had to serve as an office and the house had no telephone. The post office, a mile away, was equipped with just a single telegraph transmitter. There was only one car. The nearest railway station was thirty miles and a four-hour drive away. Instead, Lloyd George summoned an unprecedented meeting of the Cabinet to Inverness. This 'gateway to the Highlands' lay close to Culloden, scene of the last pitched battle to be fought on British soil. The doomed Bonnie Prince Charlie had held council in the town on the eve of his catastrophic final effort to overthrow the Hanoverians.[5]

The day before the meeting, Churchill motored over to the nearby Brahan Castle in Dingwall. Historic seat of the chiefs of the Clan Mackenzie, it had been put by its owners, Lord and Lady Seaforth, at the disposal of Cabinet members for the duration of the discussions. One of the Seaforth ancestors had taken part in the 1715 Jacobite rebellion only to see his men cut to pieces at the Battle of Sheriffmuir. Yet battalion after battalion of the Seaforth Highlanders had subsequently fought for the British Crown in campaigns across Europe. In this remarkable history, wrote one hopeful journalist, English eyes might see how once irreconcilable hostility had given way to 'peace, prosperity, and an intense and exuberant loyalty on the part of a race that has done probably as much as any other to build up and fortify our Empire'. The possible analogies with Ireland were obvious.[6]

It is not clear whether Churchill, historian as he was, nurtured any similar hopes. In any case, he first had to make it safely to Inverness. Highland roads were still rough and ready, and his car broke an axle on the way. Ministers still in London had to endure the fifteen-hour sleeper train from Euston station. 'This is outrageous, dragging us to Inverness,' grumbled Austen Chamberlain, who had already refused a previous summons to travel to the Highlands. 'Why did the PM not have the meeting in Edinburgh?' But there were good reasons for the Inverness choice beyond Lloyd George's personal convenience. From Dublin, the Commander of British forces Sir Neville Macready sailed directly to Gairloch on the British destroyer HMS *Sterling*, and two Sinn Fein couriers crossed the Irish Sea by ferry. Not least of the advantages of Inverness was that the King was staying at nearby Moy Hall, the historic seat of the chiefs of the Clan Mackintosh famed for its grouse-shooting. His June speech in Belfast had helped kick-start the talks, he was known to favour moderation, and his views carried considerable weight. High-level British officials well versed in Sinn Fein politics also arrived directly from Dublin. 'The eyes of the nation, and indeed of the world, are on Inverness,' headlined one Scottish newspaper that morning, 'for . . . today a long-drawn and harrowing political drama may reach the closing stages which make for a happy ending, or open up a new act of a terrible tragedy.' As ever in such staged events featuring Lloyd George, the reliable Lord Riddell stood poised to issue a press release as soon as the meeting was over.

In bright sunshine, Churchill was the first Cabinet member to arrive at the Town Hall. Dressed in a light suit worn under a heavy overcoat, he was welcomed by the Lord Provost. A crowd several rows deep had gathered to witness the historic occasion. People leaned out of windows to watch the spectacle and a few brave souls balanced precariously on the slate roofs of the surrounding houses. Perhaps overwhelmed by the gravity of the occasion, they gazed on silently as the succession of ministers entered the building. Finally, at nearly eleven thirty, Lloyd George stepped out of his car. A light breeze gently ruffled his mane of white hair.[7]

Discussions began shortly afterwards in the Council Chamber. It had already been agreed that talks with Sinn Fein should be given one last try. The main question now was whether they should be held with or without a prior commitment by Sinn Fein to accept continued membership of the British Empire under the Crown. Beneath a large stained-glass window featuring Queen Victoria flanked by Lord Salisbury, Benjamin Disraeli, William Gladstone and other of her prime ministers, the Cabinet embarked on an intense debate that lasted most of the day. From a large portrait on another wall Prince Albert, dressed in full Highland dress, looked down on the scene. Lloyd George went round the table asking everyone in turn whether they were for or against preconditions. He had started the day by having breakfast with the King. The monarch was 'anxious', he informed them, that the government's position should not resemble an ultimatum or be likely to spark hostilities. In fact, the King had objected strongly to the draft statement put in front of him and deprecated anything that could be interpreted as 'an attempt by a large country to bully a small one into submission'. This set the tone for the proceedings. The first two ministers to speak opted for unconditional talks.[8]

But not Churchill. He had driven over from Brahan Castle with Macready, who bullishly believed that his forces had the IRA on the run and could, if necessary, finish them off quickly. Thus encouraged, Churchill assured his colleagues that Sinn Fein 'had fear in their hearts', and that a strong line insisting they should come to talks only if they accepted the integrity of the Empire would bring them to their senses. Thomas Jones, the Welsh-speaking deputy secretary of the Cabinet taking the minutes, described him as 'breathing fire and slaughter'. His bellicose rhetoric prompted an abrupt response from Lloyd George. War could easily come again to Ireland, he warned. 'I do not agree with the Colonial Secretary that it [defeating the IRA] is a small operation. It is a considerable operation'. After lunch the talks continued, the large crowd outside still waiting patiently. But the tide was running strongly against Churchill and those who thought like him. By 3.45 p.m. a message for de Valera was hurriedly placed in the hands of the Sinn Fein couriers, who immediately rushed off to catch the ferry to Dublin.

'This is the pen with which I signed the [Paris] Peace Treaty, and I hope to sign the Irish agreement with it'. So Lloyd George had melodramatically told a messenger boy at Brahan Castle the previous day while flamboyantly signing the receipt for a box of cigars sent to him by a group of American well-wishers. It remained to be seen whether his confidence was justified. In a skilfully phrased letter, the Cabinet had asked for a definite reply as to whether Sinn Fein was ready to take part in a conference 'to ascertain how the association of Ireland with the community of nations known as the British Empire can best be reconciled with Irish national aspirations'. If the answer was 'yes', then talks could be resumed in Inverness two weeks later. Churchill later gave an account of the meeting in *The World Crisis*. Understandably, he omitted to mention that his harder-line approach was rejected. Annoyingly, after leaving the meeting, his car once again broke an axle. It was a rocky day all round.[9]

However, the follow-up meeting in Inverness was not to be. Displeased at the tone of de Valera's eventual reply, Lloyd George angrily cancelled it. But letters continued to flow between the two men. With even the strongly nationalist press in Ireland still in favour of talks, de Valera made conciliatory noises. Encouraged, Lloyd George once again summoned key Cabinet figures to the Highlands. This time it was to Gairloch. The prime minister was far from well. He had been suffering for days from a seriously abscessed tooth. This had finally been extracted just the day before under heavy anaesthetic and in the presence of the King's own personal physician. When Lloyd George finally awoke, it was to the sound of 'Men of Harlech' being sung by a fellow Welshman.

Still, when Churchill arrived after motoring over on the morning of Wednesday 21 September, the prime minister was well enough to take him for lunch on board a huge white yacht named the *Liberty* that was anchored offshore. Its owner was Sir Robert Houston, a Scottish-born shipping magnate whose fortune had come from carrying frozen beef from Argentina to fill hungry British stomachs. He was also a former Conservative Member of Parliament from Toxteth in Liverpool, where he was known as 'the Robber Baron' for his unscrupulous business dealings. He had also thrown a lot of his pre-war legal business – mostly litigation – to the chambers of the young and upcoming solicitor F. E. Smith, who had built his early fortune on this along with legal work for another Liverpool magnate, Lord Leverhulme. Birkenhead had actually sailed up to Gairloch with Houston. The yacht, originally built for the American publisher Joseph Pulitzer, was the largest of its kind in the world. The ever-present George Riddell called it 'a small floating palace'. During the war it had served as a Royal Navy hospital ship.[10]

Suitably entertained and refuelled by Houston, who had recently sold his company for £4 million, the two former 'terrible twins' of radical Liberalism headed back to Flowerdale House to meet their other colleagues. Churchill was now in a more conciliatory mood, but remained dead set against granting full independence and an Irish republic. Lloyd George had been copying him in on his correspondence, and he knew that the Sinn Fein leader was under pressure to compromise from within his own ranks. There was also, as always, a weighty American dimension to the issue. De Valera's apparent rigidity was not playing well with many Americans. 'Practical Patriotism' was what was needed, stressed the New York *Evening News*, in a rebuke to his often rambling discursions into the mists of Irish history. 'I still believe,' Churchill wrote confidently to Clementine the day before the Gairloch meeting, 'there will be a peaceful settlement.' It was duly decided, after long-distance consultations with

Cabinet ministers who had been unable to travel to Gairloch, to invite de Valera to a conference in London in October.

Three days later Churchill arrived in Dundee for the long-planned visit to his Scottish constituency. Here, he was to make his stance on Ireland clear to the British people. Already, the press was naming him as one of the most likely negotiators that Lloyd George would pick for the crucial talks with Sinn Fein.[11]

*

Dundee lay on the River Tay on Scotland's North Sea coast, 'a dark mass of dirty grey sandstone tenements punctuated by high chimney stacks and church spires'. The country's third-largest city with a population of some 190,000 people, it was an industrial and commercial centre renowned for the 'three j's' of jute, jam, and journalism. D. C. Thomson was a publisher of newspapers, magazines, and children's comics with sales across the whole of the United Kingdom. Unfortunately for Churchill, the sixty-two-year-old owner David Coupar Thomson also detested him. 'Mr. Churchill is a political controversialist like the three-legged symbol so favoured by the Isle of Man,' he had thundered at the time of the Liberal government's pre-war battle against the House of Lords, 'he seems to point in all directions but really concentrates attention upon himself all the time.' Thomson had never ceased pouring scorn on the city's Liberal MP, denouncing him as greedy for glory and as a 'loud-mouthed bullying place-seeker'. To make matters worse, Thomson owned both of the city's main newspapers.

The jam – mainly marmalade – was Keillor's, a brand familiar to most breakfast tables across the nation. But it was the jute industry that dominated the city to give it the sobriquet 'Juteopolis'. In some two hundred factories it employed 40 per cent of Dundee's workforce, the largest domination by a single industry of any British city. Along with its associated businesses of engineering and shipping, almost half the population depended on transforming jute – a tropical plant imported mostly from India – into the sturdy sacking and rope used in countless industries. But even the good times meant hardship. The trade employed mainly women and boys, who were paid less than men. Male unemployment always ran high. Thousands of men left the city by way of the army recruiting office. Damp and miserable slums abounded. Soup kitchens fed the starving. Alcohol-induced violence was commonplace. Churchill once said he had never witnessed such drunkenness as in the streets of Dundee.[12]

*

He had held the constituency as a Liberal since 1908, when he was already in the Cabinet as President of the Board of Trade. It was 'a seat for life', he claimed, relieved to have won it after a defeat in North-West Manchester. Then, as now, the chairman of the city's Liberal Association was Sir George Ritchie. A tall and dignified seventy-two-year-old sporting a white goatee beard, he was the owner of a chain of grocery stores and a former City Treasurer. 'We must get that brilliant young man to represent the city and put Dundee on the map,' he declared. Since then, he had served loyally through thick and thin as Churchill's political guide and friend in the city, informing him about its political temperature, organizing his visits – usually once a year, and handling local Liberal Party affairs. Dundee was a two-member constituency. In the summer, amidst widespread press rumours of an impending election, Ritchie had found a running mate for Churchill in D. J. Macdonald, the owner of a local engineering and automobile company with an impressive record of charitable giving. Ritchie confessed frankly to Churchill how he had struggled hard to find a candidate acceptable to the two opposing wings of the party, the Asquithians and the Coalitionists. 'We have had a long and merry fight to keep the unity of our Party,' he wrote. 'Had it not been out of personal loyalty to yourself I would have given it up.' He also warned of a growing discontent in Dundee with the Coalition government over expenditure, the interference of London-based authorities, and the 'arrogance of so many of the Public Officials all over'. Had there been a strong opposition with a policy of efficiency and economy, it would sweep the country. 'The only thing in your favour,' he told him, 'is the fear of a Revolutionary party obtaining power.'[13]

Ritchie's frankness prompted Churchill to make an avowal of his own. Not for the first time this year he hinted that he, too, could turn his back on politics and that life held other attractions. 'Personally,' he told him two days after strenuously justifying his Middle East policy to the House of Commons, 'I would far rather at this juncture and after all these years be free from the burden and obloquy of public office.' But he firmly added a qualifier. This was only true if he could be sure that a different government – by which he meant Labour – would do better. Here, his views remained as trenchant as ever. On his visit to Dundee the year before he had castigated 'the simpletons of the Socialist Party' for worshipping the Bolshevik idol and being 'more than ever unfitted for the tasks of responsible government'.[14]

He now seized on Ritchie's comments to reiterate the electoral message that together with Lloyd George and Freddie Guest he had been pushing since the spring. In an open letter to his constituency he had already spelled out the political threat posed by the vastly expanded electorate and especially the 'ambitions of the Socialist Party to obtain control of municipal affairs'. Now, he told Ritchie, the way the Labour leaders mismanaged their own affairs proved how utterly unfit they were to undertake 'the burden and responsibility of the Imperial Government'. Fighting socialism was rapidly heading to the top of his own political agenda. Shortly afterwards, he met with his fellow candidate Macdonald in London and suggested they should soon hold a joint meeting in Dundee, where together they could draw 'a clear line of cleavage' with the left.[15]

*

Churchill was right to be worried about the impact of Labour. 'The great extensions of the franchise which were made during the War fundamentally altered the political character of Dundee,' he wrote later.[16] The trebling of the electorate to include 8 million women aged over thirty and 5 million more men was certainly significant, although it had roundly elected him in 1918. More important was its disillusioned rejection of Lloyd George and the policies of his Coalition government.

But there was also a personal and local factor at work. To thousands of Dundonians, Churchill was by now an almost demonic figure. For one thing, his fervent support for the Black and Tans had alienated the city's significant Irish population who had once been his great supporters for his Home Rule sympathies. While he was in Cairo, the city had been visited by Archbishop Mannix of Melbourne in Australia, a keen partisan of Irish nationalism. To a rapturous audience of Sinn Fein supporters, the senior Catholic cleric declared that Churchill was 'an enemy of Ireland' whose days were numbered. Simultaneously, the *Dundee Catholic Herald* started running a 'Churchill must go' campaign, insisting that it was time for the voters 'to see that this dangerous, double-dealing, oily-tongued adventurer is not given the power to do further harm'.[17]

The Secretary of the Jute and Flax Workers' Union, John Sime, felt much the same, believing strongly that the jute workers had been badly let down during the post-war recession by Churchill, a man who was 'born a Tory, is still a Tory, and always will be a Tory'. Just before Christmas, Sime had invited Churchill to Dundee to see conditions for himself but in reply had merely received an invitation to come to London. Since then, he had bombarded him with letters and telegrams. When Sime finally turned up at the House of Commons in August requesting to see his constituency MP, he was refused. 'Here endeth the chapter so far as Mr. W. S. Churchill is concerned,' he declared, infuriated, in the Union's journal. 'It will not be necessary to waste paper and postage on [him] in the future.' Many other voters also thought that Churchill was treating the city as a mere pocket borough, out of town and out of touch.[18]

But it wasn't just his perceived failings to defend Dundee that was turning the tide of opinion against him. It was the broader swing against the National Liberals along with the capture of Liberal votes by the Left. The man already chosen as its candidate in Dundee by the Labour Party was E. D. (Edwin Dene) Morel, a campaigning journalist made famous by his pre-war exposé of Belgian atrocities in the Congo and now Secretary of the Union of Democratic Control. Founded in 1914, this was a radical pressure group opposed to conscription that campaigned for greater democratic control of foreign policy. Morel had been briefly imprisoned during the war for his pacifism. Now he was focusing on raising working-class consciousness about foreign policy and its intimate links with domestic affairs. The previous year, when Churchill's anti-Bolshevik rhetoric was at its peak, Morel had discovered that a large Russian purchase of jute bags had been stopped at Constantinople by the Royal Navy. He immediately made use of the news. 'It is the literal truth to say,' he thundered, 'that the Dundee working man is now out of employment because the figure of Winston Churchill rises between them [*sic*] and the Russian people.' Such charges easily stuck in the desperate city.[19]

Yet it was a local man who offered the greatest threat. In every election since 1908 Churchill been opposed by Edwin Scrymgeour, the leader of the Scottish Prohibition Party. In a country notorious for its alcohol-induced violence, prohibition was a powerful political force and only the year before the Scottish Trade Union Congress had passed a resolution in support of it. Scrymgeour, who was also a socialist, found his combination of anti-drink and left-wing views gaining powerful traction. For him, too, the local MP personified the evils that damned the city and was 'the man particularly associated with Imperialism and War'. Churchill later gave him some grudging respect and acknowledged that, unlike himself, Scrymgeour had regularly visited almost every household in the constituency. 'He lived a life of extreme self-denial,' he wrote. 'He represented the poverty and misery of the poorer parts of the city.' The charges of both Scrymgeour and Morel readily stuck to their target. Above all, Churchill's regular claim that Labour was 'unfit to rule' had infuriated many of Dundee's voters and convinced them that in truth the charge really applied to him.[20]

AUTUMN

FIFTEEN

'THE COURAGE AND INSTINCT OF LEADERSHIP'

B y the autumn Dundee was in crisis. Thousands of the city's army of unemployed had exhausted their benefits. While the city excitedly awaited the imminent arrival of the latest Charlie Chaplin movie *The Kid*, the city's Lord Provost made the shock announcement that the Distress Relief Committee had run out of funds and that the city itself could find work for only 400 people. Three days of violence followed. A mass meeting of the unemployed culminated with dozens of windows being smashed at the Parish Council offices. Behind a large red banner and lustily singing 'The Red Flag', a crowd of thousands also besieged the home of the Lord Provost, and his daughter was injured by a stone hurled through the window of his car. Shop windows were indiscriminately targeted all across the city. There were baton-wielding charges by the police, and dozens of arrests were made. In all, the damage was estimated to be at least £10,000.[1]

Churchill was at Inverness when the rioters took to the streets. There were outbreaks in other British cities such as Bristol, Liverpool, Sunderland and London, where unemployed workers had now also exhausted their benefits. With demands escalating for the government to do something, Lloyd George belatedly instructed a Cabinet committee to look into the problem. A delegation of Labour mayors from London boroughs even made the arduous journey to Gairloch, completing the final 80 miles of their trek north over rocky Highland roads in a motor coach.

From the Duke of Westminster's Lochmore Lodge, Churchill took his own steps to confront the crisis by contacting Sir George Ritchie with an offer to meet face to face with the City Council. To his new Liberal running mate D. J. Macdonald, the solution seemed obvious. As chairman of the Juvenile Employment Committee at the local Labour Exchange, he had been on the front line of the battle for a long time. 'The period of Unemployment should be extended,' he told Churchill. 'The Financial outlay is a mere bagatelle.' This was true, but not helpful. The period of unemployment benefit was fixed by Acts of Parliament. Only a change in legislation could alter that. Meanwhile, local authorities in Scotland struggled to help on their own; under Scottish law it was strictly illegal for them to pay relief to the able-bodied poor.[2]

*

Such was the position when Churchill finally checked into Dundee's Royal Hotel. Hardly had he arrived than he was confronted by a delegation headed by John Sime demanding the immediate recall of Parliament to amend the unemployment laws. Unable to promise this, Churchill also had to refuse the petition of another delegation carrying a local grievance. As part of its post-war restructuring of the Territorial Army, the War Office had decided to merge the 4th and 5th Battalions of one of Scotland's most famous regiments, the Black Watch. During the war, the 4th Battalion had recruited heavily from the city's jute and jam factories and suffered grievously at the Battle of Loos – which by now, on the eve of its sixth anniversary, was being hailed as 'Dundee's Somme'. Many in the city were outraged, and Churchill struggled vainly to change War Office minds by forcefully telling his successor that the affair was a matter of fierce local patriotism. The Lord Provost took the decision badly as a serious slight on his city. 'What is the meaning of this seemingly determined effort to ignore Dundee?' he demanded. 'Our trade is very bad [and] unemployment extremely prevalent.' To the Black Watch petitioners, Churchill could only promise to do his best.[3]

So when he met with the Council the next day the atmosphere was distinctly frosty. As a local MP he had his constituents' interest to promote. But being a Cabinet member meant he had to defend government policy. It was a strenuous task to do both at once. It was made worse after one of the Council's Labour members began by angrily accusing the Cabinet of a 'brutal and callous' response to the unemployed. Churchill hit back forcefully by pointing out how much the government had handed out in benefits since the war, by blaming the recent waves of strikes – and especially that of the miners – for weakening the economy, and by saying that it was really for the Scottish Office to find ways to help local authorities cope with the crisis. But the fractious and often emotional meeting left not just its audience dissatisfied. He himself was unhappy. What he had seen with his own eyes had clearly shocked him. Dozens of shops still had their windows boarded up. Many men were shoeless. Some of the children were clearly in what he described as 'a savage and starving condition'. Immediately after the meeting he sat down and wrote a heartfelt personal letter to Lloyd George, confessing he had become convinced that there was 'very great ground for complaint' about the government's unemployment policy.[4]

*

It was as a national rather than as a local actor, however, that Churchill turned his performance in Dundee into a success. On the following day, Saturday 24 September, he delivered the speech he had been carefully preparing at Dunrobin. The venue was the recently completed city hall, named after James Key Caird, a local jute baron and philanthropist who had also sponsored Sir Ernest Shackleton's ill-fated expedition to the Antarctic. With its neo-classical grandeur and acoustically top-rated auditorium, it held out the hope of a more prosperous future for the city on the Tay. To ensure a sympathetic audience, Ritchie had made the event an all-ticket affair. But this was Dundee. Hundreds of entry tickets were forged and only at the last minute were their holders prevented from entering. Outside, a crowd of several thousand sang socialist songs and an unsuccessful effort was made to rush the hall. There was a heavy police presence. Afterwards, Churchill had to exit by the back door with several police officers bundling him into his car as he hastily drove back to his hotel.

Still, despite an occasional heckler, he found a responsive audience. More importantly, the national British press gave him widespread coverage. It was a classic set-piece of the Churchillian rhetoric more generally associated with his Second World War speeches, but that he was already wielding as an effective political weapon. As a twenty-three-year-old subaltern in India during Queen Victoria's Diamond Jubilee year, he had spelled out his belief in the power of the spoken word. 'Of all the talents bestowed upon men,' he wrote in a short essay entitled 'The Scaffolding of Rhetoric', 'none is so precious as the gift of oratory. He who enjoys it wields a power more durable than that of a great king. He is an independent force in the world.' In the light of what had befallen him since 1915, the sentence that followed seemed especially apt: 'Abandoned by his party, betrayed by his friends, stripped of his office, whoever can command this power is still formidable.' This was to prove true throughout his career. Lord Moran, his later-life personal physician, noted that 'Few men have stuck so religiously to one craft, the handling of words. In peace, it made his political fortunes; in war it has won all men's hearts.'

This was exaggerated. But his close attention to words reaped him many rewards over his lifetime. 'With his great speeches he has . . . erected his most enduring monument,' said the Swedish author Sigfrid Siwertz in presenting him with the Nobel Prize for Literature in 1953. A decade later when he conferred on him American citizenship, President John F. Kennedy famously declared that he had 'mobilised the English language and sent it into battle'. Both had in mind his Second World War speeches. But for decades already Churchill had wielded the spoken word to powerful effect, deploying words, as he did his paint, to express not just facts and opinions but tone, mood, and shades of feeling.[5]

His Caird Hall speech contained many of the elements he regarded as vital to the orator: the careful choice of short and common words; a rhythm of speech resembling blank verse rather than prose; a rapid succession of waves of sound and vivid pictures enabling the audience to anticipate the conclusion so that the final words fall 'amid a thunder of assent'; striking metaphor; and extravagant language to raise the emotions and release the deepest feelings of the listener. But it was also its trajectory that demonstrated his skill. Consciously or not, his speech followed that of one of the most influential classics of British literature: John Bunyan's great Christian allegory *The Pilgrim's Progress*, a work almost certainly well familiar to his audience. In it, the everyman protagonist Christian makes an arduous journey from the City of Destruction to the Celestial City, from darkness to light, from despair to hope.

The hall was packed with between three and four thousand people. It was a grand civic event. The Lord Provost presided, and the platform included many local worthies including Sir George Ritchie as well as representatives of the Liberal and Conservative parties. As a significant straw in the political wind, the Lord Provost opened the evening by stressing that he was chairman only in an official capacity. Personally, along with many others present, he had strongly supported the government during the war. But since then, he admitted, many things had happened of which he did not approve.[6]

Thus alerted – and possibly stimulated – by this provocation, Churchill opened his speech by accepting that the present post-war period was a time of great social distress and anxiety where everyone was still suffering from 'the grievous wounds of the war', the imprint of which they would all carry to their graves. From this dark opening he guided his audience step by step towards a brighter future that echoed familiar sentiments he had been expressing throughout the year. 'I look forward confidently,' he eventually concluded – amidst cheers – 'to an ever closer association between the United States and the British Empire, for it is in the unity of the English-speaking peoples that the brightest hopes for the progress of mankind will be found to reside.'

How was this future to be reached? His answer was by following the path of reconciliation. This was the time, he declared after moving on from his sombre opening scene, 'for composing differences, for assisting each other, for leaving alone all quarrels and co-operating in the rebuilding as quickly as possible of the threatened prosperity of the country. Classes and nations must help each other.' One way was to settle war debts and re-establish a healthy and prosperous system of tariff-free international trade. Another was for the Great Powers of Europe, as well as of the Pacific, to create a climate of peaceful co-operation. He looked ahead to the near future. 'I have high hopes of this Washington Conference,' he told his listeners. 'It marks the re-entry of the United States into the responsibilities and difficulties of world politics' – and, he added, made him confident of the Anglo-American future.

Of course, perils awaited. Not surprisingly, he pronounced that the greatest of these was Bolshevism. Earlier that month the *Dundee Advertiser* had carried a full-page appeal requesting donations for famine relief in Russia where millions were starving in the aftermath of the Revolution and Civil War. Children especially were its victims, often abandoned and reduced to eating grass, roots, and rubbish. In total, some 35 million Russians were suffering. 'One of the world's greatest granaries,' Churchill declared, 'has been reduced through four years of Socialism and Bolshevism to absolute starvation.' Worse, he added, Lenin and Trotsky had killed without mercy all those who opposed them and lived off the wealth of those they had dispossessed. This claim also rang true to his audience. In a dispatch from Helsinki, the local paper had recently reported that sixty-one people had been shot in Petrograd for being implicated in the latest 'plot' against the regime; most, it seemed, were 'men of education, including two professors and a famous sculptor'. Churchill's attack on the perils of Bolshevism concluded on a familiar note. Its British supporters had been doing their best to disrupt the economy through strikes and disputes and 'to ruin us here in Britain'. Luckily, he added, in a typical aside that drew approving laughter, 'we always seem to get these foreign diseases in a less acute form'.

However, the more immediate threat lay in Ireland. This was the centrepiece of his talk, and the one his audience was most anxious to hear. Again, reconciliation was the central theme. Past quarrels now had to be put aside and this included, he stressed, differences between the Conservatives and Liberals themselves on how to deal with Ireland. But if the message was reconciliation, his tone was firm. In its offer of Dominion Home Rule to Sinn Fein, the government had gone 'to the utmost limit possible'. De Valera's response so far had been disappointing and puzzling. True, the Sinn Fein leader was 'riding a nationalist tiger', and allowance had to be made for that. Nonetheless Churchill was still uncertain where the Irish leaders stood. 'I only know,' he said, 'where we stand. We have reached the end of our tether.' This prompted cheers in the audience.

But now he added a sobering note by raising the prospect of an independent Irish Republic and what it would mean. Deliberately deploying the extravagant language recommended in his youthful essay, he painted a dark and ominous picture of what could lie ahead: a fortified frontier between North and South with hostile armies on each side; constant fear that the Irish Republic was intriguing with other countries against Britain, possibly by giving them submarine bases – a not so subtle reminder of the wartime landing in County Kerry by German U-boat of Sir Roger Casement, who was subsequently hanged for treason; a tariff wall between the two nations; and hundreds of thousands of Irishmen living throughout the British Empire immediately being declared 'aliens' if war broke out between it and the Republic. 'What a ludicrous and what an idiotic prospect is unfolded before our eyes,' he declared. 'What a crime [Sinn Fein] would commit if ... they condemn themselves and their children to such misfortunes.' To head off this dark future, a conference was clearly needed. It would be wise to be outspoken, and foolish to encourage false or dangerous hopes. It had to be a *successful* conference. 'Squander it,' he warned in words clearly designed for the ears of de Valera, 'and peace is bankrupt.'[7]

His final words linked Ireland's fate to his broader vision for Britain:

When in moments of doubt or hours of despondency we fear that the course of events we are pursuing towards the Irish Sinn Feiners is repugnant to some of our feelings ... we must cheer ourselves by remembering that a lasting settlement with Ireland – a healing of the old quarrel, a reconciliation between two races – would not only be a blessing in itself inestimable, but with it would be removed the greatest obstacle which has ever existed to Anglo-American unity, and that far across the Atlantic Ocean we should reap a harvest sown in the Emerald Isle.[8]

*

As early as Churchill's first and unsuccessful attempt to enter Parliament in 1899, one observer had noted that he was 'always thinking of the impression which his speeches would make, not on his immediate audience, but on London'. His speech did little to alter Dundee minds about his suitability as a local MP. But nationally it marked another important step in his political rehabilitation since the dark days of 1915. The press, apart from the usual suspects in the socialist and Sinn Fein press, was positive. 'The chorus of praise ... must have astonished you yourself,' purred the ever loyal Archie Sinclair. Churchill might also have been feeling flattered that month at finding himself portrayed alongside Disraeli, Gladstone, and Lloyd George himself in a book of pen portraits by Sir Henry Lucy. Having once compared Churchill unfavourably to his father, the journalist now described him as 'The Lion Cub of the Lloyd George Cabinet' in whom he saw subtle but striking reminders of Lord Randolph and 'the brilliant comet that flashed through the House of Commons in the early eighties'.[9]

More significant than such praise, however, was the emergence in the serious press of the words 'statesmanship' and 'leadership' about his performance. 'The country does not only require assistance for its unemployed,' declared *The Times*, 'even more it needs the inspiration of great leadership. Its counsels are confused; it has experienced sufferings for which it is still largely unable to account; it regards the future either with uncertainty or apprehension. These are circumstances in which great men might even now awaken the people to a true understanding of the national position.' Who such a man that might be was made explicit in an editorial. Under the heading 'An Essay in Statesmanship' it praised the breadth and lucidity of Churchill's address and pronounced that it would restore confidence in the country. Its broad appeal raised it above the common level. 'Discarding the debased coinage of party politics,' it declared, '[Churchill] used the nobler currency that once used to pass, and will, we trust, pass again between British public men and the British public.'[10]

This was not the only response of its kind. 'Mr. Winston Churchill may have faults as great as his talents,' remarked the weekly *Saturday Review*, 'but at least he has courage [and] ... often shows the instinct of real leadership ... when he speaks he is apt to speak out, and with the precision and authority of a keen and genuinely independent mind. Courage and the instinct of leadership and the habit of straight and sensible talk are valuable qualities at any time; they are invaluable now.' The periodical *Outlook*, another weekly, raised his stature even higher. 'Signs of incipient statesmanship are not readily to be discerned in most of our rulers. I have observed several of late in Mr. Winston Churchill,' declared an anonymous contributor. 'The symptoms are so pronounced that were I an ambitious young backbencher I would hitch my wagon to the star of the Colonial Secretary, a star that once seemed to be waning to telescopic dimensions, but of late has rapidly waxed from the third to the second magnitude and, in my opinion, will go on waxing. Winston seems to be the only man in the Cabinet with a sane and comprehensive view of world politics.'[11]

These were remarkable words that broke radically with conventional opinion. Who, since the Dardanelles, had uttered the words 'statesmanship' and 'Churchill' in the same breath? Who could imagine that an ambitious young politician would now wish to hitch their wagon to Churchill's star? Even more remarkable was that *Outlook* traditionally supported the Conservatives, who had long loathed him as a traitor to their cause. Here was an intriguing straw in the wind hinting at major tremors in the political world. Such changes were also picked up by two other observers. Both were journalists with a keen eye for the shifting tide of parliamentary affairs. One was the journalist Herbert Sidebotham, *The Times'* accredited observer in the House of Commons' press gallery and a former leader writer and military correspondent for the *Manchester Guardian*. Often he had gazed down on Churchill leaning forwards with his elbows on his knees, busily making paper triangles and twirling them round furiously on his thumbs as he listened intently to the proceedings. This autumn a series of his sketches written for *The Times* appeared under the title *Pillars of the State*. One of them was devoted to Churchill, whom he painted as indispensable to a Coalition starved of able men: highly intelligent, conscientious, hardworking – and one of its best debaters. 'He can create an atmosphere, he is a master of dangerous retort, and always,' claimed Sidebotham, 'there is the sense of power and mastery.' Above all, however, he made clear that he considered that Churchill's future still lay ahead of him. Should the Coalition turn towards the left, he predicted, Churchill, one day, would become a 'leader of a new Tory Party with ideas'.[12]

A similar instinct inspired T. P. O'Connor. As the nights lengthened in London, in late October the veteran MP and journalist drew attention to 'fitful stirrings in the political world that seem to point dimly but decisively towards new developments'. This was inevitable given the discordant elements within the Coalition, but it was unlikely that Lloyd George would be challenged until after he had settled the Irish question. Yet no one could know what tomorrow would bring. After all, pointed out O'Connor, one of the most extraordinary and unpredicted transformations had just taken place in journalism – the sudden devotion of the Tory-supporting *Morning Post* to Winston Churchill. 'It is known that for years there was no public man for whom [it] had so violent, ruthless, and unremitting hatred as Mr. Churchill,' he noted. Yet it had recently changed tack and appealed to him to come to the rescue of the Tories. 'It is easy to forecast where Winston would like to lead,' wrote the veteran and good-natured Irishman. 'Like his father before him he is the ideal leader for a Tory Democratic Party: with more daring even than his father, more education, more energy, and more concentration.'[13]

Churchill was of course delighted with all the publicity. So much so that it put him in the mood to respond with typically wry humour to another congratulatory letter, this one from his sometime friend, Lord Curzon. 'Thank you so much for your kind remarks about my speech,' he told the Foreign Secretary. 'The essence of statesmanship is platitude.' Such self-deprecating false modesty demonstrated that he clearly sensed that his political fortunes were taking a significant turn for the better.[14]

*

Churchill returned from Dundee distressed by the misery he had seen and troubled by its political dangers. Across the country unemployment remained high with no ready solution in sight. His public rhetoric was fiercely anti-socialist. Yet behind closed Cabinet doors he took a more liberal stance on social issues than most of his colleagues. He had argued strongly for a tax on war wealth – the amount by which personal wealth had increased between 1914 and 1918 – and over the summer had strongly resisted abandonment of the government's housing programme to appease the 'anti-waste' movement. This had hit especially hard in his own constituency. At the start of the housing scheme in 1919 the Dundee Council had estimated that the city needed 6,000 new houses to relieve the famine in working-class housing and clear the slums. Since then, it had bought land, streets had been laid out, and gas, water, and electricity mains installed, all at a cost of some £200,000. Even this was only a fraction of what was needed. Now, it had all come to a crashing halt. In July he had pointed out the irony in a protest to his Cabinet colleagues; in the name of 'anti-waste', the heavy capital expenditure by Dundee had been rendered unproductive and the cause of a substantial annual deficit in the city's budget. 'I need scarcely say that I shall find it a matter of very great difficulty to offer any satisfactory explanation to the City Council of the violent reversal of policy in which we have been led,' he protested.[15]

Since then, austerity had tightened further after Sir Robert Horne, his personal nemesis as Chancellor of the Exchequer, successfully proposed the creation of an independent committee under the Minister of Transport, Sir Eric Geddes, to make recommendations for major cutbacks in national expenditure. He both opposed this and insisted that his dissent be officially recorded in the Cabinet minutes. The Committee was formed of axe-wielding business tycoons and one of them, the shipping magnate Lord Inchcape, quickly targeted 'worthless spending on schools and houses'. Churchill was angered by this sabotage of the Coalition's social programme, and during a vigorous discussion between ministers at Gairloch he lamented that the country was 'being sacrificed upon the altar of the banks'.[16]

In London he repeated his complaint. 'Should our policy remain the austere bankers' policy?' he pointedly asked the Cabinet. 'It is not possible for a civilized State with a large portion of its members living in luxury and the great bulk of its members living in comfort to leave a proportion of its citizens with neither work nor maintenance.' To Lloyd George personally, he bluntly declared that it would be useless for him to pretend that he admired 'our post-war policy in several important aspects. The first and greatest mistake,' he stated, 'was leaving the profiteers in possession of their ill-gotten war wealth.' As for the government's wider monetary and financial policy, he believed that the Coalition was 'drifting about in a fog without a compass'. Inside him there clearly struggled remnants of the youthful radical Liberal who had once promised a Glasgow audience that 'the cause of the Liberal Party is the cause of the left-out millions'.[17]

All seemed set for yet another major row with Lloyd George. But in October his course suddenly changed tack. For the rest of the year his political energies were to be almost fully devoted to Ireland.

SIXTEEN

THE COMFORT OF FRIENDS

Back in London after the summer break, the Churchills sought to find comfort for their summer griefs by resuming their busy social life as normal. Friends were only too ready to help, and early in October Ettie Desborough invited them again to Taplow. It was exactly a year since she had been at Cassis enjoying their company in the warmth of Provence. 'Clemmie is so delicious to be with, so easy & happy,' she had noted. 'Winston's spirits and *joie-de-vivre* & the fun-per-minute that he puts into life are quite indescribable – and his absorption in his pictures (really very good) keeps him utterly happy from 7a.m. till bed-time.' The mood was more sombre now, and he spent most of his time painting quietly in the company of John Lavery.[1] A week later, with Clementine incapacitated by an ingrowing toenail, he bundled Diana and Sarah into a car along with his painting gear and thanks to an invitation from Sir Ian and Lady Hamilton drove down to Lullenden. It was blazing hot. Southern England was suffering a record heatwave and temperatures in central London were the highest in more than eighty years. He spent hours outdoors painting a picture of Lullenden's barn and the contrasting effects of light and shade that he had learned on the Riviera. He also took along his painting of the Spears' house at Ightham Moat that Lady Hamilton had bought for £50, and together they chose a spot to hang it in the dining room. Now, she was no longer sure that she liked it and wished instead that she had bought one of Cap Ferrat, but he assured her that he thought it one of his best. Meanwhile, his daughters eagerly explored the house they knew so well and pronounced their approval for the additions made by their hosts. Left unspoken between them all was any mention of Marigold. But when Churchill's eye lit upon the Hamiltons' recently adopted daughter, Lady Jean thought she detected a shadow flit briefly across his face.[2]

Another weekend took them again to Breccles to stay with Edwin and Venetia Montagu. The Saturday was Guy Fawkes Night, perfect weather with russet brown leaves on the trees and a hint of frost in the air. They arrived late and missed the fireworks display, but as usual his appearance rapidly lit things up and sparked a fiery discussion about politics. Duff Cooper was also there with his wife Diana. 'We drank a lot and argued heatedly,' he wrote in his diary. 'Winston doesn't get drunk but takes a great deal.'[3]

Hazel and John Lavery continued to be close friends of the Churchills. They had spent part of the summer playing golf and painting in North Berwick on the Firth of Forth. Hazel was a painter in her own right and since returning to London the couple had been adding a second studio to their Cromwell Road house. In October the Alpine Gallery in the West End opened a show of Sir John's landscapes from his Riviera trip as well as some of Hazel's portraits, including one of Clementine, one of Philip Sassoon's sister Lady Rocksavage, and another of herself taking an early morning cup of tea in her bed. The private viewing was a glittering event that stretched over two days and attracted the cream of London society. There was also a handsomely produced catalogue with a foreword by Churchill. As a companion and eyewitness, he was well able to capture the spirit of his teacher's *plein-air* technique. 'No painter has coped so successfully with the difficulties of this method,' he wrote in praise of Lavery's use of the 'pellucid and pleasurable' light of the Riviera. 'His practicability made it child's play to transport easel and extensive canvas to the chosen scene to stabilize them against sudden gusts of wind, to protect them from the caprice of rain. In consequence,' he added, 'there is a freshness and a natural glow about these pictures which gives them unusual charm.' The experience, as well as the skill, was also obviously his own.

But the actual words were not. They had been crafted by Eddie Marsh. Besides his literary pursuits, Churchill's private secretary was a distinguished art connoisseur and patron of the arts. Thanks to a family inheritance he had been buying paintings by young and upcoming English artists such as Stanley Spencer, Mark Gertler, and the brothers John and Paul Nash, and by now was the owner of one of the most valuable collections of modern works in private hands. That the unmarried Eddie was gay and part of a large homosexual community in London was little secret, although with male homosexuality still illegal in Britain the fact was left discreetly unspoken. It certainly bothered Clementine and Winston not at all, and spoke well for the latter's tolerance when it came to the private lives of his friends.[4]

As he scanned Marsh's draft, he removed some of the more arcane art-historical references and added a sentence or two of his own. One, revealing of his own approach to the canvas, highlighted Lavery's use of 'brilliant and beautiful colour'. The foreword prompted some gentle mockery in the press. 'Mr. Winston Churchill, as the world knows, paints pictures,' The Times reminded its readers, and regretted that some of his own were not in the show. 'Did he not paint the Pyramids some months ago,' it enquired ironically, 'at a time when he might otherwise have been painting a portrait of himself as Chancellor of the Exchequer?' – a pointed reminder, as if he needed it, of the issue that still rankled deeply. Yet he can only have been pleased to have such a spotlight shone on his efforts as an art critic. Shortly afterwards, the New English Art Club invited him to submit one or two of his paintings for a forthcoming exhibition, either under his own name or a *nom de brosse* (artist's pseudonym). The Club had been founded some thirty years previously by artists who had fallen under the spell of Impressionism, as he so obviously had himself.

If close friends such as the Laverys, Desboroughs, and Montagus provided much-needed comfort, so too did his broader network of friends. Like most men of his class, generation, and profession, he already belonged to a club, indeed to many, that catered to the capital's elite: The Turf, The Bath, the Royal Automobile, the National Liberal, and the Athenaeum all counted him as a member. But before the war he had also created one of his own crafted to his individual taste. Along with Lloyd George, F. E. and others, he had established The Other Club, a dining group that met at the Savoy Hotel on the Strand for dinner at 8.15 prompt every other Thursday while Parliament was sitting. This was now a fixed date in his social calendar. With its regular meetings and familiar faces, it provided a reassuring reminder that in the face of his personal grief the world still revolved on its familiar axis.

The Other Club's members were restricted to fifty in number divided equally between parliamentarians from both major parties and a selection of men (all members were male) from the worlds of the arts, literature, entertainment, and the press. He could regularly count on seeing such friendly faces at the table as those of Lord (George) Riddell and Jim Garvin from the world of journalism, as well as fellow politicians of different colours such as the fiery-tempered Irish peer Lord Winterton – frequently a political thorn in his side on Irish questions – and the MP Dudley Ward. Eddie Marsh and Archie Sinclair were also members. One of its earliest recruits was Anthony Hope, the author and staunch Liberal whose 1894 best-selling novel of Ruritanian derring-do, *The Prisoner of Zenda*, had inspired his own single venture into fiction with his novel *Savrola*, a Byronic romance in which the hero is a barely disguised portrait of himself, at least as he had liked to imagine it in his mid-twenties. Hope was a keen attendee, liked Churchill, and believed his exploits at Antwerp had been 'really splendid'. The club has been described as 'the most enduring monument to the F. E.-Winston friendship', a description that does a slight injustice to the significant inaugural role played by Lloyd George, but is broadly true. Churchill along with Birkenhead was clearly the animating force, and by 1921 the club's day-to-day running was largely in the hands of his cousin Freddie.[5]

Churchill also kept his pen busy this autumn by working assiduously on *The World Crisis*. In early November he sent the first three chapters of Volume One to his publisher Thornton Butterworth, requesting they be set up in galley proofs and estimated that the final text would be 100,000 words long, plus thirty or forty pages of appendices. He liked to have galley proofs in front of him so he could work on improving his text and send them out for comments and critiques to friends and experts. It was an expensive way to work, as each new set of proofs had to be set and reset, but it was one that he always followed.[6]

*

Parliament resumed sitting in mid-October. As the autumn nights drew in, his social calendar included dinners alongside Philip Sassoon at Eresby House with the Earl and Countess of Ancaster, and at the Laverys with Duff and Diana Cooper. Towards the end of November he and Clementine were also guests at a dinner at the Hyde Park Hotel hosted by Lord and Lady Beaverbrook.

The owner of the *Daily Express* and *Sunday Express* had met him before the war when he was simply Max Aitken, a newly arrived business tycoon from Canada, and had been dazzled by his brilliance. Given a peerage by Lloyd George for his wartime services – but still known as Max by his friends – the millionaire press lord knew the value of the carefully chosen gift. Over the summer he had sent Churchill the latest volume of the *Dictionary of National Biography*, an essential item for any writer's library. 'Believe me, dear Max,' he responded, 'I value much more the spirit of regard of which it is a token. I think our friendship is not only very pleasant, but fruitful both in council and in action ... I never forget,' he added with genuine feeling, 'the encouragement and help you gave me in 1916 [over Gallipoli] when I had such distracting political and personal issues to cope with.'

Other familiar faces greeted him around the table. Beaverbrook liked to entertain and preferred a round table to a long one to encourage conversation and also did away with the dismal English custom of dismissing females from the table after meals. Birkenhead was there with his wife, and so were Edwin and Venetia Montagu, as well as the ubiquitous Philip Sassoon. A much younger couple in their late twenties were also present. The Honourable Richard Norton was the son and heir to the fifth Lord Grantley. A captain in the Scots Guards with a penchant for fast cars, he had been wounded during the war and ahead of him beckoned a career in merchant banking and film production. His wife Jean was the daughter of a Scottish baronet and Brigadier-General and as a society beauty she was part of the Prince of Wales' glamorous social set. Prince Louis Mountbatten was godfather to their one-year-old daughter. Beaverbrook was an unashamed philanderer and shortly afterwards took Norton's wife as his mistress and she became his constant companion at social events until her death in 1945. Towards the extramarital affairs of his close friends Churchill was as open-minded as he was to homosexuality. Here he differed from Clementine, who strongly disapproved of adultery. She already disliked Beaverbrook and Birkenhead – both Conservatives – for the political influence she feared they had on her husband. Their sexual misdemeanours only made matters worse. Once, when she learned that Winston had invited Beaverbrook for a lunch party, she wrote him a sharp letter of admonition. 'Please do not allow any very low conversation before the Children. I don't necessarily mean "improper", but Lord B does manage to defile any subject he touches, & I hope the relationship between him & Mrs. Norton will not be apparent to Randolph and Diana's inquisitive marmoset-like eyes and ears.' It was no wonder that, more than once, she begged her husband to lock up or burn her letters.[7]

Beaverbrook had added some spice to the evening by inviting a sprinkling of celebrities. From his wide and diverse circle of friends, he had picked the novelist and playwright Arnold Bennett, one of the highest-paid literary journalists in England, as well as a fellow member of The Other Club. A devotee of the Riviera and its grand hotels, the fifty-four-year-old Bennett had spent the previous summer sailing round the Mediterranean in his private yacht with its crew of eight. Thanks to Beaverbrook's post as Lloyd George's wartime Minister of Information, he had been appointed Director of Propaganda to France and become a close friend to the press magnate. Bennett's talk that night might have lacked sparkle. Just hours before, his wife had told him she wanted a separation. As he had been expecting this for some time, however, Beaverbrook's champagne might have given him cause to celebrate rather than drown his sorrows.

But the undoubted main celebrity of the evening was a youthful star of the silver screen. Beaverbrook controlled Britain's largest chain of cinemas, and it was a fellow Canadian who joined Churchill and others round the table. Aged twenty-nine, the Toronto-born and newly minted American citizen Mary Pickford was the undisputed queen of the silent film, her Hollywood contracts worth millions. In her latest film, *Little Lord Fauntleroy*, she had masterfully played the role of both mother and son. She was slim, petite, and undoubtedly pretty. Across the Atlantic she was dubbed 'America's Sweetheart' and 'the Girl with the Curls'. Her husband, seated beside her, matched that fame. Their marriage the year before had been the first movie-star celebrity wedding. In London for the honeymoon, they had been mobbed by enthusiastic crowds and only the quick-witted response of her husband hoisting her onto his shoulders as they stepped from their Rolls-Royce had saved her from serious injury by their fans. But that was a role natural to Douglas Fairbanks. His appearance in *The Mask of Zorro* had already marked him out as a pioneer of the Hollywood swashbuckler role. Along with Charlie Chaplin, both Pickford and Fairbanks had toured the United States during the war promoting the sale of Liberty Bonds to wild success.

What kind of performance this Hollywood royalty couple put on for Churchill is unclear. But the evening surely piqued further his powerful fascination with the world of the moving image, one already made evident in his 1898 description of the Battle of Omdurman as flickering before his eyes 'exactly like a cinematographic film'. When the press magnate William Randolph Hearst later gave him a tour of Hollywood studios, he pronounced it 'a strange and amazing world . . . It is like going behind the scenes of a theatre magnified a thousandfold.' Soon after that, he tried writing a screenplay of his own entitled *The Reign of George V*, which he described to his film producer friend Alexander Korda as 'an imperial film embodying the sentiments, anxieties and achievements of the British people all over the world'. Unlike many of his more conventionally minded political colleagues, he eagerly grasped the propaganda power of film, and especially so after the arrival of the talkies. 'With the pregnant word, illustrated by the compelling picture,' he told Korda, 'it will be possible to bring home to a vast audience the basic truths about many questions of public importance.' He saw films as essentially celluloid versions of great public speeches.[8]

His friendship with Max, which was to last a lifetime, always blew hot and cold. Yet at the very end of his life Beaverbrook had generous and revealing words to say about Churchill: '[He] is essentially a man without rancour. He has been accused of being bad-tempered. It isn't true. He could get very emotional, but after bitterly criticizing you he had a habit of touching you, of putting his hand on your hand . . . as if to say his real feelings for you were not changed. A wonderful display of humanity.'[9]

*

There was little to comfort him, however, in his ministerial duties dealing with regular Colonial Office affairs. Shortly after returning from Dundee, he spoke grandly at the inaugural dinner of the Gold Coast Service Club at the Connaught Rooms in London about the vast potential of British colonies around the world. 'Here,' he pronounced, 'are assets in which you could sink two hundred million pounds in the next ten years with the certainty of getting back every penny you invested.' Yet there lay the insuperable problem – who would take the risk? Already this year he had protested to Lloyd George that the Treasury was starving his Colonial Office budget. But he was certainly not ready to have a row in Cabinet over the issue, especially given his own cost-cutting policies in Iraq. Once again, it was a matter of 'Imperialism-lite'.

Over Africa he gave obligatory ministerial attention to Kenya and Southern Rhodesia. Just the year before, Kenya had become a separate colony with its own governor, and controversy swirled around the part that immigrant Indians should be permitted to play in its affairs. Some 30,000 Indian indentured labourers had worked (and 2,500 had died) to build the Uganda Railway that crossed over 600 miles of Kenyan territory from the sea to Lake Victoria and the Ugandan border. After its completion many chose to settle with their families and by 1921 their demands for greater participation in the colonial legislature could no longer be ignored. Racial tensions were also rising.

He knew Kenya at first hand. As Under-Secretary of State for the Colonies over a decade before he had made an official visit there in company with Eddie Marsh. Disembarking from their ship at Mombasa, he had taken the Uganda Railway into the interior. 'One of the most romantic and wonderful railways in the world,' he had described it with youthful imperial fervour, 'a sure, swift road along which the white man and all that he brings with him for good or ill, may penetrate into the heart of Africa ... one slender thread of scientific civilization, order, authority, and arrangement, drawn across the primeval chaos of the world'. Nairobi, the colony's capital, was at the time little more than an overgrown assembly depot for the railway with a population of about 500 Europeans, 3,000 Indians, and 10,000 Africans. His stay there was long enough for him to grasp the toxic racial and other complexities that now faced him as Colonial Secretary. 'There are already in miniature,' he wrote, 'all the elements of keen political and racial discord, all the materials for hot and acrimonious debate. The white man *versus* the black; the Indian versus both; the settler as against the planter; the town contrasted with the country ... all these different points of view, naturally arising, honestly adopted, tenaciously held, and not yet reconciled into any harmonious general conception, confront the visitor in perplexing display. Nor will he be wise,' he concluded, 'to choose his part with any hurry.'[10]

He was no more inclined now than before to hasten to judgement about Kenya's affairs. While he urged greater partnership between the white colonists and Indians, including a ban on residential segregation in urban areas and the creation of a common electoral role that included both Indians and Europeans, he was unwilling to cause a confrontation. He even described the Indians as 'mainly of a very low class of coolie', and insisted that the reservation of the Kenyan Highlands for white settlers was 'an agreed fact' that could not be changed. This prompted a bitter row with his more liberal-minded friend Edwin Montagu. 'How angry you make me,' complained the Secretary of State for India. Still, as in other cases, political disagreement failed to dent a personal friendship and a bare three weeks later he was enjoying his Guy Fawkes evening at Montagu's home.[11]

Elsewhere in Africa, Jan Smuts was dreaming of absorbing Southern Rhodesia into the Union of South Africa. But the settlers demanded autonomy and in September Churchill agreed to a referendum, although he personally preferred the Smuts option. Here, too, he was not prepared to raise the ire of local whites and kept officially neutral. In the event, union was rejected and Southern Rhodesia became an independent Crown Colony. In both cases he pursued an essentially 'hands-off' policy that revealed once more the essentially pragmatic nature of his imperial commitment. In any case, in his own mind Colonial Office affairs remained distinctly second rank to those of the Foreign Office. In speaking to the Overseas Bankers' Association at Claridge's Hotel in late November, he made his standard encomium on the potential of the British Empire. Yet his simultaneous and powerful call for reconciliation between Germany and France made clear that his urgent concern was Europe and relations between Britain's neighbours across the Channel. That same month, Curzon complained yet again about Churchill's meddling in Foreign Office affairs but he would hear none of it. 'There is absolutely no comparison between the issues in Foreign affairs and . . . those which arise in ordinary departments,' he wrote in an acerbic minute to the Foreign Secretary. 'I have never known Foreign Affairs treated as if they were merely a departmental matter.' On second thoughts he decided not to send it. But his feelings never changed. He remained the same Winston Churchill who before the war had prompted Earl Grey of Fallodon, the Foreign Secretary, to remark wearily that 'Winston, very soon, will become incapable from sheer activity of mind of being anything in Cabinet but Prime Minister.'[12]

*

Nor did the Middle East offer much comfort. November saw the fourth anniversary of the Balfour Declaration, which sparked violence in Jerusalem between Arabs and Jews and caused several deaths. Since his frustrating encounter in August with the Arab delegates in London, he had struggled to chart a path forward that would placate both sides. He also remained heavily committed to cutting the costs of maintaining the

British garrison in Palestine, just as he was doing in Iraq. One idea he floated was to transfer the Black and Tans from Ireland as soon as they could be spared. In mid-November he repeated his familiar mantra to the head of his Middle East Department: 'Do please realize that everything else that happens in the Middle East is secondary to the reduction of expense.'[13]

In wrestling to find a middle ground, he angered both Zionists and Arabs. He pleased the former by approving an ambitious hydro-electric scheme for Palestine known as the Rutenberg Plan after the Ukrainian Jewish immigrant entrepreneur promoting it, but he simultaneously angered Chaim Weizmann by refusing to endorse the claim that Palestine would become 'as Jewish as England is English'. Once again, he tried to persuade Arabs and Jews to sort out their own differences, and arranged a joint conference that he would chair at the Colonial Office on the afternoon of Wednesday 16 November. But the day before, at a lunch given by the Arab delegation, Lord Sydenham of Combe, a former Governor of Bombay, delivered a fiery anti-Zionist speech and Churchill promptly cancelled the meeting using the excuse that he was unwell. He then delegated two subsequent meetings with Weizmann at the Colonial Office to senior officials. Richard Meinertzhagen was scathing. 'Winston is prepared to relegate Zionism to the same policy of drift which has characterized the policy of the Government since the Armistice,' he fulminated in his diary.[14] This was typically intemperate, and inaccurate. Churchill was struggling with currents of history that no single person could halt or divert, and he was tiring of dealing with opponents who appeared unwilling to compromise.

*

In addition to his private tragedies, there remained public griefs and memories of war to assuage. As Chairman of the English-Speaking Union, he soon had a front-row seat in Westminster Abbey at a ceremony that was rich in symbolism. Preparations for the Washington Conference were well advanced and the British delegation was readying to cross the Atlantic. Watched by large crowds that had been assembling for hours, shortly before eleven o'clock on the morning of Monday 17 October General John ('Black Jack') Pershing, the man who had commanded American troops on the Western Front, stepped out of his carriage in front of the Abbey. A band struck up 'The Stars and Stripes'. By the door stood the Dean of Westminster, Lloyd George, and the Duke of Connaught representing the King. Inside, American soldiers and sailors in their khaki and blue lined the nave. Near its west end, the Tomb of the Unknown Warrior was surrounded with wreaths. A Union Jack lay at its foot. The band of the Scots Guard began to play a selection of classical and modern music. The packed congregation watched as a succession of dignitaries filed into the Abbey.

Churchill was one of the first to arrive. He walked slowly the length of the nave and took his seat. The choir and the clergy in their scarlet cassocks assembled around the Tomb. Pershing, along with the American ambassador, Lloyd George, and other government ministers including Freddie Guest as Secretary of State for Air and Lord Lee of Fareham, the donor to the nation of the American-funded Chequers, joined them.

The American ambassador spoke first. By Act of Congress, he announced, President Harding had been authorized to bestow the Medal of Honour, the highest military award that could be granted by the government of the United States, upon Britain's Unknown Warrior. It was not just a military tribute, he declared, it was also a message of fraternity from the American people to the people of the United Kingdom. He was followed by Pershing. In a crisp and clear voice, the general lauded the soldier in his tomb as the latest in the long line of men and women already lying within the Abbey who had given their lives and service to Great Britain. 'His was ever the courage of right,' he declared, 'the confidence of justice.' After solemnly laying the medal with its long ribbon of watered blue silk on the tomb's grey stone, he stepped one pace back and gave a salute. The Dean also spoke a few words. 'Saxon and Norman, Plantagenet and Tudor' also lay in the Abbey, he reminded the congregation, and were part of the Anglo-American heritage. Then came the turn of Lloyd George to thank the American people for their gesture. 'The Empire to its remotest corners will not miss the deep significance of this deed,' he pronounced. 'We feel we are taking part in no idle pageant ... the homage laid today on this grave will remain as an emblem of a common sacrifice for a common purpose. It will be a reminder, not only for this generation but generations to come, that the fundamental aim of these two democracies are the same. These two mighty peoples,' concluded the man who had so recently dominated the Paris Peace Conference, 'who were comrades in the Great War have resolved to remain comrades to guarantee a great peace.'

Churchill then joined in The Lord's Prayer, and the choir sang the 'Battle Hymn of the Republic'. From the far end of the Abbey the 'Last Post' sounded its melancholy notes. The ceremony closed with the singing, to the same tune, of 'God Save the King' and 'My Country 'tis of Thee' – the British and American National Anthems. Many of the congregation joined in. General Pershing and the Duke of Connaught shared an Order of Service, and the King later sent a telegram to President Harding announcing that he would confer Britain's equivalent military medal, the Victoria Cross, on America's Unknown Warrior, who was to be ceremoniously interred at Arlington National Cemetery on the approaching Armistice Day.[15]

Churchill placed great store on ceremony and political theatre. Music and ritual moved him deeply. He had an instinctive feel for the potency of symbolism as a lubricant of power. Twenty years later he was to draw on his experience of this October day as he master-minded a ceremony of his own in the cause of Anglo-American relations. In August 1941 he braved the U-boat infested North Atlantic for his first face-to-face meeting as prime minister with President Franklin D. Roosevelt off the coast of Newfoundland. Their summit climaxed with a Sunday morning service on the deck of the British battleship, which he had carefully rehearsed beforehand. Seated side by side in the centre of a hollow square, and with ranks of British and American sailors on each side and the Union Jack and the Stars and Stripes draped together on the pulpit, he and Roosevelt sang together the hymns they had selected. 'If nothing else had happened here,' pronounced the American President, 'the joint service would have cemented us.'[16]

*

The Westminster Abbey service was not the last of the year's events to bring back memories of the scars of war. Shortly afterwards, he was the guest at the annual dinner of the Tanks Corps to celebrate the Battle of Cambrai fought on the Western Front four years before, when British tanks had accomplished a significant breakthrough at relatively little cost in lives. He had strongly pushed for their use. Soon, in *The World Crisis*, he would be accusing 'without exception all the great ally offensives of 1915, 1916, and 1917, as needless and wrongly conceived operations of infinite cost'. Instead, more and better use of tanks and other mechanized weapons should have been used. 'If only the Generals,' he lamented, 'had not been content to fight machine gun bullets with breasts of gallant men, and think that was waging war.' His pen was at work not just to vindicate his own wartime years. He was also setting out his stall as an expert on tactics and strategy for the future.[17]

*

The day of remembrance for the war dead, 11 November, was another ritual that never failed to stir his emotions, and this year witnessed the first official wearing of red poppies to recall the fields of Flanders. That evening he was due to chair the Armistice Day dinner of the English-Speaking Union, where it would officially welcome the new American ambassador to London. But only a few minutes beforehand he was urgently summoned by Lloyd George to a Cabinet meeting about Ireland and his speech was given instead by Freddie Guest. 'The one and only thing that mattered today was the fervent co-operation between the great English races,' his cousin told an audience that included the Canadian High Commissioner as well as the senior members of the United States' embassy. 'As long as they were united they need not fear any foes ... If they were divided, the road lay open to mischief and intrigue, through which they alone would not suffer, but the whole world.'[18]

Churchill's Anglo-American enthusiasms were heartfelt and sincere. He liked Americans, was excited by the energy and dynamism he had encountered personally in the United States, and he believed that the country represented the essential spirit of the twentieth century. The fact that his mother and maternal aunts were all American was important in his life. But the Churchill family was to have an American future, as well as a past. It was more than fitting that it was Freddie Guest who spoke for him to the English-Speaking Union. For Freddie was not just married to an American: all his children were American citizens, having been born in the United States. In 1921 his second son Raymond was just fourteen years old. Twenty years later he was to head the naval section of 'Wild Bill' Donovan's Office of Strategic Services – the forerunner of the CIA – in London. Shortly after that, he was elected a senator for Virginia and was subsequently appointed the US ambassador to Ireland – the very country whose future Churchill was helping determine when Raymond's father Freddie stepped into his shoes for this Armistice Day dinner. If the British and Americans are often described metaphorically as cousins, in Churchill's case it was literally true.

*

In the United States, the press continued to keep an eye on the progress of Jennie Jerome's elder son. Shortly after Armistice Day the *New York World* reported on the final state of Lady Randolph's marriage settlement to the benefit of both him and his brother. In the eyes of the *Washington Post*, this carried more than financial gain for Churchill. Under the headline, 'Churchill Made Independent', a columnist noted that combined with his earlier inheritance that year, his income now freed him from reliance on his official salary. This was noteworthy for one simple reason. 'Private means,' it declared, 'are well-nigh indispensable to public life in Britain.' It seemed self-evident across the Atlantic by the end of 1921 that Churchill could now find his own pathway through the dark thickets of British politics. Clearly, he was someone to keep an eye on.[19]

SEVENTEEN

'THE DARK HORSE OF ENGLISH POLITICS'

The Irish delegation arrived in London from Dublin on Saturday 8 October and took up residence in Hans Place, a small leafy square in Knightsbridge tucked discreetly away behind Harrods luxury department store. Its leader was Arthur Griffith, Sinn Fein's founder who had fought for the Boers against the British in South Africa. Churchill laconically described him as 'that unusual figure, a silent Irishman'. Eamon de Valera deliberately opted to stay in Dublin. This left Griffith's principal lieutenant as the IRA's director of intelligence, the thirty-year-old Michael Collins, who slipped quietly into London unnoticed two days later and stayed in a different house from the others round the corner in Cadogan Gardens. The group's secretary was the Anglo-Irish Erskine Childers, author of the best-selling pre-war spy thriller, *The Riddle of the Sands*. A wartime lieutenant-commander in the British Navy who had been awarded the DSO, he was a late and uncompromising convert to the cause of Sinn Fein.

Churchill later wrote of Collins that 'he had elemental qualities and mother wit which were in many ways remarkable'. To this he added: 'He stood far nearer to the terrible incidents of the conflict than his leader . . . His hands had touched directly the springs of terrible deeds.' Indeed, Collins' campaign to paralyze Britain's intelligence system in Ireland had been masterful and ruthless. Speaking of the British officers his squad had murdered the previous November, he declared unabashedly that 'By their destruction the very air is much sweeter. For myself, my conscience is clear. There is no crime in detecting and destroying in wartime the spy and the informer. They have destroyed without trial. I have paid them back in their own coin.' Collins had also doubled as a remarkably successful Minister of Finance for the Sinn Fein government.[1]

It was scarce wonder that Churchill described the first meeting at 10 Downing Street on Tuesday 10 October as 'not without its shock'. When Clementine had first heard of the truce in July she immediately hoped he could play an active part in the negotiations. A good Liberal, she abhorred her husband's violent language about Ireland and disliked its handling by Hamar Greenwood – 'nothing but a blaspheming, hearty, vulgar, brave Knock-about Colonial'. But her reason this time was bluntly political – his relationship with Lloyd George. 'I do feel,' she told him, 'that as long as he is P.M. it would be better to hunt with him than to lie in the bushes & watch him careering along with a jaundiced eye.' Her wish had come true. He was now one of the seven Cabinet ministers selected by Lloyd George for the negotiating team and sat almost directly across the long Cabinet table from Collins – the leader of what he had frequently denounced as 'the Murder Gang'. By now the tall dark-haired Irishman was something of a celebrity. Beaverbrook's *Daily Express* described him as 'this big, good-humoured Irishman with the rich brogue and the soft, yet decisive voice', while to *The Times* he was handsome and debonair but also 'sulky, obstinate, and forbidding'. Across the Atlantic, the *Washington Post* portrayed him as a man who hardly slept and worked his stenographers from seven in the morning until 'all three of his own girls [were] dropping from fatigue'.[2]

On his side, Collins saw in Churchill the creator of the Black and Tans that had wreaked havoc across his homeland. Anxious to have a better measure of the men he would be negotiating with, he requested background briefings on them all. Sinn Fein had many English sympathizers, and one of them obliged. The fifty-three-year-old pipe-smoking Crompton Llewellyn Davies was a former Liberal advisor on land reform to Lloyd George and official solicitor to the British Post Office. He came from a radical family: his father lost his post as rector of Christchurch in Marylebone after unwisely delivering a sermon against imperialism in the presence of Queen Victoria; his aunt was the founder of Girton College in Cambridge; and he was uncle to the boys who inspired the author Sir James Barrie to create the characters in *Peter Pan*, a favourite of many Irish nationalists, including Collins. As a student and fellow of Trinity College, Cambridge, Davies had been a member of the elite intellectual group known as 'The Apostles' that included such distinguished figures as John Maynard Keynes, the novelist E. M. Forster, and the poet Rupert Brooke. The philosopher Bertrand Russell, who was a close friend, described Davies as 'able, high-minded, and passionate'. His wife Moya was the daughter of James O'Connor, an Irish Nationalist MP who had spent four years in prison as a Fenian. Radicalized by the Easter Uprising, Moya moved to Dublin where she stored guns for the IRA in her mansion and gave Michael Collins other practical help. In 1919, when he travelled to London hoping to plead the Irish independence case with President Wilson before the Paris Peace Conference, she and her husband helped draft his submission. Davies, thought Bertrand Russell, 'admired rebels more, perhaps, than was wholly rational'.

Early in 1921, a Black and Tan raid on Moya's Dublin house turned up incriminating documents and she was detained in Mountjoy Prison for several weeks. In London, her husband was dismissed from the Post Office and joined a distinguished firm of City solicitors. But he remained passionate about the Sinn Fein cause and agreed to assist Collins with his insider knowledge about his negotiating opponents. Lloyd George he described as 'fertile in expedients, adroit, tireless, energetic and . . . skilled in political strategy'. About Churchill, he wrote:

> The 'dark horse' of English politics. Too adventurous and independent for the ordinary party ties and labels . . . Can hammer out an argument thin, and has an intellectual thoroughness which is very rare in a politician . . . In spite of his reputed 'militarism' and dictatorial air, has more real idea of freedom and care for it than other politicians, and a better understanding of its political framework, and more real regard for the future of England and the British Empire as based on freedom. Can look ahead to necessary and desirable developments.

Collins had strongly protested against de Valera's insistence on sending him to London. 'To me,' he said, 'the task is a loathsome one.' But Llewellyn Davies' profile of Churchill gave at least a glimmer of hope that the defender of the Black and Tans might also be a man the Irish could deal with.[3]

The talks were to last for eight weeks. They were difficult, fraught, frustrating, and often hovered close to collapse. The Sinn Fein delegation constantly had to refer back to de Valera and more vehemently minded Republicans in Dublin, while its members flitted regularly to and fro between the two capitals. On the British side, Lloyd George had to keep his traditionally pro-Ulster Conservative partners happy. By shrewdly choosing both Austen Chamberlain and the fiercely pro-Unionist Birkenhead as negotiators, he made sure he could win crucial Tory support for the treaty. Lloyd George also demonstrated his negotiating wizardry by quickly abandoning the plenary sessions in favour of smaller discussions by the key players on each side.[4]

Churchill's specific role in the talks was to chair a joint committee to discuss naval and air issues. 'We must have free use of the Irish coasts in peace or war for Imperial Defence,' he made clear to the Irish from the start. British control of ports, and hence the denial of any neutrality for Ireland, met instant objection by Collins and the others. Only if they could be assured of the continued unity of the whole of Ireland, stated Griffith, could they consider allegiance to the British Crown. But Northern Ireland by now had its own separate Parliament and prime minister in Belfast and abandoning it would, at the very least, be political suicide for Lloyd George. But holding out the hope that by free consent Ulster might one day in the future play a part in overcoming Irish division offered some chance, however slight, of winning Sinn Fein over to accepting Dominion status under the Crown. 'We can't give way on Ulster,' declared Churchill. 'We are not free agents.' But he could envisage trying to persuade the Northern Irish to accept some kind of loose all-Irish body in the future. In addition, the promise of adjustments to the border between North and South might help to bring Sinn Fein along.[5]

241

Beyond the practical matters at hand was the issue of trust. 'We found ourselves confronted in the early days not only with the unpractical and visionary fanaticism and romanticism of the extreme Irish secret societies,' wrote Churchill later, 'but also the distrust and hatred which had flowed between the two countries for so many centuries.' On principle the Sinn Fein delegates refused to accept any official British hospitality and kept themselves to themselves. They paid for their own accommodation and Arthur Griffith even turned down the offer of a drink during a visit to Chequers. Collins brought his own staff to London including couriers and bodyguards, and early each morning slipped out of his house alone to pray at the nearby Brompton Oratory. At nights the Irishmen mostly socialized together in Hans Place. Often Collins preferred to spend time with his sister Hanna who lived and worked in London, or with old friends he had known before or since the war such as the Llewellyn Davies. Ironically, the most important couple he visited during the negotiations were the Churchills' close friends, the Laverys. 'Do you remember how good he was in the War to us when we were in the Cromwell Road,' Clementine once asked her husband, referring to the artist. 'I used sometimes to go & sit with him in the evenings when I was anxious about you & when you came back from Flanders you used to paint in his studio.'[6]

John Lavery's dominating concern was painting and he was cautious in what he said in public about Ireland. But the much younger Hazel was passionate and outspoken about politics. Her American family had an Irish pedigree, and although she grew up as an Episcopalian she converted to Roman Catholicism. By 1921 both had made known to Churchill their views on Ireland. 'You asked me the other day what I thought of my country's state and I had not the courage to tell you,' Lavery wrote in a letter clearly prompted by Hazel. 'But if one artist may speak to another I will give you my beliefs ... I believe that Ireland will never be governed by Westminster, the Vatican, or Ulster without continuous bloodshed. I also believe that the removal of the "Castle" and all its works, leaving

Irishmen to settle their own affairs, is the only solution left. I am convinced with the knowledge I possess of my countrymen that such a situation would make her one of your staunchest allies instead of an avowed enemy of all time. Love is stronger than hate.'

Once the truce was signed, the Laverys opened their home as a 'neutral ground' where both sides might meet, and soon after the Sinn Fein delegates arrived in London they were invited to Cromwell Road to have their portraits painted. Through his sister Hazel contacted Collins personally. One morning, he turned up unannounced at Lavery's studio, 'a tall young Hercules with a pasty face, sparkling eyes, and a fascinating smile,' recalled the artist. 'I helped him with a heavy overcoat to which he clung, excusing himself by saying casually, "There is a gun in the pocket." '[7]

Lavery's portrait showed Collins with the moustache he wore for his intelligence work. The painting was subsequently lost in Ireland and the artist replaced it with another. Painted almost certainly posthumously, it portrayed him clean shaven and looking younger with unruly dark hair and casually wearing a jacket and white shirt and tie. Collins found it 'absolute torture' having to sit still while being painted and Lavery noted that he sat facing the door and was 'always on the alert'. His capture of the charismatic Collins was an artistic coup. Augustus John had also hoped to paint him, and according to Hazel her husband's fellow Irish portrait artist William Orpen was so jealous that he openly abused Lavery for 'siding with murderers'. Lavery also received several anonymous and threatening letters, including one that claimed his painting of the 'murderer' Collins would no doubt be hung at 10 Downing Street by 'his friend and fellow Republican Lloyd George'.[8]

Over the several weeks of negotiations, the Laverys threw numerous dinner parties and other functions to help bring the two sides together. Collins was always a welcome guest. Sometimes he would stay late at night reading a book from their shelves. 'I found this portion of a wonderful book in an old shop,' Hazel told him once. 'I am trying hard to get an intact copy to send you as you would delight in it I know, and be interested in all the facts about the French Revolution.' In turn Collins presented her with a Kerry Blue terrier, which she named 'Mick'.

This was when Hazel's paintings along with those of her husband were on show in London and her name was being frequently featured in the social columns of the press. She was also an inveterate hostess who readily inflated her own role in the negotiations. Shane Leslie did much to help the myth along. 'History will show,' he claimed, 'how much [she] achieved to make the Irish Treaty possible – Mike Collins, Winston and Hazel made a powerful and scintillating trio. Something had to be created and without them there would have nothing been.'[9] Leslie's family loyalty, as well as a strong sexual attraction to Hazel, clearly helped inflate matters. There were also many stories about her alleged sexual relationship with Collins. These owed much to Hazel herself, who was clearly infatuated with the young Irishman. One of those inclined to believe in an affair was Lady Diana Cooper, who along with her husband Duff – notoriously no stranger to extra-marital affairs himself – was hosted by Hazel at a dinner with the Churchills during the negotiations. Malicious rumours were also spread by Collins' enemies to discredit him in Republican ranks. Yet despite all this mythmaking, it is clear that the turbulent waters swirling round the Sinn Fein–British talks were indeed sometimes smoothed by the personal links between Collins, the Laverys, and Churchill.[10]

On Saturday 29 October he was again at Lympne with Philip Sassoon, but returned the next day to London to meet with Lloyd George and Birkenhead at his house for dinner. It was a critical moment. Lloyd George was facing a parliamentary vote of censure from diehard Unionists opposed to the talks and he needed some firm assurances from Sinn Fein to bolster his position. Urgently summoned by the assistant Cabinet Secretary Tom Jones, Griffith and Collins turned up at his house at ten o'clock that night. Lloyd George took Griffith upstairs for private talks, leaving Collins alone with Churchill and Birkenhead.

So far, Collins had little good to say about Churchill. 'Don't know quite whether he would be a crafty enemy in friendship,' he noted at one point during the talks, 'outlook: political gain, nothing else . . . Studies, I imagine, the detail carefully – thinks about his constituents, effect of so and so on them. Inclined to be bombastic. Full of of ex-officer jingo or similar outlook. Don't actually trust him.'[11] It was no surprise, either, that Churchill found the Irishman 'in a most difficult mood, full of reproaches and defiance and it was very easy for everyone to lose his temper'. But memories of the settlement with the Boers after the hard-fought South African War stood him in good stead. When Collins complained bitterly that the British had hunted him day and night and put a price on his head, Churchill instantly responded: 'Wait a minute,' he said, 'You are not the only one,' and took down from the wall a framed copy of the reward offered for his recapture by the Boers following his escape from their prisoner-of-war camp. 'At any rate it was a good price,' he pointed out to Collins, '£5,000. Look at me – £25 dead or alive. How would you like that?' Collins looked at it, paused for a moment, and laughed. 'All his irritation vanished,' wrote Churchill and from then on, so he claimed, they never lost some measure of trust – although, as he freely admitted, 'deep in his heart' there remained a certain gulf between them. But he was certainly striving hard to grasp the Irish perspective. Three days before, at a Canada Club dinner, he had spoken earnestly of the need to 'penetrate the true spirit of the Irish heart, and by understanding it to lay aside once and for all the ghost of medieval hatreds that had survived even to this hour'. That night at his home, Collins also regaled Birkenhead with tales of his many hair-breadth escapes from the police and the two men became 'good buddies'. This was a turning point for Collins. 'I trust them,' he said afterwards. 'I'm prepared to take their word.' Upstairs, Lloyd George had also reached a crucial personal understanding with Griffith that enabled him the next day easily to defeat the diehards in Parliament.[12]

Meanwhile, Churchill was doing his best to ensure mainstream Tory support for the government. A week later, when he was staying with the Montagus at Breccles for the Guy Fawkes celebrations, he argued vociferously against abolishing the British protectorate and granting internal self-government to Egypt. It was a stance that had already put him at odds with Curzon, who bitterly complained that 'Winston [wants] to concede nothing and to stamp out rebellion in Egypt by Fire and Sword.' But Duff Cooper detected something more calculating at work. The only reason Churchill was taking such an intransigent line, he believed, was that he hoped to make the Irish settlement 'more palatable to the Tories'. Churchill told Cooper and the other guests that the chances of an agreement were '7 to 2 on'.[13]

*

In Ireland, violence continued despite the truce and the IRA continued to smuggle in guns. In Dublin, de Valera kept a tight and suspicious rein on the London delegates. During the first week of November, Lloyd George grew so frustrated that he threatened to resign, but Churchill strongly urged him against it. Not only would it be an abdication of responsibility, it would precipitate 'a very great public disaster' by pitting a hard-line Conservative Party against Labour. The prime minister stayed on. Talks continued, now mainly conducted on the British side by just him, Birkenhead, and Chamberlain. Before the end of the month it appeared as though a breakthrough was close and Lloyd George summoned Griffith to Chequers.

He arrived shortly before ten o'clock in the evening of Saturday 26 November and was ushered into the Long Gallery, a room packed with mementos of English history. Above the mantelpiece hung the sword of Oliver Cromwell, and displayed elsewhere was the letter the Roundhead general wrote after his victory over Royalist forces at the battle at Marston Moor: 'The Lord made them as stubble in our hands'. What Cromwell meant for Irish Catholics and Anglo-Irish relations was best explained later by Churchill himself in his *History of the English-Speaking Peoples*: 'Cromwell's record was a lasting bane. By an uncompleted process of terror, by an iniquitous land settlement, by the virtual proscription of the Catholic religion . . . he cut new gulfs between the nations and the creeds . . . Upon all of us there still lies "the curse of Cromwell".' What effect all the Chequers memorabilia might have had on Griffith is unclear. But when Lloyd George returned to London shortly before midnight, he declared that things were 'better'. The next day a draft treaty was handed to the Sinn Fein delegates. It offered them an Irish Free State with a place within the British Empire akin to that of Canada, but with a guarantee of continued use by the Royal Navy, in both peace and war, of certain defined ports and dockyards. If Northern Ireland chose not to enter a united Ireland, then a Boundary Commission would determine the final border between the two countries.

The Irish delegates took the draft to Dublin to confer with de Valera and returned divided between themselves on how to respond. Collins by now was 'fed up' with the muddle and next day refused to meet with Lloyd George. At this point, according to Sir John Lavery, the Irishman turned up at Cromwell Place in a foul mood and only after hours of persuasion by Hazel did he agree to see the prime minister. 'Take what you can now and get the rest later,' she urged him. Then she drove him to Downing Street in her car. Clementine Churchill repeated this story later, adding that Hazel had done so dressed in her favourite opera cloak. She and Hazel were certainly close enough to have shared confidences. 'That bright, gay, beautiful affectionate [*sic*] who brought so much pleasure & animation wherever she went,' Clementine said of her when she died sadly young just over a decade later.[14]

True or not, the climax to the talks came on Monday 5 December. Newspaper headlines revealed extremes of opinion about the likely outcome. For the *Daily Chronicle* there was 'Little Hope of Settlement', while Beaverbrook's *Daily Express* announced boldly 'Irish Conference Fails'. But for *The Times* the negotiators 'have not yet given up the task', and the Late Night Special edition of the *Evening Standard* announced that 'Both the Government and the Sinn Fein leaders are undesirous of breaking the truce.' Indeed, at three o'clock that afternoon, Lloyd George, Churchill, Austen Chamberlain and Birkenhead met with Collins, Griffith, and another of the Sinn Fein delegates, Robert Barton, at 10 Downing Street. Here, Lloyd George gave them an ultimatum. Either they signed that night, or talks would end and both sides would be free to resume war. For the Irish delegation decision time had come. Griffith said he would sign even if the others refused. By contrast, in Churchill's words, Collins glowered as if he were going to shoot someone, 'preferably himself'.

During these critical hours Churchill also seemed in a belligerent mood. On the one hand, he had some fruitful discussions with the political philosopher Harold Laski, an old acquaintance from Manchester days, about constructive ways of satisfying Sinn Fein over the terms of an oath of allegiance to the Crown. Yet, as Laski told friends, he simultaneously uttered threats 'of John Bull laying about [Ireland] with a big stick'. Just half an hour before the critical meeting at Downing Street, Churchill summoned the bellicose Ulsterman and Chief of the Imperial General Staff Sir Henry Wilson to his office in the Colonial Office to consult him about Royal Navy bases in Ireland. War, he told him, seemed likely. At Downing Street itself, Erskine Childers noted Churchill's body language. 'My chief recollection of these inexplicably miserable hours,' he recorded in his diary, 'was that of Churchill in evening dress moving up and down the lobby with his loping stoop and long strides & a huge cigar like a bowsprit.' The Sinn Fein delegates then returned to Hans Place to argue bitterly between themselves about what to do.[15]

In the evening Lloyd George and the others waited in Austen Chamberlain's room in the House of Commons to receive their reply. Churchill was still in a bullish mood. If they hadn't received an answer by 10 p.m., he declared, the Irish should be left in no doubt 'as to what we are going to do'. He was ignored, and the deadline passed. So did midnight. Then, in the early hours of 6 December the Irish delegation returned and Griffith announced they were prepared to accept the treaty – so long as some 'points of drafting' could be cleared up. This took until almost three o'clock. When the Sinn Fein members finally rose to leave, the British ministers walked round the table and for the first time shook hands.

The treaty gave Ireland practically the same status within the Empire as Canada, Australia, New Zealand, and South Africa. This meant full self-government and financial autonomy, the withdrawal of all British officials, armed forces and police, and an independent Parliament. In return, it would have a Governor-General and grant the Royal Navy certain permanent harbour facilities along with others to be given in the event of Britain going to war. The six counties of the North had a month after ratification of the agreement either to become part of a united Ireland or remain separate as part of the United Kingdom. If they chose the latter, a Boundary Commission would be set up to decide the proper extent of this territory.

So far as Collins was concerned, the terms of the treaty gave 'freedom, not the ultimate freedom that all nations desire and develop to, but the freedom to achieve it'. He also knew that it would bitterly divide Sinn Fein against itself and that his enemies would use it to destroy him. That same day he wrote to one of his oldest friends, 'I tell you this – early this morning I signed my death warrant'. The next day the Cabinet discussed what should happen to Sinn Feiners who had been convicted of murder, and accepted Churchill's view that the Irish should be told privately that the death penalty would not be imposed. Meanwhile Collins and his colleagues returned to Dublin to make their case for the treaty. De Valera was bitterly opposed to Dominion status. But the majority of his Cabinet supported the deal and the treaty was duly sent to the Dail, or National Assembly, for debate. It was now up to it and to the Irish people to decide their fate.[16]

EIGHTEEN

FLEETING SHADOWS

The year had begun with music-hall songs at Lympne. But when Churchill motored down to Chequers the week before Christmas it was to find Lloyd George surrounded by Free Church ministers and a choir solemnly singing Welsh hymns. This was no surprise. Yet for the man accompanying him to the prime minister's English country-house retreat, it was a startling and novel experience.[1]

Boris Savinkov had erupted back into Churchill's life a few days earlier, a reminder that while the Middle East and Ireland had dominated most of his year the future of Russia under the Bolsheviks still ranked high on his personal if not official agenda. The chain-smoking anti-Bolshevik conspirator had spent most of the year in Warsaw plotting guerrilla uprisings in Russia. Known as the 'Greens' to distinguish them from the Reds and the Whites, they blew up trains, assassinated Bolsheviks, and ambushed Red Army patrols. Russia was still in chaos after the Civil War, mired in famine and misery which Churchill sensed could yet stoke the overthrow of Lenin. Still captivated by Savinkov's charisma, he compared the Greens positively to Sinn Fein and described them as waging 'a sort of Robin Hood warfare'. Thanks to pressure from Moscow, Savinkov had been expelled from Warsaw in September and had eventually taken refuge in Paris.

Meanwhile Churchill had met privately in London with Sidney Reilly to discuss Savinkov's schemes. While SIS had now severed its official links with the 'Ace of Spies', Desmond Morton had kept in touch with him.

'There is no doubt that Reilly is a political intriguer of no mean class', he told a colleague, '. . . he is at the moment Boris Savinkoff's right-hand man. In fact, some people might almost say he *is* Boris Savinkoff.' In a lengthy report written for Churchill, Reilly described the guerrilla leader as 'a man of courage, commanding personality, resolution, optimism, [and] shrewd and patient', and rated as high the chances of a general uprising that would produce a more moderate government in Moscow. Early in November, Edward Spears, now one of Reilly's business partners, met privately with Archie Sinclair to discuss his plans.[2]

Savinkov liked to dramatize and yearned to play the great leader. By this time he had convinced himself that Lenin's New Economic Policy meant that the Bolsheviks were desperate to widen their basis of support. Perhaps, as Reilly had suggested, they might make concessions to opponents of the regime – possibly with a place in the leadership for Savinkov himself. With this in mind, Reilly planned to meet in London with Leonid Krassin, with whom he had briefly worked during the Social Revolutionary terrorist campaign against the Tsar and who was one of the few top Bolsheviks that he respected.

But there was a problem. The Foreign Office was firmly opposed to Savinkov's visit. Since the signing of the Anglo-Soviet trade treaty that spring, it was standing firm on a policy of non-interference in Soviet affairs while it pondered the longer-term issue of establishing formal diplomatic relations with Moscow. Savinkov with his guerrilla forces was a disruptive factor in these calculations. Besides, as the senior Foreign Office official Sir Eyre Crowe noted scathingly, Savinkov was 'most unreliable and crooked'. So he was refused a visa.

Churchill, however, was setting great store on meeting him in person. The journalist Herbert Sidebotham astutely described Churchill at this time as 'not so much a member of the Government as an independent principality'. He might also have added that he often took an almost schoolboyish delight in playing cloak and dagger. 'In the high ranges of Secret Service work,' Churchill once wrote, 'the actual facts in many cases were in every respect equal to the most fantastic inventions of romance and melodrama.' Not for the first time he ignored the Foreign Office, pulled his personal intelligence strings, and was able to get Savinkov a visa issued by the Passport Control Office in Paris.[3]

Once in London, Savinkov stayed at Reilly's flat and met privately with Krassin over dinner at a private home. Ever the conspirator, he never revealed his host's name but the most likely candidate was Edward Spears. What was agreed remains uncertain. Savinkov subsequently claimed that an eager Krassin had offered him a post in the Soviet government and that he agreed to take it, but only on three conditions: the abolition of the Cheka; the recognition of individual property rights; and free elections. Hardly was the meeting over than Churchill sent Archie Sinclair to discover what had happened and breakfast was arranged for the next morning. When Savinkov arrived at Sinclair's home it was to find Churchill already seated at the table, hungry for the details. After listening carefully to his account of the meeting with Krassin, he said that the conditions would be quite acceptable to the British government but expressed his doubt that the Bolsheviks would ever agree. The next day, this time over tea at Sussex Square, Savinkov also met Birkenhead who agreed that any recognition of the Soviets had to be wholly conditional on their acceptance of Savinkov's three points.[4]

These discreet private meetings over, Lloyd George had to be brought into the picture, so Churchill and Savinkov motored down together to see him at Chequers and found him with his Welsh choir. For a while they listened politely before the Russian put his case to him. Any official dealings with Moscow, he pleaded, should be on the stringent political conditions agreed by him, Birkenhead, and Churchill.

Lloyd George had his own plans in mind for Russia and believed that the quickest route to post-war recovery was through the rapid economic and political reintegration of Russia into Europe. 'The way to help Russia and Europe and Britain is by trade,' he flatly declared. He was now planning a major European conference for the spring to which the Bolsheviks would be invited. But for this he needed support from France, and he had invited its prime minister, Aristide Briand, for talks in London the next day. Privately, Lloyd George dismissed Churchill's favourite Russian as a 'seductive nihilist'. But the views that Savinkov expressed at Chequers, at least as the prime minister presented them, proved tactically highly convenient in persuading a deeply reluctant Briand to enter into talks with Moscow. Many counter-revolutionaries predicted that Bolshevism was on the verge of collapse, Lloyd George said. But those who 'waited for dead men's shoes were apt to find themselves down at heel', and none of them were men of action who could be relied on. By contrast, he told Briand, at Chequers Savinkov had revealed himself as the only one of any strength. 'The rest were sheep,' he pronounced, whereas Savinkov 'had blown up half a dozen governments and killed a Prime Minister. He was a man of action and great determination, which was plain from his personal appearance.' This made it all the more significant that he had now urged the Allies to talk to Lenin and Trotsky on the grounds that they had become 'anti-revolutionary and were fighting their own extremist wing'. It was even Savinkov's view that it would be possible to put an end to the Bolsheviks. 'If Lenin and Trotsky knew that they had Western Europe behind them,' Savinkov had told him, 'they would defy the extremists.'

As he explained them to Briand, Lloyd George's interpretation of Savinkov's views accorded conveniently with his own, which even included seeing Krassin 'as a kind of Sir Eric Geddes, a businessman not a politician'. This was consistent with what he also told Savinkov at Chequers: that people had been predicting the collapse of Bolshevism for years but that revolutions, like diseases, ran their course. The Bolsheviks would either grow more responsible or fall out amongst themselves, as in the French Revolution, and thus open the way for more moderate leaders. Lloyd George's arguments for talking with the Bolsheviks clearly had some effect on Briand, and they agreed to meet for further talks in Cannes early in the New Year.

Only after the Chequers meeting did Churchill bother to inform Curzon about the Russian's visit. In a 'Secret and Personal' letter he wrote to the Foreign Secretary on Christmas Eve, he told him that he had 'been informed in great secrecy' that Krassin had approached Savinkov and they had met in London. This was disingenuous to say the least. Not only did he omit his own role in events, but by presenting Krassin as the instigator he suggested that Moscow was more eager for talks than in reality it was. Churchill's main goal was to ensure that in any official discussions about aid to Russia, or even the diplomatic recognition to which he remained firmly opposed, the hardest possible bargain should be struck. Aid without the strings as being demanded by Savinkov would be both wrong and foolish. 'Yet that is what I am afraid we may be led into doing if we slide helplessly into a reconstruction policy for Russia without making a good bargain for its unfortunate people,' he told the Foreign Secretary. 'If I may repeat a homely simile I have used before . . . "we want to nourish the dog and not the tapeworm that is killing the dog".' Somewhat cheekily, he added a PS: 'I presume you know of Savinkoff's lunch at Chequers & how well he got on with the P.M?'

Nothing of this episode endeared Churchill to the Foreign Office. It merely reinforced their view that he was something of a troublesome maverick. '[He] has notoriously relied on the advice concerning Russia of persons having no authority, and no direct connections with the centre of Russian affairs,' wrote an irritated Sir Eyre Crowe, 'I fear this is happening once again with Savinkov.' Nothing in the future was to change Churchill's preference for seeking out his own sources of intelligence to weigh against those of professional experts. As for both Savinkov and Reilly, shortly afterwards they were separately lured back to Moscow by a bogus anti-Bolshevik Front run by the GPU, the forerunner of the KGB, and were soon conveniently dead.[5] Later, when his secret dealings with them became an inconvenient memory, he and Desmond Morton ensured that references to them were largely excised from his papers; Reilly's name does not even appear in the relevant volume of the official biography. Alongside the fugitive references to Clare Sheridan, Churchill's private contacts with the anti-Bolsheviks have left only ghostly traces in the record, remnants of what had once been a consuming passion that was already losing its heat.[6]

*

In the meantime, thanks to his hard-working staff, he dealt with the myriad of other small requests that land routinely on ministers' desks. Would he, pleaded Vera Weizmann, be the patron of a fund-raising concert for the London-based Women's International Zionist Organization at which many well-known artists had already promised to appear? Reminding him that since the Balfour Declaration, 'the gates of the country have been thrown open to those Jews who wish to return to their ancient homeland', she went on to explain that 'Most of the immigrants are economically ruined, having come from Russia, Poland and the Ukraine. Our organisation makes it a duty to look after the welfare of these women and children on their arrival in Palestine.' Their specific aim was to build a reception hostel for which they had already purchased the land. On behalf of his boss, Eddie Marsh replied – a bit too hurriedly, as he addressed Vera as 'Sir' – that Churchill would gladly act as patron for the concert 'on the understanding that it is purely honorary'.[7] There also came a request for money from the Rector of Ardelinis Church in Carnlough, County Antrim, reminding him that Lord Herbert Vane-Tempest from whom he had inherited Garron Towers had always been a benefactor of the Parish. Aware of his new duties as the local squire, he instructed his bankers to make sure that £10 for the Parochial Sustentation Fund and a further £2 for the Sunday School Prize Fund be sent. As a reminder of the fast-approaching Christmas holidays he also wrote an open appeal to shoppers urging them to do their gift-buying as early as possible and pointing out that the Early Closing Association, of which he was President, had successfully lobbied the government to make Tuesday 27 December an additional Bank Holiday. He ended by pressing the railway companies to lay on extra trains with cheap fares for the 'millions of toilers' so that they might purchase their presents early, thus ensuring that 'there will be a good prospect of a happy Christmas for every one to bring this anxious and strenuous year to a satisfactory close'.[8]

*

It certainly closed well for him politically. After the signing of the Irish agreement both Houses of Parliament had to approve it. Two days of heated debate took place. In the Lords, Curzon and Birkenhead defended it against bitter attacks by Sir Edward Carson, the leader of the Ulster Unionists. In the Commons, with Sir John Lavery sitting in the gallery sketching the historic scene below, Churchill followed Lloyd George in putting the government's case. By this time de Valera had come out strongly against the treaty, as had a vocal minority on the Tory back benches. Churchill set out to demolish their objections and above all to reassure the mass of traditionally pro-Ulster Unionist MPs of the treaty's merits. He lavishly flattered Ulster's supporters and especially Sir James Craig, Northern Ireland's prime minister, for their continued allegiance to the Crown, their willingness to seek peace, and for not blocking developments in the south. 'Our debt to Ulster is great,' he said. So far as the Irish Free State was concerned, he stressed its similarity to other independent Dominions that gave allegiance to the Crown and offered no threat to Britain. He admitted that the treaty was a compromise but that it was no surrender by an enfeebled Britain – a nation that, after all, had just emerged victorious from the war. On the contrary, it was 'a manifestation of British genius' that would echo throughout the Empire by removing a bitter grievance. 'Whence does this mysterious power of Ireland come?' he asked. 'It is a small, poor, sparsely populated island, lapped about by British sea power, accessible on every side, without iron or coal. How is it that she sways our councils, shakes our parties, and infects us with her bitterness?' Here he resorted to words he had used during his speech to the Canada Club. 'Ireland is not a daughter state. She is a parent nation ... They are intermingled with the whole life of the Empire, and have interests in every part of the Empire wherever the English language is spoken, especially in those new countries with whom we have to look forward to the greatest friendship ... and where the Irish canker has been at work.' In Canada, the Toronto *Globe* had already expressed the same point. 'It looks as though the vile spirit which has infected Anglo-Irish relations for centuries will be exorcised at last,' it declared, while the *Montreal Star* rejoiced that the news of peace in Ireland 'will warm more hearts and set more pulses beating than even the splendid forward step taken toward world peace at Washington.'[9]

Churchill continued. Did complaints against the treaty justify once again laying Ireland 'waste to the scourge of war?' he asked rhetorically. Clearly it was high time that the main body of Irish and British opinion asserted its determination to put a stop to 'these fanatical quarrels'. Cartoonists relished portraying Churchill as a warmonger. But the tone he now struck was that of a committed, even militant, peacemaker and defender of the common people. After referring to Carson's attacks on Curzon and de Valera's on Collins, he went on to say:

> Are we not getting a little tired of all this? These absolutely sincere, consistent, unswerving gentlemen, faithful in all circumstances to their implacable quarrels, seek to mount their respective national war horses, in person or by proxy, and to drive at full tilt at one another, shattering and splintering down the lists, to the indescribable misery of the common people, and to the utter confusion of our Imperial affairs.

The next day, in a speech to the English-Speaking Union, he widened his focus to bring the United States once more into the picture. By now the Washington Conference had already oiled significant points of friction in Anglo-American naval relations. Yet Ireland remained. 'Who shall say,' he asked, 'how much we have suffered in our relations with the United States by the unceasing hostility of the Irish Americans, men who have emigrated from their country, carrying hatred of this island and its institutions all over the world?' He could not foretell the future, he told his audience in Westminster's Central Hall. 'But this I will say. If the hopes . . . which we are entitled to hold of a satisfactory adjustment of the relations of this country with Ireland, of a union of hearts between the people of Great Britain and Ireland, if those fructify . . . then you will embark in the United States upon an era in which the work of the English-Speaking Union will find none of the obstacles which in the past have confronted the efforts to bring into closer harmony the political, social, and moral action of these two great communities.'[10]

Plaudits poured in for his speech. Austen Chamberlain told the King that the case for the treaty could not have been better put and had had 'a profound effect on the House'. The Education Secretary H. A. L. Fisher wrote in his diary that 'Winston makes one of his finest speeches in defence of the settlement'. For Freddie Guest, it was the best speech he had ever heard his cousin make. 'Simplicity of style & fervor of advocacy won a genuine reception from all quarters,' he told him. 'Splendid, bless you.' For *The Sunday Times*, too, he had excelled himself. The speech was 'one of the best things he has done in this Parliament . . . Towards the end . . . Mr. Churchill attained a real eloquence, and it was noticeable that he reduced the malcontents to almost complete silence.' For Hazel Lavery, listening intently from the gallery, it was 'very long but *excellent*'.[11]

He had brilliantly made his case as a peacemaker for Ireland. A week later Lloyd George put him in charge of a special Cabinet Committee to arrange details of the handover of power in Dublin. With typical speed and energy, he took on the task by immediately pronouncing that British troops would be withdrawn from the Irish Free State as quickly as possible. 'Ostentatious preparations to quit should be made everywhere,' he instructed, and on the three consecutive days before Christmas he chaired his committee to work out the details. 'I am full of hope and confidence about Ireland,' he told the Prince of Wales. 'I believe we are going to reap a rich reward all over the world and at home.'[12]

*

Churchill spent Christmas Day with the family at home, and early the next morning left London by train with Lloyd George and Freddie Guest bound for Cannes and the prime minister's meeting with Aristide Briand. The plan was for Clementine to join him later for a short Riviera break together. He was still working assiduously on *The World Crisis* and had recently consulted Foreign Office officials about the diplomatic manoeuvrings leading up to the outbreak of the war. As they rattled their way south through France, Lloyd George read two of the chapters and made some helpful suggestions. 'I cannot help getting vy [sic] interested in the book,' Churchill wrote to Clementine. 'It is a gt [sic] chance to put my whole case in an agreeable form to an attentive audience.' And, he added, the money would make them very comfortable.[13]

In Cannes he stayed with Adele, Lady Essex, working every morning and evening on the book and painting in the afternoons. In six days he wrote some 20,000 words. The more he wrote, the more he felt that he needed to do. The first volume was almost complete with just some 'polishing' left. When he sent it to the publisher, he would receive a hefty cheque. He also lifted weights every day to strengthen the elbow he had damaged during a polo accident to get it fit for action again. Predictably, he also succumbed to a temptation that rarely left him. The casino at Monte Carlo was only a short drive away, and he made several visits to gamble at its tables. 'It excites me so much to play – foolish moth,' he confessed to Clementine, pleading guiltily that he had earned many times what he had lost by the work he had done on his book.[14]

This was good news for the family finances. But back home Clementine was wandering through what she termed 'a miserable valley'. Hardly had he stepped out of the door than one after the other the children and two of the maids started falling ill with the flu – fortunately not such a virulent or fatal strain as three years before. Bessie the maid was the first to succumb, followed quickly by Randolph. On the family doctor's advice, Sarah and Diana were sent to stay with a relative but almost immediately Diana too fell ill and was returned to be nursed at home. Soon the nursery floor resembled a miniature hospital. Clementine called in professional nurses. But one of them proved unsuitable and only after a frantic search was she replaced. By the end of the day Clementine felt like a 'squashed fly', and the doctor ordered her to bed and prescribed a sleeping pill which she thankfully washed down with a glass of champagne. Twelve hours later, after a heavy night's sleep, she wrote a lengthy letter to Winston with a detailed timetable of events. 'Now what do you think of that?' she asked. 'In a small way it is like the beginning of the Great War.'

When she sent a telegram two days later reporting that everyone was on the mend, he replied that her letter was 'Napoleonic' and suggested that once she was recovered she should come out to the Riviera while he, back in London, would 'mount guard in yr [sic] place over the kittens'. Meanwhile, he told her, he was sitting in his bed at night, 'writing, dictating and sifting paper like the Editor of a ha'penny paper'. In his mind, he added, he could imagine her at the same time about to have dinner with a glass of champagne to keep up her spirits. Then, far beyond that, 'in an outer circle of darkness ranges the wide colonial Empire and the Emerald Isle'. In ten days it would all be on top of him again. He also passed on a piece of family news. Cousin Freddie, who had by now separated from his wife Amy, was pursuing a young woman staying on the Riviera and had even mentioned marriage. 'I replied sepulchrally,' Churchill wrote, 'that she was young enough to be his daughter, & that ten years would carry us both to the brink of the sixties.'[15]

His acute awareness of the passing of the years was also heightened by the recent death of yet another of his old acquaintances. As the Irish talks came to their climax in early December, Sir George Ritchie died at the home of his son near London. He had been taken ill in Dundee and travelled to London to consult a specialist, but collapsed with a fatal brain haemorrhage before he could keep the appointment. He was seventy-two. Churchill's sense of loss was sincere and profound. 'His kindness to me was boundless and unceasing,' he wrote in a tribute, 'he has been one of the best friends I have ever had and one of the most able and far-seeing counsellors.' Ritchie's wife had died earlier in the year, and he had unburdened his sorrows to Churchill in Dundee. 'He was sustained and to some extent comforted by an absolute conviction of re-union in a happier world,' he added, 'and ... spoke to me in the accents of one for whom death [was] simply a gateway beyond which all he had loved most on earth were awaiting in a serener form of existence.' He himself had no such faith in an afterlife. What mattered was what one achieved in this life – and he was increasingly conscious of the relentless march of time.[16]

From his room at Lady Essex's home he could see the Cap d'Ail Hotel, where he had stayed with his mother just ten months before. After dining on New Year's Eve in Monte Carlo, the next morning he indulged in more melancholy reflections about the year that had passed. 'What changes in a year!' he lamented to Clementine. 'What gaps! What a sense of fleeting shadows! But your sweet love & comradeship is a light that burns the stronger as our brief years pass.'[17]

'HE WOULD MAKE A GREAT PRIME MINISTER'

fter his return from the Riviera Churchill continued to distinguish himself as one of the heavyweights in the Cabinet, shepherding the Irish Free State Bill through the House of Commons, signing a treaty with Iraq declaring it 'an independent Arab state' under a League of Nations mandate, and ensuring the backing in the House of Commons for his policy in Palestine. He was later to claim that during his time at the Colonial Office he had enjoyed 'some parliamentary and administrative success'. This was ironic false modesty clothing what he justifiably regarded as a considerable triumph. On Ireland alone, he had accomplished more than any chief secretary since the Act of Union in 1800.[1]

On the domestic front, he vigorously defended the Coalition as the only way of preventing the catastrophe of a socialist advent of power and of keeping the Centre and Right in government. In private, however, his views on Lloyd George grew increasingly caustic. 'I don't feel the slightest confidence in L.G.'s judgement,' he confided to Clementine. 'Anything that serves the mood of the moment & the chatter of the ignorant and pliable newspapers is good enough for him.' By the end of the summer he was privately predicting that 'The reign of our revered leader is, I apprehend, drawing to a close.'[2]

His family and social life continued along the well-trodden path of the previous twelve months. He frequently spent time with his brother Jack and Goonie, kept a close eye on his investments, and socialized regularly with friends such as Philip Sassoon, the Duff Coopers, the

Desboroughs, the Montagus, F. E. Smith, and Max Beaverbrook – although Adele, the Countess of Essex with whom he had celebrated the New Year, died suddenly in her Mayfair home in July, aged only sixty-three. 'The world thins very quickly in these days,' he had lamented the year before on hearing of the passing of another old acquaintance. On the anniversary of Marigold's death in August, he wrote sadly that the memory was still 'a gaping wound'. But he took enormous pleasure in his growing young family. 'The children are sweet,' he fondly told Clementine while she recovered from exhaustion on the Riviera early in the year. 'Diana is shaping into a human being. Sarah is full of life and human qualities – with her wonderful hair. The Rabbit [Randolph] has got results in 3 of his subjects.'[3] She shortly discovered she was pregnant and in September gave birth to Mary, the last of their children. That same month Winston finally bought Chartwell Manor, the house in Kent he had spotted the year before. With its purchase, he finally owned the country home he had long yearned for, and it became the political base and emotional haven that was to nurture him for the rest of his life.

Wider family affairs continued to collide with world events. 'The Union Jacks are being silently stored away,' his aunt Leonie wrote forlornly from the Leslie estate now lying just inside the Irish Free State's border with Northern Ireland, which remained a part of the United Kingdom. 'The [Sinn Fein] flag flies on the orange hall.' The tempestuous Clare returned from America as a roving reporter for the New York *World*, and her MI5 file grew thicker as the security service became convinced that she was in the pay of the Russians. 'She has conducted herself in a disgraceful manner in various countries adopting a consistently anti-British attitude,' reported the Chief Passport Officer in London. But whatever she got up to, ultimately she was still family and Churchill was ready to forgive her when the time was ripe. Twenty years later, with Britain at war with Hitler and Moscow and the Bolsheviks now allies, Clare was to spend a wartime morning sculpting his head in 10 Downing Street. She found him in bed smoking a cigar and restlessly stroking his black Persian cat. Finally, he agreed to sit still. 'I want it to be a success,' he grunted. 'We'll call it Prime Minister by Obstreperous Anarchist.'[4]

Meanwhile, he continued to nurture the personal and secret service contacts that were to remain standfast for the next two decades: Archie Sinclair was to become his loyal and dependable Secretary of State for Air during the Second World War; Duff Cooper proved an ally over Munich and was sent to Paris as ambassador to newly liberated France in 1944; Edward Spears remained a trusted source of information about France, and when that country collapsed he flew with General Charles de Gaulle to London to promote his Free French cause; and Desmond Morton soon bought 'Earlylands', the house from which he would frequently stroll over to Chartwell for dinners, games of tennis, and long and unrecorded discussions on secret intelligence affairs. In 1940 Churchill made this 'Man of Mystery' his principal intelligence advisor with an office in 10 Downing Street. Eddie Marsh served Churchill faithfully over many years and was a frequent and welcome guest at Chartwell for the next three decades.[5]

On the sporting front, Churchill suffered a seriously bad fall while playing polo and sold off his ponies, another milestone marking the end of youth. By way of compensation, he poured even more time and energy into his painting. During the summer he was joined in Biarritz by Charles Montag, who insisted that he learned to paint even on cloudy days in order to focus on drawing rather than on the brilliant colours that instinctively attracted him. Painting was to remain his balm at critical moments in his future life. After his crushing electoral defeat at the moment of wartime victory over Nazi Germany, he retreated again to the sun – this time to Lake Como in Italy – and immersed himself deeply in his canvases while he considered, once more, how to rebuild his career. 'Happy are the painters', he once wrote, 'for they shall not be lonely. Light and colour, peace and hope, will keep them company to the end, or almost to the end.' To Sir John Rothenstein, Director of the Tate Gallery, he confessed after he finally resigned as prime minister in 1955 that 'if it weren't for painting I couldn't live. I couldn't bear the strain of things.' He was to continue painting until physical weakness prevented him from doing so in his mid-eighties.[6]

He also made major progress with *The World Crisis*, and sent the final three chapters of his opening volume to the printers. The completed history more than fulfilled his goal and was to prove a bestseller when it started appearing in print a year later. Famously, it also provoked sarcasm from the former Conservative prime minister Arthur Balfour, who described it as 'Winston's autobiography disguised as a history of the world'. This was a typically flippant remark from a man who delighted in the quotable quip, especially if Churchill was its target. *The World Crisis* deserved better than that, both as history and because it laid the groundwork for its author's public reputation as a strategist and statesman with experience and understanding of both war and peace.

His prediction that Lloyd George's time in office was nearing its end soon proved correct. The Coalition collapsed in the autumn of 1922 and the general election that followed produced a political earthquake. The Conservatives won a resounding victory, for the first time in history the Labour Party emerged as the nation's principal opposition, and the Lloyd George and Asquithian Liberals were reduced to third and fourth place respectively, never again to form a British government. Churchill was also crushed at the polls and for the first time in over twenty years found himself without a seat in Parliament. Immediately before the election, he was rushed to hospital for an emergency appendectomy and missed much of the action. As he later wittily put it, he suddenly found himself 'without an office, without a seat, without a party, and without an appendix'.[7]

If his own political forecast about Lloyd George proved right, so did that about his own future made in 1921 by the journalists Herbert Sidebotham and T. P. O'Connor – that the path he was taking was clearly leading him back to the Tories. Just two years after he lost his 'seat for life' in Dundee, and following a short-lived Labour government propped up by the Liberals, he was returned to the House of Commons as a Conservative MP for Epping in Essex in the general election of November 1924. Within days, the new prime minister Stanley Baldwin appointed him Chancellor of the Exchequer, the position once held by his father – and bitterly denied him by David Lloyd George.[8]

*

It would be extravagant to argue that 1921 and the months surrounding it instantly or even totally transformed Churchill and his public image. The ghosts of the Dardanelles lingered obstinately on. In Parliament, the ambitious young Labour politician Oswald Mosley, who was later to lead Britain's Union of Fascists, denounced him as 'a private Napoleon'. David Low's cartoons continued to depict him as irredeemably bellicose. Even ardent supporters continued to harbour doubts. 'Whether he ever comes to the very top or not, will depend upon the answer to one old question,' wrote the veteran journalist and old ally J. L. Garvin. 'The tendency to rush into warlike enterprises ... has been the very bane of his life, and unless he corrects that bias all else will be in vain.' Lloyd George felt much the same after witnessing Churchill's reaction to a border incursion by the IRA into Northern Ireland, when he threatened to send in British troops. 'The PM compared Winston to a chauffeur who apparently is perfectly sane and drives with great skill for months, then suddenly he takes you over the precipice,' noted the assistant Cabinet Secretary Thomas Jones.[9]

Yet he had clearly crossed a watershed in his fortunes. His witticism about the loss of his seat and appendix was one of those literary tricks he frequently deployed to lend dramatic force to the ups and downs of his political life. Clearly, the loss of his seat and Cabinet position was an important setback. But it was also short-lived, and the quip obscured the enormous gains he had made over the previous year. Behind the headlines and alongside the acerbic comments of both friends and rivals, an alternative and more positive view was steadily gaining ground, as heralded by the laudatory press responses to his public speeches on Ireland. Another observer also recorded the shift. The journalist Harold Begbie was a defender of pacifists and conscientious objectors, a biographer of Lord Kitchener, and the author of an instant memoir about the great Antarctic explorer, Sir Ernest Shackleton. Under the pseudonym of 'A Gentleman with a Duster', in 1920 he had published a book entitled *The Mirrors of Downing Street*, a lament about the low moral tone of post-war politics and politicians that he saw embodied in Lloyd George and his government. Although he valued Churchill as an exception with many brilliant gifts, what he lacked, argued Begbie, was the unifying spirit of *character* that would give him direction. 'You cannot depend on him,' he pronounced. 'He carries great guns, but his navigation is uncertain, and the flag he flies is not a symbol that stirs the blood.'[10] This was typical for the time. But twelve months later, struck by Churchill's forceful stand over the child slavery issue in Hong Kong, he had radically changed his mind to declare that it had been 'a brave, disinterested and noble act' and that Churchill was 'a man of the highest character and of a really sincere and moral patriotism'.

Other such startling changes of view could also be found. Clementine unexpectedly encountered one while campaigning for her husband in Dundee, where she was confronted by hostile crowds who shouted her down and even spat upon her. But amidst the vicious hostility, she ran into one of his long-time political opponents, who was clearly impressed by his achievements in Ireland. 'Well,' he told her, 'I always knew that Winston was a great fighter, but I did not know he was a great peacemaker.'[11]

*

Character, as highlighted by Begbie, had always lain at the heart of judgements about Churchill. This had been transparent in the first biography, which appeared astonishingly early in 1905 when he was only thirty years old and had sat in Parliament for a mere four years. Its author was Alexander MacCallum Scott, a lawyer and journalist of the same age from Scotland making his way in Liberal politics in London. Electrified by Churchill's switch from the Conservatives to the Liberals, he boldly predicted that one day he would make history for the nation and become its prime minister. Above everything else, it was his personality and character that mesmerized Scott. His personality was marked by 'bold and striking' colours, while the salient features of his character were will, courage, originality, and magnetism. 'He has mapped out his course,' penned Scott, 'and he pursues it with a dogged persistence [uninfluenced] either by party pressure or public prejudice.' And to hostile critics who relished recalling that Churchill's father had burned out early, Scott riposted bluntly that Lord Randolph's son's survival through many life-threatening escapades suggested a very different destiny. 'He has out-distanced all his contemporaries,' he wrote, '[and] he has ruthlessly brushed aside the mediocrities who encumbered his way.'

He had stuck to this view through Churchill's subsequent misfortunes. After the Dardanelles, Scott updated his biography to argue that adversity had done Churchill nothing but good and whatever the future held he would have an important part to play:

> Those who believe that Churchill's public career is ended have not learned the lessons of history, and have no understanding of human nature, of the power of genius, and of the craving of the mass of the people for leadership. The men of destiny do not wait to be sent for; they come when they feel their time has come. They do not ask to be recognized, they declare themselves; they come like fate; they are inevitable. If Churchill be the man of genius and of power which his past career would indicate, he will come again, and he will be all the stronger and wiser for the bitter experience through which he has passed. This check may, indeed, be the very thing that was necessary to broaden his nature, to teach him restraint and caution, to temper his will like steel, so that it might bend without breaking, and to prepare him for greater tasks in the future. He had been too successful heretofore. He had never known real adversity. In the swift rush of his career he had never learned some lessons which others learn who climb more slowly. He was impatient; he was intolerant of restraint; he did not understand the long game and the waiting game.[12]

*

As demonstrated by the events of 1921, Churchill had finally learned the long game and was reaping the rewards of experience. Even those who had been seared at close quarters by his fiery temperament now believed that his record made him worthy of the highest office. Christopher Addison, who served alongside him in Lloyd George's Cabinet as Minister of Reconstruction and Health, was one. As a newly elected Liberal MP a decade earlier, he had greatly appreciated the support given him by

Churchill as Home Secretary over a difficult constituency issue. 'Whatever happens,' he noted at the time, 'I shall always have a warm corner in my heart for Winston.' His experience as a colleague had not diminished his feeling. 'Nineteen times out of twenty he will get a grip of facts as quickly and as clearly as any man and evolve a sane and practical policy out of them,' he wrote. And even though in the twentieth case Churchill's judgement seemed flawed, he argued that he would be 'a great Prime Minister'. What is noteworthy about this testimony is that when delivering it Addison was moving to the Left while Churchill was returning to the Tories, both men having been made politically homeless by the collapse of the Liberals. In due course, indeed, Addison would become an important Cabinet member of Clement Attlee's post-Second World War Labour government.[13]

Addison was not the only Liberal-turned-Labour Party member who kept faith in Churchill. Alexander MacCallum Scott also transferred his political loyalties and was soon adopted as a prospective Labour candidate for a Scottish constituency. By then the great venture that Churchill had launched in 1921 was bearing fruit with the publication of *The World Crisis*. Scott avidly devoured each volume along with the dozens of reviews that appeared in national and regional newspapers. His thoughts on Churchill's future provide an astute verdict on what he had achieved during the year explored here: 'How he found time to write the book I can hardly conceive,' he wrote in his diary. 'To judge from the reviews this book will be an enduring monument in our literature.' But, he added, 'I think it does more. In the event of another war it might secure for Churchill an authoritative position in the handling of it. It is not the work of an armchair critic. It is the manifesto of a man of action.' Churchill's appeal across the tribal lines of party politics was to stand him in powerful stead as the obvious candidate to become the nation's wartime leader.[14]

*

Admiration for his character extended beyond fellow males or politicians. Women, too, detected leadership qualities in Churchill. A man of his times, he held traditionally conservative views about their role in society and had opposed female suffrage before the war, although he had now changed his opinion about that. Yet he was no misogynist and enjoyed the company of intelligent women – in addition to Clementine – with whom he could spar intellectually. Violet Asquith was one, and historians have often mined her memoirs for insights into his character.[15] Another, rarely mentioned, was Helen Vincent.

A daughter of the 1st Earl of Feversham and a wealthy beauty of her day who had served as a nurse anaesthetist on the Western and Italian Fronts, in 1921 she was in her mid-fifties and married to Lord Edgar d'Abernon, Britain's first ambassador to the Weimar Republic. Before the war she had toured Italy by car with Churchill, and when he was en route to East Africa had lunched with him in Venice where she owned the magnificent Palazzo Giustinian on the Grand Canal. She had also lunched with him and Lloyd George at the height of the crisis over the Red Army's invasion of Poland the previous year. Along with excited discussion about the anti-war Council of Action and the dangers of revolutionary feeling in Britain, there was some fevered speculation about the possibility of an attempt to capture the War Office. 'Winston became rhetorical,' she noted in her diary, 'and talked of the War Office standing "with its back to the river in a fine strategical position".' But along with such typically warlike banter, he had also urged that the conditions leading to such revolutionary feeling should be seriously addressed – especially the deplorable housing conditions in industrial areas of the country.[16]

Shortly after he announced his plans for the Cairo Conference, she penned some thoughts about him in her diary. Years before, she had wagered at long odds that one day he would be prime minister. Nothing since then had led her to change her view: 'His star suffers frequent and semi-total eclipse,' she acknowledged, 'but I still think it will rise at length supreme.' She went on:

He is one of those rare people who seems to gather fresh strength from every reverse. In spite of certain shortcomings, his personality is attractive and winning. He has amazing talent, spirit, and vitality, is full of expedients for every situation, and although he has sometimes shown a lack of judgement he is endowed with rare gifts of imagination and vision. On the human side he is kindly and good-natured, so long as people do not stand directly in his path. A gift for painting and sensitiveness to beauty, not only in nature but in women, are qualities which serve him well, more especially as they are coupled with a sense of humour that is witty and mischievous but never malignant or mean.[17]

*

With successful high office behind him, Churchill was now poised to embark on a new phase of his extraordinary life. He had surmounted turbulence and tragedy to find welcome personal equilibrium in a world still tormented and stripped of optimism by the wounds of war. His achievements in Ireland and Iraq, his eager but cautious embrace of the rising new power of the United States, his sombre insights into the poisonous forces of ideology and nationalism festering in Europe, and his patent parliamentary, ministerial, and rhetorical skills, showed him as a man who could successfully confront this unpredictable new world and lead Britain safely along its treacherous paths. There were to be stumbles and mistakes ahead. Nonetheless, he had clearly emerged from the dark days of his eclipse and was now, more than ever, a prime minister in the making.

ENDNOTES

PROLOGUE: 'A BOLD, BAD MAN'

1. For the Abermule accident, see the Wikipedia entry: Abermule_train_collision; also, www.railwaysarchive.co.uk
2. Bonham Carter, *Winston Churchill as I Knew Him*, p. 15; Gilbert, *World in Torment*, p. 912.
3. Gilbert, *World in Torment*, p. 430; Anon., *Outlook*, 22 October 1921.

INTRODUCTION: 'A TRAGIC FLAW IN THE METAL'

1. Bell, *Churchill and the Dardanelles*, provides a definitive study of the topic.
2. See Bonham Carter, *Champion Redoubtable: The Diaries and Letters of Violet Bonham Carter 1914-1945*, entry for Wednesday 19 May 1915, p. 53; Winston S. Churchill, *Painting as a Pastime*, p. 16.
3. Black, *Winston Churchill in British Art*, p. 42.
4. Brendon, *Winston Churchill*, p. 10; Henry W. Lucy, as quoted in the *Dundee Advertiser*, 21 September 1921; Cannadine, *Aspects of Aristocracy*, pp. 132, 161.
5. Stafford, *Churchill and Secret Service*, p. 34.
6. Langworth, *Winston Churchill, Myth and Reality*, pp. 39-42.
7. Allen Packwood, 'A Tale of Two Statesmen: Churchill and Napoleon', *Finest Hour*, no. 157, Winter 2012-13, pp. 14-19. For information about the Napier, I am grateful to Richard Langworth.
8. A. G. Gardiner, 'Prophets, Priests, and Kings', p. 104, quoted in Shelden, *Young Titan*, p. 8; for the 1913 portrait, see Gardiner, *Pillars of Society*, pp. 152-8.
9. Gardiner, *Pillars of Society*, p. 121.
10. Quoted in Toye, *Lloyd George and Churchill: Rivals for Greatness*, p. 131.
11. Lord Alanbrooke Diary, 14 February 1944, quoted in Gilbert and Arnn, *The Churchill Documents, Volume 19: Fateful Questions September 1943 to April 1944*, p. 1,748.
12. Bonham Carter, *Winston Churchill as I Knew Him*, p. 146; see also on Churchill's 'fierce loyalty' to his immediate family, Cannadine, *Aspects of Aristocracy*, pp. 137, 138-43.
13. Soames, *Winston Churchill: His Life as a Painter*, p. 20.
14. Quoted in Buczacki, *Churchill and Chartwell*, p. 63. See also Randolph Churchill, *Young Statesman: Winston S. Churchill 1901-1914*, p. 69.
15. T. P. O'Connor, *The Times*, 20 March 1921.
16. Churchill and Gilbert, *Companion Volume* (*Companion Volumes* to the official biography by Randolph S. Churchill and Martin Gilbert), p. 953.

17. Gardiner, *Pillars of Society*, p. 153; Churchill, Preface to *The Aftermath*, vol. 4 of *The World Crisis*, pp. vii–viii.
18. Pelling, *Winston Churchill*, p. 258.
19. Stevenson, *Lloyd George: A Diary*, pp. 196–7.
20. Norwich (ed.), *The Duff Cooper Diaries*, entry for 23 January 1920.
21. As quoted by Harold Nicolson in his Foreword to *W.S.C. A Cartoon Biography*, compiled by Fred Urquhart, p. x.
22. Low, *Low's Autobiography*, pp. 146–8.
23. Winston S. Churchill, 'Cartoons and Cartoonists', in his *Thoughts and Adventures*, pp. 9–21.
24. Quoted in Clarke, *The Locomotive of War*, p. 85.
25. Quoted in Paul Addison, 'How Churchill's Mind Worked', unpublished paper for the Faculty Seminar at the University of Texas, 2017, with many thanks to the author.

1 'RULE BRITANNIA'

1. Stansky, *Sassoon: The Worlds of Philip and Sybil*, p. 56. Lord Riddell's diary record of the weekend at Lympne can be found in his *Intimate Diary of the Peace Conference and After*, pp. 259–62. For the Greenwoods, see Maclaren, *Empire and Ireland*, passim. For Hankey on Sutherland, see Cameron Hazlehurst, introduction to *The Lloyd George Magazine 1920-1923*, vol. 1, p. xiv.
2. Boothby, *I Fight to Live*, p. 50.
3. Stansky, *Sassoon*, p. 157. For a more recent biography of Sassoon, see Collins, *Charmed Life*, passim, and for Lympne in particular, pp. 80–6.
4. Toye, *Lloyd George and Churchill*, p. 86.
5. Gilbert, *The Challenge of War*, p. 623.
6. Michael McMenamin, 'Winston Churchill: The Untold Story of Young Winston and his American Mentor', in McNamara (ed.), *The Churchills in Ireland*, pp. 199–219; see also Churchill on Cochran in his *Thoughts and Adventures*, pp. 32–3.
7. For Churchill's view on Anglo-American naval power, see Phillips O'Brien, 'Churchill and the U.S. Navy 1919-29', in Parker (ed.), *Winston Churchill*, pp. 22–42.
8. Amery, *Diaries*, vol. 1, p. 254.
9. Rose, *The Literary Churchill*, p. 97.
10. Marsh, *A Number of People: A Book of Reminiscences*, p. 370.
11. Young, *Churchill and Beaverbrook*, pp. 28–9.
12. Colville Papers, entry for 1 April 1944, quoted in Gilbert and Arnn, *The Churchill Documents*, vol. 19, p. 2,270.
13. Maclaren, *Empire and Ireland*, p. 201.
14. Clarke, *Mr. Churchill's Profession*, pp. 76–7; Lough, *No More Champagne*, pp. 126–8; Reynolds, *In Command of History*, p. 525.
15. Riddell, *Intimate Diary of the Peace Conference and After*, p. 261.
16. Morgan, *Consensus and Disunity*, p. 129; Lee of Fareham, *'A Good Innings': The Private Papers of Viscount Lee of Fareham*, p. 197.
17. Paul Addison, 'The Search for Peace in Ireland', in Muller (ed.), *Churchill as Peacemaker*, p. 200; Bew, *Churchill and Ireland*, p. 1.
18. Bew, *Churchill and Ireland*, pp. 95, 100. See also Gilbert, *World in Torment*, pp. 443–71, 508. For further background on Ireland, see Townshend, *The Republic*, passim.
19. See Gilbert, *World in Torment*, pp. 77–9, and Riddell, *Intimate Diary of the Peace Conference and After*, p. 262. For peace feelers, etc., see Townshend, *The Republic*, pp. 223–4, and Bew, *Churchill and Ireland*, pp. 102–4.
20. Townshend, *The Republic*, pp. 193–7. For MacSwiney's funeral, see Walsh, *Bitter Freedom*, pp. 262–3.
21. Gilbert, *World in Torment*, pp. 500–6.
22. Riddell, *Intimate Diary of the Peace Conference and After*, p. 8.

23. Margo Greenwood diary, 9 January 1921, quoted in Maclaren, *Empire and Ireland*, pp. 203–4.
24. Toye, *Churchill's Empire*, p. 142.

2 FAMILY AND FRIENDS

1. Manchester, *The Last Lion*, pp. 750–6.
2. Stafford, *Churchill and Secret Service*, p. 102.
3. For Guest, see G. R. Searle's entry in the *Oxford Dictionary of National Biography* and his *Corruption in British Politics*, passim; see also David Cannadine, 'The Perils of Family Piety', in Blake and Louis (eds), *Churchill*, pp. 15–16.
4. Addison, *Churchill*, pp. 48–9.
5. See Buczacki, *Churchill and Chartwell*, for Churchill's housing arrangements during this period. For his finances, see Lough, *No More Champagne*.
6. *The Sunday Times*, 4 December 1921.
7. David Freeman, 'Eddie Marsh: A Profile', *Finest Hour*, no. 131, Summer 2006; undated note by Churchill to Marsh, but pre-1914, in Marsh Papers, Churchill College, Cambridge, EMAR1. For Marsh's own memoir, see his *A Number of People*, and for a biography, Hassall, *Edward Marsh: Patron of the Arts*, both very discreet. For Clementine (Hozier) to Marsh, see her undated letter (1908?) in the Marsh Papers, Churchill College, EMAR1.
8. There are numerous biographies of Lawrence. Here I have drawn mostly from that by James, *The Golden Warrior*, pp. 272–362.
9. For Lowell Thomas and his creation of the Lawrence myth, see Stephens, *The Voice of America*, esp. pp. 82–6 and 96–120.
10. See 'Allenby Travelogue in the Provinces', *The Times*, 13 November 1919; also Stephens, *The Voice of America*, p. 112.
11. Churchill, *Great Contemporaries*, p. 137; James, *The Golden Warrior*, p. 362.
12. Speech to the Oxford Union, 18 November 1920, in Churchill, Winston S., *Winston S. Churchill*, p. 3,027. See also Gilbert, *The World in Torment*, p. 437, and Morgan, *Consensus and Disunity*, p. 137. The Communist Party of Great Britain (CPGB) was established in July 1920. Malone was subsequently arrested, jailed, and stripped of his OBE.
13. Stafford, *Churchill and Secret Service*, passim.
14. Colville, *The Churchillians*, p. 172.
15. See Paul Addison's entry on Sinclair in the *Oxford Dictionary of National Biography*, online edition 2008.
16. Hunter, *Winston and Archie*, pp. 12–13; De Groot, *Liberal Crusader*, passim; Paul Addison, entry on Sinclair in the *Oxford Dictionary of National Biography*.
17. Stafford, *Churchill and Secret Service*, p. 99.
18. From *The World Crisis*, quoted in Bennett, *Churchill's Man of Mystery: Desmond Morton and the World of Intelligence*, p. 28. Morton, like Sinclair, helped Churchill collect and select material about Russia for the final volume of *The World Crisis*. See Gilbert, *The Wilderness Years*, pp. 298–309.
19. Bennett, *Churchill's Man of Mystery*, p. 62.
20. Gilbert, *In Search of Churchill*, p. 90. For more on Spears and Churchill, see Egremont, *Under Two Flags: The Life of Major-General Sir Edward Spears*, passim; also Colville, *The Churchillians*, pp. 203–4.
21. Churchill and Gilbert, *Companion Volume*, vol. IV, pt 2, p. 1,071.
22. From Krassin, London, to Tchitcherin, Moscow, copies for Krestnitsky, Lenin, Trotsky, Levrava, 30 December 1920, CHAR 16/74; Churchill note, 5 January 1921.

3 'HE USES IT AS AN OPIATE'

1. Diary of Alexander MacCallum Scott, 28 July 1917, University of Glasgow MS Gen 1465/8.

2. Letter from Belgium to Clementine, 23 November 1915, in Soames, *Winston and Clementine*, p. 116.
3. For a description of the day, see *The Times*, Friday 12 November 1920, 'Armistice Day: The Burial of the Unknown Soldier'. For the wider social context, see Juliet Nicolson, *The Great Silence: 1918–1920. Living in the Shadow of the Great War*, passim.
4. Major Geiger to Sir Archibald Sinclair, 13 January 1921, in Churchill and Gilbert, *Companion Volume*, vol. IV, pt 2, p. 1,307.
5. Leslie, *Jennie*, p. 239.
6. Letter from Mimizan to Clementine, 27 March 1920, in Soames, *Winston and Clementine*, p. 223; Soames, *Winston Churchill: His Life as a Painter*, p. 23.
7. Ibid, p. 46.
8. Ibid, p. 38. His 1915 portrait of Lavery, given to the artist, was exhibited in 1919 at the Royal Society of Portrait Painters.
9. Coombs and Churchill, *Sir Winston Churchill*, p. 202.
10. For Dada and Paris, see Rasula, *Destruction Was My Beatrice*, pp. 145–78.
11. Stafford, *Churchill and Secret Service*, pp. 111–12.
12. *Daily Herald*, 7 January 1921.
13. For Cassel, see the entry by Pat Thane in the *Oxford Dictionary of National Biography*, online edition 2008; Ridley, *Bertie*, pp. 334–5; and for the connections with Churchill, see Randolph S. Churchill, *Young Statesman 1901–1914*, pp. 53–4, 88–9, 195–6.
14. *The Times*, 7 February 1921.
15. Clementine Churchill to Winston Churchill, 26 February 1921, in Soames, *Winston and Clementine*, p. 234.
16. *The Sunday Times*, 30 January 1921; see also 'Riviera Notes,' *The Times*, 24 January 1921; and Howarth, *When the Riviera Was Ours*, p. 98.
17. Macmillan, *The Riviera*, pp. xi–xii.
18. Spurling, *Matisse: A Life*, pp. 336–7, 454. A decade later, when the Regina finally closed its doors to guests and was converted to apartments, Matisse was the first, and for a long time, the only buyer. Cimiez is now the site of the Musée Matisse.
19. Churchill, *Painting as a Pastime*, pp. 34–6.
20. For Bodkin, see Eade, 'Churchill as a Painter', in Eade (ed.), *Churchill by his Contemporaries*, p. 287.

4 A WORLD IN TORMENT

1. For Churchill's reaction to Hunter's suspension, see his letter of 18 February 1921 to Brigadier-General W. Horwood in CHAR 2/14. For Thompson, see his overblown memoir, *I Was Churchill's Shadow*, passim.
2. Churchill to Balfour, 26 February 1921, in Churchill and Gilbert, *Companion Volume*, vol. IV, pt 2, p. 1,379.
3. Curzon to his wife, 14 February 1921, in Gilbert, *World in Torment*, p. 528.
4. Churchill, Departmental minute, 10 February 1921, in ibid, pp. 1,342–3.
5. Sinclair to Churchill, 10 February 1921, in Hunter, *Winston and Archie*, pp. 154–5. For Sinclair's reports on Krassin, Kopp, etc. see passim, pp. 141–55; also Stafford, *Churchill and Secret Service*, pp. 131–3; for Churchill on Savinkov, see his essay in *Great Contemporaries*, pp. 125–33.
6. Minute to Cabinet Finance Committee, 4 January 1921, Churchill and Gilbert, *Companion Volume*, vol. IV, p. 1,287; speech on Air Estimates to House of Commons, 1 March 1921, in Rhodes James (ed.), *Winston S. Churchill*, pp. 3,070–83.
7. Churchill, 'Air Estimates', House of Commons, 1 March 1921, in Rhodes James, ibid, pp. 3,078–9.
8. Churchill to Curzon, 4 February 1921, in ibid, p. 1,340. Also, Stafford, *Churchill and Secret Service*, p. 144.
9. Ibid, passim.

10. Ziegler, *King Edward VIII*, p. 112.
11. Riddell, *Intimate Diary of the Peace Conference and After*, p. 286.
12. Ibid, p. 59.
13. Letter to Clementine, 16 February 1921, CSCT 2/14/16, Churchill College Archives.
14. Ibid.
15. See his letters to Clementine of 9 and 16 February 1921, ibid. For his general stance on the monarchy, see Philip Ziegler, 'Churchill and the Monarchy', in Blake and Louis (eds), *Churchill*, pp. 187–98.
16. For Jack Churchill, see Lee and Lee, *Winston and Jack*, passim; also Colville, *The Churchillians*, pp. 201–21.
17. Lough, *No More Champagne*, p. 128.

5 THE GREAT CORNICHE OF LIFE

1. Churchill to Clementine, 27 January 1921, in Soames, *Winston and Clementine*, p. 224. For Churchill and his finances, see Lough, *No More Champagne*, passim.
2. Soames, *Clementine Churchill*, p. 196; Churchill to Clementine, 6 February 1921, in Soames, *Winston and Clementine*, p. 225. For more on the Garron Towers Estate, see Lough, *No More Champagne*, pp. 130–1, and CHAR 1/151/1.
3. 'Men, Women, and Memories', *The Sunday Times*, 20 March 1921.
4. Geiger to Sinclair, CHAR 16/75, Churchill College, Cambridge; *The Times*, 28, 29, 31 January, 1, 4 February 1921; *The Sunday Times*, 4 February 1921; Clementine to Churchill, 7 February 1921, in CHAR 1/139/3-8. The official biography makes no reference to this visit.
5. Diary of Lady Jean Hamilton, 4 February 1921.
6. For Lavery's stay and painting at Cap d'Ail, see McConkey, *Free Spirit*, pp. 148–9.
7. Garvin on Churchill quoted in Rhodes James, *Churchill*, p. 91; Clementine to Churchill, 13 February 1921, Soames, *Winston and Clementine*, p. 228. In place of the biography, Garvin wrote the glowing foreword to Alexander MacCallum Scott's 1916 biography, *Winston Churchill in Peace and War*; see especially pp. ii–iii.
8. Dilks, 'The Great Dominion', p. 16.
9. For Maclean's reaction to Churchill, see Chalmers, *A Gentleman of the Press*, p. 123. For his meeting with Clementine, see her letter of 18 February in Soames, *Winston and Clementine*, p. 231.
10. *Maclean's* magazine, 15 June 1921; Hamilton, *Gallipoli Diary*, pp. ix, 242; Churchill, *Ian Hamilton's March*, passim.
11. Churchill to Clementine, 15 August 1929, in Soames, *Winston and Clementine*, p. 338.
12. J. H. Plumb, 'The Historian', in Taylor et al., *Churchill: Four Faces and the Man*, pp. 123, 139.
13. Letters of 7 and 21 February 1921, in Soames, *Winston and Clementine*, pp. 226, 233.
14. John Simkin, 'Edward Marsh', on spartacus-educational.com (2014).
15. Toye, *Lloyd George and Churchill*, p. 5.
16. *The Sunday Times*, 6 February 1921, p. 11. For 'Anti-Waste' see Morgan, *Consensus and Disunity*, esp. pp. 96–8.
17. Cowling, *The Impact of Labour 1920–1924*, pp. 166–7.
18. Wilson, *The Downfall of the Liberal Party*, pp. 117–18, and J. M. McEwan, 'Lloyd George's Acquisition of the *Daily Chronicle* in 1918', in *Journal of British Studies*, vol. 22, no. 1, Autumn 1982, pp. 127–44. For the 1920 Club, see Cameron Hazlehurst, Introduction to *The Lloyd George Liberal Magazine 1920–1923*, vol. 1, p. xiii.
19. 'The Menace of Labour', *The Times*, 18 March 1921, p. 12.
20. *The Times*, 11 February 1921, p. 12. For Guest's tour, see *The Lloyd George Liberal Magazine 1920–1923*, vol. 1, pp. 378–81.
21. Morgan, *Consensus and Disunity*, p. 115.
22. For Churchill's position on these social issues, see Pelling, *Winston Churchill*, pp. 271–7; Addison, *Churchill on the Home Front 1900–1955*, pp. 200–21; and Cameron Hazlehurst,

'Churchill as a Social Reformer: The Liberal Phase', *Historical Studies*, vol. 17, no. 66, pp. 84–92.

23. MacMillan, *Paris 1919*, p. 354.
24. Gilbert, *The World in Torment*, pp. 535–6.

6 'THIS WILD COUSIN OF MINE'

1. Sheridan, *Naked Truth*, p. 33.
2. Ibid, p. 25.
3. Clementine to Winston, Saturday 4 December 1915, in Soames, *Winston and Clementine*, pp. 125–6.
4. Leslie, *Cousin Clare*, pp. 78–9.
5. Ibid, pp. 94–7; also, Sheridan, *Naked Truth*, pp. 127–35.
6. Quoted in Cameron Hazlehurst, 'Churchill's "collection of brilliant lions": The Other Club and its Founders', p. 6, unpublished article kindly lent by its author.
7. For Birkenhead, see Campbell, *F. E. Smith, First Earl of Birkenhead*, passim; and the same author's entry on him in the *Oxford Dictionary of National Biography*.
8. Ibid, p. 143.
9. Sheridan, *To the Four Winds*, p. 87.
10. Campbell, *F. E. Smith, First Earl of Birkenhead*, passim; Leslie, *Jennie*, p. 342.
11. Stafford, *Churchill and Secret Service*, p. 111.
12. Leslie, *Cousin Clare*, p. 102; Gilbert, *World in Torment*, p. 422.
13. Sheridan, *Mayfair to Moscow*, pp. 21–5.
14. Churchill and Gilbert, *Companion Volume*, vol. IV, pt. 2, pp. 1,174, 1,182–3.
15. Sheridan, *Mayfair to Moscow*, p. 49.
16. Oswald Frewen Diary, Sunday 5 September 1920.
17. Stafford, *Churchill and Secret Service*, p. 125.
18. *The Times*, 22 November 1920; and Sheridan, *Mayfair to Moscow*, pp. 184, 187.
19. Sheridan, *To the Four Winds*, p. 210.
20. Leslie, *Cousin Clare*, pp. 134–5.
21. Sheridan, *Mayfair to Moscow*, entry for 19 October 1921.
22. CHAR 1/138/5–6.
23. Baruch, *The Public Years*, pp. 121–2; Colville, *The Churchillians*, pp. 86–7; Fishman, *My Darling Clementine*, p. 325.

7 'THE FORTY THIEVES'

1. Churchill, *History of the English-Speaking Peoples*, vol. III, p. 238.
2. The diary of Wing-Commander Maxwell Henry Coote is to be found in the Liddell Hart Centre at King's College, London, Ref.: GB 0099 KCLMA Coote. For Sir Martin Gilbert's account of the Cairo Conference, see *World in Torment*, pp. 544–7.
3. *The Sunday Times*, 13 March 1921; Thompson, *Assignment Churchill*, p. 13.
4. Manchester, *The Last Lion*, vol. 2, p. 70. Manchester himself, however, chooses the wrong hotel, claiming that the conference was held at the Mena House.
5. Hardy, *The Poisoned Well*, p. 130.
6. 'The Cairo Season', *The Times*, 2 April 1921.
7. Humphreys, *Grand Hotels of Egypt in the Golden Age of Travel*, pp. 148–57; Churchill to Warren Fisher of the Treasury, 18 March 1921, in Churchill and Gilbert, *Companion Volume*, vol. IV, pt 2, pp. 1,400–1; Hardy, *The Poisoned Well*, p. 65.
8. Barr, *A Line in the Sand*, p. 121.
9. *The Sunday Times*, 13 March 1921; *Daily Herald*, 14 March 1921.
10. Gilbert, *World in Torment*, vol. I, pp. 532–3, 537–8; for Churchill and Lawrence, see Richard Meinertzhagen, quoted in Dockter, *Churchill and the Islamic World*, p. 130; and Churchill to Shuckburgh, 18 February 1921, in Churchill and Gilbert, *Companion Volume*, vol. IV, pt 2, pp. 1,362–3.

11. Coote Diary, Friday 11 March 1921.
12. Ironside (ed.), *High Road to Command*, pp. 190–1. See also John C. Cairns' entry on Ironside in the *Oxford Dictionary of National Biography*, online edition 2007.
13. Churchill to the House of Commons, 14 June 1921.
14. See e.g. Wallach, *Desert Queen*, and Howell, *Queen of the Desert*. For 'the only female star', see Asher-Greve, 'Gertrude Bell', in Cohen and Joukowsky (eds), *Breaking Ground*, p. 163. See also Lukitz, *A Quest in the Middle East*, passim, and the same author's entry on Bell in the *Oxford Dictionary of National Biography*, online edition 2008.
15. Hardy, *The Poisoned Well*, p. 147; and letter to her father, March 1919, held in the online Bell Archive at the University of Newcastle upon Tyne.
16. Bell, letter to her father, 10 January 1921, in Bell Archive, University of Newcastle upon Tyne.
17. Liora Lukitz, 'Bell, Gertrude Margaret Lowthian (1868–1926)', *Oxford Dictionary of National Biography*, online edition 2008.
18. Coote Diary, Sunday 13 March 1921; Gilbert, *World in Torment*, pp. 546–7.
19. Coote Diary, Monday 14 March 1921.
20. Boyle, *Trenchard*, pp. 381–4.
21. Bell, letter to Frank Balfour, 25 March 1921, in Bell Archive, University of Newcastle upon Tyne; Gilbert, *World in Torment*, pp. 549–50; Catherwood, *Churchill's Folly*, pp. 135–6.
22. Coote Diary, 15 March 1921.
23. Gilbert, *World in Torment*, pp. 551–2; Churchill to Lloyd George, 16 March 1921, in Gilbert, *Companion Volume*, vol. IV, pt 2, pp. 1,396–7.
24. Coote Diary, 17 March 1921.
25. Churchill to Lloyd George, 14, 18, 21, 23 March 1921, and Lloyd George to Churchill, 16 and 22 March 1921, in Churchill and Gilbert, *Companion Volume*, vol. IV, pt. 2, pp. 1,388–415; also, Barr, *A Line in the Sand*, pp. 124–7.
26. 'Scrutator', *The Sunday Times*, 20 March 1921.
27. Gilbert, *World in Torment*, p. 557.
28. Lawrence to his brother Bob, quoted in Gilbert, *World in Torment*, pp. 556–7; Bell to Frank Balfour, 25 March 1921, in Bell Archive, University of Newcastle upon Tyne.

8 THE SMILING ORCHARDS

1. Coote Diary, 24 March 1921; Ridley, *Bertie*, p. 388.
2. Wasserstein, *Herbert Samuel*, p. viii.
3. Sebag Montefiore, *Jerusalem*, pp. 412–19; Shalom Goldman, 'The Rev. Herbert Danby (1889–1953): Hebrew Scholar, Zionist, Christian Missionary', *Modern Judaism*, vol. 27, no. 2, May 2007.
4. Gilbert, *Companion Volume*, vol. IV, pt 2, p. 1,449.
5. Coote Diary, 21 March 1921.
6. Gilbert, *World in Torment*, p. 559.
7. Storrs, *Orientations*, pp. 311, 325.
8. Sebag Montefiore, *Jerusalem*, pp. 441–3.
9. Storrs, *Orientations*, pp. 282–4.
10. Coote Diary, entries for 25 and 26 March 1921; Storrs, *Orientations*, pp. 432–3.
11. Wilson, *King Abdullah, Britain and the Making of Jordan*, pp. 3, 29–30; Graves (ed.), *Memoirs of King Abdullah of Transjordan*, p. 202; Churchill to the House of Commons, 14 June 1921, in Rhodes James (ed.), *Winston S. Churchill*, p. 3,095.
12. Wilson, *King Abdullah, Britain and the Making of Jordan*, p. 53.
13. Hardy, *The Poisoned Well*, pp. 90–1; Churchill to Curzon, 5 April 1921, in Churchill and Gilbert, *Companion Volume*, vol. IV, pt 3, p. 1,432; Wilson, *King Abdullah, Britain and the Making of Jordan*, pp. 207–15.
14. See Gilbert, *World in Torment*, pp. 562–6.
15. Coote Diary, 29 March 1921.

16. Churchill, 'Transjordania', Memorandum for the Cabinet, 2 April 1921, in Churchill and Gilbert, *Companion Volume*, vol. IV, pt 3, p. 1,430; Churchill to Curzon, 5 April 1921, in Churchill and Gilbert, *Companion Volume*, vol. IV, pt 3, p. 1,432.
17. Coote Diary, entries for 27, 28, 30 March 1921.
18. Gilbert, *World in Torment*, pp. 572–5.
19. Twenty years later the *Esperia* was torpedoed by a British submarine off the coast of Tripoli.

9 TRAGEDY STRIKES

1. See Churchill's hotel bill for 4–8 April 1921 in CHAR 1/154; Martin, *Jennie*, vol. 2, pp. 395–6. The error that Churchill rushed back to London is repeated in Roberts, *Churchill*, p. 284; Roy Jenkins simply ignores the episode.
2. McConkey, *Free Spirit*, pp. 148–9; Churchill's Foreword was drafted for him by his private secretary Eddie Marsh; *The Brooklyn Daily Eagle*, 17 December 1921. For Lavery's election to the Royal Academy, see *The Times*, 2 March 1921. Sir Martin Gilbert makes no mention of this Cap d'Ail visit in the main narrative of his official biography; it appears only as a footnote in the relevant companion volume of documents.
3. *The Times*, 28 April 1921.
4. Gilbert, *World in Torment*, pp. 581–2.
5. For Bill Hozier's death, see *The Times*, 16 April 1921; for Lady Blanche's letter to Churchill, see CHAR 1/138.
6. Letter from New York of 8 April 1921, CHAR 1/138; Bricrin Dolan, 'Clare Sheridan, an Adventuress and her Children', *Journal of Irish Literature*, vol. 19, no. 2, May 1990, pp. 3–46. In 1943 Clare was to suggest to her cousin Winston that he include her brother Oswald on a mission to Moscow on the grounds that he had driven by motorcycle with her across Russia in 1923 and hence possessed 'an exceptional understanding' of the Soviet Union. See Clare to Winston, 27 September 1943, in Gilbert and Arnn, *The Churchill Documents*, vol. 19, pp. 286–7.
7. Lady Jean Hamilton Diary, undated but February 1921.
8. Handwritten note dated 29 June 1921, sold at Christie's, New York, 23 June 2011, Sale 2456, Lot 7.
9. Martin, *Jennie*, vol. 2, pp. 396–401.
10. *Boston Evening Globe*, 29 June 1921; *Boston Post*, 10 July 1921, CHAR 1/146; Baruch, undated, CHAR 1/140/84.
11. Gilbert, *World in Torment*, pp. 605–6; *The Sunday Times*, 3 July 1921; *The Times*, 4 July 1921; Churchill to 'Dearest Millie', in Sutherland Papers, Staffordshire and Stoke-on-Trent Library Services, online www.sutherlandcollection.org.uk. I am grateful to Paul Addison for this reference.

10 PEACEMAKER

1. Mowat, *Britain Between the Wars 1918–1940*, pp. 119–29; Lee of Fareham, 'A Good Innings', p. 208.
2. For the rising internal paranoia within the IRA of early 1921, see Townshend, *The Republic*, pp. 262–6; Walsh, *Bitter Freedom*, pp. 252–7.
3. For Stenning's murder, see 'List of Suspected Civilian Spies Killed by the IRA, 1920–21' by Dr Andy Bielenberg and Professor Emeritus James S. Donnelly, at theirishrevolution.ie; for Frewen, see the biography by Leslie, *Mr. Frewen of England*, passim.
4. James S. Donnelly, 'Big House Burnings in County Cork during the Irish Revolution 1920–1921', *Eire-Ireland*, vol. 47, nos 3–4, Fall/Winter 2012, pp. 141–80; Leslie, *Mr. Frewen of England*, p. 195.
5. Charles Lysaght, 'Leslie, John Randolph ('Shane')', *Dictionary of Irish Biography*; Leslie, *Cousin Clare*, p. 163; Leslie, *Long Shadows*, p. 228.

6. Aidan Dunne, 'A Passion for the Political', *The Irish Times*, 26 July 2010; Lavery, *The Life of a Painter*, pp. 211–12 (he gives no date for this letter); Bew, *Churchill and Ireland*, p. 103. Bew claims it was a portrait of MacSwiney, but as no such portrait is known to exist it was presumably the Southwark Cathedral scene.
7. Isaiah Berlin, 'Personal Impressions', quoted in Robert Rhodes James, 'Churchill the Parliamentarian, Orator, and Statesman', in Blake and Louis (eds), *Churchill*, p. 108.
8. Soames (ed.), *Winston and Clementine*, pp. 231–2.
9. Bew, *Churchill and Ireland*, p. 105.
10. Street, *Ireland in 1921*, pp. 23–7.
11. Townshend, *The Republic*, p. 301.
12. Gilbert, *World in Torment*, p. 666.
13. 'Ireland and Anglo-American Relations', 28 June 1921, in Rhodes James (ed.), *Winston S. Churchill*, pp. 3,113–14.
14. James, 'Churchill the Parliamentarian, Orator, and Statesman', in Blake and Louis (eds), *Churchill*, pp. 506–17.
15. Duff Cooper Papers, DUFC 15/2/5, Churchill College, Cambridge; Field, *Bendor*, passim.
16. Rose, *Churchill*, p. 180; and see his article on 'Churchill and Zionism' in Blake and Louis (eds), *Churchill*, pp. 147–66; Makovsky, *Churchill's Promised Land*, passim.
17. Quoted in Cocker, *Richard Meinertzhagen*, pp. 2, 105, 268. For his ornithological frauds, see Fortey, *Dry Store Room No. 1*, pp. 281–3; see also Garfield, *The Meinertzhagen Mystery*, passim. Meinertzhagen also claimed to have rescued one of the Tsar's daughters from Ekaterinburg, and to have interviewed Hitler with a pistol in his pocket.
18. For his meeting with Churchill, see Cocker, *Richard Meinertzhagen*, pp. 148–9; Mattar, *The Mufti of Jerusalem*, pp. 26–8.
19. Gilbert, *World in Torment*, p. 583; and Cocker, *Richard Meinertzhagen*, p. 267, fn 28.
20. For the speech, see Rhodes James (ed.), *Winston S. Churchill*, pp. 3,095–111.
21. Thomas Marlowe, 'Memorandum for Lord Northcliffe', 30 May 1921, in Churchill and Gilbert, *Companion Volume*, pp. 1,477–8; Neville Chamberlain to his sister Hilda, 18 June 1921, in *The Neville Chamberlain Diary Letters, Volume Two: The Reform Years 1921–1927*, ed. Robert Self, p. 65; Churchill to Lloyd George, 17 June 1921, in Churchill and Gilbert, *Companion Volume*, p. 1,511.
22. Gilbert, *World in Torment*, pp. 598–9.

11 'WHERE ARE WE GOING IN EUROPE?'

1. *The Times*, 21 June 1921.
2. Churchill, *My Early Life 1874–1908*, p. 71.
3. Ibid, pp. 113, 215; *The Times*, 23 June 1921.
4. Sixsmith, *Russia*, pp. 8–9.
5. Stafford, *Churchill and Secret Service*, pp. 145–7; Bennett, *Churchill's Man of Mystery*, pp. 48, 54–5.
6. Ibid, 18–19 June 1921; Egremont, *Under Two Flags*, p. 97.
7. Letter to her husband, 11 July 1921, in Soames (ed.), *Winston and Clementine*, p. 238.
8. Ibid, letters of 11, 20 or 27 July 1921, pp. 238–9; Soames, *Clementine Churchill*, p. 217.
9. Memorandum for Lord Northcliffe by Thomas Marlowe, 30 May 1921, Churchill and Gilbert, *Companion Volume*, vol. III, pp. 1,477–8.
10. Toye, *Lloyd George and Churchill*, p. 196.
11. There is a considerable scholarly literature about the *Mui-tsai* system. A useful starting point is the article by Susan Pedersen, 'The Maternalist Moment in British Colonial Policy: The Controversy over "Child Slavery" in Hong Kong 1917–1941', *Past and Present*, no. 171, May 2001, from which the quotation by Churchill is taken (p. 171). For a contemporary account by anti-slavery activists, see Lt Cmdr and Mrs H. L. Haslewood, *Child Slavery in Hong Kong: The Mui Tsai System*, London, The Sheldon Press, 1930.

12. 'International Affairs', 8 June 1921, in Rhodes James (ed.), *Winston S. Churchill*, pp. 3,091–4.
13. *The Times*, 24 May 1921; see also 2 and 21 June 1921; Steiner, *The Lights that Failed*, p. 196.
14. 'International Affairs', Speech to the Manchester Chamber of Commerce, 8 June 1921, in Rhodes James (ed.), *Winston S. Churchill*, pp. 3,091–4.
15. C. P. Snow, *Variety of Man* (1969), pp. 136–8, quoted in an article by Paul Addison, 'How Churchill's Mind Worked'. I am deeply grateful to the author for sharing this with me before publication. Hitler's election as sole leader of the Nazi Party took place in Munich on 29 July 1921.
16. Graham, *Arthur Meighen, a Biography*, vol. II, pp. 76–81.
17. For Churchill's 15 June speech, see *The Times*, 16 June 1921.

12 IMPERIAL DREAMS

1. For the guest list, see *The Times*, Court and Social Section, 28 June 1921.
2. Graham, *Arthur Meighen*, vol. II, p. 84.
3. Ibid, pp. 108, 507; *The Times*, 11 April 1921; Ian McGibbon, 'Allen, James 1855–1942', *Dictionary of New Zealand Biography*.
4. 'Prince and West Indies: Mr. Churchill on Links with Canada', *The Times*, 25 June 1921.
5. Churchill, Cabinet Memorandum, 'The Anglo-Japanese Alliance, 17 June 1921', in Churchill and Gilbert, *Companion Volume*, vol. IV, pt 3, pp. 1,512–13.
6. Churchill, Cabinet Memorandum, 4 July 1921, in Churchill and Gilbert, *Companion Volume*, vol. IV, pt 3, pp. 1,539–42; Gilbert, *World in Torment*, pp. 606–7; Beloff, *Imperial Sunset*, p. 331; Neidpath, *The Singapore Naval Base and the Defence of Britain's Eastern Empire 1919–1941*, p. 41.
7. Gilmour, *Curzon*, pp. 524–5; Davenport-Hines, *Ettie*, p. 241.
8. Hancock, *Smuts*, pp. 129–30.
9. Churchill and Gilbert, *Companion Volume*, vol. IV, pt 3, pp. 1,544–6.
10. Hamill, *The Strategic Illusion*, pp. 17–30. For other useful studies of the Singapore base, see McIntyre, *The Rise and Fall of the Singapore Naval Base 1919–1942*, and Neidpath, *The Singapore Naval Base and the Defence of Britain's Eastern Empire 1919–1941*.
11. Wm. Matthew Kennedy, 'Imperial Austerlitz. The Singapore Strategy and the Culture of Victory 1917–1924', in Walsh and Varnava (eds), *The Great War and the British Empire*, p. 124. See also Hamill, *The Strategic Illusion*, pp. 25–9.
12. Toye, *Churchill's Empire*, p. xvii; Clarke, *The Locomotive of War*, p. 94, and *Mr. Churchill's Profession*, pp. 291–3.
13. *The Times*, 12, 13 July 1921.
14. Amery, *Diaries*, p. 270.
15. Churchill, Cabinet Memorandum, 23 July 1921, Churchill and Gilbert, *Companion Volume*, vol. IV, pt 3, pp. 1,563–6; Beloff, *Imperial Sunset*, pp. 341–4.
16. *The Times*, Friday 1 July 1921.
17. Quoted in Boyle, *Trenchard*, p. 159.
18. Bridge, *William Hughes*, passim.
19. *The Times*, 26 August 1921.
20. *The Times*, 8 September, 3 October 1921.

13 'I WILL TAKE WHAT COMES'

1. Churchill Cabinet Memorandum, 'The Situation in Palestine', 10 June 1921, in Churchill and Gilbert, *Companion Volume*, vol. IV, pt. 3, pp. 1,499–500.
2. 'Note of a Conversation held at A. J. Balfour's house', 22 July 1921, ibid, pp. 1,558–60; Churchill to Cabinet, 11 August 1921, ibid, pp. 1,585–90.

3. 'Conversation between Winston S. Churchill and Shibley Jamal', 15 August 1921, in ibid, pp. 1,592–1601; Churchill, 'Remarks to the Palestinian Arab Delegation', 22 August 1921, ibid, pp. 1,610–18.

4. Churchill to Cabinet, 4 August 1921, in ibid, pp. 1,576–8; Churchill to Lloyd George, 7 August 1921, ibid, p. 1,582.

5. Churchill to Trenchard, 22 July 1921, in ibid, p. 1,561; see also pp. 1,497–8, 1,547.

6. Haldane to Churchill, 14 August 1921, in ibid, pp. 1,590–1.

7. Gertrude Bell to her father Sir Hugh Bell, 20 December 1921, Bell Archive, University of Newcastle upon Tyne.

8. R. M. Douglas, 'Did Britain Use Chemical Weapons in Mandatory Iraq?', *The Journal of Modern History*, vol. 81, no. 4, December 2009, pp. 859–87; and Haldane to Churchill, 14 August 1921, in Churchill and Gilbert, *Companion Volume*, vol. IV, pt. 3, pp. 1,590–1.

9. Lough, *No More Champagne*, pp. 136–7.

10. Librairie P-V Stock, Paris, to Churchill, 28 July 1921, in CHAR 1/153/15–18.

11. Churchill to Jackson, 22 July 1921, in Churchill and Gilbert, *Companion Volume*, vol. IV, pt. 3, pp. 1,562–3.

12. Lough, *No More Champagne*, p. 138; H. A. L. Fisher Diary, 19 August 1921, in Churchill and Gilbert, *Companion Volume*, vol. IV, pt 3, p. 1,609; Barker & Co. (Coachbuilders) Ltd to Churchill, 19 August 1921, in CHAR 1/153/ 27–28.

13. Churchill to Clementine, 18 July 1921 (not in Soames, *Winston and Clementine*), CSCT 2/14/30.

14. Gertrude Bell to Sir Hugh Bell, 28 August 1921, in Bell Archive, University of Newcastle upon Tyne.

15. Soames, *Clementine Churchill*, pp. 200–2; *A Daughter's Tale*, p. 5; *Winston and Clementine*, p. 241; also Gilbert, *World in Torment*, p. 613.

16. Davenport-Hines, *Ettie*, p. 241.

17. Leslie, *Long Shadows*, p. 24; Sinclair to Churchill, undated, but August, in Churchill and Gilbert, *Companion Volume*, vol. IV, pt 3, pp. 1,621–2; Elizabeth Walden to Churchill, 19 August 1921, in CHAR 1/ 153/26.

18. *The Times*, 21 August 1921.

19. Lough, *No More Champagne*, pp. 135–6.

20. Churchill to Clementine, 19 September 1921, in Gilbert, *The World in Torment*, pp. 613–14. For the full text, see CSCT 2/14/32.

21. Churchill to Edwina Ashley, 25 September 1921, in Churchill and Gilbert, *Companion Volume*, vol. IV, pt 3, p. 1,627.

22. Clementine to Churchill, 22 September 1921, in Soames, *Winston and Clementine*, p. 242; *The Times*, 27 September 1921.

14 'A SEAT FOR LIFE'

1. Churchill, *The World Crisis 1918–1928: The Aftermath*, pp. 311–12.

2. Maclaren, *Empire and Ireland*, p. 235. The idea for the map was Margo Greenwood's.

3. For the text of the letter, and much that follows here, see Jones, *Whitehall Diary*, ed. Keith Middlemas), *Volume III, Ireland 1918–1925*, pp. 1,921–3. For De Valera's 'second-rate political margarine', see *The Times*, 7 September 1921.

4. *Dundee Advertiser*, 5 September 1921.

5. Owen, *Tempestuous Journey*, pp. 577–9.

6. 'Brahan Castle: Wise Behind the Hand', *The Times*, 6 September 1921.

7. *Dundee Advertiser*, 7 September 1921; *The Times*, 8 September 1921.

8. Nicolson, *King George the Fifth, his Life and Reign*, p. 359.

9. Jones, *Whitehall Diary*; Churchill, *The World Crisis: The Aftermath*, p. 313.

10. *The Times*, 13 September 1921; for Lloyd George's illness, see *The Times*, 21 September 1921; for Riddell, see his *Intimate Diary of the Peace Conference and Beyond*, p. 325; for Houston, see Campbell, *F. E. Smith, First Earl Birkenhead*, pp. 97–8.

11. Letter to Clementine, 19 September 1921, in CSCT 2/14/32; for Lloyd George's letter of invitation to De Valera, see *The Times*, 30 September 1921.
12. Tomlinson, *Dundee and the Empire*, p. 9; Paterson, *Churchill*, pp. 46, 48, 267. See also Jeffrey, *This Dangerous Menace*, p. 9.
13. Sir George Ritchie to Churchill, 17 June 1921, in CHAR5/24.
14. Speech at King's Theatre, Dundee, 14 February 1920, in Rhodes James (ed.), *Winston S. Churchill*, p. 2,938.
15. Paterson, *Churchill*, p. 148; for an obituary of Ritchie, see the *Dundee Advertiser*, 5 December 1921; for Churchill's letter to Ritchie on Socialism, see *The Times*, 17 February 1920; for that on the Middle East, see CHAR 5/21, final draft by Marsh with Churchill's changes, dated 1 March 1921.
16. Churchill, *Thoughts and Adventures*, pp. 159–60.
17. Cited in William M. Walker, 'Dundee's Disenchantment with Churchill: A Comment on the Downfall of the Liberal Party', *The Scottish Historical Review*, vol. 49, no. 147, April 1970, p. 99.
18. Walker, *Juteopolis*, pp. 426, 440.
19. Walker, 'Dundee's Disenchantment', p. 103.
20. Ibid, p. 104; Churchill, *Thoughts and Adventures*, p. 161.

15 'THE COURAGE AND INSTINCT OF LEADERSHIP'

1. See the *Dundee Advertiser*, all issues 6–30 September 1921.
2. Churchill to Ritchie, 11 September 1921, in CHAR 5/24; D. J. Macdonald to Churchill, 17 September 1921, in CHAR 5/24; Addison, *Churchill on the Home Front 1900–1955*, p. 220.
3. Churchill to Worthington Evans, 15 July 1921; and Alexander Spence to Churchill, 21 July 1921, both in CHAR 5/24.
4. Churchill to Lloyd George, 23 September 1921, in CHAR 5/24.
5. Winston S. Churchill, 'The Scaffolding of Rhetoric', unpublished essay 1897; Moran, quoted in Cannadine (ed.), *Winston S. Churchill*, introduction, p. xiv; Clarke, *Mr. Churchill's Profession*, pp. 294–5.
6. *Dundee Advertiser*, 26 September 1921.
7. For the text of the Caird Hall speech, see Rhodes James (ed.), *Winston S. Churchill*, pp. 3,128–31; the *Dundee Advertiser* and *The Times*, 26 September 1921.
8. Rhodes James (ed.), *Winston S. Churchill*, p. 3,140.
9. Rhodes James, *Churchill*, p. 20, fn 32; Henry Lucy ('Toby M.P.'), *Lords and Commoners*, p. 80.
10. Gilbert, *World in Torment*, p. 669; *The Times*, 24, 26 September 1921.
11. *Saturday Review*, 1 October 1921; *Outlook*, 22 October 1921.
12. Sidebotham, *Pillars of the State*, pp. 140, 149–50.
13. T. P. O'Connor, *The Times*, 23 October 1921; Addison, *Churchill on the Home Front 1900–1955*, p. 202.
14. Churchill to Curzon, 29 September 1921, in Churchill and Gilbert, *Companion Volume*, vol. IV, pt 3, pp. 1,634–5.
15. Churchill, 'Dundee and the Housing Scheme', Cabinet Memorandum, 20 July 1921, in CAB/22/126, National Archives. I am grateful to Paul Addison for drawing my attention to this.
16. Riddell, *Lord Riddell's Intimate Diary of the Peace Conference and After 1918–1923*, 15 September 1921, p. 235; see also Morgan, *Consensus and Disunity*, pp. 104–5.
17. Churchill, 'The Unemployment Situation', Cabinet memorandum, 28 September 1921; Lloyd George to Churchill 1 October 1921; Churchill to Lloyd George, 8 October 1921, all in Churchill and Gilbert, *Companion Volume*, vol. IV, pt 3, pp. 1,630–44; for the Glasgow speech, see Rhodes James, *Churchill*, pp. 40–1.

16 THE COMFORT OF FRIENDS

1. Davenport-Hines, *Ettie*, pp. 239, 241.
2. Lady Hamilton Diary, Sunday 16 October 1921.
3. Duff Cooper Diary, 5 November 1921.
4. See Hassall's entry on Marsh in the *Oxford Dictionary of National Biography* (2004–16), and Douglas Plummer, *Queer People*, p. 304.
5. Mallet, *Anthony Hope and His Books*, pp. 196–7, 221, 232. Hope's full name was Anthony Hope Hawkins; Campbell, *F. E. Smith*, p. 267. The club's official history can be found in Colin Coote's now dated 1971 *The Other Club*, while a more recent and valuable analysis of its origins and historiography can be found in Cameron Hazlehurst's unpublished article 'Churchill's "collection of brilliant lions": The Other Club and its Founders', kindly lent to the author by Professor Hazlehurst. See also Toye, *Lloyd George and Churchill*, p. 85.
6. See Marsh's (undated) draft with Churchill's amendments in the Marsh Papers at Churchill College, Cambridge, EMAR1. For the Alpine Club events, see *The Times*, 16 and 24 October 1921; C. H. Collins Baker, Secretary, to Churchill, 22 November 1921, in CHAR 1/138/123; M. Wise of Thornton Butterworth to Churchill, 10 November 1921, in CHAR 8/40.
7. Campbell, *F. E. Smith*, p. 267; Clementine to Churchill, 10 September 1921, in Soames, *Winston and Clementine*, p. 300. See also her letter of 11 July 1921, ibid, p. 238.
8. For the November Beaverbrook dinner, see *The Sunday Times*, 27 November, 1921; for Bennett, see Drabble, *Arnold Bennett, a Biography*, esp. pp. 230–61; and John Lucas, entry for Bennett in the *Oxford Dictionary of National Biography*. For Beaverbrook and Bennett, see Taylor, *Beaverbrook*, esp. pp. 54–5, 170, 234–45, 657. For Churchill's letter of thanks, see Churchill and Gilbert, *Companion Volume*, vol. IV, pt 3, pp. 1,550–1, Young, *Churchill and Beaverbrook*, p. 59. For his visit to Hollywood and the exchanges with Korda, see John Fleet, 'Alexander Korda: Churchill's Man in Hollywood', in *Finest Hour*, no. 179, Winter 2018, pp. 12–15, and, in the same issue, Churchill's description of Hollywood from the *Daily Telegraph*.
9. Taylor, *Beaverbrook*, p. 657.
10. Winston S. Churchill, *My African Journey*, pp. 3–8, 21–2; also Randolph S. Churchill, *Young Statesman*, pp. 221–38.
11. Churchill to Montagu, 8 October 1921, and Montagu's reply, 12 October 1921, in Gilbert, *Companion Volume*, vol. IV, pt 3, pp. 1,644–50.
12. *The Times*, 29 September 1921; Ronald Hyam, 'Churchill and the British Empire', in Blake and Louis (eds), *Churchill*, pp. 167–85. *The Times*, 30 November 1921; Churchill to Curzon, in Churchill and Gilbert, *Companion Volume*, 9 November 1921, vol. IV, pt 3, pp. 1,665–6; Grey, quoted in Rhodes James, *Churchill*, p. 45.
13. Churchill to Sir John Shuckburgh, 12 November 1921, in Churchill and Gilbert, *Companion Volume*, vol. IV, pt 3, pp. 1,668–9.
14. Gilbert, *World in Torment*, p. 639.
15. *The Times*, 18 October 1921.
16. Stafford, *Roosevelt and Churchill*, pp. 68–9.
17. Gilbert, *World in Torment*, p. 62.
18. *The Times*, 12 November 1921.
19. *The Times*, 'Mr. Churchill's Fortune', 17 November 1921; *Washington Post*, 3 December 1921, in CHPC 2/2/288, Churchill Archive.

17 'THE DARK HORSE OF ENGLISH POLITICS'

1. Stafford, *Churchill and Secret Service*, p. 157.
2. Clementine Churchill to her husband, 18 February, 11 July 1921, in Soames, *Winston and Clementine*, pp. 232, 238.
3. Quoted in Forester, *Michael Collins*, p. 220; see also for Crompton and Moya Llewellyn Davies, Coogan, *Michael Collins*, pp. 108–9, 284–6. Moya Llewellyn Davies later claimed

to have had a sexual liaison with Collins, but this is much disputed. See her entry in the *Dictionary of Irish Biography*. For her husband Crompton, see Lubenow, *The Cambridge Apostles, 1820–1914*, pp. 195–6; also his obituary in *The Times*, 25 November 1935; *The Times*, 11 December 1921; Walsh, *Bitter Freedom*, p. 311; and Slinn, *Clifford Chance*, pp. 71–3.

4. For Birkenhead and Chamberlain's crucial role, see Campbell, *F. E. Smith*, pp. 549–85; Maclaren, *Empire and Ireland*, pp. 239–43.
5. Gilbert, *World in Torment*, pp. 669–73.
6. Winston S. Churchill, 'The Irish Treaty', in *Thoughts and Adventures*, p. 167; Hart, *Mick*, p. 29; Clementine to her husband, 5 January 1935, in Soames, *Winston and Clementine*, p. 367.
7. Lavery, *The Life of a Painter*, p. 213.
8. McCoole, *Hazel*, p. 74.
9. Leslie, *Long Shadows*, p. 228; see also Coogan, *Michael Collins*, p. 288.
10. Coogan, *Michael Collins*, pp. 288–9; McCoole, *Hazel*, pp. 63–82.
11. Taylor, *Michael Collins*, p. 155.
12. Churchill, 'The Irish Treaty', p. 170; Jones, *Whitehall Diary*, p. 157; Mowat, *Britain Between the Wars*, p. 90; Coogan, *Michael Collins*, pp. 252–9. Owen, *Tempestuous Journey*, p. 583; *The Times*, 27 October 1921.
13. Toye, *Churchill's Empire*, p. 50; Norwich (ed.), *The Duff Cooper Diaries 1915–1951*, entry for 5 November 1921, p. 153.
14. Clementine to Winston, 5 January 1935, in Soames, *Winston and Clementine*, p. 367.
15. Churchill, *The Aftermath*, p. 321; Childers' Diary, 5 December 1921, quoted in Hart, *Mick*, pp. 317–18; Sir Henry Wilson Diary, 5 December 1921, in Churchill and Gilbert, *Companion Volume*, vol. IV, pt 3, p. 1,648; Wilson (ed.), *The Political Diaries of C. P. Scott 1911–1928*, pp. 406–7. For the meeting in the Long Gallery at Chequers, see Jones, *Whitehall Diary*, pp. 176–7.
16. Churchill and Gilbert, *Companion Volume*, vol. IV, pt 3, pp. 673–7; for full details see Frank Pakenham (Lord Longford), *Peace by Ordeal*, Appendix 1, pp. 288–93; Campbell, *F. E. Smith*, p. 572; McCoole, *Hazel*, p. 84.

18 FLEETING SHADOWS

1. Churchill, *Great Contemporaries*, p. 132.
2. Stafford, *Churchill and Secret Service*, p. 142; Bennett, *Churchill's Man of Mystery*, p. 55.
3. Sidebotham, *Pillars of the State*, p. 96.
4. Stafford, *Churchill and Secret Service*, pp. 136–7; Michael Heller, 'Krassin-Savinkov: Une rencontre secrète', in *Cahiers du Monde russe et soviétique, Janv–Mars 1985*, pp. 63–8; David Watson, 'The Krassin–Savinkov Meeting of 10 December 1921', ibid, juillet–décembre 1986, pp. 461–70; Spence, *Savinkov*, passim; David Footman, 'Boris V. Savinkov', *History Today*, 1958, pp. 73–82; for Lloyd George and the background to Genoa, see Andrew Williams, 'The Genoa Conference of 1922: Lloyd George and the Politics of Recognition', in Fink et al. (eds), *Genoa, Rapallo, and European Reconstruction in 1922*, pp. 29–40.
5. Churchill to Curzon, 24 December 1921, in Churchill and Gilbert, *Companion Volume*, vol. IV, pt 3, pp. 1,699–711; see also Gilbert, *World in Torment*, pp. 760–1.
6. Stafford, *Churchill and Secret Service*, p. 147. In 1941, in deference to his wartime Soviet ally Stalin, he had his essay on Savinkov removed from that year's edition of *Great Contemporaries*, along with that on Trotsky.
7. Vera R. Weizmann to Churchill, 2 December 1921, and E. Marsh to Mrs Vera R. Weizmann, 5 December 1921, in CHAR 2/118/ 22, 35.
8. The Rev. T. Gordon Sharpe to Churchill, 9 December 1921, Churchill to Cox & Co, 19 December 1921, in CHAR 1/151/51–55; *The Times*, 13 December 1921.
9. *The Times*, 9 December 1921.
10. Rhodes James (ed.), *Winston S. Churchill*, pp. 3,146–57.

11. Gilbert, *World in Torment*, p. 681; *The Sunday Times*, 18 December 1921; McCoole, *Hazel*, p. 83.
12. Ibid, pp. 681–3.
13. Headlam-Morley to Churchill, 10 December 1921, in CHART 8/40/199; Churchill to Clementine, 29 December 1921, in Gilbert, *Companion Volume*, pp. 1,706–7.
14. Churchill to Clementine, 4 January 1922, in Soames, *Winston and Clementine*, p. 246; Gilbert, *World in Torment*, pp. 761–2.
15. Clementine to Churchill, 27 December 1921, in CHAR 1/139/93–106, summarized in Soames, *Winston and Clementine*, p. 243; Churchill to Clementine, 29 December 1921, in ibid, p. 244.
16. Churchill's obituary statement on Ritchie, 3 December 1921, in Churchill and Gilbert, *Companion Volume*, vol. IV, pt 3, pp. 1,683–4.
17. Churchill to Clementine, 1 January 1922, in Soames, *Winston and Clementine*, p. 245.

EPILOGUE: 'HE WOULD MAKE A GREAT PRIME MINISTER'

1. Churchill, *The Second World War*, vol. 1, p. 21; Bew, *Churchill and Ireland*, pp. 7, 31.
2. Churchill to Clementine, 27 January 1922, in CSCT 2/14/1; Gilbert, *World in Torment*, p. 795.
3. Ibid, pp. 758, 791–2. Lord Ranksborough, formerly Major-General John Brocklehurst who had been present during the Siege of Ladysmith and was the Liberal whip in the House of Lords, died in February 1921; for Churchill's comment, see CHAR 2/115/3.
4. See her file in KV 2 1033, National Archives, Leslie, *Cousin Clare*, p. 249. The bust now stands in the hall at Chartwell.
5. Bennett, *Churchill's Man of Mystery*, p. 62; Stafford, *Churchill and Secret Service*, pp. 146, 185.
6. Soames, *Churchill: His Life as a Painter*, p. 199.
7. Churchill, *Thoughts and Adventures*, p. 213.
8. For the parliamentary machinations leading up to this, see Jenkins, *Churchill*, pp. 370–92.
9. Quoted in Gilbert, *World in Torment*, pp. 890–1, 909.
10. Begbie ['A Gentleman with a Duster'], *The Mirrors of Downing Street*, pp. 121–7.
11. Begbie's leaflet 'To the Women Electors of Dundee' is to be found in the National Library of Scotland. It took many years for Churchill's instructions to Hong Kong to be enforced locally.
12. Scott, *Winston Churchill in Peace and War*, pp. 252, 154–5.
13. Addison, *Politics from Within*, p. 128; Morgan and Morgan, *Portrait of a Progressive*, p. 9. In the 1930s Churchill was to ensure that Addison, by then a Labour peer and fellow opponent of appeasement, should be supplied with inside information on air defences; ibid, p. 229.
14. Diary of Alexander MacCallum Scott, 5 March 1927, in MSG 1465/22, University of Glasgow. I am grateful to Cameron Hazlehurst for bringing these words to my attention.
15. Bonham Carter, *Winston Churchill as I Knew Him*, passim.
16. D'Abernon, *Red Cross and Berlin Embassy*, pp. 8, 65–6. For her previous encounters with Churchill, see Shelden, *Young Titan*, p. 160; Randolph S. Churchill, *Young Statesman*, p. 197; Churchill to Lady Lytton, 19 September 1907, in Churchill and Gilbert, *Companion Volume*, vol. IV, pt 2, p. 679.
17. Quoted in Davenport-Hines, *Ettie*, p. 337.

BIBLIOGRAPHY

Addison, Christopher, *Politics from Within*, London, Herbert Jenkins Ltd, 1924.

Addison, Paul, *Churchill on the Home Front 1900–1955*, London, Pimlico, 1993.

Addison, Paul, *Churchill: The Unexpected Hero*, Oxford, Oxford University Press, 2005.

Amery, L. S., *Diaries, Volume 1: 1896–1929*, ed. John Barnes and David Nicholson, London, Hutchinson, 1980.

Applebaum, Anne, *Gulag: A History*, New York, Anchor Books, 2004.

Arthur, Max, *Churchill: An Authorized Pictorial Bibliography*, London, Cassell, 2015.

Barr, James, *A Line in the Sand: Britain, France, and the Struggle for Mastery in the Middle East*, London, Simon and Schuster, 2011.

Baruch, Bernard, *The Public Years*, New York, Holt, Rinehart and Winston, 1960.

Beaverbrook, Lord, *The Decline and Fall of Lloyd George*, London, Collins, 1963.

Beaverbrook, Lord, *Men and Power 1917–1918*, London, Hutchinson 1916.

Beaverbrook, Lord, *Politicians and the War 1914–1916*, London, Thornton Butterworth, 1928.

Begbie, Harold, *The Mirrors of Downing Street: Some Political Reflections*, London, Mills and Boon, 1920.

Bell, Christopher, *Churchill and the Dardanelles*, Oxford, Oxford University Press, 2017.

Beloff, Max, *Imperial Sunset, Volume 1: Britain's Liberal Empire 1897–1921*, London, Methuen & Co Ltd, 1969.

Bennett, Gill, *Churchill's Man of Mystery: Desmond Morton and the World of Intelligence*, London, Routledge, 2007.

Bentley, Michael (ed.), *Public and Private Doctrine: Essays in British History presented to Maurice Cowling*, Cambridge, Cambridge University Press, 1993.

Berlin, Isaiah, *Mr. Churchill in 1940*, London, John Murray, n.d.

Best, Geoffrey, *Churchill: A Study in Greatness*, London, Hambledon, 2001.

Bew, Paul, *Churchill and Ireland*, Oxford, Oxford University Press, 2016.

Black, Jonathan, *Winston Churchill in British Art, 1900 to the Present Day: The Titan with Many Faces*, London, Bloomsbury Academic, 2017

Blake, Robert, and Louis, Wm. Roger (eds), *Churchill*, New York, W. W. Norton, 1993.

Blume, Mary, *Côte d'Azur: Inventing the French Riviera*, London, Thames and Hudson, 1992.

Bonham Carter, Violet, *Champion Redoubtable: The Diaries & Letters of Violet Bonham Carter*, ed. Mark Pottle, London, Weidenfeld & Nicolson, 1998.

Bonham Carter, Violet, *Winston Churchill as I Knew Him*, London, Eyre and Spottiswoode, and Collins, 1965.

Boothby, Robert, *I Fight to Live*, London, Gollancz, 1947.

Boyle, Andrew, *Trenchard*, London, Collins, 1962.

Brendon, Piers, *Winston Churchill: A Brief Life*, Toronto, Stoddart, 1984.

Bridge, Carl, *William Hughes: Australia*, London, Haus, 2011.

Buczacki, Stefan, *Churchill and Chartwell: The Untold Story of Churchill's Houses and Gardens*, London, Frances Lincoln Ltd, 2007.

Cameron, Roderick, *The Golden Riviera*, London, Weidenfeld and Nicolson, 1975.

Campbell, John, *F. E. Smith, First Earl of Birkenhead, London*, Cape, 1983.

Cannadine, David, *Aspects of Aristocracy: Grandeur and Decline in Modern Britain*, New Haven and London, Yale University Press, 1994.

Cannadine, David, *In Churchill's Shadow: Confronting the Past in Modern Britain*, London, Oxford University Press, 2003.

Cannadine, David (ed. and Introduction), *Churchill: The Statesman as Artist*, London, Bloomsbury Continuum, 2018.

Cannadine, David (Introduction), *Winston S. Churchill. Blood, Toil, Tears and Sweat: The Great Speeches*, London, Penguin, 2001.

Catherwood, Christopher, *Churchill's Folly: How Winston Churchill Created Modern Iraq*, New York, Carroll and Graf, 2004.

Chalmers, F. S., *A Gentleman of the Press*, Toronto, Doubleday, 1969.

Chamberlain, Neville, *The Neville Chamberlain Diary Letters, Volume 2: The Reform Years 1921–1927*, ed. Robert Self, Aldershot, Ashgate, 2000.

Charmley, John, *Churchill, the End of Glory: A Political Biography*, New York, Harcourt Brace, 1993.

Churchill, Peregrine, and Mitchell, Julian, *Jennie: Lady Randolph Churchill: A Portrait with Letters*, London, Collins, 1974.

Churchill, Randolph S., *Young Statesman: Winston S. Churchill 1901–1914*, London, Minerva, 1991.

Churchill, Randolph S., and Gilbert, Martin, *Companion Volumes* to the official biography and their continuation as *The Churchill War Papers*, 1967–present.

Churchill, Winston S., *Great Contemporaries*, London, Fontana, 1959.

Churchill, Winston S., *History of the English-Speaking Peoples*, London, Cassell, 1956.

Churchill, Winston S., *Ian Hamilton's March*, Toronto, Copp Clark, 1900.

Churchill, Winston S., *My African Journey*, Toronto, William Briggs, 1909.

Churchill, Winston S., *My Early Life 1874–1908: A Roving Commission*, London, Fontana, 1969.

Churchill, Winston S., *Painting as a Pastime*, Delray Beach, Florida, Levenger Press, 2002.

Churchill, Winston S., *The Second World War*, vols 1–6, Boston, Houghton Mifflin, 1948–56.

Churchill, Winston S., *The World Crisis*, New York, Scribners, 1923–9.

Churchill, Winston S., *Thoughts and Adventures*, London, Odhams Press Ltd, 1947.

Churchill, Winston S., *Winston S. Churchill: His Complete Speeches 1897–1963, Volume III: 1914–1922*, ed. Robert Rhodes James, New York, R. R. Bowker and Company, 1974.

Clarke, Peter, *Mr. Churchill's Profession*, London, Bloomsbury, 2012.

Clarke, Peter, *The Locomotive of War*, London, Bloomsbury, 2017.

Cocker, Mark, *Richard Meinertzhagen: Soldier, Scientist, and Spy*, London, Secker and Warburg, 1989.

Cohen, Getzel M., and Joukowsky, Martha Sharp (eds), *Breaking Ground: Pioneering Women Archaeologists*, Ann Arbor, The University of Michigan Press, 2006.

Collins, Damian, *Charmed Life: The Phenomenal World of Philip Sassoon*, London, Collins, 2016.

Colville, John, *The Churchillians*, London, Weidenfeld and Nicolson, 1981.

Conway, Jane, *Mary Borden: A Woman of Two Wars*, London, Munday Books, 2010.

Coogan, Tim Pat, *Michael Collins: A Biography*, London, Hutchinson, 1990.

Coombs, David, *Churchill: His Paintings*, London, Hamish Hamilton, 1967.

Coombs, David, and Churchill, Minnie S., *Sir Winston Churchill: His Life and His Paintings*, Philadelphia, Running Press, 2003.

Coote, Colin R., *Sir Winston Churchill. A Self-Portrait*, London, Eyre and Spottiswoode, 1954.

Coote, Colin R., *The Other Club*, London, Sidgwick and Jackson, 1971.

Cowling, Maurice, *The Impact of Labour 1920–1924*, Cambridge, Cambridge University Press, 1971.

D'Abernon, Viscountess, *Red Cross and Berlin Embassy 1915–1926*, London, John Murray, 1946.

Davenport-Hines, Richard, *Ettie: The Intimate Life and Dauntless Spirit of Lady Desborough*, London, Weidenfeld and Nicolson, 2008.

De Groot, Gerard, *Liberal Crusader: The Life of Sir Archibald Sinclair*, London, C. Hurst, 1993.

Dilks, David, *'The Great Dominion': Winston Churchill in Canada 1900–1954*, Toronto, Thomas Allen Publishers, 2005.

Dockter, Warren, *Churchill and the Islamic World*, London, I. B. Tauris, 2015.

Drabble, Margaret, *Arnold Bennett, a Biography*, London, Weidenfeld & Nicolson, 1974.

Eade, Charles (ed.), *Churchill by His Contemporaries*, London, Reprint Society, 1955.

Egremont, Max, *Under Two Flags: The Life of Major-General Sir Edward Spears*, London, Phoenix Giant, 1998.

Ellerton, D. H., *Chequers and the Prime Ministers*, London, Robert Hale, 1970.

Feske, Victor, *From Belloc to Churchill: Private Scholars, Public Culture, and the Crisis of British Liberalism 1900–1939*, Chapel Hill, University of North Carolina Press, 1996.

Field, Leslie, *Bendor: The Golden Duke of Westminster*, London, Weidenfeld & Nicolson, 1983.

Fink, Carole, et al. (eds), *Genoa, Rapallo, and European Reconstruction in 1922*, New York, Cambridge University Press, 1991.

Fishman, Jack, *My Darling Clementine*, New York, David McKay Co. Inc., 1963.

Forester, Margery, *Michael Collins: The Lost Leader*, London, Sidgwick and Jackson, 1971.

Fortey, Richard, *Dry Store Room No. 1: The Secret History etc.*, London, Vintage, 2009.

Fromkin, David, *A Peace to End All Peace: The Fall of the Ottoman Empire and the Creation of the Modern Middle East*, New York, Henry Holt, 1989.

Fry, Plantagenet Somerset, *Chequers: The Country Home of Britain's Prime Ministers*, London, Her Majesty's Stationery Office, 1977.

Gardiner, A. G., *Pillars of Society*, London, J. M. Dent, 1916.

Garfield, Brian, *The Meinertzhagen Mystery: The Life and Legend of a Colossal Fraud*, Lincoln, Nebraska, Potomoc Books, 2008.

Germains, Victor Wallace, *The Tragedy of Winston Churchill*, London, Hurst & Blackett, 1931.

Gilbert, Martin, *In Search of Churchill*, New York, Wiley, 1997.

Gilbert, Martin, *The Challenge of War: Winston S. Churchill 1914–1916*, London, Minerva, 1990.

Gilbert, Martin, *The Wilderness Years*, London, Macmillan, 1981.

Gilbert, Martin, *World in Torment: Winston S. Churchill 1917–1922*, London, Minerva, 1990.

Gilbert, Martin, and Arnn, Larry P., *The Churchill Documents*, vol. 19, Hillsdale, Michigan, Hillsdale College Press, 2019.

Gilmour, David, *Curzon*, London, John Murray, 1994.

Graham, Roger, *Arthur Meighen, a Biography*, vol. II, Toronto, Clarke, Irwin, 1963.

Graves, Philip (ed.), *Memoirs of King Abdullah of Transjordan*, London, Jonathan Cape, 1950.

Grieves, Keith, *Sir Eric Geddes: Business and Government in War and Peace*, Manchester, Manchester University Press, 1989.

Hamill, Ian, *The Strategic Illusion: The Singapore Strategy and the Defence of Australia and New Zealand 1919–1942*, Singapore, Singapore University Press, 1981.

Hamilton, Sir Ian, *Gallipoli Diary*, vol. 1, London, Edward Arnold, 1920.

Hancock, W. K., *Smuts: The Fields of Force 1919–1950*, Cambridge, Cambridge University Press, 1968.

Hardy, Roger, *The Poisoned Well: Empire and its Legacy in the Middle East*, Oxford, Oxford University Press, 2017.

Hart, Peter, *Mick: The Real Michael Collins*, New York, Viking, 2005.

Haslewood, Lt Cdr and Mrs H. L., *Child Slavery in Hong Kong: The Mui Tsai System*, London, The Sheldon Press, 1930.

Hassall, Christopher, *Edward Marsh: Patron of the Arts*, London, Longmans, 1959.

Hattersley, Roy, *David Lloyd George, The Great Outsider*, London, Little, Brown, 2010.

Hazlehurst, Cameron, *Politicians at War*, London, Jonathan Cape, 1971.

Hazlehurst, Cameron (ed.), *The Lloyd George Magazine 1920-1923*, vol. 1, Brighton, The Harvester Press, 1973.

Hough, Richard, *Winston and Clementine: The Triumphs and Tragedies of the Churchills*, New York, Bantam Books, 1991.

Howarth, Patrick, *When the Riviera was Ours*, London, Routledge and Kegan Paul, 1977.

Howell, Georgina, *Queen of the Desert: The Extraordinary Life of Gertrude Bell*, New York, Farrar, Straus and Giroux, 2007.

Humphreys, Andrew, *Grand Hotels of Egypt in the Golden Age of Travel*, New York, The American University in Cairo Press, 2011.

Hunter, Ian, *Winston and Archie*, London, Politico's, 2005.

Ironside, Lord (ed.), *High Road to Command: The Diaries of Major-General Sir Edmund Ironside 1920-1922*, London, Leo Cooper, 1972.

Jackson, Ashley, *Churchill*, London, Quercus, 2012.

James, Lawrence, *Churchill and Empire: A Portrait of an Imperialist*, New York, Pegasus Books, 2014.

James, Lawrence, *The Golden Warrior: The Life and Legend of Lawrence of Arabia*, London, Weidenfeld and Nicolson, 1990.

James, Robert Rhodes, *Churchill: A Study in Failure*, London, Weidenfeld & Nicolson, 1970.

Jeffrey, Andrew, *This Dangerous Menace: Dundee and the River Tay at War 1939-1945*, Edinburgh, Mainstream Publishing, 1991.

Jenkins, J. Gilbert, *Chequers: A History of the Prime Minister's Buckinghamshire Home*, London, Pergamon Press, 1967.

Jenkins, Roy, *Churchill. A Biography*, New York, Plume Books, 2002.

Jones, Thomas, *Whitehall Diary, Volume 1, 1916-1925*, London, Oxford University Press, 1969; *Volume III, Ireland 1918-1925*, London, Oxford University Press, 1971.

Koss, Stephen, *Fleet Street Radical: A. G. Gardiner and the* Daily News, London, Allen Lane, 1973.

Langworth, Richard, *Winston Churchill, Myth and Reality: What He Actually Did and Said*, Jefferson, North Carolina, McFarland and Company, 2017.

Lavery, Sir John, *The Life of a Painter*, Boston, Little, Brown and Company, 1940.

Lee, Celia and John, *Winston and Jack: The Churchill Brothers*, London, Celia Lee, 2007.

Lee of Fareham (Arthur Hamilton Lee), *'A Good Innings': The Private Papers of Viscount Lee of Fareham*, ed. Alan Clark, London, John Murray, 1974.

Leslie, Anita, *Cousin Clare: The Tempestuous Career of Clare Sheridan*, London, Hutchinson, 1976.

Leslie, Anita, *Jennie: The Life of Lady Randolph Churchill*, London, Hutchinson, 1969.

Leslie, Anita, *Mr. Frewen of England*, London, Hutchinson, 1966.

Leslie, Shane, *Long Shadows*, London, John Murray, 1966.

Lloyd George, David, *War Memoirs*, vols 1-6, London, Nicholson and Watson, 1933-6.

Lloyd George, Robert, *David and Winston*, London, John Murray, 2005.

Longford, Lord, *Peace by Ordeal*, London, Sidgwick and Jackson, 1972.

Lough, David, *No More Champagne: Churchill and his Money*, London, Head of Zeus, 2015.

Lovell, Mary, *The Riviera Set*, London, Little, Brown, 2016.

Low, David, *Low's Autobiography*, London, Michael Joseph, 1956.

Lubenow, W. C., *The Cambridge Apostles, 1820-1914*, Cambridge, Cambridge University Press, 1998.

Lucy, Henry W., *Lords and Commoners*, London, T. F. Unwin, 1921.

Lukitz, Liora, *A Quest in the Middle East: Gertrude Bell and the Making of Modern Iraq*, London, I. B. Tauris, 2006.

Maclaren, Roy, *Empire and Ireland: The Transatlantic Career of the Canadian Imperialist Hamar Greenwood, 1870–1948*, Montreal and Kingston, McGill Queen's University Press, 2015.

MacMillan, Margaret, *Paris 1919*, New York, Random House, 2002.

Macmillan, The Revd Hugh, *The Riviera*, London, J. S. Virtue & Co, 1885.

Madeira, Victor, *Britannia and the Bear: The Anglo-Russian Intelligence Wars 1917–1929*, Woodbridge, The Boydell Press, 2014.

Major, Norma, *Chequers: The Prime Minister's Country House and its History*, London, Little, Brown, 2001.

Makovsky, Michael, *Churchill's Promised Land: Zionism and Statecraft*, New Haven and London, Yale University Press, 2007.

Mallet, Sir Charles, *Anthony Hope and His Books*, London, Hutchinson & Co Ltd, 1935.

Manchester, William, *The Last Lion: Visions of Glory*, Boston, Little, Brown, 1983.

Marsh, Edward, *A Number of People: A Book of Reminiscences*, New York, Harper, 1939.

Martin, Ralph G., *Jennie: The Life of Lady Randolph Churchill, Volume Two: The Dramatic Years 1895–1921*, New Jersey, Prentice-Hall, 1971.

Mattar, Philip, *The Mufti of Jerusalem: Al-Hajj Amin al-Husayni and the Palestinian National Movement*, New York, Columbia University Press, 1988.

McConkey, Kenneth, *Free Spirit: Irish Art 1860–1960*, London, Antique Collectors' Club, 1990.

McCoole, Sinead, *Hazel: A Life of Lady Lavery 1880–1935*, Dublin, The Lilliput Press, 1996.

McIntyre, W. David, *The Rise and Fall of the Singapore Naval Base, 1919–1942*, London, Macmillan, 1979.

McMeekin, Sean, *The Ottoman Endgame: War, Revolution, and the Making of the Modern Middle East 1908–1923*, New York, Penguin, 2015.

McNamara, Robert (ed.), *The Churchills in Ireland*, Dublin, Irish Academic Press, 2012.

Millard, Candice, *Hero of the Empire: The Making of Winston Churchill*, London, Allen Lane, 2016.

Morgan, Kenneth O., *Consensus and Disunity: The Lloyd George Coalition Government 1918–1922*, Oxford, Clarendon Press, 1979.

Morgan, Kenneth, *Lloyd George*, London, Weidenfeld & Nicolson, 1974.

Morgan, Kenneth, and Morgan, Jane, *Portrait of a Progressive: The Political Career of Christopher, Viscount Addison*, Oxford, Clarendon Press, 1980.

Mowat, Charles Loch, *Britain between the Wars, 1918–1940*, London, Methuen, 1940.

Muller, James (ed.), *Churchill as Peacemaker*, Cambridge, Cambridge University Press, 1997.

Neidpath, James, *The Singapore Naval Base and the Defence of Britain's Eastern Empire 1919–1941*, Oxford, Clarendon Press, 1981.

Nicolson, Harold, *King George the Fifth, his Life and Reign*, London, Constable, 1952.

Nicolson, Juliet, *The Great Silence: 1918–1920. Living in the Shadow of the Great War*, London, John Murray, 2010.

Norwich, John Julius (ed.), *The Duff Cooper Diaries 1915–1951*, London, Weidenfeld & Nicolson, 2005.

Owen, Frank, *Tempestuous Journey: Lloyd George, His Life and Times*, London, Hutchinson, 1954.

Parker, R. A. C. (ed.), *Winston Churchill: Studies in Statesmanship*, London and Washington, Brasseys, 1995.

Paterson, Tony, *Churchill: A Seat for Life*, Dundee, David Winter & Son, 1980.

Pearson, Hesketh, *Modern Men and Mummers*, London, George Allen and Unwin, 1921.

Pelling, Henry, *Winston Churchill*, London, Macmillan, 1974.

Plummer, Douglas, *Queer People: The Truth about Homosexuals in Britain*, New York, Citadel Press, 1965.

Purnell, Sonia, *Clementine: The Life of Mrs. Winston Churchill*, London, Viking, 2015.

Rasula, Jed, *Destruction Was My Beatrix: Dada and the Unmaking of the Twentieth Century*, New York, Basic Books, 2015.

Reynolds, David, *In Command of History: Churchill Fighting and Writing the Second World War*, London, Allen Lane, 2004.

Riddell, George Allardyce, *Lord Riddell's Intimate Diary of the Peace Conference and after 1916–1923*, London, Victor Gollancz, 1933.

Ridley, Jane, *Bertie: A Life of Edward VII*, New York, Vintage, 2013.

Roberts, Andrew, *Churchill: Walking With Destiny*, London, Allen Lane, 2108.

Roberts, Brian, *Randolph: A Study of Churchill's Son*, London, Hamish Hamilton, 1984.

Rose, Jonathan, *The Literary Churchill: Author, Reader, Actor*, New Haven and London, Yale University Press, 2014.

Rose, Norman, *Churchill: The Unruly Giant*, New York, Free Press, 1995.

Sandys, Celia, *Churchill: Wanted Dead or Alive*, London, HarperCollins, 1999.

Scott, Alexander MacCallum, *Winston Churchill in Peace and War*, London, George Newnes Ltd, 1916.

Scott, Alexander MacCallum, *Winston Spencer Churchill*, London, Methuen & Co, 1905.

Searle, G. R., *Corruption in British Politics 1895–1930*, Oxford, Clarendon Press, 1987.

Sebag Montefiore, Simon, *Jerusalem: The Biography*, New York, Alfred A. Knopf, 2011.

Seymour-Ure, Colin, and Schoff, Jim, *David Low*, London, Secker and Warburg, 1988.

Shelden, Michael, *Young Titan: The Making of Winston Churchill*, New York, Simon and Schuster, 2013.

Sheridan, Clare, *Mayfair to Moscow: Clare Sheridan's Diary*, New York, Boni and Liveright, 1921.

Sheridan, Clare, *Naked Truth*, New York, Blue Ribbon Books, 1928.

Sheridan, Clare, *To the Four Winds*, London, André Deutsch, 1957.

Sidebotham, Herbert, *Pillars of the State*, London, Nisbet & Co, 1921.

Singer, Barry, *Churchill Style*, New York, Abrams, 2012.

Sixsmith, Martin, *Russia: A 1,000-Year Chronicle of the Wild East*, New York, Overlook Press, 2014.

Slinn, Judy, *Clifford Chance: Its Origin and Development*, Cambridge, Granta, 1993.

Sluglett, Peter, *Britain in Iraq 1914–1932*, Oxford, St Antony's College, 1976.

Soames, Mary, *A Churchill Family Album*, London, Allen Lane, 1982.

Soames, Mary, *A Daughter's Tale: The Memoir of Winston Churchill's Youngest Child*, London, Transworld, 2011.

Soames, Mary, *Clementine Churchill*, London, Cassell, 1979.

Soames, Mary, *Winston and Clementine: The Personal Letters of the Churchills*, Boston and New York, Houghton Mifflin, 1998.

Soames, Mary, *Winston Churchill: His Life as a Painter*, London, Viking, 1990.

Spence, Richard B., *Boris Savinkov: Renegade on the Left*, New York, Columbia University Press, 1991.

Spurling, Hilary, *Matisse: A Life*, 2 vols, London, Penguin, 2009.

Stafford, David, *Churchill and Secret Service*, London, Abacus, 2000.

Stafford, David, *Roosevelt and Churchill: Men of Secrets*, London, Little, Brown, 1999.

Stansky, Peter, *Churchill*, New York, Hill and Wang, 1973.

Stansky, Peter, *Sassoon: The Worlds of Philip and Sybil*, New Haven and London, Yale University Press, 2003.

Steiner, Zara, *The Lights that Failed*, Oxford, Oxford University Press, 2005.

Stephens, Mitchell, *The Voice of America: Lowell Thomas and the Invention of 20th Century Journalism*, New York, St Martin's Press, 2017.

Stevenson, Frances, *Lloyd George: A Diary*, ed. A. J. P. Taylor, London, Hutchinson, 1971.

Storrs, Ronald, *Orientations*, London, Nicholson and Watson, 1945.

Street, C. J. C., *Ireland in 1921*, London, P. Allan, 1922.

Taylor, A. J. P., *Beaverbrook*, London, Hamish Hamilton, 1972.

Taylor, A. J. P., *English History 1914–1945*, Oxford, Clarendon Press, 1965.

Taylor, A. J. P., et al., *Churchill: Four Faces and the Man*, Harmondsworth, Penguin, 1973.

Taylor, Rex, *Michael Collins*, London, Hutchinson, 1958.

Thompson, Walter H., *I Was Churchill's Shadow*, London, C. Johnson, 1951 (US edn, *Assignment Churchill*, New York, Farrar, Straus and Young, 1955).

Tomlinson, J., *Dundee and the Empire: Juteopolis 1850–1939*, Edinburgh, Edinburgh University Press, 2014.

Townshend, Charles, *The Republic: The Fight for Irish Independence, 1918–1923*, London, Penguin, 2014.

Toye, Richard, *Churchill's Empire*, London, Pan, 2011.

Toye, Richard, *Lloyd George and Churchill: Rivals for Greatness*, London, Pan Books, 2014.

Udy, Giles, *Labour and the Gulag*, London, Biteback, 2017.

Urquhart, Fred, *W.S.C. A Cartoon Biography*, London, Cassell and Company, 1955.

Walker, William M., *Juteopolis: Dundee and its Textile World*, Edinburgh, Scottish Academic Press, 1979.

Wallach, Janet, *Desert Queen: The Extraordinary Life of Gertrude Bell*, New York, Doubleday, 1996.

Walsh, Maurice, *Bitter Freedom: Ireland in a Revolutionary World 1918–1923*, London, Faber and Faber, 2015.

Walsh, Michael J., and Varnava, Andrekos (eds), *The Great War and the British Empire*, London, Routledge, 2017.

Wasserstein, Bernard, *Herbert Samuel: A Political Life*, Oxford, Clarendon Press, 1992.

Wasserstein, Bernard, *The British in Palestine: The Mandatory Government and the Arab-Jewish Conflict 1917–1929*, London, Royal Historical Society, 1978.

Waters, Helena L., *The French and Italian Rivieras*, London, Methuen, 1924.

Wavell, Archibald, *Allenby: A Study in Greatness*, New York, Oxford University Press, 1941.

Wilson, Mary C., *King Abdullah, Britain and the Making of Jordan*, Cambridge, Cambridge University Press, 1987.

Wilson, Trevor, *The Downfall of the Liberal Party 1914–1935*, London, Collins, 1968.

Wilson, Trevor (ed.), *The Political Diaries of C. P. Scott 1911–1928*, London, Collins, 1970.

Winstone, H. V. F., *Gertrude Bell*, London, Jonathan Cape, 1978.

Wolff, Michael, *The Collected Essays of Winston Churchill*, London, Library of Imperial History, 1975.

Young, Kenneth, *Churchill and Beaverbrook: A Study in Friendship and Politics*, London, Eyre & Spottiswoode, 1966.

Ziegler, Philip, *King Edward VIII*, London, Collins, 1990.

INDEX

Abdullah, king of Transjordan, 108–9, 114, 120–1, 123, 125–8, 152
Abermule, Wales: railway accident, xi
Aboukir, Battle of (1798), 101
Addison, Christopher, 267–8
Admiralty: WSC justifies record at, 190–1
Africa: British colonies, 230
Agnew, Colin, 92
air travel: development, 180–1
Airlie, Blanche, Countess of, 47
airships, 181–3
Alexandra, consort of Edward VII, 157
Allen, Sir James, 170–1
Allen, John, 171
Allenby, Field Marshal Edmund Henry Hynman, 1st Viscount, 39–40, 103–4, 114, 117, 119
Amery, Leo, 23
Amin al-Hussayni, Al Hajj, Grand Mufti of Jerusalem, 151
Anglo-Japanese Alliance (1902), 172–3, 178
Antwerp: WSC organises defence (1914), 5
Arabs: in Palestine conflict, 148, 185, 232
Archer, Sir Geoffrey, 104
Armistice Day: celebrated, 48–9
Ashley, Edwina see Mountbatten, Edwina
Asquith, Herbert Henry: and WSC's career in Great War, 5–6; on WSC's self-centredness, 11, 81; predicts WSC's lack of political success, 13; and security services, 43; Samuel serves under, 119; calls for truce in Ireland, 145
Astor, Nancy, Viscountess, 171
Ataturk, Mustapha Kemal, 30, 85, 153–4
Attlee, Clement, 268
Augusta Viktoria, Empress of Germany, 122
Australia: and potential war in Pacific, 178

Bailey, Sir Abe, 194
Baldwin, Stanley, 264
Balfour, Arthur James, 177, 264
Balfour Declaration (on Palestine, 1917), 12, 126–7, 130, 151, 153, 185, 232
Barrie, Sir James Matthew, 240
Barry, Sir Charles, 194
Barry, Kevin, 29
Barton, Robert, 247
Baruch, Bernard, 98, 135, 138–9, 193
Beatty, Admiral David, 177–88
Beaverbrook, William Maxwell Aitken, 1st Baron: on WSC's fondness for music hall songs, 24; on French Riviera, 56–7; entertains WSC, 227–9; and Jean Norton, 228; praises WSC, 230; friendship with WSC, 262
Begbie, Harold: *The Mirrors of Downing Street*, 265–6
Bell, Gertrude: at Cairo Conference, 109–14, 115; poses on camel with WSC, 116; returns to Baghdad, 117–18; on limitations of bombing in Iraq, 188; and Faisal's election as King of Iraq, 192; sends condolences on Marigold's death, 193
Bennett, Arnold, 228
Birkenhead Frederick Edwin Smith, 1st Earl of: friendship with WSC, 90, 262; pursues Clare Sheridan, 90–2; ostracizes Clare, 96; on Palestine problem, 186; and Sir Robert Houston, 203; in The Other Club, 226; Clementine dislikes, 228; negotiates with Irish delegation, 241, 244, 246–7; and Michael Collins, 245; Savinkov meets, 252
Birley, Oswald, 89, 92
Black and Tans, 27, 207, 233, 239–40
Black Watch (regiment), 212

Blenheim Palace, Oxfordshire, 4

Blunt, Wilfrid Scawen, 7–8

Bodkin, Thomas, 59

Boer War (1899–1902), 75–6

Bolshevik Party: 10th Party Congress (1921), 159; British view of, 253

Bolshevik Revolution (1917): WSC denounces, 9

Bonham Carter, Violet (née Asquith): loyalty to WSC, 7, 269; *Winston Churchill as I Knew Him*, 7

Borden, Mary ('May'; Edward Spears's wife), 161

Brahan Castle, Dingwall, 199

Briand, Aristide, 60, 252–3

Britain: naval power, 22–3, 61–2; Coalition government, 81–3; Middle East policy, 114, 120; post-war slump and mass demonstrations, 141; relationship with USA, 180, 184; austerity measures, 221–2

British Empire: extent, 81; and Imperial Conference, 168–9; and sea power, 176; WSC's view on, 178–9, 232; and air travel, 180–1

Brooke, General Sir Alan: on WSC's impetuousness, 6

Brooke, Rupert, 38

Butterworth, Thornton (publisher), 226

Byng, Field Marshal Julian Hedworth George, Viscount (of Vimy), 170–1

Caird, James Key, 213

Cairo: Conference on Middle East (1921), 101–12, 114, 116, 185

Caix, Robert de, 128

Campbell-Bannerman, Sir Henry, 119

Canada: WSC visits, 75–7; and Irish settlement, 256

Cannes, 258

Carnegie, Mrs Andrew, 123

Carson, Sir Edward, 255, 257

Casement, Sir Roger, 144, 217

Cassel, Sir Ernest: relations with WSC, 34, 54–5; in Monte Carlo, 57; helps Jack Churchill, 68; death, 196–7

Cazalet, Victor, 162

Cenotaph (Whitehall): unveiled, 48

Chamberlain, Austen: as Chancellor of Exchequer, 115; on WSC's anger at missing Chancellorship, 133; and WSC's speech on Middle East, 154; attends Cabinet meeting in Inverness, 200; negotiates with Irish delegation, 241, 247; on WSC's speech on Irish Treaty, 257

Chamberlain, Neville: praises WSC's speech on Middle East, 154

Chaplin, Charlie, 20, 135, 229

Chartwell Manor, Kent, 162–3, 262

Chequers (house), Buckinghamshire, 78–80, 250, 252–3

Childers, Erskine, 238, 248

Chirgwin, George, (G. H.), 25

Churchill, Clementine (née Hozier): and WSC's reflections of middle age, xii; on WSC's near-breakdown, 2; marriage to WSC, 4; children, 18, 32, 47, 262; friendship with Philip Sassoon, 18; warns WSC of Lloyd George, 21, 81; 59th birthday celebrations (1944), 24; financial worries, 34, 71, 73; tennis-playing, 35, 57, 74, 191; Riviera holidays, 47, 54, 57, 73–4, 77, 80; supports WSC's painting, 51; encourages WSC's political career, 70, 74; woos Colonel Maclean, 76–7; disapproves of Freddie Guest, 83; sympathy for Clare Sheridan, 89; accompanies WSC to Cairo, 101, 106, 109, 111, 113, 116–17; in Jerusalem, 122–3; and brother's suicide, 134; on Irish unrest, 144–5; attends polo match, 157; difficult relations with Spears, 161; and acquisition of Chartwell, 162; household allowance increased, 189; stays with Westminsters at Eaton Hall, 191; and death of daughter Marigold, 192–3; and Cassel's death, 197; social life, 223; disapproves of Beaverbrook and Birkenhead, 228; on Irish truce, 239; and Hazel Lavery's support for Michael Collins, 247; campaigns for WSC in Dundee, 266

Churchill, Diana (WSC/Clementine's daughter), 32, 60, 259, 262

Churchill, Gwendeline ('Goonie'; Jack's wife): helps Jack Churchill, 6, 68; supports WSC, 7; marriage and children, 69; marriage relations, 69; and Chartwell Manor, 163; WSC's relations with, 261

Churchill, Jennie (née Jerome; WSC's mother; Lady Randolph Churchill): character and background, 3; on WSC's paintings, 51; social life, 68, 137; concern for niece Clare Sheridan, 87–8, 91, 96–7; joins WSC at Cap d'Ail, 132; relations with WSC, 136; death and funeral, 137–9, 173, 194; finances, 137; marriage settlement, 237

Churchill, John Strange ('Jack'; WSC's brother): supports WSC, 7, 68; Cassel supports, 55; career, 68; travels in Canada, 77; stays at de la Grange château in war, 119; faith in WSC's career, 132; and Chartwell, 162; attends Walden's funeral, 194; finances, 196; WSC's relations with, 261

Churchill, Johnny (Jack/Goonie's son), 33, 77

Churchill, Marigold (WSC/Clementine's daughter): childhood, 32, 60; visits Chequers with WSC, 78, 80; illness and death, 192–3; burial at Kensal Green, 197

Churchill, Mary (WSC/Clementine's daughter; *later* Soames): on WSC's painting, 51; and death of Marigold, 193; birth, 262

Churchill, Peregrine (Jack/Goonie's son), 33

Churchill, Randolph (WSC/Clementine's son): character, 6, 32; schooling, 60, 262

Churchill, Lord Randolph (WSC's father), 2–3, 55, 115–16

Churchill, Sarah (WSC/Clementine's daughter): birth, 18; schooling, 60; illnesses, 192, 259; WSC praises, 262

Churchill, Winston Leonard Spencer: inherits Vane-Tempest's fortune (Garron Towers estate, Ireland), xii, 71, 134; reputation as buccaneeer, xiii; and Dardanelles campaign, 1–2, 76, 171, 265; early political success, 1; ambition, 2; loses office in Great War, 2; family background, 3; joins Liberals, 3–4; loyalty of extended family and friends, 6; organises defence of Antwerp (1914), 6; painting, 7, 19, 26, 47, 50–3, 57–9, 69–70, 106, 113, 114, 117, 122, 132, 190, 195, 223, 263; as Minister of Munitions under Lloyd George, 8; serves on Western Front in Great War, 8, 48; hostility to Bolshevism, 9–10, 42–3, 84, 91, 92–4, 149, 159–61, 165, 216, 254; on post-Great War world, 9–10; caricatured, 11–13; reactionary views, 12–13; love of singing and the good life, 17; visits Port Lympne, 17–20, 22; appearance, 21; visits to and knowledge of USA, 21–2; love of music hall songs, 23–5; writings and literary earnings, 25–6, 70, 71, 191, 259; views on Ireland, 27, 29–30, 216–17; as Colonial Secretary, 31–2, 36–7, 76, 80, 175, 230–2; children and family life, 32, 69, 191, 261; London homes, 32–3, 36; attitude to money and finances, 36, 71, 140, 189, 196; supports security services, 43–5, 66; holiday on French Riviera with

Clementine, 47, 54, 56–8; exhibits paintings in Paris (as 'Charles Morin'), 50–1; given police protection, 61; at War Office, 61; concern over post-war European settlement, 62; meets Savinkov, 63–4; on Prince of Wales, 66–8; social life, 68, 223–4, 227, 261; supports wider family, 70; lecture tour of North America, 74–6; travels in Canada, 77; dependence on Lloyd George, 81; differences with Lloyd George, 84–5, 91, 133, 163–4; shocked at unemployment, 84; and Greek–Turkish war, 85–6; sits for Clare Sheridan, 91; and Clare Sheridan's behaviour, 93; and Clare Sheridan's flight to Moscow and USA, 95–8; attends Cairo Conference, 101–9, 111–13, 116–17; on importance of theatre in politics, 103; admires Lawrence, 105; proposes shooting army horses, 107–8; and need for budget cuts, 114; ambitions to be Chancellor of Exchequer, 115; unpunctuality, 118; in Jerusalem, 120–34; sympathetic to Zionism, 120, 128, 149; meets Abdullah, 121, 125–7, 152; changes plans for return from Middle East, 129; passed over as Chancellor of Exchequer, 132–3; Lavery paints on Riviera, 133; and mother's death and funeral, 137–9, 173, 194; inheritance from mother, 140, 237; urges truce in Ireland, 144–6, 148; addresses Commons on Middle East settlement, 148, 152–3, 155; speech-making, 148, 214, 218, 257–8; supports restriction of Jewish immmigrants into Palestine, 149; and grand mufti of Jerusalem, 151; Middle East policy, 151–2, 232–3; love of riding and polo, 158–9; at Imperial Conference, 163–5, 169–70, 173; buys Chartwell Manor, Kent, 163, 262; opposes *Mui-tsai* system in Hong Kong, 164; concern about Britain's role in Europe, 166–7; entertains imperial prime ministers and guests, 170–1; opposes renewal of Anglo-Japanese Alliance, 173; imperialism, 178–9; on Franco-German relations, 179; overseas visits to empire, 179; and relationship with USA, 180; opposes airships, 182–3; and Arab-Jewish differences over Palestine, 185; and administration of Iraq, 186; alleged use of poison gas in Iraq, 187–9; justifies wartime record at Admiralty, 190–1; buys and sells Rolls Royce motor car, 191, 193;

Churchill, Winston Leonard Spencer (contd):
and death of daughter Marigold, 192–4,
262; stays at Dunrobin Casle, 194–6;
effect of personal tragedies on, 197;
attends Cabinet meeting in Inverness,
200–2; opposes full independence to
Ireland, 203; represents Dundee, 204–7;
loses support in Dundee, 207–8; and
unemployment and unrest in Dundee,
212–14; Dundee speech, 213–18; press
praise for, 218–20; protests against
austerity measures, 221–2; club
memberships, 225–6; writes on art, 225;
on importance of ceremony, 235; military
expertise, 236; pro-Americanism, 236;
negotiates with Irish delegation in
London, 238–9, 241, 244–8; relations with
Michael Collins, 244–5; and terms of
Irish treaty, 249; intriguing and
intelligence interests, 251–4;
miscellaneous public interests, 254–5; in
parliamentary debate on Irish Agreement,
256–7; in Cannes, 258–9; chairs Cabinet
committee on transfer of power to
Ireland, 258; marriage relations, 259–60;
Clare Sheridan sculpts head, 262; injured
playing polo, 263; appointed Chancellor
of Exchequer, 264; loses parliamentary
seat, 264–5; rejoins Conservative Party
and elected MP for Epping (1924), 264;
qualities and reputation, 265–70; attitude
to women, 269; History of the English-
Speaking Peoples, 246; My Early Life, 194;
'Painting as a Pastime' (article), 52, 190;
Savrola (novel), 226; The World Crisis, xii,
9, 25–6, 29, 36, 70, 71, 140, 190–1, 198,
202, 226, 236, 258, 263–4, 268
Coates, William, 96
Cochran, Bourke, 21–2, 138, 143
Collins, Hanna, 242–3
Collins, Michael: negotiates in London,
238–44, 247; on Irish treaty, 249; de
Valera attacks, 257
Colonial Office: WSC appointed to, 31, 80;
receives copies of diplomatic intercepts, 65
Colville, Sir John ('Jock'), 25
Connaught, Arthur William Patrick Albert,
Duke of, 158, 234–5
Cooper, Alfred Duff: on WSC's reactionary
views, 11; anti-Semitism, 149; differences
with WSC, 224; and Hazel Lavery, 244;
and WSC's proposals on Irish settlement,
245–6; WSC's relations with, 261; on
Munich crisis, 263

Cooper, Lady Diana, 159, 224
Coote, Captain Maxwell Henry, 102, 106,
109, 111–14, 116–19, 121–3, 128–30
Coronel, battle of (1914), 191
Cox, Sir Percy, 105, 108, 110–11, 113, 115,
186–7, 192
Cox, Sir Reginald, 140, 189
Craig, Sir James, 145–7, 256
Croke Park stadium, Dublin: massacre
(1920), 27
Cromwell, Oliver, 246
Crowe, Sir Eyre, 251, 254
Cumming, Sir Mansfield, 161
Curtis Brown, Albert, 25
Curzon, George Nathaniel, Marquess: as
Foreign Secretary, 37; complains of WSC's
interference in foreign affairs, 62, 165,
232; agrees to Colonial Office receiving
diplomatic intercepts, 65; and WSC's view
of de Caix, 128; and WSC's mother's
death, 140; and Middle East policy, 153,
155; on Anglo-Japanese Alliance, 173–5;
relations with WSC, 174; praises WSC,
220; and WSC's policy on Egypt, 245;
WSC informs of Savinkov's visit to
Chequers, 253–4; Carson attacks, 257

d'Abernon, Lord Edgar, 269
Daily Chronicle, 83, 247
Daily Express, 239, 247
Daily Herald, 53, 105, 155
Dardanelles Expedition (1915), xiii, 1–2,
265
Davidson, Randall, Archbishop of
Canterbury, 145
Davies, Crompton Llewellyn, 239–42
Davies, Moya (née O'Connor), 240
Derby, Edward George Villiers Stanley, 17th
Earl of, 46
Derby, Edward Henry Stanley, 15th Earl of, 3
Desborough, William Grenfell, Baron and
Ethel ('Ettie'), Lady, 136, 140, 174, 193,
223, 225, 262
de Valera, Eamon, 145, 147, 198–9, 202–4,
216, 238, 241, 246–7, 249, 256–7
Disraeli, Benjamin, 78
Doyle, Sir Arthur Conan, 53
Druet, Eugène, 49
Dudley Ward, Freda, 66–8, 195
Dudley, William Humble Ward, 2nd Earl of,
226
du Maurier, Daphne: Rebecca, 162
Dundee: social deprivation and unrest, 84,
211–14, 221; WSC elected MP for, 84;

WSC's speech in, 196, 213–18; political representation, 204–5; turns against WSC, 207; WSC loses parliamentary seat, 264–5
Dunrobin Castle, near Inverness, 194–6

Eaton Hall, Cheshire, 191
Edward, Prince of Wales: and Freda Dudley Ward, 66–8; qualities and lifestyle, 66; and WSC's commitment to developing Canadian trade, 172; on air travel, 180; at Dunrobin Castle, 195; and WSC's views on Irish settlement, 258
Egypt: British policy on, 62; WSC in, 101–9; WSC opposes abolishing British protectorate, 245
Eisenhower, Dwight D., 52
Elliot, Maxine, 135
Enchantress (Admiralty yacht), 11
English-Speaking Union, 233, 236, 257
Epstein, Jacob, 89
Essex, Adele, Countess of, 73, 80, 174, 258, 260, 262
Europe: post-war settlement, 62, 166–7, 179
Evening Standard, 247
Everest, Elizabeth, 194
Ewart, Sir Spencer, 3
Ewer, William, 96

Fairbanks, Douglas, 229
Faisal I, King of Iraq, 39, 105, 108, 111, 115, 119, 152, 186, 188, 191
Falkland Islands, battle of the (1914), 191
Fearon, Percy ('Poy'; cartoonist), 12
Fielding, Henry: *Amelia*, 195
Fisher, H. A. L., 192, 257
France: interests in Middle East, 114–15, 125–6, 128; deteriorating relations with Britain, 166–7; supports Poland over Upper Silesia, 175; WSC defends, 176, 179
French Riviera: Clementine in, 47, 54, 57, 73–4, 77, 80; WSC visits, 47, 54, 56–8, 73–4, 132, 157; French painters visit, 58
Frewen, Hugh, 110–11
Frewen, Moreton, 87, 142–3, 147

Gairloch, Ross-shire: Flowerdale House, 199, 203–4, 211
Gallipoli campaign (1915): and WSC's reputation, 1–2, 7–9, 171; Jack Churchill at, 68–9; Hamilton commands at, 76
Gardiner, Alfred George (A. G.), 5, 9; *The Pillars of Society*, 5
Garron Towers estate, Co. Antrim, 71–2, 134, 189

Garvin, J. L. ('Jim'), 74, 226, 265
Gaulle, General Charles de, 11, 263
Geddes, Sir Eric, 221, 253
Geiger, Major Gerald, 49–50, 73
General Elections: 1918 ('Victory'), 81; 1922, 264
George V, King: denounces WSC, 4; WSC's low opinion of, 67; appeals for peace in Ireland, 146; attends polo match, 157; at Balmoral, 195; and Inverness Cabinet meeting, 200
Germany: post-war collaboration with Soviet Russia, 63; uses Zeppelins in war, 64; post-war settlement and situation, 166–7, 176, 179
Gertler, Mark, 225
Gill, Eric, 193
Gladstone, Dorothy, Viscountess, 165
Gold Coast Service Club, 230
Gouraud, General Henri, 128
Government Code and Cypher School, 43, 66
Grange, Baroness de la, 119
Greece: war with Turkey, 84–6, 154
Greenwood, Sir Hamar, 17, 23, 28, 61, 199, 239
Greenwood, Margo, Lady: relations with Lloyd George, 18, 31; at Port Lympne, 23, 28–9; and WSC's knowledge of Chirgwin songs, 25
Greville, Ronald and Mrs, 119
Grey (of Fallodon), Edward, Viscount, 194, 232
Grey, Lady Sybil, 170
Griffith, Arthur, 238, 241, 244–7
Guest, Amy Grant (*née* Phipps), 35–6, 51, 260
Guest, Frederick (WSC's cousin): close relations with WSC, 34–6, 51, 68; as Chief Liberal Whip, 82–3; collects sculptured heads of friends, 90; meets Meinertzhagen, 151; attends polo match, 158; as Secretary of State for Air, 181, 234; opposes airships, 182; at funeral service for R38 victims, 184; electoral policy, 206; runs The Other Club, 226; speech at English-Speaking Union, 236–7; praises WSC's speech on Irish Agreement, 257; separates from wife, 260
Guest, Ivor, 140
Guest, Raymond, 237

Hackwood House, Hampshire, 174
Haig, General Sir Douglas, 18

Haldane, General Sir Aylmer, 107–8
Hamilton, Sir Ian, 34, 68, 137, 223
Hamilton, Jean, Lady, 73, 136, 137, 190, 223–4
Hampden, John, 78
'Hands Off Russia' campaign, 96
Hankey, Sir Maurice: condemns Sutherland, 17; and WSC's appointment to Colonial Office, 31; relations with WSC, 76–7
Harding, Warren G., 21–2, 179, 190, 234
Hashemite family, 109
Hassan, Mohammed Abdullah ('the Mad Mullah'), 105
Hawkins, HMS, 176
Hayashi, Baron Gonsuke, 172
Hearst, William Randolph, 229
Herbert, Michael, 67
Hirohito, Crown Prince of Japan, 172
Hitler, Adolf, 62, 167
Hoe Farm, near Godalming, Surrey, 7–8, 50
Hong Kong: child slavery, 164, 266
Hope, Anthony (Sir Anthony Hope Hopkins), 226
Horne, Sir Robert, 131–2, 221
Horner, Sir John and Frances, Lady, 33, 162
Houston, Sir Robert, 203
Hozier, Katharine ('Kitty'; Clementine's sister), 47
Hozier, Lieut.-Cdr William Ogilvy ('Bill'; Clementine's younger brother), 134
Hughes, William ('Billy'), 12, 163, 168, 173, 178, 181–3
Hunter, Detective-Sergeant, 61
Hurlingham Park, Fulham: Anglo-American Polo Test Match, 157–9

Ibn Saud, king of Saudi Arabia, 113
Imperial Conference (1921), 76, 147, 163, 165, 168–70, 172–3, 180
Inchcape, James Lyle Mackay, 1st Earl of, 221
India: rise of nationalism, 9; status, 169
Innishannon House, Co. Cork, 142–3, 147
Inverness: Cabinet meeting on Irish settlement, 199–202
Iraq (formerly Mesopotamia): founded and British mandate, 30–1, 37; WSC's interest in, 64, 186; discussed at Cairo Conference, 106, 108–9, 113; Faisal appointed king, 111; WSC proposes financial contribution from, 114; British policy on, 152; economies, 186; Royal Air Force in, 186–9; British punitive actions in, 187; supposed use of poison gas in, 187–8; treaty of independence, 261

Ireland: political unrest and violence, 17, 26–7, 29, 141–6, 157, 246; WSC's views on, 27–8, 30; truce, 198–9; and Inverness Cabinet meeting, 200–1; in WSC's Dundee speech, 216–17; delegation in London, 238–48; treaty and settlement with, 248; Agreement debated in Parliament, 255–7
Irish Free State: offered to Irish, 246, 248
Irish Free State Bill (1921), 261
Irish Republican Army (IRA), 26, 28, 30, 141–3, 145, 147, 201
Ironside, General Sir Edmund, 107–8

Jackson, Admiral Thomas, 190–1
Jaffa: riots, 148, 152
Jamal, Shibley al-, 185
Japan: alliance with Britain (1902), 172–3; potential war with, 177–8
Jellicoe, Admiral John Rushworth, 1st Earl, 177
Jemal Pasha, 121
Jerome, Leonard: estate, 196
Jerusalem: WSC visits, 118, 121–4, 127, 130
Jewish National Council, 127
Jews: and anti-Semitism, 149; conflict with Arabs, 185, 232; *see also* Palestine; Zionism
John, Augustus, 243
Jones, Thomas, 202, 244, 265

Kamenev, Lev, 92–5
Kennedy, John F., 214
Kennet, Kathleen, Lady, 171
Kenya, 230–1
Keppel, Alice, 132
Kerensky, Alexander, 63
Kolchak, Admiral Aleksandr Vasilevich, 10, 41, 53
Korda, Alexander, 229
Krassin, Leonid, 41–2, 46, 92–5, 251–3
Kronstadt: mutiny, 160
Kurdistan, 113
Kurds: in Iraq, 188–9

Labour Party: increasing popularity, 82–3, 206; election success (1922), 264
Lansbury, George, 93, 96
Laski, Harold, 247–8
Lavery, Hazel, Lady: friendship with WSC, 50, 67–8, 74, 132–3, 136, 159, 193; painting, 224; supports Collins in Irish negotiations, 242–4, 247

Lavery, Sir John: friendship with WSC, 50–1, 67–8, 74, 132–3, 136, 224; and Irish situation, 144, 255; and death of Marigold Churchill, 193; WSC paints with, 223–4; Michael Collins visits in London, 242–4, 247; *The Bay, Monte Carlo* (painting), 133; *The Blue Bay: Mr. Churchill on the Riviera* (painting), 133

Law, Andrew Bonar: on WSC's 'unbalanced mind', 6; resigns as Conservative Party leader, 115

Lawrence, T. E. ('Lawrence of Arabia'): introduced to WSC, 37–8; image and reputation, 39–41; attends Cairo Conference, 104, 108–9, 117; criticizes luxury in Cairo, 104; WSC admires, 105; backs Faisal as king of Mesopotamia, 108–9; and Gertrude Bell, 110; poses on camel, 116; dislikes French, 119; and Palestine question, 120–1; on Meinertzhagen, 150; as advisor to WSC, 151

League of Nations: WSC's scepticism over, 62, 166; proposes ban on use of chemical weapons, 187

Lee, Sir Arthur Hamilton (Viscount Lee of Fareham) and Ruth, Lady, 78–80, 83, 163, 234

Lenglen, Suzanne, 57

Lenin, Vladimir I., 10, 41–3, 46, 63–4, 95, 159–61, 165, 216, 251, 253

Leslie, Anita, 90

Leslie, John, 88

Leslie, Sir John, 88

Leslie, Leonie, Lady, 88, 143, 262

Leslie, Shane, 88, 90, 95, 139, 143–4, 194, 244

Leverhulme, William Hesketh Lever, 1st Viscount, 203

Lewis, Percy Wyndham, 133, 161

Liberal Party: WSC joins, 3–4; and Coalition government, 82–3

Liberty (yacht), 203

Lloyd George, David: WSC's alliance with, 3; on WSC's unpredictability, 6; as wartime prime minister, 8; tolerance of Bolsheviks, 10, 42, 91, 94; on WSC's hostility to Bolshevism, 10; at Port Lympne, 17–18, 20, 22–3; view of WSC, 20–1; on Anglo-US naval relations, 22; negotiates with Irish delegation in London, 24, 239, 241, 244, 247–8; policy on Ireland, 27–8; WSC fears break with, 30; appoints WSC Colonial Secretary, 31–2, 81; and sale of honours scandal, 35, 83; encourages trade and relations with Soviet Russia, 41–2, 252; discusses German reparations with Briand, 60; Sinn Fein plots to kidnap, 61; at Laverys' party, 67; at Chequers, 78; as prime minister of Coalition government, 81–3; courts press, 83; differences with WSC, 84–5, 91, 133, 163–4; supports Greece against Turkey, 85, 155; and WSC at Cairo Conference, 111–14; and Bonar Law's resignation and successor as Chancellor, 115, 129; appoints Horne Chancellor, 131; and Irish violence, 145–6; praises Meinertzhagen, 150; Middle East proposals, 153; at Imperial Conference, 163–4, 168–9, 175; dines with WSC, 170; agrees to renewal of Anglo-Japanese Alliance, 173; on sea power and Empire, 176; appoints Committee of National Expenditure, 178; and potential war with Japan, 178; and Irish truce, 198–9; calls Cabinet meetings in Inverness and Gairloch on Irish settlement, 199–202; tooth problem, 202–3; electoral policy, 206; and social unrest and unemployment, 211, 213; secure position, 220; and WSC's opposition to austerity, 222; and preparations for Washington Conference, 234; calls Cabinet meeting on Ireland, 236; Davies on, 240; agreement with Griffith, 245; threatens resignation, 246; hymn-singing at Chequers, 250; meets Savinkov, 252–3; WSC's increasing disbelief in, 261; and collapse of Coalition, 264; on WSC's bellicosity, 265

Lloyd George, Margaret, 170

Lochmore Lodge, Sutherland, 191, 194, 212

Londonderry, Charles Stewart Henry Vane-Tempest-Stewart, 7th Marquess of, 134

Long, Walter, 65

Lords, House of: reforms, 3–4

Lorimer, Sir Robert, 194

Lou Mas (villa), St Jean Cap Ferrat, 73–4

Loucheur, Louis, 49

Low, David, 12–13, 265

Lucy, Sir Henry, 3, 218

Lullenden (house), Surrey, 33–4, 36, 73

Lutyens, Sir Edwin, 48

Lympne, Kent *see* Port Lympne

Macdonald, D.J., 205, 211

McEvoy, Ambrose, 92, 135

MacInnes, Rt. Revd Rennie, bishop of Jerusalem, 121, 123

McKinley, William, 75
Maclean, Colonel John Bayne, 75–7
Maclean's (magazine), 76
Macmillan, Hugh: *The Riviera*, 57–8
Macready, Sir Neville, 200–1
McSwiney, Terence, 29, 144
Malone, Cecil, 43, 96
Manchester: WSC visits, 165
Manchester Guardian, 165
Mannix, Daniel, Archbishop of Melbourne, 207
Marlborough, Charles Churchill ('Sunny'), 9th Duke of, 4, 149
Marlborough, John Churchill, 1st Duke of, 4, 68
Marlowe, Thomas, 153, 163
Marsh, Sir Edward, 37–8, 80, 115, 160, 184, 225–6, 231, 255, 263
Mary, consort of George V, 157–8, 195
Massey, William, 163, 168, 173, 181, 183
Matisse, Henri, 58
Meighen, Arthur, 163, 168–9, 171–3, 181
Meighen, Isabel, 171
Meinertzhagen, Colonel Richard, 150–2, 233
Mells Manor, Somerset, 33, 137
Mena, Sheik of, 116
Menabilly (house), Cornwall, 162, 192
Menzies, Stewart, 44–5
Mesopotamia *see* Iraq
MI5, 43, 66
MI6, 43, 66
Middle East: territories mandated, 37; discussed at Cairo Conference, 106–7, 148; British presence and policy in, 114, 120; French interests in, 114–15, 125–6, 128; British air power in, 130; WSC addresses Commons on, 148, 152; *see also* Palestine
Millerand, Alexandre, 49
Milner, Alfred, Viscount, 62, 164
Minto, Gilbert Elliot, 4th Earl and Mary, Countess, 75
Montag, Charles, 49–50, 190, 263
Montagu, Edwin, 85, 169, 224–5, 227, 231, 245, 262
Montagu, Venetia (*née* Stanley), 85, 193, 224–5, 227, 245, 262
Montreal Gazette, 75
Moran, Charles Wilson, Baron, 214
Morel, Edwin Dene, 207–8
Morgan, J. P. Jr, 123
Morning Post, 220
Morton, Major Desmond, 45, 250, 254, 263

Mosley, Sir Oswald, 265
Mosul, Iraq, 114
Mountbatten, Edwina, Countess (*née* Ashley), 55, 197
Mountbatten, Lord Louis, 55

Napoleon I (Bonaparte), Emperor of the French: WSC admires, 4
Nash, John and Paul, 225
National Liberal Club, 82
Nazism, 62, 167
New English Art Club, 225
New York World, 237
1920 Club, 82–3
Northcliffe, Alfred Harmsworth, 1st Viscount, 74, 163
Northern Ireland: and Irish settlement, 247–8, 256, 262
Norton, Jean, 228
Norton, Richard, 227
Novello, Ivor, 13, 24

Obregón, Álvaro, 135
O'Connor, Thomas Power, 72, 220, 264
Ogilvy, Lady Blanche (Clementine's mother), 70, 134
Omdurman, battle of (1898), 158
Orpen, William: portrait of WSC, 2; and Lavery's painting of Collins, 243
Ottoman Empire: defeated and dissolved, 9, 37, 81; *see also* Turkey
Outlook (periodical), 219
Overseas Bankers' Association, 232

Pacific: British naval power in, 176–7
Palestine: as proposed Jewish homeland, 119–21, 127; as British mandate, 120; WSC visits, 120–1, 130; Arab resistance in, 130–1; Jewish immigration suspended, 148–9, 152; Jewish–Arab unrest, 148, 185–6, 232; WSC's policy on, 151–3, 185–6, 261; WSC's cost-cutting in, 232–3
Paris: WSC visits and exhibits in, 49–53; air travel to, 65
Paris Peace Conference and settlement, 17, 39, 62, 81
Peelings (house), East Sussex, 161
Pershing, General John ('Black Jack'), 234–5
Pickford, Mary, 229
poison gas: alleged use in Iraq, 187–9
Poland, 166, 175, 269
polo *see* Hurlingham Park
Porch, Montagu (Jennie's third husband), 70, 137–8

Port Lympne, Kent, 17–20, 23–4, 28, 32, 36, 68, 244
'Poy' (cartoonist) see Fearon, Percy
Pro-Jerusalem Society, 123
Protocols of the Elders of Zion, 127
Punch (magazine), 11

R38 (airship), 181–3
Raffles, Sir Thomas Stamford, 176–7
Redmond, John, 143
Reilly, Sidney, 160, 250–2, 254
Riddell, George Allardice, Baron, 17, 25–6, 31, 66, 190, 200, 203, 226
Rishon-le-Zion, Palestine, 130, 149, 153
Ritchie, Sir George, 205–6, 212–13, 260
Room 40 (Admiralty), 43
Roosevelt, Franklin Delano, 235
Roosevelt, Theodore, 75
Rothenstein, Sir John, 263
Rothschild, Baron Edmund de, 130
Royal Air Force: WSC supports as independent service, 64; in Middle East, 112–13; in Iraq, 186–9; role in British Empire, 186
Royal Colonial Institute, 180
Royal Irish Constabulary (RIC), 27
Ruhr: Allies occupy, 166
Russell, Bertrand, 240
Rutenberg Plan (Palestine), 233

Samuel, Sir Herbert: in Palestine, 119–22, 128, 130; restricts Jewish immigration, 148–9, 152; appoints Grand Mufti of Jerusalem, 151
Sassoon, Sir Philip, 18–20, 67, 68, 149, 152, 158, 227, 244, 261
Saturday Review, 219
Savinkov, Boris, 63, 160, 250–4
Scotland: unemployment and social unrest, 211–12; see also Dundee
Scott, Alexander MacCallum, 81, 266–8
Scottish Prohibition Party, 208
Scribners' Sons, Charles (US publishers), 70
Scrymgeour, Edwin, 208
Seaforth Highlanders (regiment), 200
Seaforth, James Alexander Stewart-Mackenzie, Baron and Mary, Lady, 199
Secret Intelligence Service (SIS), 43–5, 250
secret services (British), 43
Sert, Josip Maria, 20
Shackleton, Sir Edward, 213
Sheridan, Clara (Clare's mother), 137
Sheridan, Clare (WSC's cousin): life and career, 87–90; sculpting, 89–91, 95, 136;

Lord Birkenhead pursues, 91–2; relations with Kamenev, 93–5; moves to Moscow, 95, 136; moves to USA, 97, 135; proposes self as ambassador to Moscow, 135–6, 254; relations with WSC, 135–6; and Irish unrest, 143–4; returns from USA, 262; sculpts WSC's head, 262; under suspicion by security service, 262
Sheridan, William ('Wilfred'), 88
Sidebotham, Herbert, 155, 219–20, 251, 264
Sime, John, 207, 212
Simon, Sir John, 145
Sims, Admiral William Snowden, USN, 174
Sinclair, Archibald (2nd Viscount Thurso): and British intelligence services, 44–6, 63, 64, 160; and WSC's visit to French Riviera, 73; attends Cairo Conference with WSC, 102–3, 106; illness, 111, 131; and WSC's changed plans for return from Middle East, 129; on WSC's personal tragedies, 194; on WSC's Dundee speech, 218; in The Other Club, 226; and Russian intrigues, 251–2; as WSC's wartime ally, 263
Singapore: naval base developed, 176–8
Sinn Fein (Irish political party): demands full independence, 26, 28; violence and protests, 27, 29; plots to kidnap British politicians, 61; conflict with British, 142, 145–9; election victory, 146; rejects Lloyd George's Irish settlement, 198; at Inverness Cabinet meeting, 201–2; WSC negotiates with, 204; and proposed Dominion Rule, 216–17; delegation negotiates in London, 238, 240–1, 246, 248; and Irish treaty, 249
Sitwell, Osbert, 53
Siwertz, Sigfrid, 214
Smartt, Sir Thomas, 170
Smuts, General Jan Christian, 147–8, 159, 163, 175, 181, 232
Smyrna: Greece invades, 84
South Africa, Union of, 232
Southern Rhodesia, 232
Soviet Russia: as threat, 10, 62–3, 93–4; and British intervention, 30; civil war in, 41, 250; trade delegation and deal with Britain, 41–2, 46, 92, 251; WSC's hostility to, 42–3, 254; war in Poland, 92, 269; famine and unrest, 159–60, 216; British policy on, 251–3
Spears, Brigadier Edward Louis: relations with WSC, 45–6, 159–61, 263; WSC visits, 223; and intrigues in Russia, 251–2

Spencer, Stanley, 225
Sphinx, SS, 101
Srinivasa Sastri, V.S., 163
Stanley, Venetia *see* Montagu, Venetia
Stenning, Frederick, 142–3
Stevenson, Frances: on WSC's reaction to
new world order, 10; relations with Lloyd
George, 18, 23, 199
Storrs, Sir Ronald, 123
Strand magazine, 52, 70, 190
Strube, Sidney Conrad, 12
Sukhar, Yusuf al-, 125
Sunday Times, The, 82
Sussex Square, London, 32, 34–5
Sutherland, George Granville Sutherland
('Geordie'), 5th Duke of, 194–5
Sutherland, Millicent ('Millie'), Dowager
Duchess of, 140
Sutherland, Sir William ('Bronco Bill'), 17,
21, 25, 139
Sutherland-Leveson-Gower, Lord Alastair
(Duke of Sutherland's brother), 196

Taplow Court, Buckinghamshire, 136, 140
Thomas, Lowell, 39–41; *With Allenby in
Palestine and Lawrence in Arabia*, 39
Thompson, Detective-Sergeant (*later*
Inspector) Walter Henry, 61, 102
Thomson, David Coupar, 204
Tilden, Philip, 19
Times, The: opposes reprisals in Ireland, 145;
on WSC's Dundee speech, 218; praises
WSC, 219–20; on Michael Collins, 239;
on Irish conference, 247
Tonypandy, Wales: striking miners (1910), 4
Transjordan, 120, 151–3
Trenchard, Air Marshal Sir Hugh, 64, 106,
112–13, 187–8
Trotsky, Leon, 16, 95–7, 216, 253
Truman, Harry S., 52
Tudor, Major-General Henry, 27–9, 146,
198
Turkey: conflict with Greece, 85–6, 154; and
Mesopotamia settlement, 114; WSC's
views on, 153; *see also* Ottoman Empire
Twain, Mark, 75

unemployment, 157, 211–12
Union of Democratic Control, 207
United States of America: post-Great War
position, 22; WSC's lecture tour in, 75; as
naval rival, 172–4; and Japanese naval
power, 173; relationship with Britain, 180,
184, 215–16, 234–5, 257; WSC's feelings
for, 236–7
'Unknown Soldier, the', 48–9, 157, 234
Upper Silesia, 166–7, 175

Vane-Tempest, Lord Herbert Lionel, xi–xii,
255
Venizelos, Eleftherios, 85
Versailles, Treaty of (1919), 9, 11, 166
Vincent, Helen, Lady d'Abernon, 269

Walden, Thomas, 194
War Office: WSC's retrenchment campaign,
61
Washington Conference (1921–2), 179–80,
190, 216, 233, 257
Washington, George: statue, 147
Washington Post, 237, 239
Webb, Beatrice, 151
Weizmann, Chaim, 185, 233
Weizmann, Vera, 254
Westminster Abbey: US-British ceremony,
234–6
Westminster, Hugh Grosvenor ('Bendor'),
2nd Duke of, 149, 159, 191, 194
Wilson, General Sir Henry, 94, 248
Wilson, Woodrow: on Sir Henry Lucy, 3
Wimborne, Cornelia, Lady (WSC's aunt),
33–4, 139, 193
Winterton, Edward Turnour, 6th Earl of,
226
Wodehouse, P. G., 53
Women's International Zionist
Organization, 255

York, Duke of (*later* King George VI), 158,
195

Zaharoff, Sir Basil, 124
Zionism, 120–1, 127–8, 130, 149, 185, 233